To Encourage the Others w..... the British Government to ..... – a case which had been ..... book, which provoked a m..... the author's television di..... ....ed many, ranging from the former Lord Chancellor Lord Gardiner, Lords Arran and Goodman, to authors such as Arthur Koestler, that a miscarriage of justice had occurred. This was in the years 1970 to 1973. Publication of this new edition will coincide with a campaign to persuade the current Government to open again this murder case. The purpose of that campaign: to establish once and for all the full truth of this unique and horrific story. In the author's words, 'Derek Bentley is dead, and a public inquiry into the circumstances leading to his death cannot bring him back from the grave, but it could acknowledge that he should never have been put there.'

Yallop's second book, *The Day the Laughter Stopped*, was widely acclaimed on both sides of the Atlantic as the definitive biography and posthumous rehabilitation of the silent-film star Roscoe (Fatty) Arbuckle, which also solved a fifty-year-old murder mystery. The book is also a brilliant evocation of the Jazz Age.

His third book, *Beyond Reasonable Doubt?* led directly to the freeing of Arthur Thomas, a New Zealand farmer serving a life sentence for double murder. Prior to Yallop's investigation Thomas had been found guilty by unanimous jury decisions on two separate occasions. Following publication of Yallop's book, Arthur Thomas was granted a Royal Pardon and, after a Royal Commission had deliberated, one million dollars compensation for wrongful imprisonment.

Yallop's fourth book, *Deliver Us From Evil*, was stimulated by a desire to pull a man *into* prison, the Yorkshire Ripper. Yallop's statements to Assistant Chief Constable George Oldfield in June 1980 proved uncannily accurate. If they had been acted upon at the time, Peter Sutcliffe would have been arrested before he could have carried out a further four murderous attacks.

Yallop receives letters continuously from many parts of the world asking, demanding, pleading that he investigate this murder or that alleged miscarriage of justice. He received one particularly singular request, to investigate a very special death. The request came from within the Vatican, and the death was that of Pope John Paul I.

David Yallop then began the extensive research for his fifth book, *In God's Name* (also published by Corgi), which caused a worldwide storm of controversy and to date has sold more than 4 million copies. To this day his central conclusions concerning the murder of the late Pope and the whirlpool of corruption within the Vatican remain unanswered, and the frightening accusations still stand undisputed.

Thus, David Yallop has established a reputation not merely as 'a seeker of justice', but also as the world's greatest investigative author. Now for the first time his first book is made available in paperback.

TO ENCOURAGE
THE OTHERS

David Yallop

CORGI BOOKS

TO ENCOURAGE THE OTHERS
A CORGI BOOK 0 552 13451 1

Originally published in Great Britain by W. H. Allen Ltd

PRINTING HISTORY
W. H. Allen edition 1971
Revised and updated Corgi edition 1990

This book is set in 10/11pt Plantin by Chippendale Type Ltd., Otley,
West Yorkshire.

Corgi Books are published by Transworld Publishers Ltd., 61-63
Uxbridge Road, Ealing, London W5 5SA, in Australia by Transworld
Publishers (Australia) Pty. Ltd., 15-23 Helles Avenue, Moorebank,
NSW 2170, and in New Zealand by Transworld Publishers (N.Z.)
Ltd., Cnr. Moselle and Waipareira Avenues, Henderson, Auckland.

Made and printed in Great Britain by Cox & Wyman Ltd., Reading,
Berks.

DEDICATION

This book is dedicated
to William and Lillian Bentley and their daughter Iris.
Let any who seek a definitive
example of courage
look no further than these three people.

CONTENTS

Defence copy of police plan as used during
their investigation and during the trial   10

Introduction to 1990 Edition   13

An Open Letter to the Home
Secretary, 1971   15

1 The Seeds   21

2 Two Threepennies to Croydon   53

3 Law and Disorder   83

4 The Mind of a Child   114

5 'Draw Near and Give Your Attendance'   163

6 The Season of Goodwill   234

7 'Help me, please help me!'   256

8 Lessons Learned?   285

Epilogue   310

An Open Letter to the Home Secretary, 1990   327

Appendix I
The House of Lords Debate, 14 June 1972   331

Appendix II
Dr Matheson's Second Report on
Derek Bentley's Mental Condition   385

Appendix III
Lord Goddard's Summing-up   391

Source Acknowledgements   401

Index   405

'In this country it is thought well to kill an admiral from time to time, to encourage the others.'

Voltaire

'As a realist I do not believe that the chances of error in a murder case, with these various instruments of the State present, constitute a factor which we must consider . . . There is no practical possibility. The honourable and learned member asks me to say that there is no possibility. Of course, a jury might go wrong, the Court of Criminal Appeal might go wrong, as might the House of Lords and the Home Secretary: they might all be stricken mad and go wrong. But that is not a possibility which anyone can consider likely. The honourable and learned member is moving into a realm of fantasy when he makes that suggestion.'

Sir David Maxwell Fyfe
14 April 1948
Hansard, vol. 449, col. 1007

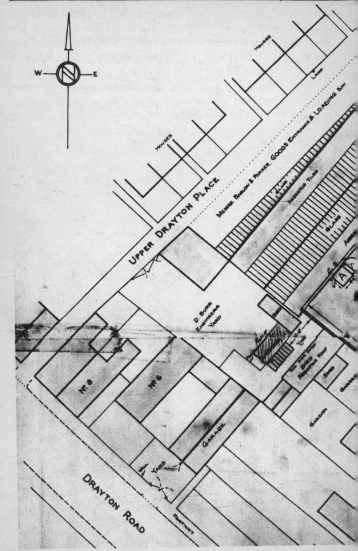

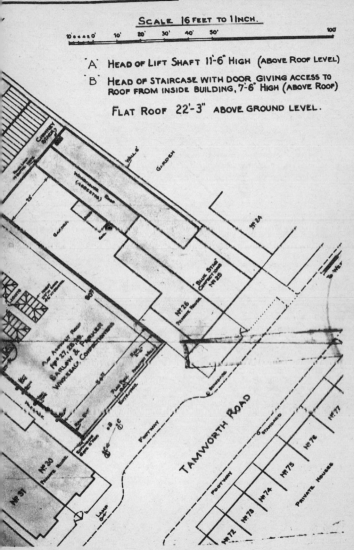

MESSRS BARLOW & PARKER.

SCALE 16 FEET TO 1 INCH.

'A' HEAD OF LIFT SHAFT 11'-6" HIGH (ABOVE ROOF LEVEL)

'B' HEAD OF STAIRCASE WITH DOOR GIVING ACCESS TO ROOF FROM INSIDE BUILDING, 7'-6" HIGH (ABOVE ROOF)

FLAT ROOF 22'-3" ABOVE GROUND LEVEL.

TAMWORTH ROAD

INTRODUCTION TO 1990 EDITION

I approach the publication of a new edition of this book with feelings that are in direct conflict with each other. My continuing desire to see, finally, a small measure of justice for Derek Bentley in the shape of a posthumous Royal Pardon is as strong as ever, but it is tempered with a reluctance to open old wounds not only in others but also myself.

The research, writing and subsequent experiences after initial publication in 1971 have left me permanently marked. They also shattered many illusions.

Prior to that publication I deeply believed in the concept of British Justice. I was aware that it could occasionally fall into serious error and sometimes even into fatal error, but I also believed that once such an error could be demonstrated everything possible would be done by the Government of the day to rectify that mistake. Surely one had but to publish a self-evident truth and it would be acknowledged? What occurred after this book was first published is, in part, recorded in an Epilogue in this edition.

By early 1973 I could take no more. Close exposure to inhumanity eventually has a deadening effect upon the soul.

I had asked for a full public inquiry. The Government had initiated a secret investigation. It was abundantly clear that any inquiry, public or secret, should be conducted by individuals who would be seen by all to be independent and removed from the issues that this book raises. The Government's secret inquiry was conducted by a senior police officer.

I was not confronted with a brick wall. Walls can be knocked down. I was faced with a large, amorphous sponge with a capacity to soak up whatever truths were presented to it without any apparent change in its shape. It seemed that there was no more that I could do.

I have discovered since then that this case will not let me be, and to judge from the many letters that I continue to receive about it, it will not let the public be either. I have come to the realization that when Lord Goodman observed in the House of Lords debate upon this case 'Time does not enable one to bury the situation', he spoke a fundamental truth.

This book begins with an open letter addressed to the Home Secretary. At the time the book was first published, the Home Secretary was Reginald Maudling. An account of his and the then Government's response is contained within the Epilogue.

The book now ends with a second open letter, again addressed to the Home Secretary of the day, who at this time of writing is David Waddington. His and the current Government's response to both that letter and *all* the evidence contained within this book will be recorded in subsequent editions.

So, dear reader. Here we go again.

AN OPEN LETTER
TO THE HOME SECRETARY, 1971

Sir,

Though personally reluctant to communicate with you via an open letter, my recent experiences with your Department have made it abundantly clear that any private dialogue between us would be one-sided. I am therefore left with no alternative other than to address my remarks to you publicly.

At the Old Bailey on the 11th December 1952 sixteen-year-old Christopher Craig and nineteen-year-old Derek William Bentley were found guilty of the murder of Police Constable Sidney Miles. Craig was sentenced to be detained until Her Majesty's pleasure be known. Bentley was sentenced to death. On the 28th January 1953 Bentley was hanged at Wandsworth Prison, one of your predecessors, Sir David Maxwell Fyfe (later Lord Kilmuir), having previously refused to interfere with the due course of justice.

In an article written shortly after the execution, Kenneth Allsop said, 'A drab and second-rate youth goes to the gallows – and a nation is in an emotional upset. I can recall only two other comparable occasions: Dunkirk and the King's death. At first thought the comparison seems irreverently incongruous. Yet the situation was very similar: each of us was momentarily entangled in a perturbation common to all.'

My purpose in writing this book was to discover exactly what had led to that execution and why so many of the people of this country considered, and still consider, that Bentley's execution was a miscarriage of justice. On the assumption that the vast lay opinion might be uninformed, I attempted to assess the conclusions of a number of distinguished men with more than a nodding acquaintance with

15

the law. Some of their comments have been made public before, others are here made public for the first time.

'However controversial the hanging question may be today, posterity will undoubtedly condemn the judicial killing of this boy, under the circumstances of his case, as a ghastly and utterly indefensible barbarity ... The hanging of this wretched boy-wrongdoer was itself wrong and unjust. Those who still "look back in anger" upon this miscarriage of justice should not cease from mental fight until such happenings in England are impossible.'

C. G. L. Du Cann, Barrister-at-Law,
Miscarriages of Justice

'I do not believe that even upon the strictest law Bentley in the circumstances of this case was responsible for a murder which he did not commit and which was committed by another more than a quarter of an hour after he had surrendered.'

R. T. Paget, QC, MP,
Hanged and Innocent

'The ritual hanging (or, if you wish, ritual murder) of Derek Bentley touched the emotions of the people of Britain. It disturbed our hangmen, for nobody knows better than they how bad a thing it is to hang an innocent man: and Bentley *did not do the deed* [his italics] ... Bentley was dead, but his name was immortalized by his hanging. For it is one to make the supporters of capital punishment tremble and blush with shame. Was it a political blunder? Whatever else it might be, it was some sort of writing on the wall.'

Charles Duff, Barrister-at-Law,
A Handbook of Hanging

'The shock to the public conscience when Bentley

died was greater than the shock to the criminals' sensibilities. Anyone who, looking back on this cloud-darkened episode, still thinks that the hanging of Bentley was justified on the grounds that it acted as a deterrent to other thugs and would-be cosh-boys certainly cannot take the slightest comfort from the published figures for violent crime, and it is difficult to see where else they could even begin to look for it.'

'There may be a good defence to put up for the hanging of Derek Bentley. Lord Goddard certainly thinks there is. One can only reply that this questionable execution seems less and less justified the more one studies it.'

Eric Grimshaw and Glyn Jones
Lord Goddard

'Yes, I thought Bentley was going to be reprieved. He certainly should have been. There is no doubt whatsoever in my mind. Bentley should have been reprieved.'

Lord Goddard, former
Lord Chief Justice of
England, and presiding
Judge at the trial of
Craig and Bentley,
in an interview with
the author.

'I have always considered that everybody connected with the case — from Lord Goddard to the most humble court attendant — entertained no doubt but that Bentley was entirely innocent of the crime with which he was charged. But many of them, including Lord Goddard, believed that it was in the public interest that somebody, anybody, should die because a police officer had been killed. In short, Bentley was a vicarious sacrifice, the innocent scapegoat released into the desert to die and thus bear away into oblivion the guilt of a whole people.'

John Parris, Barrister-at-
Law and Defence Counsel
for Christopher Craig,
in an interview with
the author.

'At any other time Bentley would have been reprieved. But at that particular time there was such a great deal of violence towards police officers, particularly from youngish men, I believe that the Home Secretary decided he had to make an example of Bentley.'

Frank Cassels, Barrister-at-
Law and Defence Counsel
for Derek Bentley, in an
interview with the author.

The above is by no means an exhaustive list, but merely a significant indication of views that are held all over the country. During my investigations, which lasted over a year, I have discovered an overwhelming amount of evidence to support those views. There is no doubt in my mind that Bentley's execution was a terrible miscarriage of justice. Indeed, I would go further and say that he was the victim of judicial murder.

During these past sixteen months I have spoken to a great many people about the Craig/Bentley case. Amongst them are: Lord Goddard, John Parris (Craig's Defence Counsel), Frank Cassels (Bentley's Counsel) and Christmas Humphreys (the senior prosecuting Counsel at the trial); Christopher Craig; the entire Bentley family; Norman Parsley; Frederick Fairfax, former Detective Sergeant, and chief prosecution witness at the trial; John Leslie Smith, former Detective Chief Inspector, and the man in charge of the police investigation of the death of PC Sidney Miles; Stanley Shepherd, former Detective Sergeant, and Mr Smith's second-in-command in the investigation; Dr Nicholas Jazwon, the doctor who initially examined and treated both Christopher Craig and Sergeant Fairfax after the shooting; Dr Gordon Hatfield, who subsequently examined and treated Christopher Craig; Dr David Haler, the pathologist responsible for the post-mortem examinations of PC Miles and Derek Bentley; and Professor Sir Denis Hill, now a world authority on human brainwaves, who performed EEG examinations on Craig and Bentley before their trial. Again, this list is by no means exhaustive; the complete total is well over fifty.

In my researches I have been given access not only to the evidence made public at the time of the case, but also to a great deal that was not. It all points to one conclusion: that Bentley was innocent.

Had many of the facts in this book been laid before the trial jury, it is my considered opinion that Craig and Bentley would have been acquitted. I have drawn a number of conclusions from that evidence, and one of them must be raised here and now.

In my mind there can be no doubt that PC Miles was not 'murdered'. I believe that not only was Derek Bentley hanged for a crime that he did not commit, he was hanged for a crime that no one committed. Furthermore, Christopher Craig was imprisoned for ten and a half years for a crime that he did not commit, either. This is but one of the frightening implications of my findings; there are many others, and they all, I submit, require immediate and earnest consideration by you.

I am asking you to find time to read this book. I am asking you, having read this book, to set up a full public enquiry into the case of Derek Bentley. If you feel, as you may well do, that such an enquiry should have the approval of the Lord Chancellor, I would advise you that Lord Hailsham, the Lord Chancellor at the time of writing, has publicly declared, during a debate in the Commons, his belief that in deciding that Derek Bentley should die, Sir David Maxwell Fyfe made a mistake.

There has never been an official enquiry into the justness of Bentley's execution.

This book raises many questions, some of which are specifically for you to answer. Can you honestly say after you have read this book that in the case of Derek Bentley justice was not only done, but that it was seen to be done? Having considered the evidence would you not agree that in the case of Derek Bentley injustice was not only done, but that it was seen to be done?

Derek Bentley is dead, and a public enquiry into the circumstances leading to his death cannot bring him back from the grave, but it could acknowledge that he should never have been put there.

Though Bentley can now only be referred to in the past tense, I am sure you would be the first to agree that that fact does not reduce the urgency of the matter. Rightly or wrongly, many, many thousands of people in this country hold the law in contempt because of what happened in the Bentley case. Once and for all let us establish whether they are right. Or is it, as so many believe, that *to err is human, to admit error is impossible*? An early answer to the questions raised not only in this letter, but in the following book, would be appreciated.

Yours faithfully,
David A Yallop.

February 1971

1

The Seeds

The effort of preventing his body descending on the spiked
gate that he was straddling was making Bentley sweat. He
swung perilously, hardly daring to breathe as a bus passed
by. Breaking into a warehouse situated in virtually a main
road was proving difficult as well as hazardous. Craig, who
had already scaled the six-foot metal gate, impatiently
called from the relative safety of the darkened alleyway
that skirted the building. 'Come on, Del! You stay on that
gate much longer, people'll think you're a bloody cat!' 'My
coat's stuck,' Bentley snapped. 'If I slip I'll get one of these
spikes up my arse.' Muttering, Craig appeared by the gate
and, tugging the coat free, helped his friend over.

Prior to the attempted break-in at the wholesalers' they
had tried the butcher's shop further down the road, only
to find it occupied. They went to an electrical shop in
the same road, but were baulked by a courting couple
in the alley.

Now the wholesalers' warehouse was to be third time
lucky. What Craig and Bentley did not know as they
explored the alleyway alongside it, was that their luck
had already run out. Nine-year-old Edith Ware, taking a
goodnight look from her bedroom window, had seen them
by the gate. In a moment her father, interrupted in the
middle of a shave, was wiping the soap from his face, hurriedly putting on a coat and ensuring the police of Croydon
some unexpected action on this quiet Sunday night.

Meanwhile Craig and Bentley were considering the
situation. The side doors of the building were firmly

locked. Entry seemed impossible. They were about to reclimb the gates and return to their Norbury homes when Craig noticed a footprint on a low window sill, and near the sill, drainpipes running up to the roof. The building was thirty feet high but he was soon on the roof and urging Bentley to follow.

Already squad cars and police vans were making the short journey from the local police station. By the time that Bentley, after considerable difficulty, had struggled on to the roof, the police were in the surrounding gardens. The roof did indeed have an entrance that led down into the building, but that too was locked. Hearing voices below, Craig and Bentley looked over the edge and saw the police at the metal gate. It would be only a matter of minutes before they had unwelcome company on the roof. It was flat, slightly larger than a tennis court and afforded little cover. In the middle of the roof were four low glass rooflights; no cover there. At the far end was the lift-head; it was a small structure, but there was no choice.

As they crouched behind it they heard the police moving about below. Then a voice from one of the gardens called out, 'You all right?' 'Yes,' came the reply, startlingly close. It had come from the roof. Then the same voice called out, 'I'm a police officer. Come out from behind that stack.' Unimpressed, Craig called back, 'If you want us, fucking well come and get us.' Detective Constable Fairfax, not a man to decline such an invitation, advanced towards the lift-head.

Bentley muttered 'I'm going out' and walked towards him to surrender himself. Fairfax grabbed him, then, unable to get behind the lift-head, dragged Bentley round the front, in pursuit of Craig. On the other side he and Craig found themselves face to face. Bentley pulled himself free from Fairfax and shouted 'Let him have it, Chris!' Craig pulled a ·45 Colt from his pocket and fired, hitting Fairfax in the shoulder. The policeman fell to the ground.

The stealth and caution that the police below had been employing was now thrown to the winds. Visibility was

22

limited on this wet, wintry, November night, and contact with each other was only possible by shouting, so shout they did. Fairfax rose groggily to his feet and found himself between his assailants; he struck out at the one nearest to him, knocking him to the ground (it was Bentley). At the same time Craig fired again; this time he missed. Fairfax dropped to the ground and, dragging Bentley up in front of himself for cover, began to move away from Craig. He edged his way around the rooflights to the comparative safety of the roof entrance. It was locked, but the wall of the entrance offered some measure of protection from the gunman. Fairfax was alone on the roof, shocked and in pain. He searched Bentley, expecting to find a gun, but found only a knuckleduster and a knife. Police Constable McDonald, having already failed to scale the pipe to the roof, was making a second attempt, urged on from above by Fairfax. Police Constable Harrison was edging along an adjoining roof towards Craig. In the darkness Craig saw him moving towards the main roof.

By now the streets below were a cacophony of noise. Fire engines, ambulances, squad cars, police vans, and a swelling crowd of sightseers milled around. Chaos abounded. In the dim light Craig watched for a moment as Harrison edged towards him; then, with his gun at the ready, he advanced on the policeman and fired. Harrison's torch clattered into the gutter below, and his body was still. Craig moved back towards the lift-head. The third shot brought even more people scurrying from the neighbouring houses; it had missed Harrison, but the policeman froze, hardly daring to breathe. After a while he began to back slowly away. By now PC McDonald had finally managed to get on to the roof and join Fairfax and Bentley. The two policemen discussed the situation, and McDonald asked his colleague what kind of gun was being used. Eagerly Bentley butted in, 'It's a ·45 Colt, and he's got plenty of bloody ammunition for it.' As if to illustrate the point, Craig fired again. He had realized that the uninjured Harrison was moving away and fired at the retreating

23

figure. At once Harrison disappeared from view. What, for the police, had begun as a routine call – 'Suspects on roof of Barlow and Parkers, Tamworth Road' – was now a full-scale battle that had already lasted nearly thirty long minutes. Fairfax had placed the knuckleduster on his hand, but knuckledusters don't stop bullets. The obvious solution was to get the roof entrance open, not only to get Bentley down, but to get reinforcements up.

Shortly after he was joined on the roof by McDonald, Fairfax had called out to Craig, 'Drop your gun.' Craig's crisp reply 'Come and get it' had left him in no doubt that the night was going to be a long one. After what seemed an eternity the two policemen on the roof heard noises from within the building. Their colleagues had finally managed to locate the warehouse manager and obtain the keys. Footsteps thundering up the stairs told the beleaguered police that help was at hand. Inside the roof entrance Police Constable Miles pushed at the door to the roof, it stuck fast, he pushed harder; the door flew open, and he jumped out on to the roof. A shot rang out and he fell with a bullet wound between the eyes. Within moments he was dead. Fairfax pulled him behind the entrance.

PC Harrison tried to come out of the entrance, ducked back inside as Craig fired. In desperation Harrison looked around for something to throw at the gunman, and in quick succession he hurled his truncheon, a milk bottle and a brick. As they crashed around him, Craig retaliated with bullets and with words, 'I am Craig. You've just given my brother twelve years. Come on, you coppers, I'm only sixteen.' He fired again. 'Come on, you brave coppers,' he shouted, 'think of your wives.' By now other policemen had climbed the pipe and were sheltering behind the roof entrance. By now, too, Harrison had leapt out on to the roof and taken cover with his colleagues. They decided to get Bentley out of the way, and rushed towards the roof entrance, shielding themselves as best they could behind their prisoner, who cried out, 'Look out, Chris, they're taking me down.'

Then all was silence on the roof, Craig's only company – the dead PC Miles.

His nerve was disintegrating fast. He saw the roof door swinging idly, forty feet away, and called out, 'Are you hiding behind a shield? Come on, you coppers.' Fairfax, armed with a police gun, called out from the roof entrance, 'Drop your gun. I also have a gun.' Craig called back. 'Yes, it's a Colt ·45. Are you hiding behind a shield? Is it bullet-proof? Are we going to have a shooting match? It's just what I'd like. Have they hurt you, Derek?' Then Fairfax heard several clicks from Craig's gun. Jumping out on the roof, the policeman fired at Craig and missed, fired again and missed again. Craig moved to the edge of the warehouse. He saw Fairfax running towards him and called out, gun pointed in the air, 'See, it's empty!' Then he dived off the thirty-foot-high building. His body smashed on to a greenhouse, then bounced on the ground. He had broken his back, his left forearm and a bone in his chest. PC Stewart leapt on the broken body, and Craig gasped, 'I wish I was fucking dead. I hope I've killed the fucking lot.'

Thus ended the battle of Croydon. The above account contains the essential elements of the Prosecution's case against Craig and Bentley. It was upon the details contained in this account that sixteen-year-old Christopher Craig was sentenced to be detained until Her Majesty's pleasure be known, a sentence which could have kept him in prison for the rest of his life. It was upon the details contained in this account that nineteen-year-old Derek William Bentley was sentenced to death and duly hanged.

I am convinced that the drama on that rooftop was by no means the whole story of the affair. I am convinced that Christopher Craig was innocent of the murder of PC Miles, and I am convinced that Derek Bentley was the victim of judicial murder.

The events in question took place on Sunday, 2 November 1952, in Croydon, a town on the fringes of South London. To understand what happened on that night and what happened in the days and weeks that followed, it is essential to examine a number of events that took place in the early post-war years. For the seeds of this flowering of violence had been planted long before and in many places.

In the general euphoria that followed the end of the Second World War the British criminal came into his own. For six years this country had lauded killing and acts of violence, provided that they were perpetrated on 'the enemy'. Now it appeared that not only were old habits dying hard, they were positively flourishing. A significant proportion of the younger generation, or perhaps a more apt term would be 'rationed generation', observing this manifestation on the part of their more violent elders, decided to join in. A land fit for criminals had been born.

The years 1945 to 1952 were vintage years for anyone of criminal inclinations living in this country. With virtually everything rationed, with the necessities of life officially declared luxuries, the situation was Savile Row tailor-made for the black market. Food, clothing, petrol, sold at two or three times the official price. But there was no shortage of customers. For a nation that had been tightening its belt for six years, the austerity of the late 1940s was only made bearable by the black market. If the prices on the market were high, no one could complain about the lack of choice; the selection ranged from orange juice to tanks. Many a middle-aged businessman owes his present successful position to the judicious buying and selling that he did in those early post-war years. The nation called these activities 'fiddling' and the gentlemen who held the violins were known as 'spivs'.

Any young man growing up in those halcyon days who did not have some first-hand knowledge, either by observation or participation, of the fiddling that abounded, could consider himself not merely lucky but unique.

The black market quickly became an accepted part of everyone's life, and those who bought the odd half-pound of butter or gallon of petrol on the side would no doubt have been shocked if they had been told they were contributing to the crime-wave.

In a country sustained by meat from the Argentine and dollars from the US, there had to be a massive reaction, and it took the form of a crime-wave unprecedented in this nation's history. While the President of the Board of Trade, Mr Harold Wilson, rightly condemned the astronomical salaries being paid to film stars, many families were endeavouring to exist on wages that today would be considered inadequate for office boys – even allowing for devaluation and inflation. While appeals were being made to Mr Wilson to condemn the New Look as 'unpatriotic' because of the amount of material required to make a dress, the majority of women still wore altered pre-war clothes. Something had to give, and what gave was the basic respect for law and order.

It has always been possible to buy revolvers illegally in this country, but never has the supply been so great as it was in those early post-war years. Undoubtedly the returning troops were largely responsible. Thousands of Lugers, Colts, Webleys, Remingtons and dozens of other makes and types of guns came into Britain in the bottoms of kitbags. This phenomenon was common to many countries. One such war trophy, an Italian ·38 Biretta, found its way into India, and into the hands of a fanatical Hindu, Naturam Godse (the name means 'the chosen one of God') – he used it to assassinate Mahatma Gandhi.

An indication of how long this plentiful supply persisted in this country is given by an incident that occurred in 1952 – the same year as the Craig/Bentley case. A sixty-year-old bus driver was sentenced to fourteen years' imprisonment for attempting to murder a policeman. During the course of his trial the police said they had found ninety-one revolvers, automatic pistols and rifles and over ten thousand rounds of ammunition at his home.

27

Interestingly, the judge in this case was Lord Goddard, the Lord Chief Justice of England, who had been waging war on the criminal fraternity for many years, and with particular vigour since his appointment as Lord Chief Justice in 1946. This appointment, which was to have such far-reaching implications, was viewed by some as a disaster, by others as an act of great wisdom. Controversy has always surrounded exactly how and why Lord Goddard came to hold this supreme judicial office. I asked him why in his opinion he had been chosen. His reply was very typical of the man. 'They had to give the job to somebody. There wasn't anybody else available, so Attlee appointed me.'

Three weeks after that appointment, Lord Goddard had given a clear warning to the criminals of this country that, so far as he was concerned, hostilities were about to recommence. A man named McBain appeared before him in the Court of Criminal Appeal, appealing against a sentence of three years' penal servitude for housebreaking. His previous application for leave to appeal against *conviction* had been refused, but as leave had been given for him to appeal against *sentence* he must have been optimistic about having it reduced. But Lord Goddard told him, 'The Court gave him leave to appeal against his sentence for one reason only, *in order to consider whether or not they should substantially increase it.*' He continued: 'The time has certainly come in the state of crime in this country now when sentences must be severe. This Court will not shrink from increasing sentences where the prisoner appeals if it thinks it right to do so.' This was an unqualified declaration of intent to all the fiddlers, spivs and gangsters that abounded in this 'land fit for heroes'.

In the event McBain merely endured a lecture; his sentence was not increased. The criminal fraternity, however, had been left in no doubt as to what would happen to the next person who had the temerity to appeal against what their Lordships considered an inadequate sentence.

28

But although Lord Goddard's words must have heartened the law-abiding citizens of this country, the criminals were unimpressed. The first post-war crime figures released in 1947 revealed some frightening facts. Indictable crime had increased over 50% on the 1939 figure. The prison population was greater than at any time since 1912. Most significant of all, the number of adolescents between the ages of seventeen and twenty-one who were convicted and sent to prison showed an increase on the 1939 figure of a staggering 250%. And this was *before* the advent of the cosh-boy era.

Undoubtedly a great many amateurs had joined the ranks of the hardened professional criminals. In the late 1940s there was an epidemic of Post Office frauds. These were mainly perpetrated in two ways.

The easier of the two involved stealing somebody else's savings book. In the early post-war years millions of people still banked at the local Post Office, and the savings book was their unsophisticated equivalent of the cheque book. Having stolen a savings book it was a relatively simple operation to go from post office to post office, forging the owner's signature and withdrawing the maximum amount of three pounds at a time until the funds in the account were exhausted.

The second method was a trifle more difficult and more dangerous, but the rewards were potentially greater. One opened a post office account with the minimum sum of five shillings. This was then altered in the savings book to read £5, £50 or whatever. The Court of Criminal Appeal, disturbed at the variety of sentences being given for this offence, issued a directive that the appropriate sentence in such cases should *not be less than three years' imprisonment*. It didn't stop the crimes but presumably some measure of satisfaction was derived from the consistency of the sentences.

Another form of crime that became popular after the War was lead-stealing. The metal was in short supply, and the price shot up accordingly. Churches and old houses

29

throughout the country, having let in thieves, started letting in rain. Again the sentences given varied considerably, to the distress of the Court of Appeal, which increased a few to the maximum of five years' imprisonment. The point was taken by the judges at Quarter Sessions, who duly followed suit. However, these punitive sentences, though they may have produced a neat order of things, did little to discourage the criminal – seven years after the War lead-stealing was still a serious problem. On 1 April 1952 Lord Goddard, rejecting an appeal against a five-year sentence for lead-stealing said, 'In this case it has been said that a sentence of five years' imprisonment is severe. The Court, however, has been saying for some time that severe sentences should be given for this type of crime. The appeal is dismissed.'

But other, and far more dangerous, crimes were prevalent during those years. Groups of men, impatient with the restricted shopping hours, were prone to go shopping at midnight, with a brick. 'Smash and Grab' became an all too familiar newspaper headline. One of the most notable thefts of this kind was a daring robbery in 1948 at the Victoria and Albert Museum during which two swords worth £15,000 vanished.

The fact that the film industry was enjoying a boom did not pass unnoticed either. Armed robberies on cinema box offices became a daily occurrence. Three years after the War many of them were carried out in broad daylight. Armed robberies of all kinds have continued undiminished ever since, possibly because gangs realize that even today, with a greatly increased police force and far more sophisticated security measures, they have an 80% chance of success. That is not the optimistic evaluation of the criminals, but of the Home Office.

The country's front-line troops in this battle against crime, then as now, were the police force. Apart from the problems that the crime-wave presented, the police were beset with internal troubles. By the summer of 1947 they were ten thousand under strength, and 30% of new recruits were resigning in their first year. By 1948 the Metropolitan Police Force *alone* was five thousand under strength, its numbers lower than at any time during the previous sixty years. When one realizes that many of its members were daily being asked to risk their lives for a basic pay of less than five pounds for a forty-eight-hour week, and that that was *lower* than a dustman's basic pay, the wonder is that there was any police force at all.

They were burdened, too, with some quite absurd regulations. A Constable was forbidden to play cards, unbutton his tunic in the canteen, own an allotment, or play rugby over the age of thirty-five. A Constable must wear a hat when in plain clothes, even if off duty, and he must consult his Chief Constable as to the suitability of his prospective wife. A policeman's lot was, indeed, not a happy one.

And if conditions at the police station were bad, conditions in policemen's homes were deplorable. The promise, in their terms of employment, that accommodation would be supplied, was broken as frequently as criminals were breaking the law. The *Daily Mirror*, recognizing the situation in an editorial on 24 March 1948, said, 'Spend less on crooks, more on police'; but it neglected to tell its readers just how bad the situation in the police force really was.

Then, as now, the pundits differed violently in their opinions on how to stem the ever-growing flood of lawlessness. Some of their reactions have an air of total unreality about them. There was the Catholic priest in Middleton, Lancashire, who protested to the local Council against what he considered a highly dangerous situation. The priest in question, Father Fairclough, stated that 'it would make children morbid and, if aroused, would add sex crimes to the present wave of thefts'. He was referring to the fact that, at the local swimming pool, mixed bathing was allowed for children between the ages of seven and eleven. What was surprising was not that the good Father held this point of view, but that when he expressed it the Council promptly banned mixed bathing, thereby emphasizing just how rationed that particular generation really was.

Another citizen who feared for the minds of the young was the Chief Constable of Gloucestershire. In 1948 he announced that the radio serial *Dick Barton, Special Agent* was 'crime propaganda', and demanded that it be banned. The *Police Chronicle*, supporting this move, declared that the programme, aimed as it was at young people at a time when 'juvenile crime is higher than ever before, is yet another example of the paradoxes of this crazy age'. It did not seem to have occurred to Dick Barton's critics that the intrepid special agent invariably managed to escape from the shark-infested cellar in Wapping or snake-infested hotel room in Brighton where he was trapped, and that the villain always got his just deserts.

In 1948 the film *No Orchids for Miss Blandish* was released. Based on a novel by James Hadley Chase, it was an English attempt to emulate the Bogart/Cagney gangster films of the thirties. It opened at the Plaza cinema and for once the film critics were unanimous. *Daily Express:* ' . . . a nasty film and a wicked disgrace to the British Film Industry . . . Its morals are about level with those of a scavenger dog.' *Daily Mirror:* 'About as fragrant as a cesspool.' *Daily Herald:* 'I advise the Plaza management to take it off at once.' *News Chronicle:* 'Contrives to insult a nation.' *Star:* 'Without doubt it is one of the most undesirable pictures ever turned out by a British studio.' *The Times:* 'A "D" certificate for disgusting.' *The Observer:* 'Repellent. All the morals of an alley cat and the sweetness of a sewer.' Dr Edith Summerskill thought that the film was 'likely to pervert the minds of the British people'. As it turned out, the British people couldn't wait to see it; there was a constant queue at the Plaza, and the manager declared, 'I haven't had a single complaint since the film started showing; business is fantastic.' But the custodians of our minds knew best. Several Watch Committees refused to give the film a licence, and eventually organizations representing over a thousand cinemas declared that they had banned the film.

I asked film critic Philip Jenkinson what he thought the reaction would be if the film was shown today. He told me, 'Not only would the sex and violence seem tame by modern cinema and television standards, but the attempt at depicting real life characters would seem as laughable as any "Carry On" farce.' But those early years after the Second World War were not the time for enlightened thinking. The young minds had to be protected at all costs, even if that meant blanket censorship. The realization that the younger generation was outstripping its elders in acts of crime struck fear into many hearts. Many refused to face the realities of the problem, but the nation's front-line troops were only too well aware of the real situation. The President of the Chief Constables' Association voiced the fears of the entire police force when he declared, 'We are becoming a law-breaking people . . . We must deal with two generations at once.' And, indeed, the younger generation had ample opportunity to observe and emulate the criminal activities of their elders.

By 1948 the Government ban on pleasure-motoring had become intolerable. There was so much commercial petrol being sold on the black market that the Government were forced to take action. It had been estimated officially that fifty million gallons of petrol per year were changing hands illegally; unofficial estimates put the figure at nearer one hundred million gallons, or two gallons for every man, woman and child in the British Isles. In an attempt to curb this vast illicit trade a system of dyeing all commercial petrol red was announced, in the hope that it would eliminate illegal sales to private motorists. Yet another task fell to a seriously undermanned police force, that of checking vehicles for the tell-tale red dye.

By 1948, too, a murder was being committed somewhere in this country every two days, and these were just the ones that the police knew about. This fact possibly explains why most of them were treated as an every-other-day event.

One murder in particular was not only widely publicized, it was also to affect the legislation of this country.

33

This was the killing of Police Constable Nat Edgar.

Edgar was shot three times whilst questioning a man suspected of house-breaking. He died on 13 February 1948, but not before he had given his colleagues vital information about his assailant. Within twenty-four hours two thousand policemen were engaged in a hunt for his killer, twenty-two-year-old army deserter Donald Thomas. Until the night of 13 February Thomas had been just one of twenty-five thousand service deserters who were still roaming the country three years after the War, cardless, couponless and desperate. Until that night he was just one of the many factors that made these dangerous times to live in; now he became rather special.

Four days later a Clapham landlady, realizing that two of her boarders were Thomas and his mistress, notified the police. Hoping to surprise him, the police stood outside his bedroom door when the landlady took in the breakfast tray, but he caught a glimpse of them, slammed the door and dived for his Luger. Three police officers burst into the room and after a violent struggle overpowered him.

Thomas's manner is sharply reminiscent of that of the teenager on the Croydon roof. Asked by the officer who had grabbed his gun if it was loaded, he replied, 'That gun's full up, and they were all for you.' On the way to Brixton Police Station he remarked to the police, 'You were lucky. I might as well be hung for a sheep as a lamb.' He had no idea that fate was about to take a hand; he was not to be hanged.

At the time of the murder of PC Edgar the Criminal Justice Bill was going through the House of Commons. When it was first published it was seen as a major measure of penal reform. It proposed many changes, including the abolition of penal servitude, hard labour and corporal punishment, which entailed whipping across the bare back with an instrument called the cat-o'-nine-tails (the tails in question being lashes of whipcord) or with the birch (made of strips of wood tied together). The birch was to be retained for offences against prison discipline, but it would no longer be a weapon in the hands of the judges of England. The Bill proposed new, enlightened methods for dealing with offenders. In view of the current crime problem the Bill was an act of great courage on the part of the Labour Government of the time. Only one of the major reforms missing from the Bill when it was published in 1947 was later added as an amendment. Destined to cause a furore that nearly destroyed the entire Bill, this reform was the abolition of Capital Punishment.

Early in 1948 it became common knowledge that such an amendment was going to be tabled. Realizing that it would be supported by a majority of the House, the then Home Secretary, Chuter Ede, may well have been influenced in some of the decisions that he made during the early part of 1948. The amendment was debated on 15 April; he had already that year considered the cases of fourteen men found guilty of murder and all but three had been reprieved.

It is generally believed that when the House debates an issue that involves a matter of conscience, such as hanging, there is a free vote, and that such matters are not, and should not be, fettered by party loyalties. That tradition was broken on 15 April 1948; the Ministers of the Labour Government had been instructed to vote against the amendment. It was the Government's belief that the time had not yet been reached when hanging could safely be dispensed with. Chuter Ede made this quite clear, pointing to the increase in crimes of violence and murders since the end of the War.

It was an ironic situation. The amendment had been introduced by Ede's own backbenchers, most notably Sydney Silverman; it was largely supported by the Labour members and opposed by the Labour Ministers and a large element of the Conservative Opposition. After a debate full of excitement the amendment was carried by 245 votes to 222. It was hailed as a great victory by the radical element in this country, for although the amendment only suspended hanging for five years, it was confidently

35

predicted that capital punishment would never return.

The following day Chuter Ede announced that in view of the vote he would be advising the King to commute all death sentences to life imprisonment until the Bill became law. As Mr Ede pointed out, he had to consider what ought to be done about the prisoners now under sentence of death and those who might be sentenced in the next few weeks. Although to have carried on hanging would have been within the strict letter of the law during that period, to have done so would obviously have been contrary to the desires of the House. There was at that time no reaction from the Opposition; to the Conservatives it seemed a perfectly reasonable procedure.

Five days after that announcement, the trial of Donald Thomas was concluded with the inevitable verdict of 'Guilty'. Thomas, who had declared during the trial that he had 'always been fascinated by guns since I was a small boy', stood as the Judge pronounced sentence of death. But there was an historic difference to the passing of this particular sentence; for the first time in four hundred years the black cap was missing from the Judge's head. Thomas, although not an avid follower of House of Commons' debates, got the point. His first words when he stepped from the dock were, 'It's good to be alive.'

He was not the only one to get the point. The following day the *Daily Express* reported the case under the headline: 4.50 P.M. AT OLD BAILEY. THE NEW DEAL FOR KILLERS HAD BEGUN. It was a New Deal that caused uproar amongst the police, who were incensed that the man who had been found guilty of the murder of their colleague was going to live. The morale of the Force, already low, was now all but shattered. Very little of their true feelings became public, for the simple reason that then, as now, they were censored. They were not allowed to write to the press or express their opinions in public, and this only increased the frustration and anger that already existed about this particular case.

A few days after the Thomas case the *Police Chronicle* made the following general comments about the no-hanging clause. 'There is little doubt that the decision of the House of Commons is being received with grave apprehension by members of the Police Service. Scarcely a week passes without a Constable being subjected to severe personal violence by criminals attempting to resist arrest. In many cases it is only a matter of luck whether death occurs or not.'

On 27 April the House of Lords debated the Criminal Justice Bill. Speaker after speaker denounced the Commons' attempt to end hanging. Eventually it was the turn of Lord Goddard to make his maiden speech in the Lords. It is significant that for four years the Lord Chief Justice of England had declined to enter the political arena of the Lords – the hanging issue ensured that he remained silent no longer.

He not only delivered a bitter attack on the Silverman amendment, he was also opposed to certain clauses of the Bill itself. With regard to corporal punishment Lord Goddard had no objection to losing the cat, a thonged legacy from the days of keelhauling, but he considered the birch 'an instrument which can be used as a very strong deterrent'. Using a debating technique with which the Upper House was to become accustomed during the ensuing years, his Lordship quoted from one of his own cases to justify his arguments.

He recounted the circumstance of a farm labourer who had been found guilty of hitting a jeweller on the head with a spanner. Lord Goddard had given him a short sentence of a couple of months and twelve strokes of the birch rod. As he explained to the listening peers, 'I was not then depriving the country of the services of a good agricultural labourer over the harvest.' Lord Goddard also quoted two particularly violent and horrific murders in detail to justify his belief that 'there are many, many cases where the murderer should be destroyed'. He did not tell the House of Lords that in these two cases both of the guilty men were grossly abnormal. But then to Lord Goddard abnormality, no matter how gross, did not absolve from hanging a man found guilty of murder. During 1947 Thomas Ley and Lawrence Smith had been found guilty of a murder that became known as the 'Chalkpit Murder'. Ley, a former Minister of Justice for New South Wales and a sufferer from acute paranoia, deluded himself into believing that his mistress was having an affair with a young barman named Mudie. Mudie's strangled body was subsequently found in a chalkpit on the North Downs, and prosecution counsel established to the satisfaction of the jury that Ley and Smith had together murdered him. Ley was declared insane and committed to Broadmoor, and Smith was thereupon reprieved, on the grounds that as he was only the accomplice it would be unjust to hang him. In later years Lord Goddard was to comment on this in no uncertain manner. In his opinion, 'insane or not, Ley should have hanged'.

The Lord Chief Justice made no reference during the April 1948 debate to Chuter Ede's announcement that in the interim period until the Bill became law all persons found guilty of murder would be recommended for a reprieve.

In May 1948 it was announced that Donald Thomas had been reprieved. Although the police could not make their views public, they made them very clear to those in positions of influence.

By early June 1948 the House of Lords had reached the committee stage of the Criminal Justice Bill. Voicing the burning indignation felt by the police, Lord Llewellyn made the following observations on the first day of the debate: 'Since the man Thomas was reprieved after he had murdered a policeman, there have been two other attacks on the police. I believe that in one case the policeman was killed, and in the other the officer sustained a ghastly stomach wound.' This speech set the tone for the entire debate.

The following day Lord Goddard spoke. He too referred specifically to the Thomas reprieve, and then delivered a scathing attack on the Home Secretary for suspending hanging until the amendment became law, declaring that such action was contrary to the Bill of Rights. 'And if this is not altering the law by administrative action,' he added, 'I do not know what is.' His attack on the Commons was equally bitter. He considered that to end hanging was to fly in the face of public opinion; for the executions of Timothy Evans, Derek Bentley, Ruth Ellis and James Hanratty were still in the future, and public opinion polls indicated that over 80% of the population still wished to retain hanging. This fact, Lord Goddard felt, could not be ignored. He told the Lords that he firmly believed in the principle of 'Vox populi, vox Dei'. The voice of the people is the voice of God. 'If the law of the country is to be respected,' he declared, 'it must be in accordance with the public conscience.' It was a commendable philosophy; in Chapters 7 and 8 we will examine how much attention was paid to it in the case of Derek Bentley.

The catalysis of the Thomas reprieve had come at exactly the right moment for Lord Goddard. Then seventy-one years old, he voiced attitudes more in keeping with the Victorian era of his youth, but he found many kindred spirits in the Lords that day. When they voted on the Silverman amendment it was rejected by the massive majority of 181 to 28. There can be no doubt that if the function of Parliament is to reflect the wishes of the people then the Lords Spiritual and Temporal had fulfilled their function on that June day in 1948. For Lord Goddard it was a particularly memorable day. He returned to the House of Lords after dinner and in a virtually deserted Chamber moved an amendment to retain birching; it was passed – in the presence of less than fifty members. The police reaction to the Thomas reprieve had proved an invaluable weapon in the hands of the Lords. Moreover, it left a mark on the minds of many politicians, among them Sir David Maxwell Fyfe, who within three years was to acquire overall responsibility for the police force.

The day after the Lords' debate, Mr Anthony Eden, the then Deputy Leader of the Opposition, raised in the House of Commons, not the issue of Lords against the Commons, but the issue that he obviously considered had greater potential advantage for the Conservative Party. He gratefully took up Lord Goddard's allegation that Chuter Ede's automatic recommendation of reprieves was unconstitutional. After Eden had spoken long and righteously about this grave breach of the Constitution, the Leader of the House, Mr Herbert Morrison, replied. He expressed surprise that the Opposition had not raised 'this grave issue' when the Home Secretary had made his original statement about reprieves *two months previously*.

The fact that the Opposition had not realized the situation until it had been pointed out by Lord Goddard did nothing to reduce their ire. The Conservative Press were quick to take up the point. The *Daily Mail* said that Morrison was a 'Wide Boy'.

In Chuter Ede's mind, however, there was no doubt at all. He was later to say, 'There was never any worry in the Cabinet about it. I was breaking the Bill of Rights, but it was a matter of common sense that those reprieves should be granted.'

In the event the Lords severely mauled the Criminal Justice Bill that June. The Government, realizing that to continue with the no-hanging amendment would mean the virtual death of the entire Bill, urged the Commons to drop the clause. It had become clear that the Lords were in no mood for compromise, and that if the Commons persisted, a much needed measure of reform would be lost. So Silverman and his supporters withdrew the amendment, but only after Chuter Ede had promised to instigate an early exploration of what practical means there were for limiting the death penalty. For the radicals, all had not been lost. Ede had become convinced during the debates that there was a general desire to modify the all-embracing death penalty to which the country was now reverting. Lord Goddard's amendment on corporal punishment was roundly defeated in the Commons, and their Lordships decided not to press the point, but to concentrate their energies on the hanging issue. So when the Criminal Justice Bill became law, corporal punishment was abolished except for serious breaches of prison discipline. Importantly, it could no longer be ordered as a punishment by the Courts, a fact that Lord Goddard viewed with something less than equanimity.

In 1950, immediately after he had sentenced the atom bomb spy Klaus Fuchs to fourteen years' imprisonment for passing secret information to the Russians, two young boys were put up before Lord Goddard in the Central Criminal Court. The dock that a few moments before had held a man who in Lord Goddard's opinion had 'done irreparable and incalculable harm both to this land and to the United States . . . merely for the purpose of serving your political creed', now held two youths whose actions equally troubled the Lord Chief Justice. James Watson, aged seventeen, and Roger Eves, aged fifteen, both pleaded guilty to robbery with violence. Armed with a revolver and a heavy cosh they had attacked an elderly woman on a train, battered her nearly senseless and taken her money, then stuffed her under a seat in the compartment. They had planned the robbery during a visit to the Probation Office which they were then both attending. As Lord Goddard listened to the evidence his face became like stone. In passing sentence he said, 'I think that this is the most shocking and disturbing case that has ever come to my notice during my seventeen years as a judge. This case and others like it must give one seriously to think whether the modern methods of dealing with young criminals are not to some extent responsible for these outrages.'

This echoed Lord Winterton's view that the Criminal Justice Bill was 'a gangster's charter'. Lord Goddard continued, 'You, and other hooligans like you, think that you can escape punishment, that there is nothing for you but

41

approved schools, and that if you are older the most that can happen to you is detention in a Borstal establishment from which you can escape at the earliest possible moment. That ought not to be regarded as a punishment and it ought not to be thought, when a grave crime has been committed, that it is enough. If there is no punishment, how can you expect any diminution in juvenile crime? I consider that this constant binding-over is very largely responsible for crimes. I am going to punish you both very severely.

'The sentences I am going to pass upon you may be a warning to others of like kidney. It is not for me to criticize the wisdom of Parliament that prevents me from doing what I might have done eighteen months ago, when I could have had you well whipped and given you a short sentence. I am going to pass a long sentence, as I am satisfied that there is no other way of dealing with it. This is not a case for Borstal, but a case of callous brutality. The sentence of the Court is that you, Watson, go to prison for seven years; and that you, Eves, are detained for seven years at such a place as the Secretary of State may direct.'

If nothing else is clear concerning these post-war years, one fact shines out like a beacon. The more punitive the sentences that Lord Goddard and his fellow judges dispensed to the younger generation, the greater was the increase in juvenile crime. It is almost as if the youth of post-war Britain regarded the harsh treatment of their contemporaries as a direct call to arms.

In 1952, referring to the sentences that he had passed on Eves and Watson, Lord Goddard remarked, 'To pass a sentence of seven years on people of seventeen and fifteen years of age is a terrible thing to do . . . no judge likes doing that.' The harshness of his actions obviously left a deep impression on Lord Goddard. However, the criminal fraternity that harshness was specifically designed to inhibit were singularly unimpressed.

In May 1951 Sergeant Gibson was murdered by a gunman as he sat in a police car. In June 1951 a twenty-year-old youth, Derek Poole, engaged in a furious gun battle with police and troops, having previously shot and killed PC Alan Baxter. After holding out with a Sten-gun for some hours he was eventually shot to death by one of his pursuers. In July 1951 Detective Inspector Fraser and PC Jagger were both shot and killed by poacher Alfred Moore.

One of the consequences of this succession of police murders was a tremendous agitation to improve the pensions paid to police widows. The inadequacy of these pensions had been a running sore with the police since before the Second World War. When Edgar had been killed in 1948 there had been great public outcry about the pittance that · his widow received, amounting to less than three pounds a week, but the authorities ignored all the protests. It was left to newspapers and other organizations to take up a collection; the public gave generously, and Mrs Edgar was relieved of immediate financial worry. But many other police widows, not so fortunate, had to live on a pension of *sixteen shillings* a week. Austerity or not, this was truly a disgraceful situation. The fact that, if a policeman was killed, his widow received a pension that was totally inadequate for her needs, is perhaps the most eloquent comment that one can make about this country's post-war values.

While the police rightly demanded adequate pensions for their next of kin, the authorities were engaged in attempting to understand the phenomenon that was putting so many of those police lives at risk.

The 'cosh-boy' menace was at its height, and the young thug had replaced the weather as the topic of conversation. The solutions proposed were many and various, but for Lord Goddard the answer was obvious. He was convinced that the Criminal Justice Act of 1948 was the root cause, and that it had indeed become a 'gangster's charter'.

On 3 July 1952, during a banquet for judges at the Mansion House, Lord Goddard condemned 'the great and disturbing increase of crime which is disgracing this country at present, and more especially the crimes of violence which are so prevalent'. It could be traced, in his opinion, to the fact that 'the discontinuance of flogging and birching has led thugs to believe that violence is worth while'. He offered no evidence to support this contention – but then Lord Goddard had never been a person to be inhibited by lack of evidence. In a clear call to arms to all supporters of whipping and beating, he declared that *the remedy is to restore corporal punishment and to extend it, not to limit it*. He spoke at great length, using phrases like 'the man who smashes a tumbler on a public-house counter and jabs it into the face of a man with whom he had quarrelled' and 'the man who beats up an old man or old woman in the streets'. Undoubtedly such incidents had occurred since whipping had been abolished. They had also occurred during the years when this country resounded to the sound of birches and whips being administered to bare backs. Lord Goddard, not surprisingly, chose not to mention this fact. As his port grew warm, he pursued the theme of his hypothetical hoodlums. 'It is those who have been encouraged in their violence by the knowledge that flogging, or the birch, which is more effective, because it brings ridicule with it, can no longer be imposed. Is not the time come when all this has got to be reconsidered? In the administration of criminal law, I believe that for years past we have thought too much of the criminal and not enough of the victim. It may be that a change of heart may now come over those in authority. If public opinion gets seriously disturbed by the amount of crime that is prevalent and I have been to the Assizes and heard that old people have dreaded to answer a knock on the door because they don't know what thug may be standing there to take their life savings, there will be a strong tendency (for people) to take the law into their own hands.' It was speeches like this that made Lord Goddard the darling boy of the whippers, hangers and floggers of this country.

His speech was fully reported the following day, but there was precious little comment. No one saw fit to point out the most glaring error in the speech – that crimes of violence, which prior to the Criminal Justice Act had been the chief crimes punishable by whipping or flogging, had not risen, but fallen significantly since the abolition of corporal punishment. In 1947 there had been 841 such cases; in 1951, 633. The punishment had been softened, and the criminal had responded. But the audience at which Lord Goddard had aimed his remarks were no more interested in such facts than he was. In fact, if a group of people has ever had the courage of its prejudices it was these supporters of the whip and the birch. A Liverpool schoolmistress, for example, organized a one-thousand-name petition demanding the return of flogging, and at Croydon, a public meeting launched a ten-thousand-name petition. This was not the first time that the people of Croydon had commented in public on the crime problem.

During 1948 they had complained long and loud about the state of affairs. Croydon Local Councillor Kendell declared, 'Young gangsters are attacking police in the streets of Croydon.' The Reverend Peskett declared, 'Boys and girls are acting like savages.' There was an appeal to the Home Secretary 'to deal with the serious lawlessness among young people in South London'. Another group declared that 'the local magistrates are too soft in Croydon'. (Ironically, when a few years later, a writer took all these people at their word and published a book that labelled Croydon as a 'crime town' its citizens were outraged.) But in July 1952, as they organized their petitions, they could not have known that they were about to have the problem brought to their very doorsteps, in an event that was to focus national attention on their town.

At the time of Lord Goddard's Mansion House speech one policeman had already died on duty during 1952. In Cardiff, PC Beattie was run over and killed while trying to arrest two men. In September, at the other end of the country, in Glasgow, an eighteen-year-old bank clerk named Edward Finley, about to be questioned in connection with a missing £900, shot a policeman dead, wounded another, and then killed himself.

Lord Goddard's speech meanwhile had undoubtedly touched a receptive nerve in certain sections of the community. The Conservative Women's Central Advisory Committee, the Women's Guild of Empire and the National Chamber of Trade, all considered that Lord Goddard had found the answer. One clergyman (it seems that clergymen were rather given to pronouncements of this kind at that time) justified corporal punishment by recalling that 'Our Lord used a whip, with some devastating results'. He omitted to mention that among those results was Our Lord's crucifixion.

A group of old-age pensioners in Wimbledon considered that the suggested measures were far too weak, they advocated the return of the stocks so that the public could observe the criminals being whipped.

In the general clamour the quiet voice of reason was altogether submerged. The Chairman of the Howard League for Penal Reform declared, 'No penalty has been so thoroughly investigated as has flogging. Data stretching back nearly one hundred years was investigated by a Departmental Committee appointed in 1937 by Lord Simon. The report of this Committee established two things. First that the arguments most frequently used to defend flogging, that it stamped out garrotting and that Mr Justice Day put down an outbreak of violence by use of the cat, were legends without even a substratum of fact, and secondly, that it was impossible to find any evidence whatsoever to show that it was more effective than ordinary imprisonment.' But he might just as well have blown in the wind.

Nevertheless, by October 1952 it was apparent that the Conservative Government were not going to be panicked into legislation to bring back the cat or the birch. They rightly regarded suggestions that would put the clock back, not merely to 1948, but, if all the suggestions were adopted, to 1822, as unbecoming to a civilized country.

It was a view that was particularly unpalatable to the Government's traditional supporters. In a four-hour House of Lords' debate on 22 October, Earl Howe called attention to 'the continuation of crimes of violence towards women and other defenceless persons'. The Earl asked whether 'the existing penalties which the Courts had the power to inflict in such cases are adequate to protect the public. Flogging was abolished in 1948, and I should like to know whether anyone can tell us what symptoms of reform it has been possible to detect in gangsters since that date.' The awkward fact that the Magistrates Association had recently voted *against* the return of corporal punishment by 219 votes to 166 was easily overcome by the Earl; he did not feel that the Association was truly representative of a body with thousands of members. Most of the speakers who followed, including, of course, Lord Goddard, supported Lord Howe's views. But the Lord Chancellor, Lord Simonds, rejected his plea for a return to the good old days of whipping. Point by point he answered the arguments and firmly declared that the Government would not be a party to panic legislation.

Into this seething cauldron were about to step two young men. During the years covered in this opening chapter they had been emerging from childhood, affected in no small measure by all that had been going on around them. Now, as two teenagers, they were about to walk into the maelstrom of the law and order issue. The nation's unease and anxiety about the state of its youth was about to be focused upon these two adolescents. They were Christopher Craig and Derek Bentley. Craig was about to become the symbol of wayward youth. Bentley, the drab Bentley, was about to become much more. On Sunday, 2 November 1952, he walked into history, and joined a most select band of men and women. It isn't every day that we judicially murder a teenager.

The awful uniqueness of Bentley's fate extended even beyond that. He was to become the only man in our entire

47

legal history to be executed for a crime for which he was only vicariously responsible when the principal actor could not be executed.

Craig was the baby of a middle-class family, the youngest of nine children. His father had served in the London Scottish in the First World War, became a captain at the age of twenty-two, and was mentioned in dispatches. Mr Craig had been a keen rugger player in his youth and had also won prizes for amateur boxing. In the Second World War he had been a Company Commander in the Home Guard. By 1952 he held a responsible position in a London bank. His wife was later to be described as a 'gentle and educated person, sensitive and with a love of poetry, which she could quote extensively from memory'. She took an active interest in social work and had on one occasion given a talk over the radio on juvenile delinquency. Of their many children, all had done well in their chosen professions. Niven Craig, the eldest son, had had what was by any standards a colourful life. During the Second World War, when still a schoolboy, he had broken into a Home Guard store, stolen firearms and ammunition and set out with another boy to cross the English Channel in a rowing boat, apparently to fight the German Panzer divisions. Although found guilty of breaking and entering, the two lads were lauded by a chauvinistic press. Young Craig and his friend presumably epitomized all that was fine and honourable about the British, the 'fight them on the beaches' philosophy at its finest.

Niven Craig had two other convictions as a juvenile and one as an adult, but for some reason these did not catch the national imagination. Then in 1945 he again showed his flair for the unusual. While serving with the Gordon Highlanders he escaped from an escort in Austria and made his way to Italy; on the way he four times held up at pistol-point drivers of Army vehicles and drove off, leaving them to gaze at the exhaust fumes. It is possible that this time he intended to flush out El Duce singlehanded but the Army authorities took a different view, and gave him five years in a Service prison to demonstrate to him just how much of a man's life it was in the regular Army.

After his release in 1950 Niven somehow managed, despite not having a job, to dress in the more elegant fashions of the day and drive large American cars. It was just such a car that led to his next court appearance. During March 1952 a Buick that he owned was found a few miles from the scene of an armed robbery. On 30 October he appeared before Mr Justice Hilbery in No. 2 Court, Old Bailey. He was found guilty of armed robbery. He was also found guilty of possessing an automatic pistol with intent to endanger life. The police had stated that at the time of his arrest at a hotel in Paddington he had gone for the gun. Niven Craig strongly denied this allegation, declaring that the gun had been removed by the police from under his pillow.

Before he passed sentence, Mr Justice Hilbery said: 'I have watched you carefully during the course of this trial and I can say that with regard to both matters in respect of which you stand convicted I do not remember in the course of some seventeen years on the Bench trying various crimes of violence a young man of your age [twenty-six] who struck me as being so determined as you have impressed me as being.

'You are not only cold-blooded, but from my observation of you I have not the least hesitation in saying I believe that you would shoot down, if you had the opportunity to do so, any police officer who was attempting to arrest you or indeed any lawful citizen who tried to prevent you from committing some felony which you had in hand.

'I have little doubt it was you who held the gun and that these others were men of rougher material, at any rate the man standing by your side in the dock acting under your directions.' The judge then sentenced Niven Craig to twelve years' imprisonment. Craig had protested throughout his trial that on the night in question he had been in Norfolk staying at a friend's farm. He called the farmer, who confirmed this. It was also stated that staying at the farm that weekend was Niven's younger brother, Christopher. But the jury preferred to believe the case for the Prosecution. After Niven's trial Christopher helped his sobbing mother from the court; as they passed two of the policemen who had just given evidence against his brother the young Craig heard one of them remark, 'Well, we've put that bastard away for a while.' This was on 30 October. Three days later Christopher Craig was to extract a terrible revenge for what had happened to his brother – at least this was how his actions were to be interpreted by a shocked public in general, and the experts in particular. They were, however, wrong.

Christopher's criminal record was insignificant by comparison with his brother's. It started in September 1951 when he was fifteen. He disappeared from his home, taking with him for company a boy of twelve, a ·45 Webley revolver, and a quantity of ammunition. The two boys were found under a boat on Brighton beach. The pundits were later to draw a parallel between this and his brother's wartime attempt to cross the Channel. To them this was a clear example of an attempt to emulate his brother's dubious achievements. When I questioned Craig about this incident, however, he assured me that at the time he had not even known of his brother's exploit. He'd run away because his almost total illiteracy was proving a severe handicap at the garage where he worked. 'I worked in the stores,' he explained to me. 'When one of the mechanics came in for a part I had to get them to spell the word for me. They took the mick out of me and made jokes about it. The thing was I knew more about cars than any of them. I should have been the one out there repairing them.' The story is a good example of people jumping to the wrong conclusions. Craig's behaviour was nothing to do with hero-worship, but simply a manifestation of a profound inferiority complex. At the time of the incident nobody took the trouble to find out what the real cause was.

If they had, two men who are now dead might still be alive. Instead of which Craig was fined 35/- and the revolver was confiscated.

Christopher Craig's subsequent criminal activities proved more successful. During the summer of 1952 he was very 'busy'. With Bentley, he broke into a large number of properties, stealing anything that they took a liking to. Without exception all the crimes that these two teenagers committed together were completely non-violent. When Craig developed an inclination for more violent forms of crime he discovered that Bentley would not even entertain the idea, and Craig had to acquire a new companion for such ventures. A mere two weeks before the rooftop battle Craig committed an armed robbery. His companion on the robbery was another sixteen-year-old boy, grammar-school-educated Norman Parsley.

Craig still recalls the robbery vividly. He had broken into a greengrocer's belonging to an elderly couple called Howes. Finding nothing of value, he reasoned that Mr Howes had the takings at his home, so he and Parsley, with trilby hats pulled over their eyes and scarves masking their faces, knocked at the Howes' South Croydon house. Mrs Howes opened the door, and they pushed her inside. Both had revolvers. Mr Howes came out into the kitchen to find his wife writhing and moaning on the floor. They demanded his wallet, but he waved a sheaf of receipts at them, protesting that he had just paid £71 worth of bills. On the sideboard was a paper money bag which the old man handed to them, telling them to get out. As they were about to leave, Mrs Howes got to her feet and tried to pull the scarf from Parsley's face. He waved her off with his gun, and she exclaimed, 'They're toys!' Parsley showed her the nickel-tipped bullets in the chamber. 'Take a look at those, lady, they aren't toys.' Then he and Craig left with the money-bag. It contained less than five pounds. It is doubtful if they would ever have been apprehended had not Craig and Bentley decided two weeks later to break into the butcher's shop.

This then was Christopher Craig. Derek Bentley was quite a different proposition. His background and character were so unusual as to make Craig's seem almost normal by comparison. Because of this, and because it has a bearing on the fact of his being hanged, I have devoted most of Chapter 4 to an examination of Bentley.

At 2.30 on the afternoon of Sunday, 2 November 1952, Police Constable Sidney Miles was at his Surrey home preparing to go on duty. It was to be the last time that his wife would see him alive.

A few miles away, in Norbury, Derek Bentley was also about to go out, to see a Betty Grable film, *The Lady from the West*. It was the last film he would ever see.

A few streets away, Christopher Craig was also getting ready to go to the pictures, in his case to see a film called *My Death is a Mockery*, in which the hero is hanged after a French policeman is killed in a gunfight. A few short hours later the fantasy world of the cinema was to become a frightening reality.

The seeds of violence that had been so diligently sown during the years since 1945 were about to flower.

2

Two Threepennies to Croydon

As Derek Bentley sat in his home in the quiet working-class district of Norbury on the evening of Sunday, 2 November 1952, his parents could tell that for once the television was not holding his entire attention. Shortly after lunchtime he had developed a headache that gradually increased in its intensity. It hadn't stopped him going to the Betty Grable film, but the headache became so severe that he left the cinema before the end of the programme. His parents attributed his restlessness to the fact that the pain was still troubling him. It undoubtedly was, but Bentley had other problems. In his pocket were the keys to a butcher's shop in West Croydon that Bentley had stolen the previous afternoon when the butcher's back was turned.

Now, as a television programme, *The Passing Show*, churned out songs from old stage shows, he was anxiously awaiting a knock at the front door. It came just before eight thirty, but before he could get to the door his mother had told the caller that Derek was out. The caller was Christopher Craig.

Bentley's parents had been trying since March of that year to prevent the association between the two boys. In their opinion Craig was an evil influence that their son would do well to avoid. The events of that evening would show just how right they were, but the events of the past were already adequate justification for the Bentleys. They were fully aware that their son was an epileptic and that he was mentally subnormal. And they considered that one spell in an approved school was more than enough for him.

53

In fact they had done more than merely forbid the association. A mere eight days before this Sunday, Mr Bentley had gone to Norbury Police Station and appealed to the police to help him in his efforts to break the relationship. The desk sergeant had listened politely, then (incorrectly) advised Mr Bentley that there was nothing they could do to help him. Yet another opportunity had been lost to avert what by now had some of the elements of inevitability normally associated only with Greek tragedy.

For Craig and Bentley this particular Sunday evening was to be spent breaking into the butcher's shop in West Croydon. Mrs Bentley had unwittingly thwarted the plan, but Craig was a resourceful boy and a few minutes later there was another knock at the door. This time when Mrs Bentley opened it she was confronted by a well-spoken youth, Norman Parsley. He made a more favourable impression, and the youth with him, Frank Fazey, was equally polite. Derek joined them on the street corner, where they were waiting with, of course, Christopher Craig. After a few minutes' conversation, Parsley and Fazey departed, leaving Bentley and Craig waiting in the rain for a bus. A No. 109 came into sight, and they ran for it.

As they climbed to the upper deck they must have looked a curious couple. Both wore wide-brimmed hats, calf-length overcoats, drape suits with fingertip-length jackets and crêpe-soled shoes, known to the teenagers of the period as 'brothel-creepers'. This style of dress, peculiar to the younger generation of 1952, created the illusion that they were both much older than they actually were (Craig was sixteen, Bentley nineteen). Craig's youthful, unlined, almost feminine face and black hair, cut in a Tony Curtis style, would have sharply contradicted his clothes. Bentley, although more powerfully built, looked equally immature, despite his fashionable marcel-waved hair and brightly coloured shirt.

Craig also affected a tough-guy American drawl. This was not a constant trait; when he became excited his accent would revert to the same as Bentley's, South London. The American influence in Craig's speech is hardly surprising; at this time he was going to the cinema three or four times a week, and the only reading matter that he could comprehend was comics.

The fact that they were on their way to commit a crime did not frighten them. Breaking into a shop was a bit of a giggle, a way of relieving the tedium. To their way of thinking there was precious little else to do on a wet Sunday night.

The conductor came upstairs, and Craig bought two threepenny tickets to West Croydon Station. Neither had been in the Boy Scouts, but they had certainly adopted that organization's motto. They were very well prepared. Bentley had a sheath-knife in his inside pocket, and Craig also gave him a little toy that he had made at the garage where he worked, a knuckleduster with a metal spike protruding at one end. Craig himself was carrying a knife and a loaded ·455 Eley Service revolver (commonly known as a ·45 Colt). He also had a spare clip of ammunition, tommy-gun bullets, in his top pocket.

In view of the fact that much publicity was given to these weapons subsequently, for they were to play an important part at the Old Bailey trial, it is worth considering why they were carrying enough weapons to rob a bank in broad daylight, let alone an empty butcher's shop. Bentley's knife was to deal with any locks that his keys wouldn't turn; I have called the knuckleduster a toy, because it was just that to Bentley. When asked at the Old Bailey why he had accepted the knuckleduster from Craig, Bentley replied, 'Something I have never had, something I had given to me, and I just put it into my pocket.' I have interviewed a great many people who knew Bentley personally. Many were highly critical of him, but none ever suggested, or had any knowledge, that he had ever been physically violent. He was a young man of immense strength, but there is no evidence that he ever in his life used that strength against another human being. To have accepted the knuckleduster was an act of bravado; to have used it would simply never have occurred to him.

Craig was quite another matter; the knife was carried for the same purpose as Bentley's, to effect an entry, but the gun? I asked Craig why he had a gun on him that night, and extra ammunition. I must admit that I was inclined, more than seventeen years after the event, to agree with the opinion that Prosecuting Counsel Christmas Humphreys expressed at the time of the trial. He asserted that the gun showed a clear intent to use whatever violence was necessary; that it was a desperate measure taken by a desperate youth. The truth is rather more complex.

Craig had carried a gun of one sort or another with him every day of his life since the age of eleven. Pocketing a gun when he got dressed in the morning was a habit; he did it in the way an ordinary youth would put on socks. He took a gun with him quite literally everywhere; to work, to the cinema, on a visit to a relative, even on a night out with his girlfriend. At school he had shown guns around quite openly in the classroom. In the neighbourhood where he lived his curious interest in revolvers was widely known. He even slept with a gun and a knife under his pillow, because he was frightened of the dark.

I asked Christopher Craig if Bentley knew that he was carrying a gun on that Sunday night – for the proof of Bentley's guilt at his trial depended crucially, as Lord Goddard said, on Bentley's being aware that Craig was armed, and intending with Craig to offer violent resistance. Craig's answer was most illuminating. 'The gun didn't come into what we were going to do. If he'd thought that I was likely to get a gun out of my pocket he'd never have come out with me that night.' When I asked him how he could be so sure, he told me about the armed robbery he had committed two weeks before that fateful Sunday night.

He'd wanted to do the job with Bentley, but as soon as his friend realized the nature of the crime, he would have nothing to do with it. *To Bentley anything that*

56

necessitated carrying a gun, let alone using one, was out.
In the event Craig took Parsley with him on the raid on
the greengrocer that I have already described. So Craig
insisted that when he and Bentley went to Croydon, not
only had there been no agreement to use any violence, the
subject had not even been discussed. Indeed, at their trial
not one shred of evidence was put forward to contradict
this. The Prosecution relied on the fact that the two
youths were carrying weapons to substantiate the claim
that there had been an agreement between them to use
whatever violence was necessary. To the adult mind this is
perhaps reasonable, the assumption being that you do not
carry weapons unless you intend to use them. But Craig
and Bentley did not have adult minds. They did not even
have normal adolescent minds. The medical evidence that
would have confirmed beyond any doubt whatsoever that
Craig and Bentley were not adults, nor adolescents but two
retarded children, was never presented at the trial. When
considering why these two youths were so extravagantly
armed the normal yardsticks of common sense and adult
intelligence have to be suspended, if for no other reason
than that Craig and Bentley did not possess one iota of
common sense and adult intelligence between them.

Arriving at West Croydon, Craig and Bentley jumped
off the bus and made their way down Tamworth Road,
fiddling with their hats and walking with that exaggerated
sway of the shoulders that, like their clothes, was so much
a part of London youth in the early 'fifties. To any onlooker
they would have presented the funny sight of two boys
aping grown men, but there were no onlookers – yet.
Arriving at the butcher's shop they saw to their dismay
that the upstairs light was on, indicating, as they believed,
that the butcher was working late. Any professional burglar
would have been able to tell them that it could just as well
have indicated precisely the opposite. They stood outside
the shop for a few minutes, then Bentley suggested that
they try their luck at an electrical shop they had passed

on the way. So, shoulders swaying, they marched up Tamworth Road and crept into the alleyway by the side of the electrical shop, only to discover that it was occupied already by a young couple swearing eternal devotion – something they hadn't bargained for, particularly as it was pouring with rain, or, as Craig put it, 'Bit wet for a knee-trembler.' Fate seemed to decree that they return home, but Bentley was equal to anything that fate decreed, and suggested Barlow and Parkers, a confectionery wholesalers, also in Tamworth Road. So like the famous Duke of York's men they marched down the hill again.

Arriving at the forecourt of the wholesalers' they were confronted with a pair of solid doors. Craig, still fiddling with his hat, told Bentley to check if the doors were locked. Obediently Bentley charged at them with his shoulder and promptly bounced back like a rubber ball. It was not quite the technique that Craig had had in mind, but it gave them the answer. Craig was uneasy; a frontal break-in was out of the question, their actions would be observed by any chance passer-by, then he noticed the six-foot, spike-topped, iron gate at the side of the building. He glanced up and down the road, but there was no one about on this wet Sunday evening. Quickly he climbed over the gate and dropped out of sight, calling for Bentley to follow him. Pausing for a moment to let a bus pass by, Bentley approached the gate and followed suit. He had a nervous moment with the spikes, but in a moment he half-climbed, half-fell over into the alleyway. Stumbling after Craig, he managed to walk straight into a dustbin, knocking it over with a clatter. They froze; but there was no reaction from the house next door. All was quiet. Their luck seemed to be holding.

In fact their luck had already run out. Directly across the road at No. 74, nine-year-old Edith Ware had taken that final look out of her window before going to bed that had revealed the two youths standing outside the wholesalers', and commented to her mother that they looked like burglars. Her mother had watched them climb over the spiked gate, then told her husband to call the police. Craig and Bentley had looked left and right before climbing the gate, but neither had given a thought to looking directly opposite. The time was 9.15 p.m.

In the alleyway the two youths explored their surroundings. So far their attempt to break into the warehouse was meeting with little success. The side doors were securely locked and there was no apparent way of forcing an entry. By now Bentley was all for calling it a night and returning home, but Craig again showed his resourcefulness. He was on the point of agreeing with Bentley, who was flip-flopping up and down the alleyway making enough noise with his 'brothel-creepers' to awaken the dead, when he noticed the footprint on a low window sill, and close by, the drainpipe running up the side of the building to the roof. Presumably someone had been there before them, for whatever reason, and that footprint gave Craig the idea of climbing up the drainpipe, on to the roof and then perhaps down into the building through the roof entrance.

By now Mr Ware had dressed and was walking away from his house, slowly in order to avoid attracting the burglars' attention. When he was clear he broke into a run, dashed to the police-box at the end of the road and dialled 999. Meanwhile, pausing only to survey the run of the drainpipe and telling his friend to keep a look-out, Craig began to climb. Although he lacked Bentley's superior strength, Craig was very fit. He had never smoked or drunk alcohol, and at school he had been considered a natural athlete. He had been a member of the school swimming team and his teachers considered that with application he could have become a top-class athlete. He preferred, however, to take less orthodox methods of exercise. Quickly scaling the pipe, he reached the roof without difficulty, and called down to Bentley to join him.

In the CID office at Croydon Police Station, Detective Constable Fairfax was typing a report about a theft from a gas meter. It looked like being a quiet, routine evening. Even the phone message 'suspects on premises, Tamworth

Road, Croydon' was fairly routine. Fairfax stopped typing his report and went out into the station yard. There he collected PC Norman Harrison who had forgotten to bring any sandwiches when he came on duty and was on his way to the staff canteen. One urgent word from Fairfax, 'Buzz!' was enough to make him forget about food. With Police Constables Pain and Bugden they jumped into a police van.

Back in the alleyway, Bentley had managed to climb about eight feet up one of the drainpipes, but the combination of his natural clumsiness and his crêpe-soled shoes was proving too much, he could get no higher. With Craig on the roof impatiently telling him to hurry it up Bentley descended and moved to the pipe that Craig had scaled; this time he made better progress, but when he had climbed to a height of fifteen feet he was overcome with a bout of dizziness. The ground swayed beneath him and he grimly clung to the pipe. (This dizziness could have been caused by the height, but I believe there was a far more serious reason, which is examined in Chapter 4.) With Craig's encouragement he eventually continued his climb and was hauled to the comparative safety of the roof.

Police car 7Z was patrolling the streets of Croydon when it received from Scotland Yard the message, 'suspects on roof'. Radio operator Police Constable James McDonald acknowledged, and his driver, Police Constable Sidney Miles, put his foot hard down on the accelerator. The car roared along the London Road towards central Croydon at over 70 mph arriving at the wholesalers' at virtually the same time as the van carrying Fairfax and Harrison. After a brief conversation with Mrs Ware to establish exactly what she had seen, Fairfax joined McDonald at the foot of the drainpipes in the alleyway. McDonald had by now discovered the footprint on the sill that had led the youths up on to the roof. Fairfax started up the drainpipe, but it swayed dangerously. He recalled, 'I didn't know whether to pray to God or to curse the plumber who'd put it there.'

On the roof Craig and Bentley saw the lights below them and hearing Fairfax's voice giving instructions to the other policemen, they were in no doubt as to who was down there. They looked around for an escape route.

The roof was long and flat. It was fifty-four feet wide and ninety long. Roughly in the middle, four rooflights rose like miniature greenhouses to a maximum height of four feet six inches. Half-way down the alleyway side was the roof entrance that led to the warehouse below. At the far end was the head of the lift-shaft, rising eleven feet six inches above roof level, and beyond that, running away into the distance, a series of asbestos and glass roofs rising and falling as far as they could see. To escape the way they had come was impossible – a quick glance over the edge showed them Fairfax and McDonald in the alleyway. The building was thirty feet high; jumping off would mean serious injury, perhaps death. The entrance into the building was locked. They were left with only two alternatives, to await the arrival of the police and give themselves up, or buy time by getting behind the head of the lift-shaft at the far end. Craig was in no mood for surrender, and before Bentley could consider what he wanted to do he was being urged to follow. The two teenagers walked quickly to the lift-head and got behind it. They waited hoping, like ostriches, that if they could not be seen by the police, then the police would go away and everything would be all right. The voice calling out from the direction of the alleyway told them the police had not gone away. 'Are you all right?' And the reply gave Bentley and Craig a profound shock; it was only one word, 'Yes', but it was spoken so close to them that they knew for certain that there was someone else on the roof. In fact Fairfax was by now standing some twenty feet away from the lift-head that sheltered them. He called out in their direction, 'I'm a police officer. Come out from behind that stack.' Fairfax was later to say during the trial that Craig's reply was, 'If you want us, fucking well come and get us.' When I interviewed Craig last summer he denied that he made any reply at all, a denial that was perhaps to be expected. But when I interviewed Fairfax, he said – although this was eighteen years later he did repeat this three times – that Craig had made no reply. As an isolated incident this is probably of little importance, but to me, seeking the total truth about what happened on that Croydon rooftop, then all incidents, small and large, are important. Pull one card out of the house of cards and the rest begin to wobble. Particularly when you remember that the next remark alleged to have been made was the one that hanged Bentley.

Fairfax stood there for a moment deciding on his best course of action. While he waited Bentley decided he'd had enough; he turned to Craig and simply said, 'I'm going out.' As he moved out, Fairfax, who had by now continued walking towards the lift-head, grabbed him. So far, with the exception of that first remark, there is little variation between the subsequent versions of what happened. At this point those versions begin to diverge. As Fairfax was arresting Bentley, PC McDonald was clambering up the drainpipe to join his colleague. However, he was having trouble doing so, being rather stocky in build, and was in fact clinging to the pipe some six feet from the top, and had just decided to go down again. Whether he was actually going down or was merely clinging motionless to the pipe is unclear, mainly because his own account was unclear. In either event he was at the very least sixty feet away and out of sight. PC Harrison meanwhile had got into the garden of No. 26 Tamworth Road and climbed on to another part of the warehouse roof, immediately behind No. 25. He too was at least sixty feet away and below the main roof level.

Having grabbed Bentley, Fairfax made his way around the front of the lift-head in pursuit of Craig. This is how he described in his deposition what happened. 'I then took Bentley round the stack with a view to closing in on Craig and as we got round the other side we came face to face with Craig. Craig was then on the westerly side of the stack. Bentley then broke away from me and as he did so he shouted "Let him have it, Chris". There was a loud report and a flash and something hit my shoulder which caused me to spin round and fall to the ground. It was my right shoulder which was hit. As I was getting up I saw one man moving away on my left and one on my right. I rushed at the man on my right, who was Bentley, and I closed on him and struck him with my fist, causing him to fall to the ground. As he did so, there was a second report and a flash and I dropped down and pulled Bentley in front of me as a shield.'

He then went on to describe how, having searched Bentley and removed his knife and knuckleduster, which he put on, he used Bentley as a shield and worked his way round to the safety of the wall behind the roof entrance. McDonald, who was then somewhere on the drainpipe, also swore that he heard the remark 'Let him have it, Chris' and the shots. Harrison also stated on oath that he had seen Bentley break away, and shout 'Let him have it, Chris'. He also stated that he heard the two shots fired in fairly rapid succession and that Fairfax had fallen after the first shot. This then in essence was the police version of the opening stages of an event that was to stun the nation.

Craig's account is somewhat different. Having grabbed Bentley, Craig says Fairfax made his way towards the roof entrance. He passed it, and arrived at the point where he had climbed up on to the roof. Seeing McDonald just below him on the pipe, Fairfax instructed Bentley to wait there and began to retrace his steps towards the lift-head. Craig was by now standing on the westerly side of the lift-head. At this point the police officer had no reason for suspecting that the youth was armed, so although he approached him warily there was no particular reason for caution. When he was thirty feet from Craig, the young boy, who had by now removed the revolver from his pocket, raised it, pointed it at the ground between himself and the policeman, and fired. Fairfax was hit and fell to the ground, but quickly recovered. He got to his feet and ran to various sides of the building shouting to his colleagues below that the men were armed, and telling his fellow police officers to surround the building and send for reinforcements. When he ran to the front of the roof and called down into Tamworth Road, Craig fired again, this time completely missing. At no time did Fairfax strike Bentley, at no time did Bentley shout 'Let him have it, Chris'. On this point Craig was insistent. There was no doubt in his mind whatsoever. Craig asserted, 'The remark that hanged Bentley was never uttered.'

The reader will doubtless arrive at his own conclusions. I would suggest, however, that he consider the following facts.

On Fairfax's evidence, Craig was only a few feet from him when the first shot was fired – in the police officer's own words 'within six feet . . . face to face'. Fairfax was hit in the shoulder by a ·45 bullet. Ballistics experts have advised me that, had he been a mere six feet from Craig, a bullet of this calibre would have either shattered the shoulder or drilled it; either way, the wound sustained would be very serious. When Fairfax was examined at Croydon General Hospital it was discovered that the bullet had hit his shoulder, travelled up the outside of his body, down his back and finally come to rest at the back of his braces. When he removed his coat in the hospital the bullet fell to the floor. It had hit the body by the right collarbone, there was no fracture to the bone and the doctor who examined Fairfax stated that the bullet had *passed over the surface of the skin and had not penetrated it*. Fairfax's jacket did not have the normal neat hole that a bullet frequently makes, but a jagged tear. It was stated during the trial that this particular bullet was slightly undersized for Craig's gun, the effect of which would be to produce a shot that was not as powerful as a bullet of the correct calibre. This was the prosecution's explanation for the incredibly slight injury that had been sustained, allegedly at point blank range, but an indication of just how powerful these undersize bullets actually were can be gauged from the fact that another undersize bullet of exactly the same calibre was found ninety feet away, by the front of the roof. The position of this second bullet is also a confirmation of Craig's account of the policeman's position at the time of the second shot. (It will be recalled that Craig contends that Fairfax was at the front of the roof at that time.) Fairfax's own testimony – 'There was a flash and a loud report, and I felt something strike my shoulder which caused me to *spin round and fall to the ground*' – is quite consistent with the impact of such a bullet. But the wound that he received and the tears in his jacket and waistcoat are inconsistent with the impact of a bullet fired directly from six feet by a ·455 Eley, whether the bullet was undersize or not. This aspect clearly worried the jury at the trial; when they were about to retire to consider their verdict, the foreman of the jury asked for just one exhibit to take with them into the jury room, and that exhibit was Fairfax's coat and waistcoat.

According to the prosecution's case, Bentley and Fairfax were virtually within touching distance of Craig when Bentley said 'Let him have it, Chris'. Yet the remark was heard by Harrison, at least sixty feet away on the roof behind No. 25 Tamworth Road, and by McDonald, clinging to a drainpipe below the warehouse roof level. If all three officers could hear this crucial remark at their respective distances it must be assumed that the remark was shouted. To have carried as far as McDonald and Harrison it must have been quite a loud shout. PCs Pain and Bugden were only a few feet further away than their colleagues, and the occupants of Nos. 26 and 30 Tamworth Road (the adjoining houses) were now in their gardens. If any of these had heard the remark it seems a pity that the Court did not have the benefit of their testimony.

It has commonly been supposed that all three officers stated specifically that it was Bentley who made the remark. In fact PC McDonald, although pressed to say that it came from Bentley, refused to do so. He declared that he was unable to recognize the voice. Analysis of

McDonald's evidence shows a considerable variance in some respects with the evidence of his two colleagues. In his original deposition, given at the preliminary hearing at Croydon, he stated that he followed Fairfax up the drainpipe. He then continued, 'I could not get up approximately the last six feet and on to the roof. *I climbed down again* and while I was doing so I heard someone shout "Let him have it, Chris." When I reached the ground I heard two or three shots fired. I shouted up to Detective Constable Fairfax and I then climbed up the pipe again and he helped me over the last few feet. When I got on to the roof I saw Fairfax, who had the accused Bentley with him. They were standing by the staircase head.' At the Old Bailey trial McDonald stated under cross-examination that at the time the all-important remark was said he was '*trying to get his footing to go down*'. He also said that the time it took him to get back down the pipe was 'minutes'; when pressed by Lord Goddard this became 'a minute'; when further pressed by the Judge it became a time that he doubted he could have counted sixty in. McDonald's precise position has a self-evident importance in view of what he said he heard. The time it took him to get down the pipe is equally important, when one remembers that Bentley's remark and the first shot were events that, according to Fairfax's trial evidence, '*happened practically simultaneously*'.

I find it hard to accept that if McDonald had heard a shot or shots while still clinging to the drainpipe he would have continued down to the ground, only to re-climb the pipe immediately; there can be little doubt that he was indeed on the ground when the first shots were fired. Hence the pressure on him by Lord Goddard during the trial to reduce the time-lag between shout and shots. His trial evidence seems to be a contradiction of Fairfax's statement, and also of Harrison's statement that after he had heard Bentley shout "Let him have it, Chris", two shots were *immediately* fired from the direction of the lift-shaft. I believe it is equally inconceivable that if McDonald had heard the alleged remark he would calmly have started to climb *down* the pipe. Why, having heard that incitement when he was a mere few feet from the roof rail, did he not wait for the outcome? The time-lag that McDonald insisted took place is a powerful confirmation of Craig's version of this critical incident. Like so much else this confirmation passed unnoticed at the time of the trial.

With regard to the evidence of the third policeman, PC Harrison, there are certain factors which cast doubt as to whether he was on the roof, let alone by the chimney stack, at the time Bentley was alleged to have made the remark, and I examine this in Chapter 5. Other aspects of his evidence also give food for thought. In his deposition he said: 'From that roof I could see Fairfax on the flat roof. I saw him take hold of a man on that roof and I saw the man break away from Fairfax. I spoke to Detective Constable Fairfax; I spoke just over normal voice and asked if everything was all right. He replied to me. It was just after that that the man broke away from his grasp. The man cried out "Let him have it, Chris". Immediately afterwards two shots were fired. I saw Fairfax spin and drop to the ground. I saw him get up again. At this time I was by the chimney stack which is marked on the plan.'

Apart from the fact that Harrison was able to recall a conversation with Fairfax of which the latter had no recollection, there is another far more worrying consideration. If Fairfax was correct in his description of the sequence of events leading to the firing of the first shot, and if he is correct in his description of the positions of himself, Bentley and Craig, *how could Harrison have seen what had happened? From his position his view would be masked by the lift-head. An examination of the roof plan will confirm this. I have been on the roof and checked the eyeline. In the excitement of the 'battle' these discrepancies are perhaps inevitable. One would expect, however, that in the calmness of a courtroom such discrepancies would be subjected to close examination. In the Craig/Bentley trial it is an expectation that is not realized.*

For a man who had just urged his friend to use violence, Bentley's subsequent behaviour was singular. On all the available evidence he submitted totally to arrest. Neither youth had contemplated violence at the butcher's shop or the electrical shop. Bentley was later to tell his solicitor that after Craig had fired and hit Fairfax he had called out to his young friend 'You bloody fool!'

For the past eighteen years no one has been able to agree on the exact meaning of the words, 'Let him have it, Chris'. Did Bentley mean that Craig should give up his gun, or did he mean that Craig should offer violence? The phrase has indeed become a classic example, frequently quoted, to show the ambiguity of our language.

For me there is no ambiguity. For my part I am far from convinced that the remark was ever uttered at all. There are too many inconsistencies, contradictions and errors in the whole case: the statements made by Fairfax, Harrison and McDonald, statements that are in serious conflict with each other; the ballistics and medical evidence relating to the injury sustained by Fairfax, plus the total absence of powder burns on the jacket – burns that would certainly have been present if the police officer's evidence was even substantially correct; the physical positions of the three police officers; the regrettable absence of any member of the public – and there were plenty within earshot – or any police officer, to substantiate the evidence of the three men; the unexplained absence from the witness box of PC Pain and PC Bugden, and the absence of any deposition from these two men. All these facts may lead the reader likewise to feel that Craig's account of what happened during those crucial moments is the correct one. There are many other facts that justify this conclusion; they are dealt with later on.

Now what happened next?

From the moment that the first shot was fired, all was noise and confusion. Apprehending two young suspects on a roof was one thing. Arresting an armed youth who had displayed a willingness to fire was quite another. As Fairfax fell to the ground Bentley ran to him and pulled back his jacket to examine the wound, asking 'You all right?' The sound of Bentley's voice jerked Fairfax back to life. Although the injury had been slight, he was suffering from a high degree of shock. He jumped to his feet, ran to the edge of the roof and shouted down into the garden of No. 26, 'They've got guns! Get the place surrounded!' He ran to the front of the roof and again shouted down to his colleagues in Tamworth Road, 'They've got guns! Radio for more men!' Craig fired at him again, this time missing completely. Bentley, still standing at the spot where Fairfax had fallen, shouted across to Craig, 'You bloody fool!' Hearing the shout, Fairfax ran to Bentley and pulled him behind the cover of the roof entrance. It occurred to him that Bentley too might be carrying a gun and he searched him, taking the sheath-knife. Bentley took out the knuckleduster and said, 'That's all I've got, guv'nor. I haven't got a gun.' Resistance was the last thing in Bentley's mind. Having meekly handed over his weapons, he stood there accepting his arrest as a fact of life. At this point Fairfax's position was highly vulnerable. He was alone on the roof, wounded in the shoulder, in a state of shock and outnumbered. Bentley knew all this, yet he made no attempt, either then or at any later time, to escape and rejoin Craig.

'*Let him have it, Chris*'?

Standing at the bottom of the drainpipe in the alleyway McDonald shouted up to Fairfax. He told his wounded colleague that he had been unable to get on to the roof. Fairfax shouted back down, urging him to try again.

By this time there were six fire engines on the scene, and several ambulances. The chaos and the confusion were growing by the second. A crowd of several hundred had magically appeared from nowhere, and was growing ever larger, providing the police with an additional unwanted problem. The whole area was alive with activity. People living in the nearby houses who, a few minutes before, had been thinking about going to bed, now had police officers rushing through their houses as they sought alternative access to the rooftop.

If the teenager with the gun was trapped on the rooftop, then assuredly Fairfax was trapped as well. Somehow his colleagues had to get aid to him. As far as they knew he was confronted with not one, but two, desperate gunmen. Displaying great bravery PC Harrison began to edge his way along the glass/asbestos roof towards the main roof, and towards Craig, lurking by the lift-head. What happened next has been the subject of as much contention for the past eighteen years as the earlier events. Did Craig then fire at Harrison? Or did he, as his Defence Counsel insisted, fire across the rooftops to frighten Harrison away? Here, in Craig's own words, is the account he gave me during the summer of 1970. Its candour must strike anyone as quite remarkable.

'I couldn't make out who he was. It was dark, there was a lot of noise. I'd heard the fire engines and I thought he might be a fireman. I left the lift-head and walked towards him to get a better look at him. He was lying with his back on the asbestos roof and edging towards me. I didn't want to shoot a fireman. I hadn't got any grievance with them. I called out and asked him if he was a copper. He didn't reply, just kept getting nearer. I still couldn't make out what kind of uniform he was wearing so I called out again, asking him if he was a fireman. He still didn't reply, just kept getting nearer. There was nothing for it. I had to stop him. I took aim and fired at him and heard his torch clatter down the roof. (It was later found in the gutter.) He didn't move, just lay there on the roof very still, so I went back to the lift-head.'

Fortunately Craig had missed. Harrison lying flat on his back and staring up into a dark sky, was unaware that Craig had retreated. For a moment he hardly dared to breathe. He kept still for what must have seemed an eternity, then slowly started to edge his way back in the direction he had come from, wisely realizing that to continue would be to invite a more carefully aimed shot.

McDonald was later to give evidence that when Craig fired at Harrison the teenager was to the *left* of the lift-shaft

– his original position. In the light of the remarkable testimony given to me by Craig, and also the evidence of PC Harrison at the time of the trial, it seems to me logical that, at this point in the proceedings, PC McDonald had still not succeeded in gaining access to the rooftop.

My task in investigating these matters would have been so much easier had PCs Harrison, McDonald and Jaggs consented to be interviewed by me: they were the only three persons who did not allow me to interview them.

A properly constituted tribunal of enquiry would not labour under this difficulty. It would have the power to subpoena any witnesses whose evidence might help to resolve these questions.

If the exact moment of McDonald's arrival on the roof is uncertain, there is no doubt that at some point he did eventually get up that drainpipe and, assisted by Fairfax, gain access to the roof. Again Bentley was totally free to do what he liked; there was no restraining hand on him, nothing at all to stop him from rejoining Craig if he had chosen to do so, yet he stood quietly watching as McDonald was finally hauled on to the roof. The numbers were now even.

Fairfax called out to Craig, 'Drop your gun', and defiantly he called back, 'Come and get it'. Fairfax wisely declined the invitation. Harrison, meanwhile, had begun to edge his way back towards the relative safety of the chimney-stack. Suddenly Craig sensed the movement, wheeled round and fired in his direction. Harrison later alleged that the bullet hit the chimney-stack, but no mark was ever found to substantiate this. Before the teenager could consider firing again Harrison had dropped from sight.

Fairfax and McDonald with Bentley between them were still pinned down behind the roof entrance. For the police the situation was critical; the very area of the operation, a high rooftop, debarred any co-ordinated effort.

During the entire period of the battle each policeman was his own master, each acting independently of all the others. It was this very fragmentation, this lack of knowledge of what the left hand was doing in relation to the right, that was to cause, if I am right, the ultimate tragedy.

The manager of the wholesalers' had by now been contacted and PC Miles had collected the keys and was speeding back to the battle.

The problem of the sightseers had by this time become so acute that the police had cordoned off the entrances to Tamworth Road. Every radio car in the area had been directed to the battle, every available policeman in the Division, and a number from outside, were brought in. At Croydon Police Station, Station Officer Sergeant Watson issued all the guns that the Station possessed – subsequent reports put the number of guns issued at between six and forty. Croydon Police Station were not able to confirm this. Here again a tribunal of enquiry should be able to elicit the exact number of guns, what type they were and how many bullets were fired.

Oblivious of these developments, the two policemen on the roof waited, and while they waited they discussed the situation. McDonald asked his colleague what kind of gun Craig was firing. He later stated that at this point Bentley interjected with the remark, 'It's a ·45 Colt and he has plenty of ammunition for it.' Fairfax's recollection of the interjection was somewhat different, but in essence the same. Bentley categorically denied making any remark of that nature.

Now the four people on the roof heard a new sound to add to the noise, chaos and confusion that already abounded. PC Miles had finally arrived with the keys, and with Harrison behind him, was running up the inside stairs towards the roof entrance. Arriving at the door, Miles pushed the bar, but it was stuck, and did not yield easily; he pushed again, this time with considerable force, and the door swung open and banged against the wall that was serving as a protection for his colleagues. Standing just inside the entrance he called out to Fairfax, who replied, warning him that Craig was to his left and that they were to his right. Miles jumped out on to the roof. A shot was fired and he fell dying almost at Fairfax's feet. The bullet entered his head just above the left eyebrow, passed right through and exited at the back of his head. Sidney Miles who, but for changing duties to help a friend, would have been at home with his wife on this evening, had died courageously. That tragic moment set forth a train of events, the effects of which are still felt eighteen years later.

Everyone has assumed that it was Craig who shot at and killed the unfortunate policeman. He even accepts it himself. But there is one other possibility that has never been considered, and therefore never checked; a possibility equally consistent with all the evidence. *It is that PC Miles was the victim of a tragic accident; that the bullet which killed him was not indeed fired from Craig's gun.*

Undoubtedly Craig had been deliberately firing at policemen earlier on. Undoubtedly he was later to fire in the general direction of the roof entrance that sheltered policemen. But when Miles jumped out on to that roof in an attempt to join Fairfax and McDonald, did he fire *directly* at PC Miles? If he had fired directly at the policeman and had aimed accurately then Miles would still be alive today. According to evidence from a ballistics expert, at a distance of thirty-nine feet – the distance between Craig and Miles – Craig's ·455 Eley was inaccurate to a degree of at least six feet. That night Craig was completely ignorant of this fact. But he was fully aware that behind that roof entrance was Bentley, so any shots he fired in that area were directed well wide of the roof entrance and were aimed over the garden of No. 30. His chances of hitting and killing PC Miles with his sawn-off ·455 Eley and his mixture of undersize and correct-size bullets were described during the Old Bailey trial as 'a million to one'. Only one policeman was later to say that he saw Craig fire his gun at that moment, and that was PC McDonald, *who was sheltering behind the roof entrance*. His description of Craig's position, moreover, was at variance with Harrison's. In McDonald's mind Craig was at that point to the left of the lift-shaft and lying on the asbestos roof. Harrison put his head out of the roof entrance immediately after Miles had fallen and described seeing Craig, gun in hand, emerge from *behind the lift-shaft*. A number of police officers subsequently described hearing two shots fired in rapid succession. Either of these shots could have been fired by one of the police marksmen. At the moment that Miles had jumped out on to that roof at least six of them had taken up positions overlooking the main roof. If the police evidence, and Craig's, is correct the police marksmen had opened fire before the roof entrance door was opened. Fairfax was later to swear on oath that there had been eight or nine other shots *before* the fatal shot. McDonald swore on oath that there had been at least six shots *before* the fatal shot. There is no reasonable doubt that before that fatal shot Craig had only fired four times. The question then arises, where did these additional shots come from? The occupants of Nos. 26 and 30 Tamworth Road were to describe after the gun battle how armed policemen had gone through their homes and gone out into the gardens to seek positions that would enable them to fire at Craig. They were not called upon to describe these events during the trial. It is for an official enquiry to establish why they were not called. Nothing has ever been said officially to indicate how many of those police guns were fired that night, or their calibre, with one notable exception. On the evidence of Fairfax, we know that after Miles had died, and after Bentley had been taken down below, Fairfax returned to the roof with a ·32 revolver and fired twice at Craig. Of the other guns issued, and used, we know nothing. The pathologist's report on the dead policeman states:

'There were two wounds in his head. One was at the inner side of the left eyebrow and was a typical wound of entry of a large-calibre bullet. The other, slightly to the right at the back of the head, was the exit wound of the same bullet.' The report concludes that mercifully 'death would have been virtually instantaneous'.

74

When the pathologist, Dr David Haler, gave evidence during the Old Bailey trial, the information elicited was basically the same as in the report. His appearance in the witness box was brief and, perhaps understandably, neither Defence Counsel cross-examined him. If they had, just two or three questions might well have shattered the Prosecution's case. When I interviewed Dr Haler I asked him if he could define the term 'large calibre bullet' more precisely. *He had privately formed the opinion that the wound could have been caused by a bullet of a calibre between ·32 and ·38. Craig was firing a ·455 Eley. If Dr Haler's estimate of calibre is right then either Craig shot PC Miles between the eyes, firing a ·38 bullet from a ·455 gun (which a ballistics · expert showed me was impossible) at 39 ft in the dark, or Craig did not fire the fatal shot.*[1]

The more one studies the available evidence, the more one realizes the truly frightening amount of support there is for the contention that Miles was not killed by the teenager. If the police had been able to produce the bullet that killed the unfortunate policeman the issue would have been settled irrevocably. *The bullet that killed Miles was never found.* I asked Dr Haler who, apart from being a vastly experienced pathologist, has had a lifelong interest in guns, how far the fatal bullet would have travelled after passing through the policeman's head. He said it was extremely difficult to be specific because so many external factors had to be taken into consideration, but the maximum distance would have been fifty yards. The morning after the gun battle there was an extensive search, not only of the roof area, but also of the entire surrounding areas. A number of bullets were found, and a number of cartridge cases, but the bullet that killed Miles presumably was not.

When a man is on trial for his life every possibility should be considered, every avenue explored. If the

[1]   Dr Haler subsequently denied giving me this information. An account of this denial and the subsequent events is contained in the Epilogue.

rush to judgment had been halted, the possibility that the crime with which Bentley and Craig were charged *had never been committed* might have percolated through to the Executive minds.

When I first interviewed Christopher Craig I believed, as everyone had at the time of the case, that he had killed PC Miles. Craig himself had accepted it as a fact at the time, and never contested the issue. As we spoke it became clear that he still accepted it. He had been firing in the direction of policemen on the roof and had ultimately killed one of them, or so he believed; but a chance remark that he made to me caused me to re-examine in detail the precise circumstances surrounding the death of PC Miles. Craig told me that any shots he had fired in the direction of the roof entrance had been directed well away from the door and were aimed over the garden of No. 30. The reason was that he knew that behind that door, as well as two policemen, was his friend Derek Bentley. Describing the moment when Miles had jumped out on to the roof Craig said, 'What I've never been able to understand is how I shot him between the eyes when *he was facing away from me and was going the other way.*' There can be little doubt that Craig's recollection of this is accurate. On Fairfax's evidence, when PC Miles opened the roof door he was advised of the positions of the police, and of Craig. Miles was aware that Fairfax had been wounded, that guns had been sent to the scene of the battle, that Harrison had been shot at twice. Is it conceivable that he should have advanced, unarmed, towards Craig? Presumably he would have turned sharp right towards his colleagues. Yet he was killed by a bullet that entered his head virtually in the middle of his forehead, just below his peaked hat.

Fairfax moved out from the cover of the wall and crawled on his knees towards his dead colleague. McDonald moved out to help him. Craig, watching them, saw Harrison begin to come out of the roof entrance. In quick succession Harrison threw his truncheon, a milk bottle and a brick in Craig's direction, but the youth stood his ground as the objects crashed around him and kept on firing, thus preventing Harrison from joining his fellow officers. Harrison was later to give evidence that he had heard the bullets thudding into the roof entrance, yet no bullet marks were found there. In all probability the shots were directed yet again over the garden of No. 30.

So although the police had succeeded in getting the door open, at the terrible cost of Sidney Miles' life, they were still pinned down, still unable to capture the desperate teenager. Craig called out, 'Is he dead?' Bentley shouted back, 'Yes he is, you rotten sod.' What had begun as a bit of a giggle now had all the ingredients of a nightmare.

One incident that then occurred is of such significance that it should be told exactly as Craig recounted it to me.

'To me one of the most terrible things that happened,' he said, speaking with considerable feeling, 'was Bentley turning against me. Helping the police like that. They got him to come over to me to persuade me to give myself up. Bentley walked towards me and called out, "For Christ's sake Chris, what's got into you?" I realized what he was up to and I told him to stop or he'd get it too. Bentley stopped for a moment, then he started to move towards me again, not in a straight line, but as if he was trying to work his way behind me. I told him that I knew what he was up to, that he was trying to get behind me to get at the gun. Again he asked me, "What's got into you Chris?" I told him to "get back or I'll shoot you. Get back or I'll shoot you." For a moment I thought he was still going to come on. Then he turned and walked back to the police.'

To appreciate the importance of this one must remember that before Bentley could be found guilty of murder two basic points had to be proved beyond all reasonable doubt. I cannot better Lord Goddard's words in his summing-up, when he said: 'And when two people are engaged on a felonious enterprise, and warehouse-breaking is a felony, and one knows that the other is carrying a weapon, and there is an agreement to use such violence as may be

77

necessary to avoid arrest, and this leads to the killing of a person, both are guilty of murder.'

It would be difficult to find a more graphic illustration that there was no agreement to use such violence than this incident on the roof. At the time that PC Miles died, Bentley had been under arrest for at least fifteen minutes, and I believe it was nearer twenty-five. He was not only under arrest but on Craig's evidence was acting in complete concert with the police. According to Craig he was risking his own life in an attempt to help the police arrest Craig.

I questioned Craig closely about this incident, and the most important aspect that emerged was his attitude. For him it was a particularly bitter moment, the moment when his close friend, encouraged by the police, turned against him. For Craig it brought to him the realization that at that moment he was totally alone, physically and mentally. He obviously considers it on the debit side of his relationship with Bentley. He was uncertain as to when exactly the incident occurred. Together we tried to place it precisely, and came to the conclusion that it had happened shortly after PC Miles was shot, though it could equally well have happened shortly before. I asked Craig why this incident had not been brought out at the trial. His reply was illuminating. 'It was bad enough that I was firing at policemen. If it had come out that I was prepared to shoot my mate, it wouldn't have done me any good at all.' I told him that it would certainly have done Bentley some good, but he couldn't see how.

When I interviewed Frederick Fairfax I questioned him about this incident. He was not prepared to state categorically that it had not happened, that it was a figment of Craig's imagination – he could not recall it.

That left Bentley. If this had happened surely he would have told his Counsel, Frank Cassels? When I interviewed Frank Cassels he could not recollect such a statement from Bentley, and it is certainly not contained either in the statement that Bentley made to the police or in the much more detailed statement that he subsequently made to his solicitor.

There are two explanations for this; one is Craig's, the other mine. Craig contended that the realization that he had betrayed a friend would have prevented Bentley from mentioning it; 'he didn't want that hanging over him,' as Craig put it. Right up to the eve of his execution Bentley thought that he would serve a few years in prison and then be released. To have it made public knowledge that he had assisted the police against his friend would be something that he could not live with, it would put him in the same category as a 'grass' – a police informer. That is Craig's explanation. Mine is simpler. *Bentley did not have the basic intelligence to realize the full implications of that incident.* Eighteen years afterwards, Craig, a by no means stupid man, couldn't see the significance. What likelihood was there that Derek Bentley could have done? The average nineteen-year-old would probably fail to grasp the full significance and, as is made clear in Chapter 4, Derek Bentley was no average nineteen-year-old.

As Harrison stood in the doorway throwing everything that was to hand, Craig retaliated not only with shots but with words. 'I am Craig,' he cried. 'You've just given my brother twelve years. Come on, you coppers, I'm only sixteen.' With great courage Harrison leapt from the doorway and joined Fairfax and the others. Police Constable Jaggs clambered up the drainpipe and joined them. He put his head round the wall to get a look at Craig, who, firing again, shouted, 'Come on, you brave coppers, think of your wives.' Bentley uttered a gratuitous warning, 'You want to look out, he'll blow your heads off.' Jaggs was quickly followed up the drainpipe by yet another policeman, PC Stewart.

It was getting uncomfortably crowded in the small area where they were protected from Craig, and Stewart, at Fairfax's instigation, left as quickly as he had come, back down the drainpipe. Fairfax had by now come to

79

the conclusion that, before a final attempt was made to capture Craig, they would be better off with Bentley out of the way. Using him as a shield they rushed towards the entrance. In view of what had just transpired, Bentley was in no doubt as to Craig's attitude; panic-stricken, he called out, 'Look out, Chris, they're taking me down.' As he was bundled down the stairs, Craig heard him cry out in pain. He called out, 'Are they hurting you, Derek?' But there was no answer.

For the moment Craig was alone on the roof except for the body of PC Miles. At ground level the noise and confusion that had become an integral part of the night had by now reached a crescendo. During the earlier stages of the battle the police on the ground had considered using the water-jets of the fire engines to wash Craig off the roof, but had decided against it. The whole road was ablaze with life and light. Estimates of the number of police in the area at the height of the battle were later to vary between forty and two hundred; but undoubtedly there were a great many by any standards of British crime.

Arriving on the ground, Fairfax handed Bentley over to one of his colleagues and was given a ·32 automatic. Disdaining for the moment any treatment for his wounded shoulder, he went back into the building and began to make his way up to the roof entrance.

Craig, bewildered by the lack of action and frightened by the implications of what had occurred, was beginning to disintegrate fast. He saw the door of the roof entrance swinging backwards and forwards and in the darkness thought it was some kind of bullet-proof shield brought in by the police. He called out, 'Come on, then, are you hiding behind a shield?' There was no answer. He was fast running out of ammunition and his main concern was to conserve what little he had left. He called out again, 'Is that thing bullet-proof? Are you all right, Derek?' But by now Bentley was in the back of a police car. Fairfax stopped inside the roof entrance and called out to Craig, 'Drop your gun. I've got a gun.' Craig, still clinging to the remnants of his defiance, called back, 'Come on then, copper, let's have it out. Are we going to have a shooting match? It's just what I'd like.' From the roof entrance Fairfax took aim and fired. Craig stood his ground and fired back. Both bullets missed. Craig raised his gun to fire again, and at that moment he was close to death – not from Fairfax's gun, but from his own, for he had decided to take his own life. He pointed the gun at his head and pressed the trigger, but there was just a click. He examined it for a moment, pointed it again at his head and fired again. Again the only result was a loud click. Two bullets had failed to fire. Fairfax, realizing that there was something wrong, emerged on to the roof. Craig was by now moving towards the edge of the roof. Fairfax took aim again and fired, but the bullet whistled harmlessly over the rooftops. Craig held his gun high in the air and called out, 'See, it's empty!', then ran to the edge of the roof and dived over, shouting as he fell, 'Give my love to Pam.' As he plummeted downwards from the thirty-foot-high roof his body struck the edge of a greenhouse, bounced off and crashed to the ground. As he lay there it was later alleged that he said 'I wish I was fucking dead. I hope I've killed the fucking lot.' But the last that Craig remembers is being out in mid-air. The rooftop battle was over.

The two threepenny tickets that Craig had bought on the No. 109 bus had exacted a terrible cost. They had cost him a fractured spine, a broken breast-bone and a fractured forearm. They were also going to cost him the next ten years of his life. They had cost courageous Sidney Miles his life. They had cost Detective Constable Fairfax a wounded shoulder and an evening when he had looked death in the face. They had cost a number of other policemen, particularly PC Harrison, moments of terror, and the thought that they too were about to die. For Derek Bentley they were to mean death by hanging.

When Craig jumped off the roof the time was 10.05 p.m. A mere fifty minutes had elapsed from the moment that little Edith Ware had taken her goodnight look out of her bedroom window. Over eighteen years later the events of those fifty minutes are still the cause of serious public concern.

Those fifty minutes contained all the essential elements to produce what, in my view, is the greatest miscarriage of justice that this country has ever known. If English justice means anything, if our version of democracy represents anything, the time has surely come for a final reckoning in the case of Bentley and Craig. The time has surely come for Justice to prevail.

3

Law and Disorder

What had begun for the Croydon Police as a routine evening had now become a full-scale murder investigation.

The body of PC Sidney Miles was taken to the Mayday Mortuary in Croydon. The wounded Detective Constable Fairfax was taken by ambulance to Croydon General Hospital with, for company, several of his police colleagues and the unconscious Christopher Craig, temporarily oblivious of the havoc he had wreaked. During the journey PC Stewart searched Craig and removed his sheath-knife and wallet.

Derek Bentley, in the back of a police car speeding towards the local police station, was conscious. From his point of view it would have been preferable if he, too, had been unable to talk.

In the car with him were three police officers. The driver was PC Henry Stephens, and squashed in the back seat with Bentley were Police Sergeant Edward Roberts and PC James Leslie Alderson. Bentley's subsequent version of what transpired during the journey was very simple. According to him Roberts asked the name of the other youth on the roof, and Bentley told him. He was also asked what kind of gun Craig had used, and told the police that he did not know.

The version recounted by *two* of the police officers was rather different. Sgt Roberts stated that *after the shooting was over* Bentley was brought downstairs from the roof and handed over to him. He then formally cautioned Bentley who replied, 'I didn't have a gun, Chris shot him.' Bentley

83

was then taken into the car and they drove off. As they approached the police station, Bentley said, 'I knew he had a gun but I didn't think he would use it. He's done one of your blokes in.' The evidence of driver Stephens was virtually identical, with the addition that he recalled that after Bentley had made the damaging remark indicating prior knowledge of the gun, he had again been cautioned by Sgt Roberts.

Sgt Roberts was quite clear about when Bentley was brought down. In his mind 'it was after the shooting was over'. In view of the fact that this is contradicted by the evidence of at least six people, including at least four police officers, there can be little doubt that Roberts' recollection of the exact sequence of events is somewhat hazy.

According to his recollection, however, there was nothing incorrect in the strict formality that Roberts accorded his prisoner. With bullets still flying on the roof, with his colleagues in very real fear for their lives, with fire engines and ambulances clanging, over a thousand onlookers writhing about, armed police scattered round the rooftops, police vans and police cars quite literally everywhere in sight, and the whole area ablaze with life, *Sgt Roberts calmly proceeded to give Bentley an official caution*. It is worth recalling exactly what the intrepid policeman said: 'You are not obliged to say anything unless you wish to do so, but anything you do say will be taken down in writing and may be given in evidence. I am now going to take you to Croydon Police Station, where you will be detained in connection with the shooting of PC Miles.' How anyone can accept that all this was said in those circumstances is to me incredible. Yet every word was uttered, or so the punctilious Roberts assured the Central Criminal Court. If his memory of the *exact* sequence of events was faulty then surely his memory of the *precise* words that he, or others, spoke on the evening of 2 November is also open to question? We can derive comfort from the fact that when Sgt Roberts gave evidence at the Old Bailey five weeks after the events in question his notebook was open and ready,

84

and before answering any question, he referred to it at great length, a habit that caused Lord Goddard to ask, 'Do you not remember without your notes, Officer?' Sgt Roberts, it transpired, did not remember without his notes.

The whole episode of Bentley's journey to the police station, and the remarks that he is alleged to have made, has about it an Alice in Wonderland quality. The evidence of two policemen was that Bentley was asked no questions during the journey, but that near the end of that journey, quite out of the blue, he spontaneously said, 'I knew he had a gun but I didn't think he would use it. He has done one of your blokes in.' The most sensational incident in their entire police careers has just occurred, a close colleague has, as far as they know, been murdered, another colleague shot in the shoulder. Every national newspaper in the country will be carrying headline stories in a few hours. They have with them one of the principal participants of the drama, a young man who, in theory, knows more than anybody else about exactly what happened on the rooftop. Yet they sit there in stolid silence, not uttering a word, no one speaks until the journey is nearly over, then Bentley suddenly feels an irresistible urge to talk, and succeeds, in one brief sentence, in supplying the evidence essential to fulfil one of the two basic points that had to be proved before he could be found guilty of murder – the knowledge that Craig was armed. It has an air of unreality.

Perhaps the *most* remarkable aspect of this incident is the evidence of the third policeman, Police Constable James Leslie Alderson. It will be recalled that Alderson was sitting in the back seat next to Bentley. What is remarkable about Alderson's testimony is that it does not exist. No deposition by him was produced in Court. *He was never called to give evidence at either the Magistrates' Court or the Old Bailey. If Bentley had made the remark that was to do him so much damage Alderson must have heard it. If he heard it he was obliged, by law, to make a written statement. If he had made a statement containing such important evidence he would certainly have been called by the Crown Prosecution.*

But Alderson joined the ranks of the silent witnesses.

Three policemen, Pain, Bugden and Alderson, were all present at vital moments. All in a position to confirm or contradict the evidence of fellow officers. Evidence which, if accepted by the jury, would hang Bentley. All three were missing from the witness box. All three failed to make statements that could go forward to assist the prosecution's case.

Seventeen policemen gave evidence during the trial at the Old Bailey. There is no doubt that if Pain, Bugden and Alderson had severally heard what their fellow officers alleged that they had heard, these three men would have been called to give evidence. The fact that Pain and Bugden were present during a vital period of the gun battle was not disclosed during the trial. Bentley's counsel, however, established on the first day of the trial that Alderson had been in the car. It was also established by the prosecuting counsel on the first day of the trial that Alderson was available if wanted. In view of the fact that the prosecution were still presenting their case *well into the second day* they had ample opportunity to contact PC Alderson and produce him as a witness, thereby ending any speculation as to why he had not been called, but they did not do so. In his speech to the jury, Bentley's counsel commented: 'There were three police officers in the car, members of the jury, and you have seen a large number of police officers giving evidence in this case. We have heard from two of those officers. We have not heard from the third one who was there. You are perhaps entitled to wonder why. You may wonder whether or not that police officer heard the remark which was made, according to the other two, by Bentley.'

I believe that we are entitled not merely to wonder, but to demand an explanation for PC James Leslie Alderson's absence from the witness box. I also believe we are entitled to demand an explanation for the absence of his two colleagues, Pain and Bugden. The evidence concerning Bentley's remark on the roof, the evidence concerning Bentley's remarks in the car – this is evidence of paramount importance.

It was the evidence that hanged him. Policemen were called to give evidence of far lesser importance. The absence of these three men constitutes one of the mysteries of this case.

Arriving at the police station, Bentley was instructed to turn out his pockets. The possessions he laid on the reception counter were of the most ordinary kind: a comb, a handkerchief, cigarettes, keys – hardly the personal effects of a 'desperate gangster', as the morning papers described him. But then the two most interesting items, the knuckleduster and the knife, had already been taken from Bentley. After preliminary questioning he was locked up. The time was 10.15 p.m.

While Bentley was being shown to a cell in the police station, Detective Chief Inspector John Smith was being shown to the rooftop in Tamworth Road, accompanied by Detective Sergeant Stanley Shepherd. These two men were now in charge of the investigation. As they took their first look at the scene of the gun battle, Craig's gun was found below them in a greenhouse where it had fallen when the youth had plunged to what he thought was his death. Pocketing the gun, Smith went to the mortuary to examine the body of his dead colleague. Shepherd went to the hospital to talk to his more fortunate friend, Fairfax.

The irony that had dictated that Fairfax should travel to hospital in the same ambulance as his adversary, had continued at the hospital. The injured policeman was placed in the next cubicle to Craig. By the time Shepherd arrived at the hospital Fairfax had received medical attention and was resting on a bed with his right arm in a sling. Shepherd discussed the evening's events with Fairfax, then moved to the next cubicle. According to his subsequent evidence he then had a conversation with Christopher Craig.

Having advised Craig who he was, Shepherd then asked the teenager how he was feeling. Craig's reply was, 'It's my back, it hurts.' A little later Craig volunteered, 'I had six in the gun. I fired at a policeman. I had six tommy-gun bullets.' It is a remarkable coincidence that in virtually the first remarks that either of them made after the battle, Craig and Bentley both succeeded in making statements that were subsequently to prove vital to the Prosecution's case. In that one line Craig fulfilled all the basic points that had to be proved against him before he could be found guilty of murder: admittance that he was armed, that he had fired deliberately at the police, and that he knew they were police.

After he had made this incriminating remark, he was cautioned. The Detective Sergeant subsequently declared in evidence that Craig's reply to the caution was 'Is the copper dead? How about the others? We ought to have shot them all.'

Craig's recollection of his first evening in hospital is very different. He had lost consciousness in mid-air when he had dived off the roof, and the next thing he recalled was 'coming round in hospital, being hit in the face and being called a murdering bastard'. His next recollection was 'being pushed down a corridor on a trolley and being run into walls and over bumps so they could hurt me'. He did not know what time these events took place or who was responsible. He had no recollection of speaking to Shepherd, and in fact declared during the Old Bailey trial that the first time he had seen Sergeant Shepherd was on the morning of 11 November, the day of Craig's first court appearance.

The police officer also stated in evidence that when he had spoken to Craig at approximately 11 p.m. on the Sunday evening, the teenager appeared quite normal, and in the policeman's opinion, he was not distraught with pain. This was less than an hour after Craig had dived off the roof, breaking his back, his left wrist and a bone in his chest. If Craig was fit enough less than an hour after sustaining such injuries to have held a lucid conversation, during which he appeared quite normal and was not distraught with pain then he was endowed with a remarkable strength and even more remarkable self-control. That, at least, was my view until I interviewed Frederick Fairfax.

From him I first learned that he had shared an ambulance with Craig and had then been placed next to him in the hospital. *He also stated that Craig was unconscious when placed in the ambulance and that he remained that way until well into the next day.* Detective Sergeant Fairfax (as he became shortly before the trial) was quite certain about this. His exact words were, 'Craig did not talk to anyone either voluntarily or any other way until the following day. He was *out* and stayed that way.'

Sergeant Shepherd claimed that Craig was quite normal and was not distraught with pain. PC Vincent Denham, who was on observation duty at Craig's bedside *over seven hours later,* was of the opinion that Craig 'was not normal, and was in great pain'. This was after Craig had been given drugs to relieve the pain, a luxury he had not been accorded at the time Shepherd apparently talked to him.

Again and again my analysis of the police statements and their subsequent evidence reminds me forcibly of the comments of Lord Justice Devlin in *The Criminal Prosecution in England.* 'The fault to be looked for today, just as it was in 1929 [a reference to a Royal Commission investigating police powers and procedure], is not the frame-up, but the tendency to press interrogation too hard against a man believed to be guilty.' Devlin felt that this was 'a very understandable fault'; it was not corruption or the desire to pervert justice that made the police less fair and dispassionate than they might to be, but '*honest indignation*' such as the ordinary citizen experiences if he is brought into contact with some '*despicable or pestilential crime*'. In the opinion of the then Home Secretary, Sir David Maxwell Fyfe, it was impossible to imagine a crime more despicable or pestilential in the eyes of those Croydon policemen than the killing of a much-liked fellow policeman. In Sir David's opinion, and he was referring specifically to the death of PC Miles, 'the murder of a police officer is justly regarded as the most heinous of crimes by the police force'.

In their dealings with Craig the police were labouring under a singular disadvantage. The police machinery could not be brought effectively to bear upon him. The trappings of police officialdom that Bentley endured at Croydon Police Station – the search, the cell, the long wait, the assurances that all was known, the interrogation – none of these could be applied to Craig. Although in great pain, he was at least cocooned in a hospital bed away from the full potency of police procedure.

I do not believe that it was so much in their interrogations of Craig that the police erred, but more in their subsequent recollections. To quote Lord Devlin again: 'The police have to be sure of themselves and what they have seen and done. If they are not, they are of no use to prosecution, for the prosecution has to present a case that makes the jury sure of the prisoner's guilt.' It is manifest from the events described on the rooftop that the police had an overwhelmingly powerful case against Christopher Craig, but nothing was left to chance. Aspects that did not fit the picture of Craig that the police were determined to present to the jury were discarded, ignored, or forgotten. This determination seems to me to be the only rational explanation for Sgt Shepherd's evidence of his conversations with Craig. On the evidence given at the time, and on the information given subsequently to me, I am forced to the conclusion that this conflict of testimony could be resolved only by a public enquiry.

At 11.25 p.m. Mrs Miles was advised that her husband was dead. At approximately 11.30 p.m. Detective Sgt Shepherd was joined at the hospital by his superior, Detective Chief Inspector Smith. They talked to Fairfax, then walked to the next cubicle. The Inspector advised Craig that he had just seen the body of PC Miles at the mortuary and that as a result of the enquiries he had made he was charging Craig with being concerned with another man in murdering Miles. Craig was again formally cautioned (the number of cautions that Craig and Bentley received that night is truly remarkable). Craig's reply to the caution was, 'He's dead, is he? What about the others?' The Inspector advised Craig that he would be detained at the hospital until fit to be removed, but Craig was in no condition to reply, let alone be moved. It must have been apparent to the Inspector that any questioning of Craig at this stage was a waste of time.

At the Bentleys' Norbury home all was quiet. The family, with the exception of Derek's twenty-one-year-old sister, Iris, had retired for the night. Iris had decided to stay up until her brother returned. There was between the two a close bond, and for some reason his absence disturbed her.

Suddenly at 1.30 a.m. there was a violent hammering at the front door. Warily, Iris opened the door, to be confronted by three men in plain clothes who informed her that they were police officers and began to search the house. Bewildered, the young woman asked if their visit had anything to do with her brother. Detective Inspector Close, who was leading the search, paused for a moment: 'Your brother has killed a man.' While Iris Bentley attempted to digest this shocking statement, Close added, 'We shall have to search the house.' Iris aroused her parents. Mr Bentley, who was at the time suffering from fibrositis, came slowly downstairs and asked the police the reason for their visit. The Inspector merely repeated, 'Your son has killed a man.' By now Mrs Bentley and her daughter had collapsed on a couch, confused and frightened.

The police searched the loft, but there was nothing there. Derek Bentley shared a bedroom with his Uncle Albert, who watched as cupboards and drawers were emptied. Amongst the boy's toys the police found a sheath-knife that he had bought when employed by a furniture remover, to rip up old unwanted furniture. To the police it obviously had a more potent significance. Ignoring the sheath, the officer took the knife and went downstairs. Mrs Bentley tried to snatch it from him, shouting, 'You're not going to say he had that with him.' Inspector Close assured her that it would not be used in evidence. An unsheathed knife was subsequently produced in Court. Bentley presumably had two knives. As the police were departing Mr Bentley asked where his son was. 'Croydon Police Station' was the reply, then the police were gone, leaving a shocked Bentley family to collect their shattered thoughts. Mr Bentley had been too dazed to ask if the police had a search warrant; there had been precious little time to get one. The search of the loft had a special significance. Fifteen minutes earlier the police had conducted a search of Craig's home, and in the loft Detective Sgt Shepherd had discovered a sawn-off piece of gun-barrel, later to be identified as a part of the gun that Craig had used during the rooftop siege.

Shepherd also found the boy's private arsenal hidden in the loft – one hundred and fifty rounds of assorted ammunition. For good measure he also found a ·45 bullet under the boy's pillow. Craig's parents must have been as shocked as the police officer was surprised, for they insisted that they had no previous knowledge of this ammunition.

The Craig and Bentley households were not the only ones visited in Norbury that night. During a moment of consciousness Craig evidently muttered the name of Norman Parsley. The well-spoken boy who had so favourably impressed Mrs Bentley failed to have quite the same effect on the police. Although in the initial stages of his interrogation he denied that he had ever been criminally involved with Craig, within twenty-four hours he had admitted his part in the robbery of the elderly greengrocer, and given the police the gun he had used on that raid. (He had not yet finished with Craig and Bentley. His case was heard by Lord Goddard while the Craig/Bentley jury were considering their verdict.)

It had been a long night for the men of Croydon Police Station, and it was going to get longer. At three o'clock in the morning Superintendent Greeno of Scotland Yard, who had been called in to assist, arrived at the police station. His first task was to confer with the men in charge of the case. Waiting beneath him in a cell was Derek Bentley. About an hour later Bentley was brought before Detective Chief

Inspector Smith and Detective Sergeant Shepherd. The result of that confrontation was the following statement. It must be borne in mind when reading this statement that, according to the subsequent evidence of the two police officers, it was taken completely and entirely at Bentley's dictation. No questions, it was said, were asked by either policeman. The entire statement was made by Bentley, *voluntarily and spontaneously*.

I have been cautioned that I need not say anything unless I wish to do so, but whatever I do say will be taken down in writing and may be given in evidence.

(Signed) Derek Bentley. ·

(Signed) Derek Bentley. ·

I have known Craig since I went to school. We were stopped by our parents going out together, but we still continued going out with each other – I mean we have not gone out together until tonight. I was watching television tonight (2 November 1952) and between 8 p.m. and 9 p.m. Craig called for me. My mother answered the door and I heard her say I was out. I had been out earlier to the pictures and got home just after 7 p.m. A little later Norman Parsley and Frank Fazey called. I did not answer the door or speak to them.

Signature *D. Bentley*   Signature witnessed
by *J.S.*

My mother told me that they had called and I then ran after them. I walked up the road with them to the paper shop where I saw Craig standing. We all talked together and then Norman Parsley and Frank Fazey left. Chris Craig and I then caught a bus to Croydon. We got off at West Croydon and then walked down the road where the toilets are – I think it is Tamworth Road. When we came to the place where you found me, Chris looked in the window. There was a little iron gate at the side. Chris then jumped over and I followed. Chris then climbed up the drainpipe to the roof and I followed. Up to then Chris had not said anything. We both got out on to the flat roof at the top. Then someone in a garden on the opposite side shone a torch up towards us. Chris said: 'It's a copper, hide behind here.' We hid behind a shelter arrangement on the roof. We were there waiting for about ten minutes. I did not know he was going to use the gun. A plain

Signature *D. Bentley*   Signature witnessed
by *J.S.*

clothes man climbed up the drainpipe and on to the roof. The man said: 'I am a police officer – the place is surrounded.' He caught hold of me and as we walked away Chris fired. There was nobody else there at the time. The policeman and I then went round a corner by a door. A little later the door opened and a policeman in uniform came out. Chris fired again then and this policeman fell down. I could see he was hurt as a lot of blood came from his forehead just above his nose. (Signed) D. Bentley The policeman dragged him round the corner behind the brickwork entrance to the door. I remember I shouted something but I forget what it was. I could not see Chris when I shouted to him – he was behind a wall. I heard some more policemen behind the door and the policeman with me said: 'I don't think he has many more bullets left.' Chris shouted 'Oh yes I have' and he fired again. I think I heard him fire three times

Signature: *D. Bentley*   Signature witnessed
by *J.S.*

altogether. The policeman then pushed me down the stairs and I did not see any more. I knew we were going to break into the place. I did not know what we were going to get – just anything that was going. I did not have a gun and I did not know Chris had one until he shot. I now know that the policeman in uniform is dead. I should have mentioned that after the plain clothes policeman got up the drainpipe and arrested me, another policeman in uniform followed and I heard someone call him

'*Mac*'. *He was with us when the other policeman was killed.*

tis as B
This statement has been read to me and is true. Sgd.
Derk Derek W. Bentley.

*Statement taken by me, written down by Det Sgt Shepherd,
read over and signature witnessed by J. Smith, DI.*

This statement displays a number of peculiarities that require explanation. Some are dealt with now and some in the following chapter.

The official procedure to be adopted by policemen taking statements is covered by what are known as the Judges' Rules. In the *Police Review* of 30 May 1952, in an article headed *Statements Made by Prisoners*, there appeared the following remarks: 'The most important thing to remember is that the procedure for taking statements from prisoners is laid down by the Judges' Rules. Although these rules are not law, non-compliance with them usually means that the statement will not be accepted by the Court. The statement should be in the *exact* words used by the prisoner, *it should not be edited or corrected for grammatical errors.*'

The following chapter will question whether Bentley was mentally equipped to dictate a statement couched in these terms.

Another of the aspects that the Judges' Rules are quite clear about is that the time the statement was begun and the time it was completed *must be recorded*. In Bentley's statement the times are conspicuous by their absence. When the two policemen in question gave subsequent evidence it was stated that the statement began to be taken at *about* 4.00 a.m., that the time taken to obtain the statement was *about* an hour, and that Bentley was charged with the murder of PC Miles at *about* 5.30 a.m.

This vagueness about times is in marked contrast to the very precise procedure adopted by the police in giving

95

cautions to both the accused. On the evidence of various police officers, by 5.30 a.m. the semi-conscious Craig had been cautioned twice, and Bentley had been cautioned no less than six times.

Bentley's statement was taken, not in the heat of the battle, but some six hours afterwards, in the comparative calm of the Inspector's office. There appears to be no justification for vagueness about the time factors when a man's life is at stake.

Another peculiarity of the statement is the number of times that Bentley signed it. Normal procedure would have been for him to sign the statement twice – after the caution, and again at the end of the statement. No reason has ever been given for the fact that Bentley signed his statement no less than seven times. Two of the signatures, those immediately following the caution, were accounted for by Detective Sgt Shepherd who stated during the trial that 'Bentley was asked to write the second (caution) signature after we inspected the first.' Bentley duly obliged *without assistance*. Yet at the *end* of the statement when he attempted to write his full name he was unable to spell 'Derek' without assistance. So right at the beginning of the statement he signs his name *twice without assistance* from the two officers, yet at the end of the statement he attempts to write his name, fails, and can only do so when the name is spelt out for him. The inference to be drawn from this is that the caution was inserted and duly signed *after* the statement had been taken down and *after* Bentley had had his Christian name spelt out to him at the end of the statement.

At the end of the statement the words 'tis as B' appear. This was an attempt by Bentley to write 'This statement has been', the first words of the sentence that appears immediately below. It was the best that the illiterate, mentally subnormal Bentley could manage.

Bentley's behaviour during this period is of paramount importance. The only comment made about it during the trial was by Detective Chief Inspector Smith: 'Sergeant

96

Shepherd would repeat what he had written before, and occasionally Bentley would ask "What have I said before?" He was very deliberate about this and thought quite a long time before he spoke and obviously occasionally he got a little out of his context.'

The picture one gets from that description is of a calm young man, in perfect control of himself, thinking and speaking quite deliberately, and occasionally getting a trifle confused. The truth is somewhat different, and it explains, as that description does not, the multitude of signatures. Bentley kept breaking down. He was full of remorse for what had happened, very disturbed and distraught. Every time he broke down Shepherd assumed the statement had been completed and made Bentley sign it; then Bentley would get control of himself and continue. This description of Bentley's behaviour was given to me by Detective Sgt Shepherd himself, as well as by a number of other people, both policemen and civilians. I have no doubt whatsoever that the description I have given is completely accurate.

Bentley's behaviour is worth recording, for without knowing about it, no one could accurately evaluate the statement he made, or the likelihood of it having been made voluntarily and spontaneously, without being led by police questions. Bentley's mental condition at the time increases the doubt that all requirements mentioned were met.

One cannot help but wonder what effect this would have had at the time had it been made public. Both defendants were to be roundly castigated by all and sundry for their total lack of remorse. But Bentley's attitude during the taking of that statement conflicts sharply with the picture of an unrepentant police-killer which was presented to the nation by the press and the Prosecution. If this had been known it would undoubtedly have had a profound effect on press, public, judge, jury and Home Secretary. This, combined with Bentley's attempt, at great personal risk, to persuade Craig to give himself up, the remarks he *admitted* uttering on the roof, remarks that were contained in his Counsel's brief, but not drawn upon during the trial – these facts *alone* should have saved him from the gallows.

To secure a conviction, Prosecuting Counsel Humphreys had to convince the jury that Bentley knew Craig was armed and that, with Craig, he was prepared to use that gun. Humphreys also considered he had a third task, to totally discredit Bentley in the eyes of the jury. *The fact that at the time PC Miles died Bentley had been under arrest for at least fifteen minutes* makes it obvious why Humphreys set himself this third task. His final remarks to the jury were directed specifically to it: '*At no time, or for one moment, throughout the whole of that twenty or twenty-five minutes did Bentley make a sound, either shouting to Craig or even to the police officers, to show that his mind had ceased to be with Craig, and that he was trying to stop Craig shooting and to throw away the gun.*' Like the bulk of the case against Bentley, those remarks are completely rebutted by the evidence in this book. It is for an official enquiry to ascertain why they were not rebutted at the time.

While the police were interrogating Bentley, his father and uncle arrived at the police station having walked from Norbury. Apart from Detective Inspector Close's statement, 'Your son has killed a man', Mr Bentley had no knowledge of the night's events. Now he identified himself and asked to see his son, he also asked for details. He was advised that a policeman had been murdered, and the Desk Sergeant advised the two men that they could not see Bentley. When his father insisted, he was told crisply, 'You can see your son in the dock later this morning.' For the first time Mr Bentley felt absolutely helpless and impotent. It was a feeling that was to be his constant companion for the next eighty-seven days. He and his brother had no alternative now but to begin the long walk back home.

At approximately 5.30 a.m. Derek Bentley was charged with the murder of PC Miles. His stunned reply was, 'Craig shot him. I hadn't got a gun. He was with me on the roof and shot him between the eyes.' It was the comment of an inarticulate youth totally ignorant of the very real danger in which he stood.

The first information his family were to have of the night's events was from a variety of newspaper reporters who called at their house in the middle of the night, and gave them garbled and totally distorted accounts of what had transpired. The reason for the reporters' presence was not, of course, to give the Bentleys information, but to acquire it, and also all available photographs.

By the time Bentley had been charged, the early morning editions of the national newspapers were on the streets, and a shocked nation was reading the first accounts of the events on the Croydon rooftop. The accuracy of that information in many instances left a great deal to be desired. This, for example, is how the *Daily Mail* told its readers about it:

CHICAGO GUN BATTLE IN LONDON
GANGSTERS WITH MACHINE-GUN ON ROOF KILL DETECTIVE, WOUND ANOTHER
'Sidney-Street' rages an hour, then hand-to-hand fight. ARMED POLICE SHOOT BACK.

The London crime wave reached a new peak last night. A detective was shot dead and another seriously wounded in a second 'Battle of Sidney Street'. They had seen the flash of a torchlight in the warehouse of Barlow and Parker, wholesale confectioners, Tamworth Road, Croydon, just after 10 o'clock. They entered the building. They cautiously edged their way in. Inside, the raiders were so far undisturbed. Ambulances and fire brigades had been summoned. Then as the bandits realized they had been trapped by a police cordon, shooting began. The gangsters armed with a Sten-gun hit one of the officers as he climbed the fire escape towards the bandits. He was Detective Constable Miles, in plain clothes, of Z division, a married man, two children, with 22 years' service. He was killed. His colleague, PC Frederick Fairfax, who was in a police patrol car, dashed into an alleyway leading to another fire escape up which the gunmen had climbed.

As he went to help Miles there was another shot and people coming out of the Sunday cinemas heard one of the gunmen cry 'You won't get me'. PC Fairfax fell wounded in the shoulder. By this time 200 police were there, thirty of them armed with revolvers. Shots were exchanged. The gunmen dodged from vantage point to vantage point, firing at everything . . . police, ambulances, fire brigade officers. Scotland Yard sent reinforcements. In a few minutes an area a quarter of a mile round the buildings was sealed off. The bullets still flew. The police dodged and ducked. For nearly an hour the gunmen fired to prevent any attempt at their capture. They seemed to have an unlimited supply of ammunition as bursts from the Sten-gun hit the streets. Then the end came. As three officers, crouching low, sprung on to the rooftop the Sten-gun was flung into their faces. The ammunition had run out. Then began a chase over the roofs after the gunmen. They dodged behind chimney-pots. One of them attempted to lower himself by a stackpipe at the rear of the premises. By this time more police were on the roofs, and there were hand-to-hand battles before the two gunmen were finally overpowered, handcuffed and brought to street level. Here one of the gunmen was found to be injured, and was taken to Croydon General Hospital. When the shooting began Scotland Yard mobilized all police officers and C.I.D. men from Kent and the Metropolitan area. 'Get them at all costs', was the order to the 200 police officers in the battle.

The story continues in a similar vein for another two columns. The whole piece is a classic justification for not believing all you read in the newspapers. Hardly a sentence is accurate – the staff reporters responsible should have got some kind of inverted Pulitzer Prize for a historic piece of misreporting.

The *Daily Mail* was by no means alone among newspapers as a distorter of the truth (although in this case it was in a class by itself); it was from articles like this that not only the general public, but also Mrs Miles and the Craig and Bentley families, first learned the 'facts'. It is hardly surprising that public reaction was immediately violently hostile towards the two teenagers. Accurate reporting of the facts would not have lessened the sympathy for Mrs Miles; it is not certain that it would have reduced the anger about Craig and Bentley; but it would undoubtedly have contributed to a fair trial. Reading those newspaper accounts may have been the twelve men who were to hold the fates of the two boys in their hands.

The jury were advised during the trial to put from their minds all that they had read about the case, and all the conversations that they had had with their friends about it. Excellent advice, but those men were not machines, but human beings like the rest of us. Responsibility for the hanging of Derek Bentley rests on many shoulders; some of those shoulders are probably still hunched over typewriters in Fleet Street today.

The confusion about what had happened was not confined to Fleet Street. *Five days* after the battle, the *Police Review* carried an article stating that Fairfax had fired *before* he was hit. Since the rest of that article is completely correct, and the *Police Review* gets its information direct from source, this suggests a possibility that an official enquiry into the case may well find worth exploring.

On the morning of 3 November, Derek Bentley made a brief appearance at Croydon Magistrates' Court. The crowds outside the courtroom were so large that he was brought from his cell via a tunnel to the court. He was formally charged with the murder of PC Miles. 'Not me, Sir,' he replied. As the packed court listened to the magistrate remanding Bentley in custody for a week, they must surely have marvelled that this quiet young man could have caused so much havoc the night before. His friend Christopher Craig could not be moved from his hospital bed, so the public had to be content with gazing at Bentley.

His parents, however, had not come to gaze, but to talk. They were doubly disappointed; all that they could see was the back of his head, and after the one-minute hearing their son was taken immediately to Brixton Prison.

It was nearly seven o'clock in the evening before they were allowed to speak to Derek. Almost twenty-four hours had elapsed since they had last spoken to him. Their first close look at him gave them a profound shock. Somewhere, somehow, in those twenty-four hours he had acquired a badly marked face. When his mother and father began to question him about his injuries, the warder officiously intervened to tell them that such questions were not allowed. At a subsequent visit Derek told his parents that he had been kicked in the face. Broken nose or not, there were far more serious problems which the Bentleys now had to cope with.

The implications of the charge the teenager faced were too great for the Bentley family to grasp, and mercifully remained so until after the Appeal hearing.

Bentley had been granted legal aid and his father engaged a Croydon solicitor. More by good luck than judgment he picked a good one. John Stevens, whatever his personal feelings, worked to the best of his not inconsiderable ability on behalf of his young client. Stevens offered the brief to barrister Frank Cassels and so began the task of creating a defence to save Bentley from the gallows.

Upon the shoulders of a brilliant young northern barrister, John Parris, fell the impossible task of trying to save Craig. If all that had apparently transpired on the roof was not enough to damn the sixteen-year-old boy, he seemed determined to put the issue beyond any doubt whatsoever. In the week that followed the gun battle Craig lay in a hospital bed. His broken wrist had been re-set during an operation and at various times he was given drugs to ease the pain from his broken body. These drugs were to play a sensational part during the subsequent trial. They were all his Defence Counsel had to justify the stream of remarks that a variety of police officers swore poured from the teenager's lips. Twelve hours after he had been admitted to the hospital Craig awoke, saw a policeman sitting by his bedside, and asked: 'Is he dead?' The policeman asked him who he was talking about. Craig replied, 'That copper. I shot him in the head and he went down like a ton of bricks.' When PC Denham recounted this conversation in Court he added the not surprising observation that Craig was in pain and was not normal at the time.

On the evening of 3 November he awoke to find a PC Smith by his bedside. His dark brown eyes stared for a moment at the officer, then he remarked, 'You're coppers. Ha. The other one is dead, with a hole in his head.' Pointing to himself he continued, 'I'm all right. All you bastards should be dead.' On 5 November he turned to PC Thomas Shepherd and enquired, 'Is the policeman I shot in the shoulder still in hospital? I know the one I shot in the head is dead.' Shepherd made no reply. An hour later Craig remarked, 'What do you get for carrying a knuckleduster? Bentley had mine.' Then a few minutes later he added, 'Did you see the gun I had? It was all on the wobble so I took it to work and sawed two inches off the barrel.' Possibly the most damaging remark that Craig allegedly made from that hospital bed was on 6 November, four days after he had been admitted and well after the period when his body had been full of drugs. This time his listener was PC Brown. 'If I hadn't cut a bit off of the barrel of my gun I'd probably have killed a lot more policemen. That night I was out to kill because I had so much hate inside me for what they'd done to my brother. I shot the policeman in the head with my ·45. If it had been the ·22 he might not have died.'

At his trial Craig denied that he made any of these remarks. He also stated that while in hospital he was in such pain and so full of drugs that for most of the time he was unconscious, and when he was conscious he was not lucid. In view of the nature of the remarks, such a denial was predictable. They show such a malevolence, such a calculated contempt for human life, such a capacity for evil, that they are truly frightening. They show an attitude of mind that one would find hard to credit in a hardened criminal, yet they came from a sixteen-year-old boy.

One aspect of this stream of sustained hatred that has never been considered is that the remarks contain information that could only have been given to Craig by the police themselves during those bedside conversations. Notwithstanding Craig's denial, I believe that his remarks *are* an accurate reflection of his attitude at that time. During the Old Bailey trial, when Fairfax left the witness box and passed close to Craig, the boy turned to a prison warder and said, 'I ought to have killed that fucker as well.' At sixteen Christopher Craig's capacity for evil was boundless.

*　　*　　*

During that week, as Craig lay in his hospital bed, Chief Inspector Smith worked quite literally round the clock. He had left his home on the Sunday evening of the rooftop battle to take charge of the case, and it was three days before he returned to it.

Added to the major task of assembling the evidence for the Prosecution was another, more unusual, duty. For within forty-eight hours of the gun-battle the Chief Inspector had been instructed to prepare an immediate report on the case. Officially he was advised that this was for the Home Secretary. Unofficially he was told for whom the report was really intended: Prime Minister Winston Churchill. It was an indication of just how political the question of Bentley's execution had become.

In the midst of important affairs of state, including his calculations of the possible effect on Great Britain of General Eisenhower's election to the American presidency, Churchill thought the Croydon gun-battle important enough to call for an immediate report on it.

This action may of course be considered quite right and proper. But why, in that case, had the Prime Minister not called for a full report on the death of PC Beattie in Cardiff, earlier that year? Why had he not called for a full report on the death of Detective Constable MacLeod and the wounding of Detective Constable Macdonald in Glasgow? Miles wasn't the only policeman to be shot in 1952 – so what prompted the Prime Minister to take such an interest in the Croydon affair?

I believe that this was the first sign of the Government's determination to use the Craig/Bentley case as an example. Many people were convinced that the country was poised on the brink of anarchy; something had to be done about it, and done quickly; and the Executive's manner of handling the Craig/Bentley case was the answer to those fears.

One of the most striking effects of the rooftop battle was the fresh life it gave to the campaign for the return of whipping and birching. It will be recalled that Earl Howe had dismissed the magistrates' vote against corporal punishment at the Mansion House as being not truly representative of the main body of their fellows. Perhaps if the three-hundred-odd votes had agreed with the noble Earl's own views he would have considered their decision of greater significance. Nevertheless the Magistrates' Association, being a democratic organization, decided to send out ballot papers to all of its 9,350 members. The *Sunday Express* decided to send a telegram to every MP asking 'Would you support a Bill, if introduced now, for the return of the birch or the cat?' Only two hundred MPs obliged with a reply but what was significant was that nearly all those in favour of the restoration of whipping were Conservatives, and the vast majority of those opposed to it were Labour members.

In the meantime Mrs Miles was exposed to fresh ordeals. At the Coroner's Inquest on her late husband she was required to tell how she had identified her husband's body at the mortuary. The only other witness was pathologist Dr David Haler, who stated that the policeman's death had been caused by a gunshot wound in the head. The Coroner adjourned the inquest indefinitely 'in view of the proceedings now being taken elsewhere'. Before he adjourned, however, the Coroner, Mr J. W. Bennet, took the opportunity of making a speech to the jury that subsequently appeared in the national press under the heading THIS BRAVE AND FEARLESS FORCE. 'The body of men forming the police forces of this country have a great variety of duties to perform. Sometimes these are of a very dangerous nature and invariably they do them bravely and fearlessly, for the protection and safe-guarding of the public. It was in the performance of such duties that this Police Constable met a most untimely death.'

One cannot but agree with the sentiments expressed by the Coroner, but the wisdom of such public utterances prior to a trial is highly questionable. As John Parris, Craig's Defence Counsel, was subsequently to say, 'Coroner's inquisitions, when a trial is pending, serve no useful purpose, and in the circumstances of this case, to require Mrs Miles to identify her husband's body and then speak of it in public was an agony she might well have been spared. The only result was to increase public indignation towards the two accused, and possibly prevent them receiving an impartial trial.' One curious feature of the Coroner's Inquest was the fact that, although it was adjourned indefinitely, the body of PC Miles was cremated within three days of the post mortem. From Mrs Miles' point of view, obviously, the quicker the distressing funeral service was over the better. From the point of view of the two defendants, any opportunity of testing the prosecution's contention of how Miles had died was now eliminated. Among the 1,200 mourners at PC Miles's funeral was the Home Secretary, Sir David Maxwell Fyfe.

Any possible doubts about the extent of popular indignation would have been dispelled by the scenes that attended Craig's first appearance at Croydon Magistrates' Court on 11 November. As the ambulance carrying Craig stopped outside the court the crowd surged forward. The policeman in attendance doubtless thought at first that this was the natural mawkish curiosity that was a feature of all murder trials. But when the ambulance doors swung open and

Craig was carried out on a stretcher, the crowd pushed even closer and suddenly there were shouts of 'He ought to swing!' and 'Let's get hold of the dirty bastard and choke him!' Craig was only saved from physical attack by the dead policeman's colleagues. After a three-minute hearing Craig was remanded for seven days.

On the following Monday, with both youths in the dock together for the first time, the Prosecution were ready to proceed. It was also the first time that the public and the press heard full details of the case for the Prosecution. Both defendants were now additionally charged with the attempted murder of Detective Constable Fairfax. The two teenagers pleaded Not Guilty to both charges, reserved their defence for the trial, and, apart from a few questions asked on their behalf by their respective solicitors, took no direct part in the proceedings. The hearing belonged entirely to the Prosecution. As a series of policemen entered the witness box and recounted their involvement on that fateful Sunday night there was complete silence in the courtroom, broken only by the occasional sob from Mrs Craig. Her youngest son listened to the entire proceedings lying on a stretcher in the well of the court. At 4.00 p.m. precisely, the Chairman of the Court committed the two teenagers for trial at the Old Bailey. He advised them that the trial would commence during the first week of December, in less than three weeks' time. In view of the fact that one of the doctors who had given evidence for the Prosecution had just stated that Craig would be on his back for at least a month, it was clear that Justice could not wait until the sixteen-year-old boy was fit. The rush to judgment had begun.

After their clients had been committed for trial both defence solicitors, 'having regard to the nature of the evidence', applied for a special Defence Certificate for two counsel. The application was denied. If the defendants had been able to pay for their defence they could have had two counsel, but as the State was paying, under what was so aptly called the Poor Prisoner's Defence, the decision as to whether they could have more than one man to defend them was in the hands of the magistrates.

Lest it be thought that by exercising this privilege the State was saving the taxpayer a vast amount of money, it should be added that Counsel was paid a pittance for a Poor Prisoner's Defence. The fee for John Parris' defence of Craig worked out at 4¾d (2p) per hour for the time spent on the case, and it cost him £250 in expenses and lost briefs.

In the brief period between committal and trial Bentley's solicitor worked diligently on behalf of his client. There was precious little time and John Stevens moved quickly. He made a number of visits to Derek Bentley at Brixton Prison and obtained from him a long and detailed statement, containing much information of immense value. It gave a fairly detailed history of Bentley's life, which was substantiated by information from a great many other sources; Bentley's parents, teachers, doctors. This information, together with police depositions, photographs and a plan of the rooftop, and a considerable quantity of other information, was sent to Frank Cassels with the following brief:

'Counsel is kindly asked to appear on behalf of the accused Derek William Bentley, who pleads Not Guilty to the two offences with which he is jointly charged with Christopher Craig.'

There then follow details of the committal proceedings, and the brief continues:

'It is not known what course Craig is taking, but, so far as Bentley is concerned, the whole matter seems to revolve about the question of whether or not he knew Craig had a revolver in his possession, when they embarked upon this criminal undertaking.

'If the evidence of the various Police Officers is even substantially correct, then there can be no doubt that Bentley did know that Craig had a revolver and ammunition.

'It may well be contended that mere knowledge of the possession by Craig of the revolver is sufficient to make Bentley guilty and that it is not necessary for the Prosecution also to prove that he knew Craig would use it, or was likely to use it, on the ground that Craig could only have had it in order to carry out the unlawful purpose at all costs.

'Archbold (32nd Edition) at page 1468 states "*it is not sufficient that the common purpose should be merely unlawful: it must either be to commit a felony, or, if it is to commit a misdemeanour, then there must be evidence to show that the parties engaged intended to carry it out at all hazards*".'

The brief continues: 'Had the Accused been arrested on the roof without any question of a revolver, they could only have been charged with attempted warehouse-breaking, which is a misdemeanour.

'On the other hand, the intention was to break into the building which, if achieved, would have been a felony.

'Bentley denies having said anything which could indicate knowledge that Craig had a gun or ammunition and that, in fact, he did not know he had them.'

There were also comments in the brief questioning seriously the veracity of police evidence given in the lower court.

The brief continues with details of what further action John Stevens was taking on behalf of his client.

In fact Derek Bentley *had* been arrested on the roof 'without any question of a revolver'. From the moment that he had been grabbed by Fairfax he was under arrest and at that point, as the brief makes quite clear, he could only be charged with a misdemeanour. The fact that the charge had escalated to the most serious that a man can face in this country was completely beyond Bentley's powers of comprehension. It also was, and still is, beyond the power of comprehension of some of the finest legal minds in the country, and they, unlike Bentley, are conversant with the doctrine of Constructive Malice.

If the brief to Frank Cassels was well documented and informative, then the brief to John Parris on behalf of Craig was a masterpiece of brevity. It contained the police depositions and the following sentence, 'Counsel will have all the information he needs from depositions enclosed herewith and conference with client.'

Parris received that brief two days before the trial was due to commence. He was at that time engaged in a protracted trial at Leeds Assizes that would certainly be in progress on 4 December, when the Craig/Bentley trial was due to start. As things stood he would not be able to be at the Old Bailey, let alone have 'conference with client'. Leaving a colleague to sit in for him at Leeds, he caught a train to London and at his request all Counsel concerned in the case saw Lord Goddard, the Lord Chief Justice of England, in front of whom the case would be tried, at his Old Bailey chambers. Parris argued for an adjournment until Tuesday, 9 December. He received little support from either of the other Counsel, for they were ready to proceed. Lord Goddard was disinclined to grant the adjournment. He told Parris that in his opinion there was no defence in the case of Craig. When Parris disagreed, Lord Goddard asked him what the defence would be. It should be remembered that this entire conversation took place in front of Christmas Humphreys, the Prosecuting Counsel for the State. Parris said that Craig's defence would be one of manslaughter. His Lordship was openly contemptuous of the validity of such a defence. Again it should be remembered that this was the trial judge. After they had argued for thirty minutes, Parris played an ace. He was aware that the Lord Chief Justice was due to attend a Criminal Court of Appeal hearing on Monday, 8 December. Parris pointed out that if the trial commenced on the 4th, it would certainly last longer than two days, which, with a weekend intervening, would mean its continuation on Monday the 8th, and Lord Goddard would not get to his Appeal Court. It was finally announced that the trial would begin on 9 December.

On 8 December John Parris saw Frank Cassels at the latter's chambers for a joint defence conference. Cassels, the man on whom all Bentley's hopes rested, greeted his colleague with the words: 'I think both the little bastards ought to swing.' This view was widely held during the pre-trial period, but coming from the man who was professionally committed to his client, it indicated a remarkable lack of commitment.

Cassels urged his colleague to persuade Craig to plead guilty. He reasoned that if Craig did otherwise he would have to go into the witness box, and this might well damage Bentley's case. In Cassels' opinion the view that had been expressed the previous week by Lord Goddard was the correct one. Craig had no defence. Therefore, Cassels reasoned, why not plead guilty? There was no danger of Craig hanging, his age debarred that. The worst he could expect was imprisonment for life. Cassels argued that Bentley, on the other hand, ran the risk of hanging. Parris did not bend to this argument. In his opinion Craig had a very real defence, based on the argument that Miles' killing was not murder but manslaughter. He pointed out that if he was successful in reducing the verdict against Craig, then Bentley could not possibly be found guilty of murder. Undoubtedly, Parris was also influenced by the belief that even if Bentley was found guilty, he would certainly be reprieved. In the end neither man convinced the other. Come hell or high water Craig would not plead guilty and Parris would fight to the bitter end to obtain a verdict of manslaughter.

Craig and Bentley spent the evening of Monday, 8 December 1952, in the hospital block of Brixton Prison, in separate cells.

At John Parris' request Mr and Mrs Craig had taken their son some sombre clothes that day to replace his present flamboyant attire. Now they sat by the fire in their Norbury home with their one remaining child, eighteen-year-old Lucy Craig. As they sat, they remembered happier times.

Mr and Mrs Bentley had spent the day buying Derek a Christmas present. Then they visited their son bringing him new clothes for his court appearance, and a sprig of

111

white heather. Bentley was going to need all the luck he could get.

Christmas Humphreys, the Prosecuting Counsel, who on the morrow would be doing everything within his powers to ensure that Craig and Bentley would be convicted, was also President of the London Buddhist Society. He spent the evening giving his fellow members a lecture on 'The Strenuous Application of Buddhism in Daily Life'.

John Parris occupied himself that evening quietly going over all the evidence he had personally collected, including a long statement from Craig. His colleague, Frank Cassels, spent the evening watching a television performance of *Faust*. Frederick Fairfax, newly promoted Detective Sergeant, relaxed with his wife and eight-year-old son in his Sanderstead home. And Lord Goddard? A few days before Lord Goddard had tried the case of two young brothers who had pleaded guilty to robbing two other boys. 'Nowadays the cane is never used at school,' he said. 'It would have done them good if they had had a good larruping. What they want is to have someone who would give them a thundering good beating, and then, perhaps, they would not do it again. I suppose they were brought up to be treated like little darlings, and tucked up in bed at night.' Then, looking squarely at the two boys, he continued, 'You are two detestable little bullies. Nowadays courts cannot deal with you boys as you ought to be dealt with. Magistrates can do nothing to you, and this Court can do hardly anything to you.' The elder of the brothers, aged seventeen, was sent to Borstal, the younger, aged fourteen, to an approved school. Had Lord Goddard asked for a report he would have discovered that the two boys came from a broken home and for some time had been beaten every night. Lord Goddard spent 8 December as he spent most days, in dispensing Justice. That day he refused two fifteen-year-old boys leave to appeal against being sent to an approved school.

The irresistible force that had been generated on that

Croydon rooftop by Craig and Bentley had ensured that, in the pre-trial period, the two teenagers came to personify all that ailed the youth of this country. That irresistible force was now about to meet an immovable object, in the form of Lord Goddard, who personified to the whip-them, beat-them and hang-them brigade all that they held dear.

4

The Mind of a Child

Before examining what occurred at the Old Bailey it is essential to examine in detail Derek Bentley's history and a number of the events immediately prior to the trial.

One of the matters that greatly concerned John Stevens, Bentley's solicitor, was Bentley's medical and social history. He was not alone in displaying an interest in this quarter. The Principal Medical Officer at Brixton Prison, Dr Matheson, was obliged by law not merely to collate Bentley's history but to submit an opinion on the young man's mental condition to the Crown Prosecution, the trial judge, and the Defence Counsel.

Upon his admittance to Brixton Prison Bentley was immediately examined by Dr Matheson and then placed in the hospital wing. This enabled Matheson and his colleagues to keep Bentley under close observation, watching his general behaviour and his ability to adjust to his new environment.

Bentley was admitted on 3 November. Matheson's report to the Court is dated 5 December. So the prison staff had just over a month to learn about his background and to arrive at conclusions concerning his present mental condition. The information that was available is only marginally less disturbing than Matheson's final conclusions.

Derek Bentley was born shortly before midnight on 30 June 1933. His parents at that time had two other children, Joan, aged six, and Iris, aged two. Several hours after his birth a second son was born. There had been no indication of twins during Mrs Bentley's pregnancy, and in fact the midwife had left after Derek was born. The second baby died two hours after birth. An hour later the Bentleys were in grave danger of losing Derek too, for he had contracted bronchial pneumonia. He was rushed to Guy's Hospital and placed in an oxygen tent. The doctors at Guy's considered his condition so critical that Mr Bentley was advised to have the child baptized immediately. However within forty-eight hours the father had given the first of a number of blood donations to help in the fight for his son's life, and the baby eventually rallied. But it had been desperately close. Derek Bentley's entry to this life was as dramatic as his exit, nineteen and a half years later.

At the time of his birth the Bentleys were living in a slum area in Blackfriars. Conditions there were so appalling that shortly before their son was born they had sent their eldest daughter, Joan, to live with her grandmother, to ease the pressures on their two-roomed flat. Joan was to remain there for the rest of her short life.

At the age of three, Derek enrolled in the Nursery section of Friar Street Elementary School. A year later he had an accident that was to have far-reaching repercussions. Whilst playing in the street with some friends, he climbed on a parked lorry loaded with huge rolls of paper destined for the Fleet Street presses. Having exhausted themselves, the older boys jumped from the lorry, leaving Derek to make his own way down. He fell fifteen feet on to the pavement, hitting his head on the concrete. His nose and head bled profusely, then his eyes became glassy, his mouth was flecked with foam and he began to convulse. His parents fought to control his flailing body, an ambulance was summoned, and for the second time in his life Bentley was rushed to Guy's Hospital. After his wounds had been dressed and he had been sedated his parents were advised by the Casualty Doctor that their son had had a major epileptic fit, caused by the blow to his head. Warning them of the seriousness of the attack, the doctor advised them that there were liable to be recurrences from time to time, and that any blow to the head could trigger off another attack.

The next recorded attack took place when Bentley was six years old. He fell down while playing, and the attack followed twenty-four hours later. His jaw became tightly clenched and his parents described his face as 'going blue'. On this occasion he was admitted to Lambeth Hospital. Presumably because there were a number of unusual post-epileptic symptoms, Bentley was admitted as an in-patient. He was drowsy and he had a high temperature. During his five-day stay at the hospital an infection developed on one of his fingers, and this was also treated. His parents were warned again to expect the epileptic attacks, possibly at shorter intervals now.

During the latter part of 1940, Bentley, his sister Iris, and their mother narrowly survived a bombing attack that demolished the air-raid shelter where they had taken refuge. Shortly after this Mrs Bentley's mother and sister were killed during a bombing raid on London; Joan Bentley, aged twelve, was also killed. Seven-year-old Derek, who had become increasingly withdrawn since the onset of the epileptic attacks, was profoundly affected by the death of his sister, and he grew increasingly nervous and fearful.

This change in Derek, combined with the fact that Friar Street School had been closed as a result of bomb damage, prompted the Bentley family to move to Edgware, where they had friends. There the two Bentley children contracted chicken-pox and scarlet fever as a result of which they were in Tooting Isolation Hospital for three months. During this period Mrs Bentley gave birth to another son, Dennis.

Having recovered from their childhood ailments Derek and Iris attended Camrose Avenue School, Edgware. Attendance records at the school confirm that they went there from August 1941 to December 1943. Early in 1944 the Bentleys' Edgware home was completely destroyed by what Londoners had come to know as a 'flying bomb', one of Dr Werner von Braun's more sophisticated inventions. The family escaped unhurt and returned to the Blackfriars area, to a flat in Hillingdon Street, Southwark. Mr Bentley was by now serving in the Army and, like millions of other fathers, saw his children only rarely. There is no indication in any known records that Derek suffered any epileptic attacks during this period, but he frequently experienced severe headaches and bouts of sickness. During this period there also developed a blueness in his skin which became very deep, and as the months progressed even his lips and fingernails went blue. Dr McManus, their family doctor at the time, is stated to have dismissed the symptoms and advised the parents they were 'probably caused by strain and lack of sleep'. In the doctor's opinion the headaches and bouts of sickness owed their origins to the same causes.

In September 1944, their flat was badly damaged by yet another 'flying bomb', and the ceiling fell on Derek as he lay in bed, completely burying him. Rescue workers dug him out and he was examined by Dr McManus. There were no external injuries and after treatment for shock he was allowed to return home. It had not been a total escape, though; the headaches that had been his constant companion from the age of four now increased in severity. In view of Bentley's history of epilepsy it is surprising that he was not immediately subjected to a neurological examination. Doubtless the War was a contributing factor to this oversight, but the Bentley case is so very full of oversights.

Derek Bentley was now eleven and his parents were getting worried by the many breaks in his formal education due to illness and the frequent moves. They now arranged for him to attend the John Ruskin School at Walworth, and it was from this school's Headmaster that the Bentleys received their first indication that epilepsy was not the only serious problem affecting their eldest son. A week after he had joined the school the Headmaster called on Mrs Bentley, and informed her that Derek was totally illiterate.

It was the first inkling of this situation, and it came as a profound shock to her. How long Derek Bentley had been illiterate is a mystery. It seems inconceivable that a congenital lack of intelligence could have passed unnoticed during eight years of school life, but this is exactly what appears to have happened. I have been unable to trace any school reports on Bentley covering the first eight years of his education. His father was later to write that the teachers at the Nursery School in Friar Street considered him of above average potential; whether this was a declaration of faith on the part of the father, or on the part of the Friar Street teachers, is debatable; there appears to be no evidence to support Mr Bentley's contention. When Bentley was executed he was still totally illiterate, so he had laboured under this handicap for at least the last eight and a half years of his life; the facts would appear strongly to support the view that it was an innate, rather than an educational, defect. This was the considered opinion of Dr Munroe, the physician in charge of the Department of Psychological Medicine at Guy's Hospital, when he examined Bentley in 1949.

When his wife told him of the situation, Mr Bentley wrote to her, instructing her to take their eldest son to the family doctor. It will be recalled that Dr McManus had already shown a marked disinclination to share the Bentleys' anxieties about Derek. Now he showed it again. In his opinion the child's educational backwardness was due to 'wartime conditions'. He arrived at this diagnosis without giving Bentley a comprehensive medical examination and he again felt no need to send the child for neurological examination. The number of oversights was mounting rapidly.

During 1945 the Bentley family moved to Norbury, and Derek was enrolled at the school where he ultimately met Christopher Craig. The beat-'em and whip-'em brigade of 1952 would doubtless have been greatly heartened to know that the last school to be responsible for the immature Craig and the feeble-minded Bentley had a teaching staff who were great believers in corporal punishment. Shortly after the Craig/Bentley trial an article about the school appeared in a local paper. In view of the then recent activities of two of its former pupils the headline was more than a little surprising, SCHOOL WHERE CANE IS USED – NO DISCIPLINARY PROBLEMS. The Headmaster was reported as having said, 'We use the cane . . . We are still old-fashioned enough to believe that if a boy kicks over the traces then he should be made to realize that punishment is going to be swift and automatic. I don't think I can recall one boy who has resented corporal punishment . . . A couple of good handers and it is all over, and you are quite good friends with the master after the smarting has died down!'

This, then, was the enlightened régime that Bentley now joined. Whether he smilingly accepted his hands and backside being lashed with a piece of wood is a moot point. As a contemporary of Bentley's also attending a school in South London, I find it difficult to recall such a philosophical attitude among any of my classmates.

What is beyond doubt is that Derek Bentley developed a dislike for the *entire* régime. His illiteracy set him apart from his classmates, and they were quick to realize it. If there is one thing that a group of twelve-year-old boys is very quick to react to, it is a markedly abnormal academic performance on the part of one of their number. A boy who is exceptionally clever invariably has to endure labels such as 'teacher's pet' or 'book-worm'. A boy who is exceptionally stupid frequently has to endure taunts and abuse of a much more basic nature. So it was in Bentley's case. He arrived home in tears more often than not, for he could not stand up to the playground insults. The situation was further aggravated by the absence of his father who was still in the Army. When his father came home on leave and realized what was going on, he advised his son to 'give them a pasting', but it was useless advice. Although Derek was above average size, he lacked that peculiar quality that enables a person to stand up and give and take physical violence. His inability not only to cope with this aspect of school life, but also with the simplest academic problem, produced an inevitable reaction. He truanted. Bentley was far happier sitting on Streatham Common, watching the world go by, than when he was sitting behind a desk, failing to comprehend the smallest fragment of that world.

During this period the epileptic attacks returned. Again they were heralded by a serious fall. The stair banisters of the first-floor landing at his Norbury home broke, sending the youth hurtling on to his head in the hall below. He lost consciousness, and on recovering, he immediately convulsed and thrashed about. He fought madly until one of the two doctors who had been called quietened him down with an injection.

By May 1946 his truanting had become so frequent that the authorities decided to take action. At this time Bentley was still totally illiterate and one would have expected the authorities to at least contemplate transferring Bentley to a school for educationally subnormal children (ESN school). What they did was to bring Bentley before a local magistrate and recommend that he be transferred to another secondary school, called Ingrams. On the magistrate's 'suggestion' Bentley was duly transferred. This decision was hotly contested by Mr Bentley, who argued that as Ingrams was two or three times further from his home than Norbury Manor, all that would be achieved would be to keep his son away from home even more than at present. He could also see no academic advantage for his son, as he considered Ingrams the inferior of the two schools. He insisted that he had the right to choose where his son was educated. Although he was ignorant of the fact, Mr Bentley had to support him in this contention, the 1944 Education Act. So, after four months at Ingrams, Derek Bentley found himself back at Norbury Manor.

It is indisputable that throughout this entire school period Bentley was educationally subnormal. Sixteen months' intensive research failed to reveal that any member of the teaching profession, either on the staff of Ingrams or on the staff of Norbury Manor, or on the staff of the local authority ever showed in any practical way that they were aware of this fact. Shortly before the Old Bailey trial Chief Inspector Smith was advised by the teachers at Norbury Manor that in their opinion Bentley had a mental age of nine years. Yet they had done nothing to remedy the situation. This undoubtedly was the most serious oversight to date.

When I interviewed the two men who were Headmaster and Deputy Headmaster at Norbury Manor during the periods that Bentley was a pupil there, they both had difficulty in giving an opinion of Bentley's ability. Both said that he was hardly ever there. 'If he attended once a week we were lucky,' was how Mr Bonnetto, the Deputy Head, put it. Both teachers blamed his absence on over-indulgent parents. They were both aware of his total illiteracy, yet were powerless to remedy the situation. A situation they felt could be remedied was Bentley's association with a younger boy (not Craig); the teachers felt the combination was harmful to both youths, so in July 1947, after ten months at Norbury Manor, Bentley found himself back at Ingrams School.

Anticipating a hostile reaction from Mr Bentley, the authorities this time had had an attendance order made by a local magistrate, naming Ingrams as the school Bentley was to attend. An interesting device for driving a coach-and-four through the 1944 Education Act. Five months later, during January 1948, Bentley went back to Norbury Manor, his father's point of view, magistrate's order or no magistrate's order, having prevailed. If the focus of this situation had not been a young boy in desperate, urgent, constant need of help, the sight of a dogmatic father fighting equally dogmatic authorities would be high farce. Bentley was now approaching his fifteenth birthday and he still couldn't write his name. The epileptic attacks were now frequent, but they certainly played no part in the teachers' evaluation of Bentley. In Bonnetto's opinion Bentley was 'like a great lump of lard, an utterly worthless piece of humanity'.

To both teachers Bentley was a total nonentity, unloved and unwanted, but Christopher Craig was a different proposition. It was during the last of Bentley's flying visits to Norbury Manor that Craig came to the school, though there was no involvement between the two boys during this period. Both teachers were full of praise for Christopher Craig. For them it was a case of 'chalk and cheese'. If Bentley was dull and uninteresting, Craig, though barely able to cope with the rudiments of reading and writing, compensated in other areas; his teachers found him a 'boy full of life, one who excelled in anything verbal, and a natural athlete.'

Those two teachers who blamed parental over-indulgence for Bentley's weaknesses were uniquely qualified to recognize over-indulgence. Craig took a companion to school with him every day: a gun. During the period that he attended Norbury Manor he owned over forty guns, at least one of which accompanied him everywhere he went. It was only after he bored out a starting pistol, and thereby created a lethal weapon, that any action was taken. He was taken to the police station and given a lecture. He continued, however, to bring guns to school, not merely starting pistols and antique guns, but also revolvers. No action was taken. His teachers were fully aware of this, they told me that he used to display guns in the classroom. The Headmaster's comment was particularly illuminating: 'It was a harmless hobby. What I had to be on the watch for was any of the boys turning up at school with a knife; you can do a lot of damage with a knife.' It is easy to be wise after the event, but surely professionals like teachers and policemen are paid to be wise at the time. The attitude of Bentley's teachers is highly relevant. For while the two teenagers were awaiting trial in Brixton Prison, it was to these men that the police turned for information – information that was to assist Dr Matheson, as I shall show.

Shortly before Bentley returned to Norbury Manor, during January 1948, his mother gave birth to another boy, Roger.

The child was a mongol (mongolism is a form of feeble-mindedness with characteristic physical abnormalities) and he died eleven months later.

The fears of the Norbury Manor teachers concerning Bentley's association with a younger boy were shown to be justified. During March 1948 the two boys appeared at Croydon Juvenile Court and were found guilty of attempting to break into a store, and also attempting to steal 10/- (50p) and a quantity of bus tickets from a bus conductor's cash-box. They were bound over for two years. One of the conditions was that the two youths should cease to associate. Yet again the magistrate made an attendance order on Bentley, naming Ingrams as the school (the possibility of moving the younger boy never seems to have occurred to anybody). So in March 1948, only a few months before he left school completely, Bentley was moved yet again. This was at least the ninth transfer during his school life.

If the maxim of a change being as good as a rest is true, then Bentley must have been the most rested youth of his generation. Every child that changes schools has adjustment problems of varying seriousness. The problems that Bentley had to cope with were not only completely beyond his capacity, they appear to have been beyond the capacity of his many teachers. It is an indictment of the educational system of this country that a feeble-minded epileptic could be shunted from school to school without it once occurring to anyone that he needed specialized training, specific help, in short *professional* handling. To his teachers he was lazy, stupid, and a regular truant. At fourteen years of age he was undoubtedly already showing an inclination towards criminal activity as an outlet for energies that were not being academically utilized.

In a book published a few months before the Craig/Bentley trial exploded on an incredulous nation, J. Pearce, the Physician in charge of the Department of Psychiatry at St Mary's Hospital and Queen Elizabeth Hospital for Children, had this to say:

'Retardation in educational attainment means that the child is out of step with his colleagues, and if he is seriously behind this may prevent him, in spite of good intelligence, from progressing in class . . . and in addition to a sense of futility he may even come to be looked on as merely stupid and lazy, especially if a new teacher takes over the class and does not know the child's personal history. This type of experience may be an important factor in a history of delinquency later on. It may entail sufficient dissatisfaction to precipitate truancy, with its attendant problems. It is out of various combinations of circumstances such as these that a vicious circle of emotional difficulties and reactions thereto develops, or it would be more precise to say, not a vicious circle, but a vicious spiral girdling a line of time.'

For Derek Bentley that 'vicious spiral girdling a line of time' was, by March 1948, well set on its upward path. It was to reach its zenith on the night of Sunday, 2 November 1952.

I am totally convinced that if just one of the many *professionals* through whose hands Derek Bentley passed before that night had acted correctly, he would still be alive. I am equally convinced that that thought has never occurred to them. Indeed, it is easy to imagine that after Bentley's arrest these same people were nodding wisely and declaring that it confirmed their own opinions: 'I always knew he was a bad lot.' The possibility that *they* were culpable would be beyond them.

In the summer of 1948 Bentley finally left school. It must have been a sweet relief, but it was a short one. He began looking for a job, but the opportunities for an illiterate fifteen-year-old proved limited. The magistrates at Croydon Juvenile Court supplied the solution. For the second time in six months Bentley appeared before them. With another youth he had wandered on to a building site and begun playing with some tools that had been left there. A public-spirited citizen telephoned the police, with the result that both youths were arrested, charged with stealing the tools and found guilty. The value of the tools was

18/- (90p). The magistrate, for some reason that only he and God knows, then asked Bentley to spell 'fluorescent'; it will come as no great shock to the reader to learn that this was quite beyond him. Before Bentley was sentenced he was remanded for a variety of reports, which I have been unable to trace; the Croydon authorities have advised me that they have been destroyed. Perhaps an official enquiry into the Bentley case will be able to succeed where I have failed.

Undoubtedly those reports would make interesting reading, for after receiving them the magistrates took a course of action which is another of the mysteries of this case. They sentenced Bentley to a three-year period at an approved school. The other boy received a similar sentence. Bentley was sent to the Kingswood Approved School at Bristol. During his stay at the approved school, Bentley was given an IQ test.

It was estimated as a result of that test that his IQ was 66 and that he had a reading age of four and a half.

Mr Pearce, in the book just quoted, gave the following interpretations of IQ levels.

Grade	IQ
Superior	125+
Above Average	115–125
Average	85–115
Dull and Backward	70–85
Feeble minded (ESN)	50–70
Imbecile	20–50
Idiot	0–20

The World Health Organization, in its report on mentally subnormal children (1954), recommended the term 'mild subnormality' for those in the IQ range 50–69.

The Royal Commission on the Law relating to Mental Illness and Mental Deficiency, 1954–1957, opined that 'severely subnormal' was a term that should be applied to all patients in the IQ range 0–49 and also to some of the patients in the IQ range 50–69.

The Stanford–Binet scale of testing gives Bentley a mental age of ten years.

It becomes, therefore, a question of definition. To Pearce, Bentley's IQ would have indicated that the youth was 'feeble-minded', to the World Health Organization that he was 'mildly subnormal', to the Royal Commission that he was possibly 'severely subnormal', and to Stanford and Binet that he had a mental age of ten. We shall see in a moment what it indicated to the staff of Kingswood Approved School at Bristol.

In the Royal Commission report referred to above, the following observation appears: 'We would consider a mental age below seven and a half to nine years, or an intelligence quotient below 50 to 60 on the Stanford–Binet scale, as being a pointer strongly indicative of a personality so seriously subnormal as to make the patient incapable of living an independent life. *But in some cases it may be true to say that patients are seriously subnormal and are incapable of living an independent life even if their intelligence quotient is, say, 60 or even higher, if they have serious defects of personality in addition, resulting in a general subnormal personality which makes them incapable of managing their own lives or places them in serious danger of being taken advantage of by other people.*'

How pertinent those remarks are in relation to Bentley's condition can be gauged from the fact that the IQ test he was given has an error margin of at least six points; Bentley's IQ, therefore, was, at the time of the Kingswood test, between 60 and 72. The particular test given to Bentley was probably one of the Stanford–Binet range, which were in common usage in 1948. In Stanford–Binet terms Bentley's mental age was between nine and ten and a half.

I have said 'probably' because the authorities at Kingswood refused to give me any details. I explained to the present Principal of the school, Mr J. L. Burns, that details of the IQ test that Bentley had would greatly assist in presenting a clear picture of his mental condition.

His reply was, 'What have IQ tests got to do with his mental condition?' At which point Mr Burns terminated the conversation.

If the reports that the Croydon magistrates had called for on Bentley indicated his mental level, then the decision to send him to an approved school was a serious breach of the law. The decision that kept him there after the tests is equally unjustifiable. There was provision under the Mental Deficiency Act for persons of Bentley's level to be transferred to a mental deficiency school by order of the Home Secretary. The Royal Commission states in its report that any children in approved schools who are found to be seriously subnormal are usually transferred if and when a vacancy can be found for them. It continues, 'These arrangements are also sometimes used to transfer to mental deficiency hospitals, as feeble-minded or moral defectives, children or young people of slightly below average or even above average intelligence who have shown persistent abnormalities of behaviour – whether inadequate or aggressive – of the types we have described, which do not respond to the approved school régime and which may be considered evidence of pathologically incomplete or arrested development of personality. Others are sometimes sent for treatment in mental hospitals.'

So the machinery was there, but it was not used. In the opinion of the approved school, Bentley 'was being encouraged by his father to make complaints about his treatment so that he would be granted an early licence'. They considered that, 'At all times he gave the impression at the school that he conserved his energy only for eating and talking; that he was self-satisfied, indifferent to training and content to let others do the work.' That was the opinion expressed by the school to Dr Matheson in November 1952.

Yet again gross negligence in Bentley's case is cloaked by an attack on his parents. The inference that Mr Bentley was wielding an unhealthy influence over his son is particularly interesting. The Bentley family lived at Norbury, the

127

school is in Bristol, their visits were never more than once a month, their son's total illiteracy precluded the exchange of letters. Yet in some Svengali-like, long-range manner, Mr Bentley is supposed to have controlled his son's attitudes. The staff at the approved school, with all their knowledge and expertise, all their vast experience of dealing with juvenile delinquents, were powerless against Bentley's simple-minded working-class father. It is not, nor has it ever been, my intention to sanctify Derek Bentley, but God knows the attempts to blacken not only him but his entire family are truly pathetic. The breakdown in communication between the Bentleys and officialdom appears to have been as near complete as is inhumanly possible. If as much effort had been spent by all concerned in helping the youth as was spent in passing the buck, there would probably have been no buck to pass. As it was, Derek Bentley spent his entire life in the bottom 2·5% – in terms of intelligence – of the population of this country.

The severe headaches that had been Bentley's constant companion became even more severe during this period. The school authorities, presumably viewing them as yet another manifestation of his malingering, took no action. His family doctor, Dr Doris Reynolds, was more diligent, however. While Derek was on home leave, in June 1949, she referred him to Guy's Hospital. Unable to trace the causes of the headaches, she rightly decided to place her patient in the hands of the specialists. At Guy's, he was given a general medical examination, a special neurological examination and finally referred to the Department of Psychological Medicine, where he was examined by Dr James Munroe, who subsequently made the following observations.

'The results of my examinations were as follows:
(1) Derek did not co-operate well in examination. *My impression was that he was feeble-minded.*
(2) The three attacks of unconsciousness he had at the age of eight or nine were probably epileptic fits and these might have been the result of a head injury about age five when

he was said to have fallen fifteen feet on to his head and been unconscious.

(3) His father wanted me to arrange that Derek should be at home with him.

(4) My recommendation was that Derek should return to Kingswood under Mr Collinson's care (a member of the staff) and in due time be examined at the Bristol Child Guidance Clinic.'

In his report to the Principal of Kingswood School Dr Munroe said: 'There is no doubt that Derek is very backward intellectually and that most of this is the result of *congenital lack of intelligence*. The father thinks it was quite wrong to commit Derek to an approved school and he looks forward to having the boy at home to work in his electrician's business. In due time I think this would be a satisfactory solution.'

That report is dated 11 August 1949. The 'due time' before Bentley was allowed to leave the approved school was nearly a year. Meanwhile, he returned to Bristol, taking with him the anti-convulsive pills that Guy's had prescribed to control his epilepsy.

The examination at Guy's was the first glimmer of hope for Bentley. It was followed with further examinations by doctors and specialists.

Following Dr Munroe's advice, the approved school sent Bentley to the Bristol Child Guidance Clinic. The Clinic have declined to make their conclusions on Bentley available to me. Again one can only hope that an official enquiry will succeed in eliciting this information where I have failed. The Clinic's report would undoubtedly make interesting reading, not only with regard to their diagnosis of Bentley's mental condition, but also what treatment, if any, they prescribed to control his epilepsy in succession to the treatment prescribed by Dr Munroe, probably a course of phenobarbitone. How little the medical profession knew about epilepsy at this time can be gauged from the following extract from the *British Medical Journal* (8 January 1949).

'All that we have learned about epilepsy in recent years can still be fairly described as a knowledge of what happens when things go wrong. We have been elaborately and successfully recording the speed of a galloping horse that has escaped from the stable door. All our pharmacological remedies are at best little more than strings with which we tie up the door, and which the horse from time to time breaks. But the door has a lock, and we have to find the key.'

Three drugs were used at this time in the treatment of epilepsy. *Phenobarbitone* was considered an effective anti-convulsant. Its side-effects, not at that time readily appreciated, included increased irritability. Sudden cessation from taking the drug often led to a return of the attacks. *Epanutin* – which was then the most powerful anti-convulsant known. Unfortunately its use on epileptics frequently had toxic effects, including constant nodding, double vision and loss of control over the arms and legs. Both these drugs controlled major seizures, but they often had no effect at all on petit mal, and indeed Epanutin quite often increased the frequency of such attacks. It will be remembered that Bentley at this time was suffering from petit mal. *Tridone*, which had just become available, was more effective in the control of petit mal, but it was not an anti-convulsant; indeed it frequently increased convulsant seizures.

One can only speculate what effect the drugs given to the sixteen-year-old Bentley had upon him.

Lest it be thought that the medical profession were floundering around in the dark, as regards the treatment of epilepsy at this time, the reader should take heart from the considerable progress that had in fact been made. When one remembers that for a long time the medical profession had had the idea that epilepsy was caused by masturbation, and that in 1880 a paper was read at the annual meeting of the British Medical Association at Cambridge on the treatment of epilepsy by castration, it will be realized just how far the medical profession had come.

Not only had Derek Bentley suffered from epileptic attacks from an early age, there was also a history of epilepsy in his family. A cousin of his mother's had died during an epileptic attack. There is a standard laboratory test for establishing whether or not a person suffers from epilepsy and on 16 November 1949 Bentley was sent to the Burden Neurological Institute at Stapleton, Bristol, for an examination with an electro-encephalograph (EEG). An EEG is an instrument which records on moving paper the fluctuations in electrical activity on the surface of the brain as detected by a number of electrodes attached to the scalp. The record so obtained (the electro-encephalogram, also called an EEG) consists of a complex trace of waves of different sizes and frequencies. Characteristic changes occur in all normal people during sleep, when looking with attention at an object, when relaxed with the eyes closed, and when conscious awareness is impaired from any cause. During waking hours, the general character-istics of the EEG pattern remain constant throughout life from maturity to senility. These characteristics, however, develop during childhood and change greatly up to the age of eighteen. They may also be changed as a result of brain injury or disease.

Standards of normality which hold good for 90% of the population have been established for EEG patterns. Abnormalities may be specific and indicate that the subject, for example, is epileptic, suffers from a brain tumour or abscess, or has a local area of brain damage from injury or disease. They may be unspecific, but indicate a severe change from normality. Or they may be unspecific and mild. It is generally accepted that a specific epileptic EEG pattern conclusively establishes the existence of epilepsy, though some persons who are clinically known to be epileptic do not show the characteristic EEG abnormality, and its absence does not therefore disprove the presence of epilepsy.

In Derek Bentley's case there was no doubt. His EEG merely confirmed what he had accepted as a fact of life from the age of five. 'There was nothing abnormal in any area while resting,' said the report. 'The patient was uncooperative and would only perform hypernoea (over-breathing) for one minute, but this evoked some low potential theta activity.

'Photic stimulation evoked several "single wave and spike" discharges spreading from the occipital lobe. This finding is diagnostic of petit mal.'

On 9 February 1950 Bentley was sent to the Institute for a further EEG. The response to photic stimulation was again abnormal, further confirming Bentley's condition. The 'spike and wave' disturbance that occurred during these EEGs is a classic indication of epilepsy.

When Dr Munroe had concluded that Derek Bentley was 'feeble-minded', he used the terms of reference of the Mental Deficiency Act that was applicable throughout the entire period of Bentley's short life. In the terms of this Act 'feeble-minded persons' are those in whose case there exists mental defectiveness which, though not amounting to imbecility, is yet so pronounced that they require care, supervision and control for their own protection or for the protection of others or, in the case of children, involves disability of mind of such a nature and extent as to make them, for the purposes of section 57 of the Education Act 1944, incapable of receiving education at school. IQ 40–70. Mental Age, six to eleven years. The IQ and Mental Age quoted are not hard and fast guide-lines. In practice there is considerable latitude and the demarcation lines may become blurred.

The Act also defined the term 'mental defectiveness'. This is a condition of arrested or incomplete development of mind existing before the age of eighteen years, whether arising from inherent causes or induced by disease or injury.

The Royal Commission on Capital Punishment (1949–1953) arrived at the conclusion that 'A mental defective, therefore, as has often been said, is a person who has never possessed a normal degree of intellectual

132

capacity, whereas in an insane person faculties which are originally normal have been impaired by disease.'

By that definition, and I must stress that it is not mine but a Royal Commission's, *there was a case to be made that Derek Bentley was insane*. If the evidence of his father, that at his first school (Friar Street) Bentley was considered of above-average potential, had been or could be substantiated, then faculties in Bentley that had been normal were now undoubtedly impaired by disease. The fact that no adverse school report was received by his parents before he reached the age of eleven, would appear to be further evidence that somewhere along the line something inside him had snapped. Balanced against this is the expert opinion of Dr Munroe of Guy's, that Bentley's condition was due to a 'congenital lack of intelligence', strongly suggesting mental defectiveness rather than insanity. In either event these were issues that should have been clarified in front of the Old Bailey jury, *and never were. The issue was never raised*. The evidence that I have acquired and the conversations that I have had with doctors, psychologists and psychiatrists concerning that evidence, *make a powerful case to substantiate the view that Bentley was unfit to plead and unfit to stand trial. These issues were never even put before a jury*. Like the issue of Bentley's sanity, they remained aspects that were not only kept from the jury's consideration, but also from the public's.

Concerning 'fitness to plead', the Royal Commission on Capital Punishment observed that 'If an idiot or imbecile were charged with murder in England, it is likely that he would be regarded as unfit to plead and found insane on arraignment; *and there may sometimes be a similar finding in the case of a feeble-minded person*.'

The legal definition of insanity was, at the time of Bentley's case, completely governed by the M'Naghten Rules, *that had been formulated in 1843 and not altered one jot from that time*. Their implementation over the years had sent to the gallows an astonishing number of men and women who were total lunatics by any medical definition, because by legal definition they were sane. In his interesting book *The Unquiet Mind*, Dr William Sargant demolishes the M'Naghten Rules with the following comment, 'It should be observed that only about one half per cent of what amounts to the modern equivalent of certified medical lunatics are M'Naghten mad, all the rest still being fully responsible in criminal law.' Any further comment on the M'Naghten Rules would be superfluous.

After the EEG examinations Bentley continued to suffer from severe headaches, and he also had a number of blackouts. Added to these discomforts, he developed an abscess that perforated an ear drum, and a skin rash that covered his body.

On 28 July 1950 his parents received a letter from the school authorities. It is worth recording this letter in full.

'The Order of the Court was that your son should be detained in an approved school until 29 September 1951, but I am glad to be able to tell you that the Managers have now decided to release him from the school as from tomorrow, 28 July 1950.

'All boys sent to an approved school for training remain in the care of the Managers for a period of up to three years *after* the period of detention ordered by the Court. Until 29 September 1954, Derek will, therefore, be in the care of the school Managers and during this period he should notify the Managers at once of any change in his circumstances. *Failure to do so, or to behave unsatisfactorily* (sic), *may mean that he will be required to return to the school.*

'We hope Derek will do well, and we shall be glad to see him or hear from him. Please endeavour to see that he writes as often as possible to let us know how he is going on, and we shall always be glad to see him at Kingswood if he is able to visit the school. Always remember that it is our job to help Derek, and we are anxious to do so.' The letter was signed by the Deputy Headmaster, John Fidoe.

The whole tone of the letter is strangely inconsistent with the school's other recorded opinions, highly critical,

134

of Bentley and his family. The most pertinent point is the decision to release Bentley from the approved school *fourteen months earlier than the magistrates had ordered.* This was hardly consistent with the views of Bentley that they expressed to Dr Matheson, the Brixton Prison Medical Officer.

When Mr Bentley received that letter he not unnaturally concluded that his son's behaviour at the school must have been exemplary and that the authorities had the fullest confidence regarding his son's future behaviour. The approved school maintained control over Bentley from then on up to the moment of his arrest on the Croydon rooftop. Mr Towes, a Home Office Welfare Officer, paid thirty-one visits on the school's behalf to the Bentley home during that period. Something is radically wrong somewhere. Bentley could have been recalled to Kingswood Approved School at any time. He wasn't. One can only conclude that not only were the school completely confident at the time of Bentley's release that his future behaviour would be satisfactory, but that his subsequent behaviour proved them right. The critical reports they made to Matheson immediately before Bentley's trial appear to me to be a classic attempt by the school and the Home Office Welfare Officer to take out an insurance policy to protect their own necks. Yet in doing so they stand condemned. If Bentley's behaviour at the school and his subsequent behaviour after release on licence are accurately reflected in the reports, why was he given a premature release? Why, having been given a premature release, was he not recalled? More oversights?

Upon his return home from the school in July 1950 his parents were shocked by his appearance. He appeared to be both physically and mentally ill. The headaches were as severe as ever and he had great difficulty in sleeping. Dr Reynolds prescribed phenobarbitone for these ailments, but there was nothing she could prescribe for his state of mind.

Bentley's twenty-two months at the approved school had done nothing to improve his intelligence; he was still totally illiterate.

He refused to leave the house. He told his parents that he could not face people. He thought that everyone knew that he had just been released from an approved school. He believed that his criminal record was public knowledge. 'If I go out people will laugh at me and call me a thief,' he told his mother. During this period Mr Towes, the Welfare Officer for Home Office Schools, was paying regular visits to the Bentley household. He may have attempted to help Bentley with what was obviously a serious problem, but I can find no record of it in his subsequent reports and my conversation with Mr Towes failed to elicit any indication that he took measures to remedy the situation.

Bentley remained in the house for over six months. Finally Albert Bentley, the boy's uncle, persuaded him to go for a walk, and after that he became more rational in his attitude towards the outside world.

Early in 1951 he started work with a firm of furniture removers. The work was hard, the hours long, yet the seventeen-year-old boy thrived on it. Was this the same Bentley who, in the opinion of the approved school, 'conserved his energy only for eating and talking', who in their opinion was 'self-satisfied, indifferent to training and content to let others do all the work'? The enthusiasm that he brought to his work proved his undoing. Trying to lift a piano unaided, he strained his back, and was advised by his doctor to find a less strenuous form of employment. This was in March 1952. His employer regretted losing Bentley, and was later to speak highly of him. Bentley himself was sorely disappointed. During the course of his work he had developed an interest in body-building, and although his body was poorly developed he had acquired a phenomenal strength. To be told that he should find a less taxing job could not but be a blow to his pride.

A month previously Bentley had attended a National Service medical board (two years' service in one of Her

Majesty's Forces was then compulsory). When he attended for his medical at Kingston-on-Thames he brought with him a certificate from Dr Reynolds saying that he was subject to epileptic attacks. This, on its own, was not sufficient to justify Bentley's rejection from National Service, for the examining doctors on such boards had a healthy suspicion of such evidence. Bentley's mental capacity was tested, however, and he was found to be mentally so subnormal that he was placed in the lowest grade possible, Grade IV.

This decision, that Bentley's mental capacity was so low that he was unfit to bear arms and that he was incapable of even simple labouring duties under supervision, would only have been reached after a psychiatric examination.

The effect on Bentley of the constant official confirmations that he was not as other young men can only be guessed at. What is beyond speculation is the fact that by this time he had a young friend to help him forget his worries, Christopher Craig. The rooftop in Croydon was already beginning to beckon.

In May 1952 the two youths were 'invited' to Norbury Police Station and questioned about some stolen petrol. Their association with the missing fuel could not be proved, however, and no charges were preferred.

Their fathers, realizing that the combination could prove dangerous, instructed their respective sons to break the friendship, but with little effect. Craig was a frequent caller at the Bentley household and, although often turned away by Bentley's parents, he still managed to associate with his friend. During the summer of 1952 a considerable number of the house burglaries that took place in the Croydon and surrounding areas were the work of these two teenagers. Craig's childhood ambition, to be not an engine driver, but a 'villain', was being realized.

During this period Bentley's health remained poor. He continued to suffer with his ears, and the attacks of epilepsy persisted. After leaving the furniture removers he had become a dustman with Croydon Corporation. Within a few months he had achieved the unique if dubious distinction of being demoted from dustman to road-sweeper, and in July 1952 the Corporation decided that even this humble occupation was beyond his capabilities, and dismissed him.

Now all Bentley had to occupy himself was assisting his father from time to time in the repair of televisions and radios and his expeditions with Craig. The 'vicious spiral girdling a line of time' was now irresistible.

In his book *My Son's Execution* Mr Bentley vividly describes the very real fears that he and his wife had about Craig's influence over their son. He also describes their attempts to keep the two boys apart. If indeed there was a battle that year for Bentley's soul, it was won by Craig, for Bentley himself was his willing ally. The victory was not total, however. Bentley would have nothing to do with any crimes of violence. House-breaking was one thing, armed robbery was quite another. He undoubtedly knew of Craig's penchant for guns; in the neighbourhood where they lived it was common knowledge, even amongst the women who threw up their hands in horror at Craig's exploits at the time of the trial. Once, when Craig was fifteen, he decided to go camping for the weekend with a friend. The friend's mother calmly made Craig promise 'that he would not take one of his guns'. Needless to say Craig broke the promise – not that he intended to use the gun on that occasion, but to go out without a gun would have been, for Craig, like walking down the High Street stark naked. One of his guns went *everywhere* with him.

Bentley knew this. He was equally aware that there had never been the slightest indication that Craig would *use* a gun; it served him as cigarettes serve many others – as a crutch, a hand-prop. When Craig discussed the armed robbery of the greengrocer, however, even Bentley with his limited intelligence, realized what it would involve. He jibbed. In Craig's own words, 'When he was aware that the gun would be out of the pocket, he would have nothing to do with it, he told me he didn't want to know. Nothing I said could budge him.' If this had been said at the Old Bailey trial its tremendous significance would have been seen, for it clearly shows Bentley's attitude towards violence and violent robbery. For Bentley, breaking into an unoccupied house was an attractive proposition; but holding someone up with a loaded revolver was a proposition he would not even entertain.

Countless thousands of criminals are caught because of their 'modus operandi'. The vast majority of criminals commit the same type of crime in the same way time after time. A section of Scotland Yard is entirely built on this fact; it has been responsible for the detection, and subsequent arrest, of most of the criminals caught in this country. If Bentley and Craig had not been caught by the police on that Croydon roof, if Bentley had continued his criminal activities, he would undoubtedly have been caught in due course – his pattern was already clearly established. He kept risk to the minimum by never breaking into occupied property, he never became involved in violent crime, he was simply a thief and, because of his very low mentality, a petty thief. *There is no record that he ever offered violence to anyone, either socially or criminally. Ten months after Bentley's execution the Home Secretary confirmed this.* Asked by Marcus Lipton, MP, 'What remedial treatment is provided for juvenile delinquents at approved schools where medical tests reveal a mental state conducive to crimes of violence? And what action did your Department take, in connection with such evidence available in the case of Derek Bentley two years before his execution?' Sir David Maxwell Fyfe replied, 'The responsibility rests on the School Managers to seek medical advice as necessary and to secure that suitable medical treatment is provided for children in approved schools, including children judged to be subject or liable to special mental or emotional disturbance. *No evidence purporting to show that Bentley's mental state was conducive to crimes of violence was submitted to the Managers of the approved school where he was detained*

from October 1948 to July 1950, or to the Home Office.'
   'Let him have it, Chris'?
   In the light of all the evidence contained in this chapter,
I would ask the reader to read again the statement that
Bentley was alleged to have made to the police, pages
93-5. Bentley, the feeble-minded epileptic with the mind
of a child, who was unable to write his name unaided.
The youth who, in the witness box at the Old Bailey,
used phrases like 'Sergeant Fairfax come and took me,
Sir, because I couldn't see nothing where I was standing,
Sir, and he come and took me, Sir, and walked me across
the roof, Sir.' The same youth was able, when making a
statement to the police, to distinguish on three occasions
between the words 'come' and 'came', an ability he did not
once demonstrate during the trial. The same youth who,
when making that statement, used articulate phrases such
as, 'We hid behind a shelter arrangement' and 'I should
have mentioned'. The inconsistency is disconcerting.
Surely it was situations like this that Lord Justice Devlin
had in mind when he wrote, 'Often in the past, when the
prisoner has gone into the witness box and the jury has
had an opportunity of contrasting the voluble incoherences
which every question – even the kindest from his counsel
– touched off, with the lucid and well-punctuated flow
of statements taken at the police station, they must have
known that the police account of the way in which the
interview was carried on was nonsense.'
   Bentley insisted at his trial that he had not dictated the
statement. He said that it was compiled from a series of
answers to the questions of Detective Sergeant Shepherd
and Detective Chief Inspector Smith. He emphatically
denied that he had said 'I didn't know he was going to
use the gun'. Indeed this is directly contradicted later on
in the statement itself. Bentley of course had never been
able to read that statement; it was read over to him and he
then signed it. The only remark really damaging to Bentley
in relation to the charge of murder is the one I have just
quoted. During his pre-trial conversations Bentley told

his solicitor, John Stevens, that, throughout the taking of the statement, he had insisted many times that he did not know Chris was armed. Working-class London speech is a language full of flat vowels and slurred words. The vowels in 'a' and 'the' sound much the same in the middle of remarks made at conversation speed. Is it not possible that Sgt Shepherd, not to put too fine a point on it, misheard? The remark was held to indicate that Bentley had *prior* knowledge that Craig was armed. Is it not possible that too literal an interpretation was placed on the remark? The statement was made six hours after the gun battle, by which time not only Bentley, but the entire Metropolitan Police Force, several hundred newspaper reporters, and many thousands of the general public, knew that Craig was armed. If a Professor of English had then used the phrase attributed to Bentley it might not be unreasonable to give it a special significance. To attribute such significance to an alleged remark made by a teenager with the mind of a child is to stand logic on its head. What could be more natural than that Bentley, who by the time he made the statement had heard countless people refer to 'the gun', should echo those words? A phrase frequently used in courts in this country is 'common sense'. If 'common sense' had been applied to Bentley's statement, Justice might have featured more prominently at his trial, instead of being conspicuous by its absence. But assuming it to be perfectly right and proper to place such a literal interpretation on his remarks one could at least hope for consistency. It is a hope that remains unfulfilled. *The most important remark contained in Bentley's statement was entirely ignored, and has remained so to this day.* 'I should have mentioned that after the plain clothes policeman got up the drainpipe and arrested me, another policeman in uniform followed and I heard someone call him "Mac". He was with us when the other policeman was killed.'

Even if everything in this book that throws doubt on the authenticity of Bentley's statement is invalid, even assuming that Bentley's statement had been taken in a

141

correct and proper manner and that nothing was added or deleted or altered – *and this assumption was made at the trial and the subsequent appeal – the two words 'arrested me' were sufficient to save Bentley's life*. In Chapter 6 I explain why.

This, then, was Bentley's history. I have not given an exhaustive account. Other information that has not been made available to me was available to Dr Matheson. One would expect therefore to find all the relevant details that I have recorded, plus a great deal more, in Dr Matheson's report on Bentley. That expectation is not realized.

One week before the commencement of the trial, Bentley was sent to the Maudsley Hospital for an EEG examination. Such an examination on a person accused of murder was, by this time, standard practice in England. The doctor at the Maudsley Hospital who examined Derek Bentley was Denis Hill. Professor Sir Denis Hill, as he now is, is recognized as a world authority on human brainwaves. The following report went with Bentley to the Maudsley.

H.M. PRISON
BRIXTON S.W.2
26.11.52.

Dr Denis Hill, MB, FRCP,
The Maudsley Hospital,
Denmark Hill S.E.5.

Dear Hill,
    8664, BENTLEY, Derek William, aged 19 years
Herewith a history of the above-named who is going to the Maudsley tomorrow for an EEG examination. He is involved in the Croydon Murder case where a policeman was murdered and another policeman injured. Bentley had no active part in the shooting which was done by his co-defendant, Craig, a boy of 16. Craig I am not sending for an EEG, because he has a crush fracture of the 7th dorsal vertebra, a fracture dislocation of the sternum and a fracture of the left radius. If, however, you think that such disabilities would not be insurmountable in the taking of an EEG I would send him along to you. It would, of course,

have to be in the near future, as the trial may commence on the 3rd of next month, i.e. a week today. I will 'phone you some time tomorrow when you have read this letter and get your views.

As regards Bentley. *No morbid family mental history has been elicited. Personal History.* When Bentley was 24 hours old, his father tells me, he was sent to Guy's Hospital suffering, he says, from bronchial pneumonia. He had blood transfusions and was nursed in an oxygen tent.

In infancy, the father states, he had one or two falls on the head but apparently they were not serious.

During the war he was buried once when the house was struck. Again, the father says, most of the rubble was on his head (the father is, in my opinion, an extremely poor informant).

There is a history of fits; the first one when he was aged between 3 and 5 years. He was sitting at a meal when he said he was not feeling well and asked permission to leave the table. He arose from the table and then, the father says, he collapsed – his head shook first, then his jaw clenched and then he stiffened. He did not lose control of his sphincters on this occasion. He had 4 subsequent fits all of the same nature – the last fit it is stated took place when he was aged 8 years.

He went to school when he was aged 5. His behaviour at school was very bad; he truanted a lot and quarrelled with the pupils and with his teachers. In consequence he was shifted to another school where he remained for two years. Then he was transferred back to his first school which he left in March 1948. He was in the top class of the inferior group when he left.

In 1948 he was before a Juvenile Court for store-breaking and stealing and was bound over for 2 years. Six months later he was again before the Juvenile Court for store-breaking and stealing and on this occasion was sent to an approved school. At this approved school it was found that his IQ was 66 and that he had a reading age of 4½ years. The school authorities felt that he was being encouraged by

143

his father to make complaints about his treatment so that he would be granted an early licence. At all times he gave the impression at the school that he conserved his energy only for eating and talking; that he was self-satisfied; indifferent to training and content to let others do all the work.

In June and July of 1949 he attended the department of Psychological Medicine at Guy's Hospital where he was given small tablets to take twice a day. I have written to Guy's Hospital for a report but have not yet received it. The school authorities, however, say that Guy's Hospital considered that the boy was influenced by his father and therefore tended to be uncooperative. While at the school an EEG was done at Burden Neurological Institute. The result was as follows:

'There was nothing abnormal in any area while resting. The patient was uncooperative and would only perform hypernoea for one minute but this evoked some low potential theta activity. Photic stimulation evoked several "single wave and spike" discharges spreading from the occipital lobe. This finding is diagnostic of petit mal.'

(sgnd) A. L. Winter
Assistant Electro-encephalographer.'

He was finally licensed from the school in July 1950, and then passed into the care of a Home Office Welfare Officer. A report from this Welfare Officer states:

'Materially the home is reasonably good and well kept. However, his parents have no influence upon him at all. There is an older sister and a younger brother, neither of whom apparently have been any trouble. The parental attitude is inconsistent and over-indulgent and there was little or no family training. Since leaving the school he has had little work and has been allowed his own way in everything. He had one period of employment with a removal contractor for seven months and his employers state that his character was very satisfactory. He was then employed by the Croydon Borough Council at first as a dustman, from which job he was demoted on account

144

Derek Bentley in the summer of 1952.

Christopher Craig shortly before the rooftop battle.

Top left, Bentley with his mother and, right, body-training; below,
Christopher Craig with friends.

On the night of 2nd November 1952, nine-year-old Edith Ware chanced to look out of her bedroom window, and saw the two teenagers climb a metal gate to gain access to these drainpipes (far left). They climbed up them to the warehouse roof (top); in the background is the lift-head from behind which Craig fought a 45-minute gun battle with the police, and in the foreground, the staircase head where Detective Sergeant Fairfax sheltered with Derek Bentley. This picture was taken the morning after the battle. The door stands open and shattered – the entrance through which PC Miles stepped to his death.

Below left, a view from ground level of the thirty-foot-high warehouse from which Craig finally dived to the ground after failing to shoot himself. Right, the view that confronted the sixteen-year-old boy in that moment of desperation; the hole in the greenhouse roof was made by his gun as he fell.

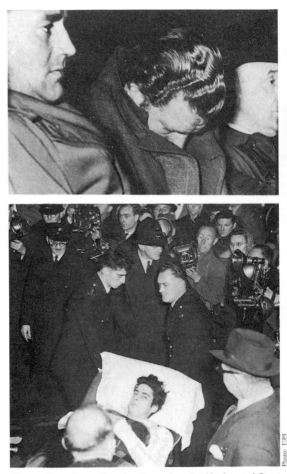

Photo: UPI

Above, after a three-minute hearing at Croydon Magistrates' Court on 3rd November, Bentley is driven to Brixton Prison; on his right, Detective Sergeant Shepherd. Below, Craig's arrival at Croydon Court. In the right foreground is Detective Chief Inspector Smith. Seconds after this photograph was taken the crowd attempted to break through the police cordon and wreak their own justice on the teenager.

Above, Mrs Bentley with her daughter Iris and her nine-year-old son Dennis arriving at the Old Bailey for the first day of the trial. Below, Mr and Mrs Craig arriving at the Old Bailey in the Rolls Royce hired for them by the *Sunday Pictorial*.

Photo: UPI

Photo: PA

Photo: Syndication International

Left above, PCs Harrison and Jaggs; below, left to right, Detective Sergeant Fairfax, Detective Chief Inspector John Smith, who was in charge of the police investigation of the Craig/Bentley case, and his second in command, Detective Sergeant Stanley Shepherd. Right, PC James Christie MacDonald.

PC Sidney Miles who died in the course of his duty on 2nd November 1952.

of being unsatisfactory, to a road-sweeper. He then was dismissed from his job because he was unreliable and was a bad time-keeper.'

The Welfare Officer reports that early this year he developed a very 'spivish' style in dress and was very truculent and arrogant in his manner.

While in custody here he has shown himself to be a very immature, careless adolescent. He blames his co-defendant, Craig, for all the trouble, and is frightened at the position in which he now finds himself. When he came in his hair, as it still is, was marcel-waved and he was wearing a very gaudy flower-pattern shirt.

He cannot read. He says that when he first went to school he tried to learn but then, on account of shifting, he gave up the effort and nobody, apparently, bothered about him. It would appear that by the time he reached the approved school his lazy habits were so strong that they could not teach him how to read.

Mental tests, however, show him, on the Wechsler scale, to have a verbal IQ of 71; Performance IQ 87; Full Scale IQ 77.

On the Kent oral tests he reaches – on the mid-scale 11 years; and on the upper scale 12 years.

Although of low intelligence it cannot be said, I think, that he is certifiable as a feeble-minded person as the defect is probably an educational one.

There has been no evidence of any epileptic manifesta-tion while he has been in custody here.

I have not yet seen the depositions but from the press reports it appears that he knew quite well that Craig was armed when they set out to break into the warehouse for the purpose of stealing money.

While there is little good to be said about this lad, in fairness to him I think it should be pointed out that his parents, especially his father, are largely, if not wholly, responsible for his present situation. His mother, I under-stand, is a small woman and crippled, and the prisoner could easily hold her off when she attempted to inflict corporal punishment. The father who is employed at the Electricity Works at Croydon is, as I indicated earlier in this report, a poor type. He is very satisfied with himself, very confident and will not admit that there is anything evil in his son. Last year, he bought an old Rover motor car for about £200 and gave it to his son. For what purpose it is hard to imagine unless to keep the boy quiet.

Physically there is nothing abnormal except that there is a history of double otorrhoea but his ears at present are clean.

Yours sincerely,
(Sgnd) J.C.M. Matheson
Principal Medical Officer.

I am not sure what the report told Professor Sir Denis Hill about Bentley. It tells me a great deal about Dr Matheson. For a start, it is crammed with errors, in a situation where there is not room for a single one. A young man has been charged with the most serious crime that a person can commit in this country. If found guilty he will be sentenced to death. If his Appeal fails his fate will rest entirely in the hands of the Home Secretary. If the Home Secretary declines to intervene, then Bentley will hang. Any report that directly affects that chain of events must be completely and entirely accurate. Hanging by the neck until dead is an exact business. All decisions leading to that event must be equally exact.

Using the evidence contained in this chapter alone, the reader can at his leisure list the errors in Matheson's report. The following observations may be of assistance in that task.

1. Matheson refers to 'the Croydon Murder Case', and also to the events 'where a policeman was murdered', begging the entire issue to be tried. It shows a prejudgment of the situation that would be considered hasty if it came from a layman; coming from the Principal Medical Officer of Brixton Prison, whose official task it is to

146

determine Derek Bentley's *exact* mental condition, it is unforgivable.

2. Matheson states that, 'No morbid family mental history has been elicited.' A cousin of Mrs Bentley's died during an epileptic attack. Two hours after Bentley's birth a second son was born and died two hours later. On 29 December 1947, Mrs Bentley gave birth to a mongol boy who died on 23 November 1948.

3. Matheson considered Mr Bentley 'a poor informant'. The Prison Medical Officer had at his disposal every conceivable facility — the police, the Courts, Governmental authority to demand information from any source. He had but to ask and he would have received. The information the father supplied could be checked instantly by one of the vast battery of officials that the doctor had at his disposal. The information about Bentley's crisis at birth, for example, could be verified by a simple 'phone call to Guy's Hospital.

4. The history of Bentley's epilepsy is totally incorrect, the most serious error being the statement that the last attack occurred when Bentley was eight. Matheson omits to mention that Bentley continued to suffer from epilepsy throughout his life, *or that his last attack had occurred less than a month previously*. Describing Bentley's examinations at Bristol, he refers to one EEG when in fact there were two. There is also no mention of his attendance at the Bristol Child Guidance Clinic.

5. The whole school history is full of errors. Matheson states that Bentley began going to school at the age of five. Bentley began his schooling at Friar Street at the age of three. There is no record whatsoever that, prior to his attendance at Norbury Manor School at the age of twelve, Bentley was a source of trouble to his teachers. The incidents that Matheson refers to only occurred during Bentley's last three years at school. The information about his school transfers is quite wrong.

6. The details of Bentley's previous convictions are incorrect; for example his first offences were *attempted*

store-breaking and *attempted* larceny. This may be considered pedantic, but when a man's life is at risk there is no room for the slightest error.

7. The most disastrous statement in the entire report is Matheson's expressed opinion that Bentley was not certifiable as a feeble-minded person 'as the defect is probably an educational one'. In one sentence all Bentley's history – the IQ test at Kingswood, Dr Munroe's considered opinion, the National Service Medical examination – is completely cast to one side. Suddenly, miraculously, Bentley is no longer feeble-minded. His IQ has risen and he is now merely 'of low intelligence'. He is still completely illiterate. His mental age, judged by tests not involving scholastic knowledge, is still only between eleven and twelve, yet he is not feeble-minded. Somewhere along the way, if one accepts that IQ rating, Bentley had acquired additional intelligence. It must have been after he left the Kingswood school at the age of seventeen, for there he had an IQ of 66 and was totally illiterate. It must have been after his general medical examination, his neurological examination and his intensive examination at Guy's Hospital in 1949, for Dr Munroe, the Physician in Psychological Medicine at Guy's, considered that Bentley *was* feeble-minded. It must have been after his National Service Medical on 11 February 1952, when Bentley was considered so mentally deficient that he was placed in the lowest possible grade (this last item finds no place in Matheson's report). This new-found intelligence of Bentley's must therefore have been acquired in the period between that medical and his arrest. A period when Bentley was employed as a dustman, demoted to road-sweeper, then finally dismissed as unsatisfactory.

8. The references to the press reports are illuminating. This is probably the first recorded instance in this country of a doctor arriving at conclusions with regard to his patient based on the evidence of Fleet Street. One hopes that doctors do not often base their assessment of their patients on such fallible sources of information.

9. Matheson was, of course, perfectly entitled to form a critical opinion of Bentley's parents, provided the opinion was based on facts. There is, however, a disturbing amount of emotional subjectivity present in this report. 'The father is a poor informant' has already been commented on. 'He was *finally* licensed from the School in July 1950', following highly critical comments attributed to the school authorities, completely hides the fact that Bentley was released fourteen months earlier than the period ordered by the Court. The fact that the nineteen-year-old Bentley was dressed in the teenage fashion of his period obviously disturbed Matheson. Bentley's 'marcel-waved hair' and his 'very gaudy flower-pattern shirt' must have held special significance for the doctor. One would not quibble with the remarks if they had come from the Editor of *The Tailor and Cutter*, but coming from the Prison Medical Officer they are merely emotive. The quality of the doctor's thinking processes is clearly demonstrated in his closing remarks referring to Bentley's father. Having already blamed the wretched man for the fact that his son had been charged with murder, the doctor continues, 'He is very satisfied with himself, very confident and will not admit that there is anything evil in his son. Last year, he bought an old Rover motor car for about £200 and gave it to his son. *For what purpose it is hard to imagine unless to keep the boy quiet.*' I would very much like to know where Matheson obtained this information it certainly wasn't Mr Bentley, who has never bought a Rover car in his working-class life. Derek Bentley never owned a Rover, or any other kind of car.

I would again remind the reader, for it cannot be stated too frequently, a man's life was at stake. At this stage of the case Bentley's fate was entirely in the hands of Dr Matheson. If he concluded that Bentley was insane, or unfit to plead the indictment, or unfit to stand his trial, then Bentley would be beyond the reach of the Courts.

Upon receiving this report Dr Hill telegraphed Dr Grey Walter, the Principal of the Burden Neurological Institute, requesting the loan of his EEG records on

Derek Bentley. He must have been more than somewhat surprised to discover that Bentley had had not one, but two, EEGs at the Institute. Dr Hill performed his own EEG examination on Bentley and wrote the following report to Dr Matheson.

'He was in a fasting state, his blood sugar being 96 mgm%. The resting EEG had normal characteristics. The dominant rhythm in the postcentral areas was 9 c/sec of moderate voltage, symmetrical and blocked to visual attention. No abnormal potentials were seen and over-breathing changed the record very little. On photic stimulation minimal abnormal responses appeared in the form of low voltage spikes associated with some slowing of the rhythm. At 14 flashes per second single high voltage sharp waves occurred repeatedly.' Dr Hill then commented on the two EEGs performed at Bristol.

'The resting records in both cases are essentially the same as that taken here. On the other hand the responses to photic stimulation were on both occasions at Bristol fairly abnormal and of epileptic type.

'The responses to photic stimulation in epileptics undoubtedly vary from time to time, but the evidence of these three EEGs is certainly compatible with and suggestive of a diagnosis of epilepsy. No focal abnormality has occurred to suggest brain damage.'

So, despite the fact that he had been seriously misled by his colleague concerning Bentley's epileptic history, Dr Hill had correctly diagnosed Bentley's *present* condition.

On 2 December 1952, Christopher Craig was sent to the Maudsley Hospital for an EEG examination. An illustration of how antiquated and absurd the Lunacy and Mental Deficiency Acts then were, can be gauged from the fact that his medical examiners at Brixton Prison could confidently state that Craig was not certifiable under the Mental Deficiency Act and that he was legally sane. The 16-year-old Craig was recently termed psychopathic by Dr William Sargant; in 1952 the law considered him fully answerable for his actions.

Sir David Henderson described the 'psychopathic personality' in his evidence to the Royal Commission on Capital Punishment.

'The individuals who form this group constitute the biggest, most serious, and most controversial medico-legal problem. They are social misfits in every sense of the term, persons who have never been able to adapt themselves satisfactorily to their fellow-men, and appear to be entirely lacking in altruistic feeling. Their life-histories are illuminating and show how from a tender age, and from a variety of causes, they have proved a problem to themselves and to the world at large. They are the "sports" of the human race. The more I see of them, or read about them, or deal with them, the more confirmed I become that they are persons who have failed in their psycho-biological development. Such a failure may not be due to any fault of their environment or education, although that possibility should always be considered, but is essentially constitutional, something which is inborn, something which is akin to the lack of intellectual development which characterizes the mental defective. Irrespective of all the efforts which are made to assist, often from their earliest days, they remain at an immature, individualistic, egocentric level. On this account they fail to appreciate reality, they are fickle, changeable, lack persistence of effort and are unable to profit by experience or punishment. They are dangerous when frustrated. They are devoid of affection, are cold, heartless, callous, cynical, and show a lack of judgment and forethought which is almost beyond belief. They may be adult in years, but emotionally they remain as dangerous children whose conduct may revert to a primitive, sub-human level . . . On the surface they can behave as ordinary, likeable, attractive human beings, but they harbour in their inner depths instinctive forces which on occasions overwhelm them. In conversation and under controlled conditions no special flaw may be discovered to enable medical certification to be effected; it is impossible in such cases to define sanity or insanity, but it is surely obvious to everyone that we are dealing with conduct abnormality of such a degree and type as to constitute the greatest potential danger to the individual and his victim. They are in the most deplorable of all conditions, not sane enough to be at large and not insane enough (in terms of certifiability) to be suitable for Bedlam. *If our ethical code feels justified in sending them to the gallows then let it be so, but at the same time let us clearly understand that such persons are driven by what may be called their collective unconscious to deeds of violence which are as uncontrollable as a tidal wave.*'

In many respects this describes the sixteen-year-old Craig. Ignorant of his true mental condition in the weeks that followed the rooftop battle, a nation wondered what could drive a young boy to such violence. When the details concerning his elder brother Niven were revealed, the press, the pundits, and the public were sure they had the answer. It was a classic case of revenge. 'I'm Craig. You've just given my brother twelve years. Come on, you coppers, I'm only sixteen.' Then later: 'That night I was out to kill because I had so much hate inside me for what they'd done to my brother.' The younger Craig, burning with a sense of injustice because the brother whom he hero-worshipped had been unjustly sentenced to twelve years' imprisonment, had wreaked a terrible vengeance on the police. His remarks on the roof, and later in hospital, conclusively explained Craig's violence, his boundless capacity for evil. Thus did the nation and her pundits rationalize the irrational. The truth, that the young man was suffering from severe emotional retardation, would have been even more disquieting. It was easier to stick labels like 'gangster' and 'hoodlum' on the youth and leave it at that. Why search for the truth when ready-made half-truths are so instantly available?

Craig's hatred of authority in general, and the police force in particular, had no connection with his brother's twelve-year sentence; it may have been the final nudge that pushed him over into the cauldron, but even that is not certain.

I questioned Craig closely about his teenage hatred of the police. He told me that it dated back to early childhood, but he was unable to offer any explanation for it. Of one thing he was quite sure; it was unrelated to his brother's exploits. Without any assistance from Niven he had acquired, at about the age of ten, an ambition to be a 'villain'. As he put it, 'My friends wanted to be engine drivers or Generals, I wanted to be a villain.' He told me of an incident that occurred about a year before the rooftop battle. He was out one evening with Bentley and a group of their friends when they had been stopped by a policeman who knew Bentley. It was merely a casual encounter, the policeman was virtually passing the time of day with Bentley. During the conversation Craig kept very quiet, not wanting to draw attention to himself, for the very good reason that in his pocket was a loaded Remington revolver. If the policeman had made a move towards Craig he would in all probability be dead now, for Craig told me he was tensed ready to use the gun. *This was a year before the rooftop battle. A year before Niven Craig was caught and sentenced to twelve years' imprisonment.* One wonders what motives the pundits would have ascribed to Craig if that incident had ended in tragedy. His teachers confirmed to me the extent of Craig's feelings about authority in general and the police in particular. *It was, they said, an attitude that prevailed throughout his secondary education.*

Craig recounted to me the childhood fantasy picture he had had of his death. He felt that it would come in a gun battle with the police. It would be fought in his own home, and end with him diving through his bedroom window to his death.

There can be little doubt that the boy who excelled in sport to such a degree that every year he was Victor Ludorum of the school, suffered from a profound mental disturbance. This was totally ignored at the time of his trial.

After a period of time in Wakefield Prison Craig became a model prisoner and since his release has been a model citizen. Those who screamed for his blood in 1952 would do well to realize that the youth who was thought beyond redemption now leads an exemplary life. Those, too, who think that anyone convicted of murder should be hanged or incarcerated for life should consider the case of Christopher Craig. Without doubt he responded completely to prison treatment.

Having received from Dr Matheson a report on Christopher Craig, Dr Hill duly performed an EEG examination. His report to the Brixton Prison Medical Officer was as follows.

'The dominant rhythm in the postcentral areas is at 9 c/sec and shows the normal characters of alpha rhythm. There is a gross excess of bilateral central 6–7 c/sec theta rhythm and in both posterior temporal regions a high voltage focus of 2 per second activity is seen. The focus on the right side is more prominent than that on the left, but in both instances the foci are related to the visual mechanism, appearing on eye closure and blocking on eye opening. Photic stimulation produced normal responses and tends to block the slow wave phenomena. Owing to his recent injuries it was not possible to over-breathe adequately.

'This EEG shows two of the main types of immaturity phenomena and shows them in severe degree. The posterior temporal slow wave foci are extremely prominent. It is of interest that these EEG abnormalities are associated in this case, as in many others, with a history of bed-wetting in late childhood, deep sleep and personality immaturity.'

It is equally of interest that the immaturity phenomena present in Craig's EEG are classic indications of a psychopathic personality.

Dr Matheson's reports on Craig and Bentley were written a few days before the original date for the commencement of their trial. Undoubtedly, if fate had not intervened the reports would have gone forward to the Court as the Prison Medical Officer's final conclusions, but fate did intervene, in the shape of John Parris. As recorded in the previous chapter, Craig's Counsel managed to persuade the Lord Chief Justice to postpone the hearing until 9 December. The extra week afforded Matheson the opportunity of correcting many of the errors contained in his report on Bentley. Five days before the new trial date, his report on Derek Bentley was submitted to the Court, the Crown Prosecutor, and, in theory, to Bentley's Counsel.

A verbatim copy of the report is included in Appendix II.

A copy of the report was sent to the Director of Public Prosecutions, for whom it had been specifically prepared. A copy was also sent to the Old Bailey for the trial judge, Lord Chief Justice Goddard, though the purpose of supplying this information to the Judge *before* the trial is by no means evident. In *The Unquiet Mind* Dr William Sargant commented on this curious action.

'The judge, of course, must not let any such information influence him in his summing-up, or convey it to the jury by the least hint – which must be as difficult as the nursery feat of thinking about a piebald horse without thinking of its tail.'

A third copy of this report should, by law, have been supplied to Bentley's Counsel by the DPP before the start of the trial. I have been unable to confirm that, prior to the trial, a copy was given to Frank Cassels either directly by Dr Matheson, or via the Public Prosecutor. When I interviewed Frank Cassels I showed him a copy of the Matheson report. *He stated that that was the first time he had seen it*. In the files of Bentley's solicitor (who is now deceased) is a letter, dated 4 November 1952, from Dr Matheson, with which was sent a copy of the EEG carried out at the Maudsley by Dr Denis Hill. The covering letter also states, 'I hope to get a copy of my report to the Court into the post tomorrow to you.' There is no indication in that file that the report ever arrived. There is no indication in the Bentley file at the office of the Director of Public Prosecutions that a copy of the report was given to Bentley's Counsel. Was the law complied with? One thing is beyond all doubt; *at no time during the trial did Frank Cassels refer to that report, and no use whatsoever was made of its contents by the Defence Counsel.*

Analysis of Dr Matheson's final report on Bentley reveals that although a number of the errors contained in his earlier report to Dr Denis Hill have been corrected, there are still many disturbing aspects.

1. *Family History:* There is no mention of Bentley's eldest sister Joan, killed in a wartime bombing raid when Bentley was seven, or of the effect the tragedy had on Bentley. There is still no reference to Derek's twin who died within two hours. His mother's cousin did not merely suffer from epilepsy, she died during an attack.

2. *School:* The information about Bentley's education is riddled with inaccuracies. The information about Bentley's criminal record is inaccurate. The information about Dr Munroe's conclusions is so seriously incorrect that the reader should compare Dr Munroe's conclusions, recorded on pages 128-9 of this chapter, with Matheson's version of those conclusions in Appendix II. Matheson's version of his colleague's first two sentences is particularly interesting. Dr Munroe said, 'Derek did not cooperate well in examination. My impression was that he was feeble-minded.' In Matheson's report it becomes, 'Dr Munroe considered that he might be feeble-minded but that he did not co-operate well in examination.' Matheson's is a travesty of Dr Munroe's carefully considered conclusions but nobody who relied solely on the Brixton Prison Medical Officer's report could possibly be aware of this.

The omissions are formidable. No mention of the fact that Bentley was prescribed phenobarbitone to ease his condition. No mention of his treatment by the Bristol Child Guidance Clinic. No mention of the second EEG examination carried out at the Burden Neurological Institute. No mention of the reasons why he did not work after

156

his release from the approved school until early 1951. This, like all the other facts that are omitted, were available to Matheson; indeed some of that information *can be proved, beyond any doubt whatsoever, to have been supplied to Dr Matheson*; he chose not to record it. One example of this is his misinterpretation of Bentley's National Service Medical Examination. Anyone who believes that National Service could be evaded with a doctor's certificate is a fool. If Bentley had been considered suitable for National Service in every other regard, the information supplied to the Medical Board about his epileptic condition would have been rigorously checked; they were spared this task because of one fact alone. Bentley was considered so mentally sub-standard after he had undertaken intelligence tests and had been subjected to psychiatric examination, that any further investigation was unnecessary. He was unfit *mentally* to carry out the most menial tasks in any branch of Her Majesty's Forces.

3. *Medical History:* One of the many truly astonishing aspects of this report, not merely this section, but the entire report, is, if one accepts the list of informants as being accurate, that Dr Doris Reynolds was not indeed contacted by Dr Matheson. Bentley had been under her care from 1945, and she was therefore an immediate and obvious source of a great deal of accurate information, but Matheson chose to ignore her.

The details of Bentley's falls and epileptic attacks are also inaccurate, and the remarks about his first epileptic attack are quite inexplicable. The earlier accounts, recorded in this chapter, of the first attack, accounts which Dr Munroe referred to, accounts included in the statement of Mr Bentley made to John Stevens at the same time as Matheson was compiling his information, bear no relation to Dr Matheson's version. What he calls the first attack was in fact a subsequent attack.

The report implies that Bentley ceased to suffer from epileptic attacks at the age of eight. All the available evidence confirms that he continued to suffer from epileptic attacks for the rest of his life – the last recorded attack was less than a month before his arrest on the Croydon rooftop.

The remark 'the father tells me the falls were never serious' is entirely inconsistent with all the information that was available at the time this report was made, including information supplied by Mr Bentley to his son's solicitor. As is quite clear from the remarks in his report to Hill, Dr Matheson had a low opinion of Bentley's father and chose to disregard a great deal of the information he had obtained from him. But if he had taken the trouble to check that information he would have discovered that it was entirely accurate. By his failure to make such checks, the gross inaccuracies that abound in the report were inevitable.

4. *Present Condition:* From the evidence of the police and civilian witnesses that I have interviewed, Bentley's mental attitude after his arrest was one of profound shock. He frequently broke down, was overcome with remorse that a policeman had died, was white-faced, shaking and very frightened. By the time he arrived at Brixton Prison, he had passed a sleepless night in a police cell, endured police interrogation, been charged with the murder of a policeman, made a public appearance in Court and been publicly charged, and he had not seen his family since eight o'clock the previous evening. For a normal nineteen-year-old to bear all this without reacting would have been miraculous, for the abnormal Bentley it would have been impossible. I cannot believe that Bentley underwent so dramatic a mental transformation once the doors of Brixton Prison closed behind him.

On the other hand, Matheson's conclusion that Bentley did not show any real appreciation of the peril in which he stood is undoubtedly correct. Up to a few days before his execution, Bentley still believed that he would be going back to Kingswood Approved School. At the time of the case, the issue of 'fitness to plead' was resolved before a jury. The test was whether the accused understood the charge, could distinguish between a plea of guilty and not guilty, had the ability to challenge jurors, to examine witnesses, to instruct counsel, to follow the evidence and to make a proper defence. Who can doubt that Bentley did not possess the ability required to perform any of these functions? In the opinion of various members of the medical profession with whom I have discussed Bentley's history, Derek Bentley did not have the ability to comprehend a fraction of his trial at the Old Bailey. For all that he could understand it might just as well have been heard in Kurdish.

I have already commented on the mental tests in my observations on Dr Matheson's report to Dr Denis Hill. The validity and accuracy of those tests should be judged in conjunction with the validity and accuracy of the report as a whole.

For Dr Matheson's comments on Bentley's mental level to have any objectivity it was of paramount importance that Dr James Munroe's contrary conclusions be recorded in the report; like so much else those conclusions are conspicuous by their absence. *The conclusions of the Head of Psychological Medicine of Guy's Hospital are totally ignored.*

I have been advised that a strong case can be presented to support the contention that Bentley's true mental condition was more serious than mere feeble-mindedness. This may well be; I wish to put the case no higher than that he was, within the definition of the Mental Deficiency Act, feeble-minded. As the Royal Commission's report on Capital Punishment indicates, that would have been sufficient for the issue of his fitness to stand trial to be put before a jury. Matheson's conclusions on this issue fly not only in the face of the considered opinion of a very experienced colleague, but in the face of all the known evidence.

The same can be said of his conclusions about Bentley's epilepsy, and particularly of the implication that it was a thing of the past. *There is a significant amount of evidence that on the evening of Sunday 2 November, Bentley was affected by his epileptic condition.* During the course of the afternoon he began to develop a severe headache that increased to such an intensity it forced him to leave the cinema early. All

159

his previous epileptic attacks had been heralded by such a headache. The conditions of the attempted break-in at Barlow & Parkers were near perfect for the inducement of an epileptic attack. The physical effort of climbing the iron gates, great nervous excitement, the additional physical effort of climbing a thirty-foot drainpipe, the resultant over-breathing (breathing hard); indeed Bentley told his solicitor that when he was barely half-way up that pipe he was overcome with dizziness. His subsequent statement to the police jumps from point to point, and large parts of the incident – Craig's firing at Harrison, for example – are forgotten. The possibility that Bentley suffered that evening an epileptic attack, or that the events were for him an epileptic equivalent, should have been seriously considered. In view of the fact that Dr Matheson was obviously working on the premise that Bentley's attacks, or, to use his word, 'fits', had terminated when the youth was eight, it is evident that the Prison Medical Officer did not take this aspect seriously.

Certain comments of the Royal Commission on Capital Punishment, which had just finished sitting at the time of this case, may be thought relevant.

'An epileptic equivalent is some kind of experience or behaviour which is not, like a general convulsion, itself of a characteristically epileptic kind, but, though due to the same causes, assumes a different form of abnormality. An attack of motiveless rage may in some cases be an epileptic equivalent. As, however, the abnormal state will not have been obviously epileptic, the difficulty will be to establish that it was in fact the "equivalent" of an overt epileptic attack due to the same causes. If there is clinical evidence, perhaps supported by an EEG, that the accused suffers from epilepsy, and if he remembers nothing of the crime, or his memory of it is clouded, and if his actions at the time of the crime show signs of mental confusion, it will be reasonable to assume that the crime was an epileptic equivalent . . . The question whether a crime was an epileptic equivalent must be decided by the appropriate

160

authority, whether this is the jury or the Secretary of State, in the light of all the evidence in each particular case. It will seldom be possible to establish this positively; but we have no doubt that, where it is established, *the accused shall be treated as wholly exempt from responsibility.*' The possibility that Bentley was suffering from an epileptic equivalent was never raised before Bentley's jury. The Secretary of State *was made fully aware of this aspect,* though not by Dr Matheson; Chapter 7 records his reaction.

Professor Sir Denis Hill has assured me that a vast body of medical opinion believed in 1952, and still believes today, that if an epileptic person is involved in the type of act that Bentley had been accused of, the possibility of the disease being a direct causation can never be safely ruled out. In Bentley's case it *was* ruled out.

I believe that the conclusions of Dr Matheson, on the evidence made available to him, are incorrect, and that his opinion, that Bentley was fit to plead to the indictment and fit to stand his trial, is an opinion that is simply not borne out by the facts.

In view of the situation recorded in this chapter, one particular passage in the report of the Royal Commission on Capital Punishment has a savagely ironic ring. It refers to the wisdom of an accused's mental condition being established solely by the Prison Medical Officer.

'Thirdly, it is all-important that evidence of insanity presented by the Crown should bear clearly the stamp of independence of judgment. No responsible person questions that prison medical officers in fact exercise their professional judgment with complete independence. But they are salaried officers of the Crown; the prosecution is being brought on behalf of the Crown; and this gives an appearance of identity of interest which may create in the mind of the public, and perhaps the jury, the impression that a wholly unbiased opinion can hardly be expected from witnesses in that position.'

The Commission went on to recommend that the mental state of every prisoner charged with murder should be examined by two doctors, of whom one, at least, should have no connection with the prison medical service. They recommended the immediate adoption of this practice; but when it was eventually adopted, it was too late to help Derek Bentley.

On the morning of Tuesday, 9 December 1952, the two teenagers left Brixton Prison on their journey to the Old Bailey.

The State *v.* Christopher Craig and Derek Bentley. The State *v.* a sixteen-year-old psychopath with the emotional responses of a child, and a nineteen-year-old, feeble-minded, totally illiterate epileptic with a mental age, even by Dr Matheson's standards, of no more than eleven. Craig and Bentley were about to go into battle against the full majesty of the Law, the power of the State and the trappings of what we are pleased to call Justice.

5

'Draw Near and Give Your Attendance'

It was cold and foggy in London on the morning of Tuesday, 9 December 1952, but the inclement weather did not deter the public. They came to the Old Bailey in their thousands. Many arrived early to ensure they obtained a seat in the public gallery. Many more came merely to stare at the principal participants of what had already been dubbed by the press 'the most sensational murder trial of the twentieth century'. Some were so anxious not to miss a word of the trial that they queued throughout the bitterly cold night. The inevitable parasites were quick to capitalize. Mingling with the vendors selling everything from peanuts to newspapers were a number of fast-talking gentlemen in long overcoats and fedora-type hats. I have remarked that in those days one could buy anything on the 'black market': tickets to the public gallery of No. 2 Court changed hands for as much as £30. And the public gallery, like any West End theatre, had two daily performances, morning and afternoon. The principal participants had no need to indulge in such extravagance, their places were already booked, and they arrived from Brixton Prison each in his own police van.

Gradually the court came to life, as it filled up with the essential personnel, clerks, solicitors, barristers, all helping to contribute to an atmosphere that became more charged by the minute. There was always something special, something unique about a murder trial during this period when capital punishment was the supreme penalty.

The Bentley family travelled from their Norbury home by public transport, and arrived at the courtroom on foot. The Craig family, decidedly more flamboyant, drew up at the steps to the Old Bailey in a Rolls-Royce, by courtesy of the *Sunday Pictorial*. The hired car was not merely a philanthropic gesture. The Sunday newspaper had signed Mr and Mrs Craig and their daughter Lucy, on an exclusive basis, for £350, and the Rolls-Royce was to assure the *Pictorial*'s investment maximum protection from rival newspapers, whose reporters might have felt inclined to talk to the Craigs.

The man entrusted with the task of ensuring that the innermost thoughts of the Craig family remained inviolate was Harry Procter. In his autobiography *The Street of Disillusion* he recalled the task. 'For weeks Madeline (his colleague) and I, as paid and skilled journalists, had the tough task of keeping away the opposition reporters and photographers. The opposition never allowed us a day or a night free from anxiety; but this girl reporter and I were the perfect team, we succeeded. When the trial opened at the Old Bailey I had to organize my forces like a military operation. My long experience of the Old Bailey made me realize that the task of taking Mr and Mrs Craig, and their daughter Lucy, to that great Court of Justice every day for perhaps a week without allowing even a "yes" or a "no" for quotes to the opposition, was a formidable one. Madeline and I were determined that it should be done. The ordeal was almost as mentally shattering for us as it was for the tragic Craig family.'

Shattering ordeal or not, Procter, as he says, succeeded. He was able to boast that not one opposition reporter got one word out of the Craigs. An interview that the rival paper, the *Empire News*, published of a conversation with Lucy Craig was, according to the indignant Procter, fictitious.

So in this three-ring-circus atmosphere the forces of Justice assembled for the trial of the two teenagers charged with the most serious offence in English law.

Craig and Bentley were not the only people specially attired for the occasion. At precisely 10.30 a.m., Lord Goddard, wearing £500 worth of robes, ermine and wig, took his place in the Judge's chair.

After both youths had pleaded Not Guilty, the seventy-five-year-old Judge eyed them for a moment, then said, 'Craig may sit down.' The courtesy that all men may sit during their trial was not to be extended to Bentley. That Craig could stand at all was little short of miraculous. On the evidence, given at Croydon Court, of a prosecution witness, who was a specialist, the sixteen-year old boy should still have been on his back. The rush to judgment was not to be halted for irrelevancies however. Somehow he was standing, and the stretcher had been replaced with a wheel-chair.

The jury were sworn but not before Craig's Counsel had made his first mark. Upon the appearance of a woman juror, John Parris leapt to his feet and challenged her. She was removed. When another woman appeared the same thing occurred. Eventually a jury of twelve men was sworn in.

The reasons for the objections were manifold. Parris was a great believer in courtroom psychology. He considered that a trial was a 'battle of personalities, in which one personality, the judge or one of the counsel, will dominate'. As long as this country insists on a legal system that is based on accusation rather than on enquiry there is enormous value in such a philosophy.

The same thinking was behind Parris' insistence that Craig should not wear his usual clothes at the trial. The youth had pleaded to be allowed to wear his suede jacket, bright blue trousers and even brighter suede shoes with thick crêpe soles, but in vain. As he sat in the dock, wearing a conservative sports jacket and flannels, he looked the model of conformity.

By challenging the women jurors, Parris also hoped to throw the Prosecuting Counsel, Christmas Humphreys, who was about to deliver his opening speech, off-balance.

A well-timed intervention could send all those carefully rehearsed phrases spinning into the ether. His main reason for the objections was more basic. Parris feared that they would identify with the widow of PC Miles. Frank Cassels considered their removal unwise – in his opinion the women would have identified with the accused's mothers – but Parris prevailed.

Christmas Humphreys rose to make the opening speech. He introduced the various Counsel, then, after reminding the jury of the charge, he continued:

'You may have read something of this case in the press; you may have read how these two young men were found on the roof of a building in Croydon, that there was what was described as a gun battle, as a result of which one police constable was killed and another wounded [although the additional charge of attempting to murder Fairfax was not proceeded with, evidence relating to it was submitted during the trial], and of a spectacular jump or dive by the boy Craig from the roof of the building, as a result of which he was injured and had to appear at the Magistrates' Court on a stretcher, and of the alleged confession of Bentley that he knew Craig had a gun. On behalf of the Prosecution I ask you to forget everything you have read about this case up to the moment. This case will be tried, as cases are in every English Court, upon the evidence before you and on that alone.'

By reminding them of the press accounts and advising them to forget them, Humphreys ensured that, whatever else the jury remembered, they would remember the press accounts. It would be interesting to know, for example, how many of those twelve men were regular *Daily Mail* readers. If the jury's recollections of the events of 2 November were based on that particular newspaper's veracity, then the defendants' cause was lost before the trial had begun. The Prosecution Counsel warmed to his theme.

'The case for the Prosecution is this: that Craig deliberately and wilfully murdered that police constable and

166

thereafter gloried in the murder; that Bentley incited Craig to begin the shooting and, although technically under arrest at the actual time of the killing of Miles, was party to that murder and equally responsible in law.'

That was a clear declaration of intent on the Prosecution's part. But those opening remarks, apart from sending the listening reporters hurrying to the phone with an instant lunchtime headline, *CRAIG GLORIED IN MURDER*, had a special significance. The Prosecution Counsel had clearly admitted that Bentley was under arrest at the time of Miles' death. The Oxford Dictionary states that 'technical' means 'legally such, in the eyes of the law'. So in the Prosecution's opinion Bentley was legally, in the eyes of the law, under arrest at the time PC Miles died. This is one of the central issues that still disturbs many legal minds when they consider the Bentley case. Although it became a main issue on appeal, for some astonishing reason it was not an issue at all during the trial.

Humphreys then recounted the police version of the events leading up to the moment when Fairfax was shot in the shoulder. He stated how all three officers, Fairfax, McDonald and Harrison, in their various positions heard Bentley say 'Let him have it, Chris.'

'All three heard it, and all three heard the shot which followed *immediately* upon it. That statement, in the submission of the Prosecution, was a deliberate incitement to Craig to murder Sgt Fairfax [he had been promoted to Detective Sergeant since the Croydon incident]. It was spoken to a man who he, Bentley, clearly knew had a gun. That shot began a gun fight, in the course of which Miles was killed; that incitement, in the submission of the Prosecution, covered the whole of the shooting thereafter; *even though at the time of the actual shot which killed PC Miles, Bentley was in custody and under arrest.*'

As has been seen, all three officers did not hear a shot follow the alleged remark immediately. The in-built contradictions in the Prosecution's statement are manifest. *If* Bentley had uttered the fateful remark, and *if* he had

167

meant by it that Craig should fire, the object of the violence was Fairfax, not Miles. Moreover, if we take Christmas Humphreys' logic to its ultimate conclusion, are we to assume that if Craig had escaped from the roof, and if Miles had caught up with him and been shot a day, a week, a year later, then Bentley would still be guilty of murder? If Fairfax or McDonald had ordered Bentley to climb down the drainpipe instead of waiting for the roof entrance to be unlocked would Bentley still have been guilty of murder? There must surely come a point in a joint enterprise when, as a joint enterprise, it is ended. No evidence was ever offered to show that Craig and Bentley's joint enterprise involved resisting arrest by the use of firearms. Their joint enterprise was the attempt to break into the warehouse. It ended at the point of Bentley's arrest – at least that is the opinion of the many legal experts whom I have interviewed. The reason that Bentley stood facing trial for an alleged murder committed not by his hand but by another's was due to a law commonly referred to as the 'doctrine of constructive malice'. Under this law, that has its origins in the Old Testament, if a Police Officer was killed while attempting to make an arrest then the law assumed automatically that the person who committed the act had intended to do so. This inflexible rule gave Craig little hope of acquittal, but what of Bentley? In law Bentley was considered 'a principal in the second degree'.

A simple illustration of this law is the following example. If two people agree to commit a burglary and one of them stays outside to keep watch, he is in law present at the commission of the offence and is a principal in the second degree and therefore equally guilty. Before Bentley could be found guilty it had to be shown beyond reasonable doubt that there was an agreement between the two teenagers, not only to break into the warehouse but also to use violence to resist arrest. Not one iota of evidence that satisfied this latter requirement was ever produced. Even assuming that there was between Bentley and Craig an agreement to use violence to resist arrest, and that assumption, unsubstantiated, was made in Bentley's case, there is still the issue of his arrest.

How he could possibly be considered to be acting in concert with Craig fifteen minutes after he had been arrested defies explanation. An indication of the Executive's determination to obtain a finding of Guilty against Bentley could be gauged from the fact that the 'doctrine of constructive malice' had not been applied *in any case this century prior to the Craig/Bentley trial*. It is ironic that when this obsolete law was dragged from the archives and dusted over, it was applied to a case in which it was not applicable. The issue should have been put to the jury for them to consider and decide upon, and the fact that it was not, must rest squarely on the shoulders of Lord Goddard and Frank Cassels.

Humphreys continued to recount the incidents on the rooftop, as described by the police depositions, and came eventually to Bentley's statement. After reading an extract of it he made the following comment:

'May I say at once, of course, that the statement by Bentley is in no sense any evidence whatsoever against Craig; because their concerted action of meaning to break and enter these premises and steal what they could and to resist their lawful apprehension by such violence as they might think necessary was over, *and the moment they are arrested, what they severally say is not evidence against the other.*'

So we have a bizarre situation where what they *say* when they have been arrested is not evidence against the other, but what they *do* is. Consequently, Bentley was now being held responsible for actions illegally perpetrated by Craig fifteen minutes after his (Bentley's) arrest.

Having recounted to the jury the various statements that Craig was alleged to have made while in Croydon Hospital, the Prosecuting Counsel concluded by repeating his contention that Craig had gloried in the murder of the policeman and that the boy's only regret was that he had not killed more policemen. His final assertion was that, while the Prosecution admitted that 'Bentley was under arrest at the time of the actual murder – that he was nevertheless still mentally supporting Craig in all that Craig continued to do, and that in English law, and you may think in common sense, was in every sense party to that murder.'

Since not one shred of evidence was produced to prove that Bentley remained mentally with Craig throughout the gun battle; since all the evidence proved the contrary point of view; since the issue of when a joint adventure exactly ended had never been established in English law, Christmas Humphreys' closing remarks are, in my opinion and having regard to the evidence, a travesty of the truth. But in fairness to Humphreys, it should be pointed out that he was involved in a rush to judgment, and such an exercise leaves very little time for discovering the truth.

The Prosecution then proceeded to call its witnesses. After several policemen had given evidence, submitting plans and photographs of the roof, a grave-looking Niven Craig Senior walked to the witness box. Within the space of three days he had seen his middle-class world crash around his ears. On 30 October, his eldest son had been sentenced to twelve years' imprisonment in this same court. On 2 November, his youngest son had taken a bus ride to Croydon as a result of which Mr Craig once again heard his name called to give evidence. On that previous occasion Christopher had been by his parents' side giving them what comfort he could. Now the handsome teenager watched with his deep brown eyes as his father gave evidence confirming his youngest son's age. The Prosecution had been obliged to call Mr Craig for this specific purpose; now John Parris rose to cross-examine.

Slowly he built up, through question and answer, a picture of Christopher Craig that bore as much resemblance to a desperate gunman as Jesus Christ does to the devil. The Court learned that Christopher suffered from 'word blindness' (dyslexia), a disability that makes the printed word incomprehensible to the sufferer. The only books

170

that Christopher knew were the works of Enid Blyton, which had been read to him by his sisters. The jury listened as Mr Craig recounted his own interest in guns, and his ability as a marksman. He had encouraged his sons to shoot well at target practice, with air-guns and air-pistols. Christopher had been the exception; his only visit to a range had produced a very poor score. Nevertheless his father's encouragement gave him an interest in guns, and Christopher Craig had developed an ambition to be a gunsmith, which his parents had *not* encouraged. Mr Craig told the Court that his son had attended Bible classes at a church in Streatham until the age of fourteen, and that the youth only left because he feared that he might be asked to read a lesson. In answer to further questions Mr Craig recalled how his son's inability to read was mocked by other boys and he was made to feel inferior.

All this of course was intended by Parris to break down the picture of Craig that had been so assiduously put in the jury's minds by the press. Undoubtedly a great deal of the press treatment prior to the trial accurately reflected young Craig's character. But the total freedom on the reporting of committal proceedings that the press then enjoyed posed a dilemma: any restriction on our newspapers should be viewed with the greatest suspicion, but total freedoms are open to abuse. In this case the pre-trial press coverage had ensured the impossibility of an impartial trial.

Christmas Humphreys must have felt that the gentle cross-examination had left its mark on the jury. Upon re-examining Mr Craig, he attempted initially to discredit the witness by referring to an occasion when he had been fined for possessing a firearm without a licence. Humphreys, under the impression that this had occurred only a few months before the gun battle, obviously saw a connection. The ploy did not pay off; the offence had been committed in 1951 and there was no connection. Indeed it was a gambit that Humphreys must have regretted for the Lord Chief Justice then asked for details of Christopher Craig's Brighton exploit (recorded in Chapter 2). When these were given they merely confirmed the picture of the youth that Parris had been at such pains to paint. Changing his tack Humphreys asked about the veritable arsenal that had been found in the attic of the Craig home. Niven Craig lamely confessed that prior to the police search he had not known that his son had had over a hundred and fifty rounds of assorted ammunition hidden in the loft.

After Mrs Ware had given evidence concerning the two unidentified men she had seen climbing over the gates of Barlow & Parkers, the Prosecution called one of its main witnesses, Detective Sergeant Fairfax.

Fairfax said that on the evening in question visibility was very restricted away from the street lights. He told how he had climbed up the drainpipe on to the roof. He had no torch with him, so he must have had very good eyesight, for he recounted how he could see the two teenagers seventy feet away. He described how, when he walked towards them, they backed behind the lift-head and he had then called upon them to come out. Craig's reply was, 'If you want us, fucking well come and get us.' (A remark that Craig was later to deny making, and that Mr Fairfax is now unable to recall.) He recalled how, having reached the right-hand side of the lift-head, he had grabbed Bentley and pulled him out, then moved round the front of the stack in pursuit of Craig, pushing Bentley in front of him. As they rounded the left-hand corner they came virtually face to face with Craig. It was at this point, according to Fairfax, that Bentley broke away from him and said, 'Let him have it, Chris.' Chris had fired, hitting Fairfax on the right shoulder, the impact causing him to spin round and fall to the ground. When he got to his feet Craig was on his left and Bentley was on his right. As he had just described how Bentley was on his left before Craig fired, *Bentley must have crossed Craig's firing line to get to the other side of Fairfax*. Quietly, Fairfax continued. He told Prosecuting Counsel how he attacked Bentley, knocking him to the ground. Craig fired again, this time completely missing him, and he pulled Bentley up in front of him to act as a shield. If this was true, Bentley undoubtedly saved Fairfax's life by allowing him to do this. Fairfax then alleged that he worked Bentley round the roof until they had reached the comparative safety of the roof-entrance wall. On the way he had searched Bentley, and found the knuckleduster and the knife, which he described as a 'dagger type'. He pocketed the knife and placed the knuckleduster on his hand.

The next incident that Fairfax remembered was helping McDonald on to the roof. As he and McDonald held Bentley, he said he had shouted to Craig to drop his gun. The sixteen-year-old boy, still full of defiance, had shouted back, 'Come and get it.' When McDonald asked Fairfax what kind of gun it was, Bentley had answered, 'He's got a ·45 Colt and plenty of bloody ammunition too.' Fairfax did not recall any other conversation between himself and McDonald in which Bentley had intervened.

He did not recall any of Harrison's involvement either, for the next incident he recounted was the death of PC Miles. Fairfax heard a shot and Miles fell virtually at his feet. As Fairfax moved to his fallen colleague there was a second shot. Fairfax had no recollection of the next sequence of events, involving Harrison; in his mind the next thing was when Harrison left the safety of the roof entrance and joined him behind the wall. Then, describing how Bentley was rushed around the door and down the stairs, he recalled that Bentley had shouted out, 'They're taking me down, Chris.' As far as Fairfax was concerned there was no reaction from Craig. He described how he was given a ·32 automatic pistol and returned to the roof, and engaged in a gun battle with Craig, and how as he ran towards Craig the youth dived over the edge of the roof.

When the officer was cross-examined by John Parris, he remembered that in all ten or eleven other shots had been fired, but did not know who by, or at whom.

When Frank Cassels rose to cross-examine, he attempted to clarify Fairfax's exact physical position when the first shot was fired. Fairfax then totally contradicted the evidence that he had given a few minutes earlier to the Prosecution Counsel. This is not a pedantic point. Nor is it a question of magnifying every minor error. This particular sequence of events covered the remark that was to hang Bentley, and cannot, therefore, be too closely examined. (When questioned by the Prosecution Counsel, Fairfax asserted several times that he had *pushed* Bentley around the lift-head in pursuit of Craig. When questioned by Frank Cassels, however, he equally dogmatically stated several times that he had *pulled* Bentley round the lift-head.) Cassels then continued his cross-examination.

CASSELS: Up till that time had he said or done anything?
FAIRFAX: No, Sir.
CASSELS: Then I suggest to you that you took Bentley towards the staircase head?
FAIRFAX: No, Sir.
CASSELS: Was that your intention?
FAIRFAX: I don't think I had an intention at that time, Sir. My intention was to get hold of the other fellow as well.
CASSELS: Now, at that stage you had hold of Bentley with your right hand, had you?
FAIRFAX: Both hands, I think, Sir.
CASSELS: Both hands?
FAIRFAX: Yes, Sir.
CASSELS: Which part of him did you hold on to?
FAIRFAX: His left arm, Sir.
CASSELS: So that you are standing beside him holding like this his left arm?
FAIRFAX: That is so, Sir.
CASSELS: Now, when Bentley, as you say, broke away, in which direction did he go?
FAIRFAX: He must have actually gone to the right, Sir.
CASSELS: Do you mean to the right of the lift-shaft?
FAIRFAX: To the east, Sir, or north-east.
CASSELS: Much obliged. Did you turn to follow?
FAIRFAX: No, Sir, not at that time.

CASSELS: Well, did you turn in any direction?

FAIRFAX: Yes, I spun round.

CASSELS: No; I am talking of before the shot was fired. Did you spin round as Bentley broke away?

FAIRFAX: No, Sir; it was practically simultaneously, Sir.

CASSELS: You see, you told my Lord and the jury you were shot here. (BY THE BOTTOM LEFT-HAND CORNER OF THE LIFT-HEAD.)

FAIRFAX: That is right, Sir.

CASSELS: If you are holding Bentley like that and he breaks away, is your right shoulder then presented to Craig on the other side of the lift-shaft?

FAIRFAX: Yes, Sir.

In fact it would have been the *left* shoulder of Fairfax that would have been presented to Craig in this position, but this, like the contradiction of whether Bentley was *pushed* or *pulled*, was allowed to pass unchallenged. Fairfax then produced the jacket and waistcoat he had been wearing that night, and Cassels questioned him about the tear in the shoulder.

CASSELS: Would you just hold up the jacket so that the jury may see? It shows the hole; it is a jagged tear, is it not?

FAIRFAX: Yes.

CASSELS: Not the normal neat hole that a bullet frequently makes?

FAIRFAX: I cannot answer that.

CASSELS: You do not know?

FAIRFAX: No, Sir.

CASSELS: You see, what I am suggesting is this: that when that shot was fired you were not directly facing Craig.

FAIRFAX: Yes, Sir; we were actually diagonally with him; because we were approximately at the bottom left-hand corner of the stack, lift-head, and Craig was half-left of me, and I was then *pulling* Bentley by his left arm.

*　　*　　*

175

These interchanges are yet further illustrations of the inconsistencies that exist in the police evidence. (See also Chapter 2.) Before the cross-examination was completed Frank Cassels obtained confirmation from Detective Sergeant Fairfax that as far as he was concerned, when Bentley had been rushed downstairs, Craig had not fired. The most disturbing information, however, had been elicited during Fairfax's examination by John Parris.

PARRIS: Now, let me see if I understand your story correctly. You say it was the third shot that was fired that was the fatal shot; is that right?

FAIRFAX: The shot that hit PC Miles, Sir? Oh no; to my recollection there were several other shots; but I don't know what he was firing at.

PARRIS: You see, you have not mentioned that hitherto, have you?

FAIRFAX: No, Sir.

PARRIS: You said there was one shot which struck you first of all, then another shot and the third shot you mentioned was the shot which hit PC Miles?

FAIRFAX: That is the shot which hit PC Miles; but it certainly was not the third shot, Sir.

PARRIS: What other shots were there?

FAIRFAX: I should say there were somewhere like six or seven other shots, Sir.

PARRIS: *Before the fatal shot?*

FAIRFAX: *Before the fatal shot, yes.*

PARRIS: Do I understand you correctly: are there six or seven other shots in addition to the ones you told my Lord and the jury about?

FAIRFAX: That is so, yes, Sir.

PARRIS: You had not said a word about those shots until a few moments ago, had you, Officer?

FAIRFAX: No, Sir.

PARRIS: *Did you see where they came from?*

FAIRFAX: *No, Sir.*

PARRIS: *Where were you when they were fired?*

FAIRFAX: *I was then round about the doorway marked 'B' and the bottom left-hand roof-light, Sir.*

The myriad questions provoked by that interchange hung unasked, and therefore unanswered, in the Old Bailey air. *Based on the trial transcript, there is no doubt whatsoever that prior to the moment when PC Miles stepped out on the roof, Craig fired just four shots, no more, no less. Apart from the two fired at Fairfax, the officer swore on oath that there had been six or seven other shots before the fatal one. Of these six or seven Craig fired just two. These were the shots fired at Harrison. Who then fired the others? The only people with guns, apart from Craig, were police officers. At least six guns were issued to the police. Taken in conjunction with the facts about the death of PC Miles contained in earlier chapters, particularly those recorded in Chapter 2 relating to the ballistics evidence, Sergeant Fairfax's sworn testimony is a powerful and frightening confirmation of my belief that Craig and Bentley were put on trial for an offence that was never committed. If the Prosecution had been able to produce that bullet, a bullet that had travelled right through PC Miles' head and in the opinion of pathologist Dr Haler would have come to rest within fifty yards of the policeman's body, then the matter would have been resolved.*

The details that were made public during the pre-trial period, the trial, and the post-trial period, produced a textbook example of what psychologists call 'mental set', a predisposition towards a certain line of thought or action. (A simple illustration is to ask someone to pronounce f-o-l-k, then ask them to pronounce s-o-a-k, then ask them to pronounce c-h-o-k-e, finally ask them what the white of an egg is called and the answer will invariably be Yolk!) Equally, given the knowledge that Craig was armed with a ·45 gun and was firing that gun in the direction of various police officers, if one is then told that a police officer was subsequently shot through the head then one concludes that Craig fired the shot, but if it had been generally known that prior to PC Miles' death, other armed persons were firing from positions that scanned the roof, the conclusion is radically different, particularly when the attendant evidence then given supports the different conclusion.

At the lunchtime adjournment Craig himself displayed how powerful a 'mental set' could be. As Fairfax left the witness box, Craig remarked, 'I ought to have killed that fucker as well.' Craig, better than anyone else, knew he had been firing at police officers. He read how he had killed PC Miles, he was told by a variety of police officers that he had killed PC Miles, therefore he *had* killed PC Miles. It was a dangerous, if natural, assumption for the teenager to make. For the Court to make it was, as far as Bentley was concerned, fatal.

Unlike the Craig family, the Bentleys had not heard the morning's evidence. They had been patiently waiting in the corridor outside the courtroom, under the impression that Mr Bentley was to be called as a witness to give evidence concerning his son's overcoat. Fairfax had stated that after he had recovered from the first shot he had got to his feet and knocked Bentley to the ground. Bentley was wearing a camel-hair overcoat, yet the wet, tar-covered roof had not left a mark on the coat. Bentley's father felt that this point should be made known to the jury. It never was. Mr and Mrs Bentley were also expecting to give evidence of their son's medical history; again they were disappointed. Frank Cassels, in fact, had never had any intention of calling any of the Bentley family, but this point was not made clear to them and they sat patiently in the corridor throughout most of the trial. The realization that they were not going to be called only dawned on them when John Parris had virtually finished making his final speech to the jury.

Frank Cassels had a good, practical reason for not calling Derek's parents. If he called any witness apart from Bentley himself then, as Defence Counsel, he would lose the right of the last word to the jury, the final speech before the judge summed-up. *To call any witness other than the defendant would mean forfeiting that privilege to the Prosecution.*

Cassels considered it vital that the last words the jury heard from any of the three Counsel should be his. He was denied an opening speech, only the Prosecuting Counsel was granted that privilege. By this procedure Defence Counsel not only started at a disadvantage but perhaps remained so for the entire trial. Prosecution witness after Prosecution witness was called, and, unless it was revealed by cross-examination, the jury would remain ignorant of the Defence case until the entire Prosecution case had been put.

A perfect illustration of how outrageously unfair these rules of procedure were is recorded by Barrister C. G. L. Du Cann. A man had been charged with unlawful wounding at Lewes Assizes. The Prosecution concluded its case with the customary words to the Court, 'That is the case for the Prosecution, my Lord', signalling that it was the Defence's turn at last.

'Taking no notice for the moment, the judge went on writing. The foreman of the jury, a long, nervous-looking man, glanced sharply along the front and back rows of the jury. Receiving a few swift nods, he shot up like a released jack in-the-box on springs. 'Guilty, my Lord,' he proclaimed with emphasis.

'There was a second's shocked silence. Dropping his pen, the judge glared at the foreman with amazement.

'"Really, Mr Foreman. You've not heard a single word of the Defence. You can't possibly find any prisoner guilty at this stage. And you have not been asked for your verdict. Really!"'

The jury was discharged, a new jury empanelled, and the trial had to begin all over again.

The trial extracts in this book are taken entirely from a verbatim transcript of the trial. The jury could not avail themselves of this facility when considering their verdict. They were not even allowed copies of Counsels' final speeches, or of the Judge's summing-up. They had somehow to retain in their heads the thousands of words spoken during the course of three days.

If the Bentley/Craig jury had displayed initiative and produced their own pens and paper to make notes, they would have run the risk of being found guilty of Contempt of Court. As C. G. L. Du Cann observed, in *Miscarriages of Justice*, 'even in *Alice in Wonderland* the jury were allowed slates to add things up on'. (He also observed that it took the Second World War to abolish the quill pen from the Courts.)

There can be no doubt, however, that a great deal of the quill-pen mentality existed in our Courts long after that period. By 1952 we had moved a little way along the path of enlightenment from the time that a Scottish Judge, Lord Braxfield, summed up to the jury with the words, 'Come along, gentlemen, and help me to get some of these scoundrels hanged before breakfast.' How far we had moved along the path is a moot point.

So it was then, that English Justice forced Frank Cassels *either* to call witnesses who could aid Bentley's cause, and there were others as well as the parents whom he could have called, and by so doing lose the right to make the last speech, *or* to jettison part of his client's defence, thereby leaving Bentley as the only Defence witness. The previous chapter demonstrates how pathetically inadequate Bentley was as a human being. Now, aided by a Counsel who had stated that both Craig and he should hang, he was robbed by the law of whatever assistance additional witnesses would have contributed.

After the lunch adjournment the Prosecution continued to present its case. Policeman after policeman took the stand; they undoubtedly had a brave story to tell, but it was riddled with contradictions. When John Parris attempted to elicit from PC McDonald precisely how many shots had been fired, the Lord Chief Justice intervened, 'I wonder how anybody could be expected to be accurate on a matter like this, on a night like this, when these men are being fired at, in fear of their lives, and now they are being asked weeks later to count how many shots were fired.' This was perfectly fair comment as far as it went; its unfairness lay in the fact that it did not go far enough. One might also reasonably wonder how these men could be expected to be accurate when recalling what had been *said* under the conditions described by the Judge. Whether words like 'Let him have it, Chris' were an entirely accurate recollection? Lest it be thought that the police officers must have made notes shortly after the gun battle, it is worth recording that the only officer asked about such notes, Detective Sergeant Fairfax, admitted that he had *never made any*.

If this aspect occurred to the jury it occurred without the assistance of the Judge. The most remarkable aspect of PC McDonald's recollection of the conversations on the rooftop, conversations that had taken place, that is, *before* he had actually climbed on the roof, was that it was confined to one line: 'Let him have it, Chris.' He declared that there had been other conversations but he had not been able to hear them clearly. Craig's shouted remark to Fairfax, 'If you want us, fucking well come and get us', had not carried to McDonald. But McDonald *had* heard Bentley's remark spoken to his friend when they were face to face. He refused, however, although pressed by Humphreys and Goddard, to attribute the remark to Bentley. Lord Goddard, obviously unhappy about this, took the opportunity to intervene when Cassels was cross-examining.

CASSELS: Did you hear anything else said on the roof apart from this remark?

MCDONALD: I could not make out any more of the conversation, Sir; there was conversation but I could not make out what it was.

CASSELS: You just did hear this particular remark?

MCDONALD: Yes.

CASSELS: I am suggesting you never heard that remark used by Bentley if it was used by anybody else.

MCDONALD: I could not say whether it was Bentley who used it or not, Sir.

THE LORD CHIEF JUSTICE: Well, did you hear the word 'Chris' used?
MCDONALD: I did, my Lord.
L.C.J.: So far as you know there were three people on the roof?
MCDONALD: Yes, my Lord.
L.C.J.: There was Sergeant Fairfax and the two men?
MCDONALD: Yes, my Lord.
L.C.J.: And you heard 'Let him have it, Chris'; is that right?
MCDONALD: Yes, my Lord.
L.C.J.: Very good.

Thus the Judge applied his own well-known brand of common sense. The possibility that *if* the remark or one like it was made, it was a fellow police officer calling to James *Chris*tie McDonald, was, of course, not worthy of consideration. Like the possibility of Miles being killed by a police bullet, it did not bear thinking about, or at least not in that Old Bailey courtroom. As in the circumstances of Miles' death, so in McDonald's evidence of the remark that hanged Bentley; a dangerous 'mental set' was applied.

One fact that emerged from PC Harrison's evidence was his truly astounding talent for climbing walls, fences and roofs at superhuman speed. Harrison and Fairfax arrived at the warehouse together. The latter, after a few brief words with another officer, climbed the small metal gate at the side of the building and then shinned up the drainpipe. While Fairfax was making his way up the pipe PC Harrison had gone right round the block to the back of the premises in Upper Drayton Place, climbed over a fence and on to the roof of the factory backing No. 25 Tamworth Road, then crawled from there across the warehouse roof and dropped down into the garden of No. 26. He then roused the people in No. 26, made his way right through the house and out into Tamworth Road. Presumably he had not gone out into Tamworth Road to admire the view, but to establish what his colleagues were doing and also to report that he had not as yet established contact with the two reported intruders: this would have necessitated walking completely along the front of the building to the small metal gate, and possibly climbing that metal gate; he would then have retraced his steps, gone back into No. 26, through the house out into the garden, climbed back on to the warehouse roof that ran along one side of the garden, then crawled along the asbestos roof and made his way to the chimney-stack. He apparently achieved all of this and was standing by the chimney-stack before Fairfax got to the top of the pipe.

Harrison then recounted a conversation he had had with Fairfax as his colleague walked down the roof towards the lift-head and grabbed Bentley – a conversation that Fairfax had been unable to recall in the witness box. Harrison said Fairfax had then taken Bentley *towards the entrance to the roof* and on their way Bentley had broken away from Fairfax and shouted 'Let him have it, Chris'. Here there is a serious conflict between the two versions. If Fairfax's version is correct then Harrison's cannot possibly be. On the evidence of Fairfax he, Craig, and Bentley were at that crucial moment *totally masked from Harrison by the lift-head*. If the evidence of Fairfax is correct, it follows that Harrison could not possibly have witnessed what he said he saw. Equally, if Harrison is right then Fairfax is mistaken. The same applies in relation to the evidence of Harrison and McDonald concerning Craig's position when he was firing at Harrison. It will be recalled that McDonald placed Craig, at that particular moment in the gun battle, to the left of the lift-head, while Harrison placed him to the right. There is a total contradiction.

Yet another of the many contradictions was established when Harrison described the moment that Miles died. Questioning him was Humphreys' colleague, John Bass.

BASS: What did Miles do when he got to the top of the stairs?

HARRISON: Well, he went straight at the door, *he pushed the bar and he kicked the door open and stepped out and as he stepped out a shot was fired from the direction of the lift-shaft* and he dropped.

BASS: When he had dropped did you see somebody?

HARRISON: I did.

BASS: Who was that?

HARRISON: I saw the prisoner Craig come *from behind the lift-shaft*. He was still holding the revolver in his two hands.

There are three worrying aspects to that interchange. Firstly, Harrison's account of what happened when PC Miles arrived at the closed door differs significantly from that of Fairfax, who in his original deposition had said: 'At this stage the door of the staircase head burst open and I heard officers calling to me. I told them I was round to their right and that the fellow with the gun was round to their left. I then saw PC Miles jump from the doorway of the staircase head and as he did so there was a loud report and he fell to the floor.'

Secondly, although he was inside the staircase head, Harrison was able to identify the direction from which the shot had come, yet a little later, Fairfax, in an identical position, was unable to hear a subsequent shot, let alone identify the direction from which it came.

Thirdly, Harrison's description of Craig's position. Immediately Miles fell, Harrison looked out and saw Craig come *from behind the lift-shaft*; this makes it very likely that *when Miles was shot there was a concrete building nearly seven feet thick between him and Craig*. And according to McDonald, Craig was up on the sloping roof when Miles was shot.

The contradictions are too many and too numerous, the inconsistencies too frequent. The various versions do not even tally in substance.

One would have expected these contradictions and these inconsistencies to have been the subject of considerable comment during Lord Goddard's address to the jury but *there is not one single reference to them.* A man's life was at stake, yet the same carelessness, the same inattention to detail that had characterized Matheson's report on Bentley, was now a predominant feature of the trial. On occasions in the past Lord Goddard had seen fit to adjourn a court in order to visit the scene of the event. Indeed a few years later Iris Bentley appeared before Lord Goddard in a case in which she claimed damages from her employer after a fall down some steps and Lord Goddard adjourned the Court and everybody went to Streatham to look at the cinema steps. If he had taken the same course of action and gone to the Croydon rooftop, Derek Bentley would be alive today. As it was, as Bentley's trial progressed, the Judge was content to let confusion, inconsistency, and contradiction run rife. Injustice was not only being done, it was being seen to be done.

A stream of policemen came to the witness box. But three who did not appear were PC Pain, PC Bugden and PC Alderson. Like the three monkeys they had heard nothing, seen nothing, and now they were saying nothing.

When Dr Jazwon, the physician who had treated Fairfax at Croydon General Hospital, gave evidence, John Parris tried to establish the exact nature of the police officer's wound and also exactly how it had, in the doctor's opinion, been caused. He established that the bullet had passed over the surface of the skin and that there had been no penetration. He established that the injury indicated that the bullet was travelling upwards and over the shoulder. He established that the bullet had come, therefore, from a low level. That was all he was allowed to establish. When Parris tried to find out if the injury that Fairfax had sustained was consistent with a bullet ricocheting upwards from the ground, Lord Goddard quickly intervened, questioning Dr Jazwon's competence to answer such a question. When the doctor replied that he did not really think he was competent to answer the question, Parris had lost, through the Judge's intervention, a vital opportunity to establish, from an independent source, the validity of the Defence version of how Fairfax had been shot. Having brought the cross-examination to a full stop with his intervention, Lord Goddard then apologized to Dr Jazwon for the inconvenience of having to travel from Manchester to give evidence and opined that his evidence could have been read from the doctor's original deposition made at the Croydon Court. Parris however, in his closing speech, rightly remarked that the doctor had contributed something that did not appear in his original deposition: the bullet that hit Fairfax had come *upwards*. It was a powerful confirmation of the Defence contention of the circumstances surrounding the firing of the first shot, that Fairfax, having walked Bentley from the lift-head to the roof entrance, left him there and then came back for Craig. The sixteen-year-old then produced his gun, pointed it at the ground between himself and Fairfax and fired, *without any prompting from Bentley, who had not opened his mouth*.

The next witness was pathologist Dr David Haler. His evidence was confined to a few formal details concerning the post-mortem that he had performed on the body of PC Miles. If either of the Defence Counsel had risen and asked just one question – what was the calibre of bullet that killed Miles? – the trial of Craig and Bentley would have had a very different course, for it would, in my opinion, have shown that whoever did kill PC Miles it was certainly not Christopher Craig.[1] But Dr Haler left the witness box without the questions being asked. Normally after giving evidence Dr Haler remained in court to hear the rest of the trial. On this occasion he had an urgent appointment and left immediately. Had he stayed, the implications of the knowledge, that at that time he may have possessed, might well have

[1] These observations are based on the comments that Dr Haler made to me when I interviewed him on 6 March 1971. As previously indicated, he subsequently denied the statements that I have attributed to him. This aspect is dealt with in the Epilogue.

been apparent to him before the Prosecution had finished their case.

Dr Freebody then gave evidence of Craig's injuries. In cross-examination he agreed that Craig could have been concussed by his dive from the roof. The doctor could not be categoric, for he had not examined the teenager until three days after the gun battle. Christmas Humphreys, obviously seeing the enormous damage that could be wreaked to the Prosecution case if it could be established that Craig had been unconscious when admitted to the hospital, confined his re-examination of the witness to this specific area.

HUMPHREYS: It has been put to you that he was possibly concussed. You were called in as an expert to examine what his injuries were. Is that right?
FREEBODY: Yes.
HUMPHREYS: Did you find any evidence as you saw him, or indeed, in the clinical report that was given to you, that he was in the least concussed?
FREEBODY: No.
LORD CHIEF JUSTICE: There was no injury to his head, was there?
FREEBODY: No, my Lord.

Dr Freebody was of course basing his conclusions on an examination of Craig carried out three days after the time in question, and a colleague's report. There was no question about Craig's consciousness on Wednesday, 5 November. What was in dispute, and still is, was his condition at 10.30 p.m. on Sunday, 2 November. If Counsel had questioned the doctor who had examined Craig on his admittance to hospital, yet another mystery might have been solved. It would then have been possible to establish if Fairfax is correct in recalling – as Craig himself recalls – that Craig was unconscious during the journey to hospital and the remainder of the night, or if, as Detective Sergeant Shepherd and Inspector Smith contended, they had spoken

187

to Craig less than an hour after the youth had been admitted to the hospital.

In view of the remarks that the two policemen in charge of the investigation attributed to Craig, it was surely in the interests of justice to establish beyond any doubt whatsoever whether he was conscious at the material time. But the jury had to rely on the inconclusive evidence of Dr Freebody. Considering that the witness box had been occupied only a few minutes before by Dr Jazwon, and that it was Jazwon who had initially treated Craig on the night of Sunday, 2 November, this was a truly extraordinary situation. When I interviewed Dr Jazwon he was unable to refer to the notes he made at the time of Craig's admittance to Croydon General Hospital, since these would have remained in Craig's file at the Hospital, and that file has regrettably now been destroyed. The doctor's observations, therefore, were based only on his memory of the events. *His recollections nevertheless confirmed the accounts of Craig's condition that were given to me by Fairfax and Craig himself. Craig was unconscious when he was admitted to Croydon.*

With regard to Detective Sergeant Fairfax, Dr Jazwon was able to elaborate on the evidence he gave at the trial. There was no trace either on the policeman's clothes or on his shoulder of any powder burns. If he had been hit by a ·45 bullet fired at virtually point blank range, there would undoubtedly have been powder-burn traces.

The next witness was yet another doctor, who gave evidence about the various drugs that had been given to Craig after his admittance to Croydon Hospital. John Parris established that one which had been administered several times was pentathol. This is commonly known as a 'truth drug', although that is something of a misnomer. When administered in a certain manner, however, it does undermine the recipient's will and remove inhibitions, so that the patient talks more freely than he normally would. Parris' intention was clear: he hoped to demonstrate to the jury that the terrible remarks that had poured from Craig's

188

lips as he lay in a hospital bed were caused by drugs. (If the jury had heard the lunch-time, drug-free, comment that Craig had made about Detective Sergeant Fairfax, they might have been in a better position to evaluate this contention.)

When Detective Sergeant Shepherd gave evidence he read out the statement that Bentley was alleged to have made at Croydon Police Station. The vagueness about the time factor passed unnoticed. Neither was there any comment about the number of times that Bentley had signed the statement. In view of the evidence recorded in the previous chapter, the opening passages of Shepherd's cross-examination by Frank Cassels are of particular interest.

CASSELS: Sergeant Shepherd, I just want to ask you about this statement. First of all, it is right, is it not, that Bentley is illiterate? He cannot read or write?

SHEPHERD: So he says.

CASSELS: Well, can he write, do you think from what is said, anything apart from his own signature?

SHEPHERD: He appeared to have difficulty in writing his name, Sir.

CASSELS: From the enquiries that have been made in the case is it right that he is close to being a feeble-minded person? Do you know that?

SHEPHERD: No, Sir, I do not know that.

That was it. Bentley's whole history dismissed in a few words. Although Detective Sergeant Shepherd was second in command in the investigation, he apparently did not know the truth about Bentley's mental level. Since Shepherd and Inspector Smith had been personally responsible for getting Dr Matheson much of the information contained in the Prison Medical Officer's report, this interchange seems, in my opinion, to disclose a rather unhealthy anxiety to secure Bentley's conviction. Here was the second-in-command dismissing, without comment or acknowledgment, all the evidence summarized in Chapter

4. He was assisted in this by Frank Cassels, who, instead of pressing the issue, allowed it to pass. Even assuming that a copy of Matheson's report had not been given to Cassels (an assumption that I am not prepared to make), Bentley's Counsel still had at his fingertips all the information that John Stevens had collected. *All this information was contained in Cassels' brief but he used not one jot of it.* After the trial a number of observers commented that judging by his performance in the witness box, Bentley needed protection from himself.

If Bentley needed help, he was entitled to expect more from his Counsel. Cassels admitted to me that prior to the trial he had told John Parris 'that both the little bastards ought to swing'. He has not veered from that viewpoint and still holds it today. When I showed him Bentley's mental history, and suggested that if the truth about Bentley's condition had been brought out at the trial it would have had a tremendous effect he said, 'Yes, but that would have meant he'd have gone to Broadmoor, and who wants that?' Frank Cassels' view is that 'anybody who carries a gun and kills a policeman ought to hang'; the fact is that Bentley did neither of these things.

Continuing his cross-examination of Shepherd, Cassels tried to show that the statement had been obtained by means of a series of questions, and was not spontaneous. Shepherd could not be shaken in his assertion that the statement was obtained in an entirely proper manner. After he stood down, six more policemen gave evidence, mainly concerning the remarks that Craig may or may not have made in hospital. Thus ended the first day of the trial. The Bentley family were still waiting patiently in the corridor to be called.

On the second day, the only reference to Bentley's mental capabilities occurred during Frank Cassels' cross-examination of Detective Chief Inspector Smith, the man in charge of the investigation.

CASSELS: Mr Smith, you have made enquiries, no doubt, with regard to the accused, Bentley?

SMITH: Yes, Sir.

CASSELS: Do you agree with me that he is below average intelligence for his age?

SMITH: Oh yes, Sir.

CASSELS: Well below it?

SMITH: Below, Sir. I cannot say well below.

CASSELS: So far as you can ascertain, is he capable of reading and writing anything else but his own name?

SMITH: He can. His schoolmaster said he could, but with difficulty.

CASSELS: With difficulty?

SMITH: Yes, Sir.

And again that was it. From this, and the interchange with Shepherd, the jury would be correct in assuming that although Bentley was perhaps a little dim, there was nothing seriously wrong with him. No mention of the IQ tests, either of those made at Kingswood and showing, a few days after he left the school where 'the master considered that he could read and write but with difficulty', that Bentley had an IQ of 66 and a reading age of four and a half years, or of the tests at Brixton Prison. No mention of the repeated findings of epilepsy, or the frequent epileptic attacks. No mention of Dr Munroe's diagnosis. No mention of the National Service Medical. *No mention, in fact, of any of the information contained in Chapter 4.*

Eighteen years after the trial, Mr Smith was able to recall, during my interview with him, that he had been advised by Bentley's teachers that the youth had a mental age of nine. It seems he had been unable to recall that fact during the Old Bailey trial.

The evidence of the final witness for the Prosecution revealed a number of highly pertinent facts, several of which escaped the notice of the entire Court. This final witness was Lewis Nickolls, the Prosecution's ballistics

191

expert. The police had given Mr Nickolls Craig's revolver, the sawn-off barrel found in Craig's loft, and an assorted collection of bullets and cartridges found on the roof. Obviously he had not been given the bullet that had killed PC Miles. Guns are rather like fingers; they leave unique marks. Give a ballistics expert twelve spent bullets and twelve revolvers and after microscopic examination he will say with 100% accuracy which gun fired which bullet. In the case of the fatal bullet there would undoubtedly have been blood traces on it, a point that was made abundantly clear when John Parris opened his cross-examination.

PARRIS: Mr Nickolls, Exhibit 8 is, in all probability, the fatal bullet, is it not, found near the staircase head?
NICKOLLS: *I could find no evidence of blood on it whatsoever. Therefore, in all probability, it is not the fatal bullet.*

Undoubtedly all the bullets handed to Mr Nickolls were subjected to an intensive microscopic examination. If any of the bullets had given the slightest indication of being the fatal bullet this point would, no doubt, have been immediately established by the Prosecution Counsel. *The fact is that there was not at any time, either before, during, or after the trial, any ballistic evidence to prove that Craig had fired the shot that killed PC Miles. In fact there was a startling amount of ballistic evidence to prove his innocence.*

PARRIS: Turning to the revolver, one of the effects of sawing the barrel off is, of course, that you remove the sight.
NICKOLLS: You do.
PARRIS: The second thing is this, that when rifling is removed the weapon becomes wholly inaccurate.
NICKOLLS: It becomes less accurate.
PARRIS: Well, how inaccurate would you say that would make it?
NICKOLLS: I should say that this weapon, certainly in the hands of a person unaccustomed to firing it, was quite an inaccurate weapon.

PARRIS: Then you agree with me that it would be wholly inaccurate?

NICKOLLS: Not quite, no Sir. I think a person could train himself to use it.

PARRIS: May I put it to you that it would be inaccurate to the degree of six feet at a range of thirty-nine feet.

NICKOLLS: Oh yes.

PARRIS: Quite as much as that?

NICKOLLS: I think it would be of that order, yes.

No evidence was at any time offered that Craig had fired this particular gun prior to that Sunday evening. (He had in fact previously fired one bullet into his bedroom ceiling, which can hardly be called 'training himself to use it'.) Mr Nickolls considered that the undersize bullets (·44 calibre) that Craig had used would make the revolver 'completely inaccurate'; as for the other bullets, it was not established how accurate they would be fired from Craig's revolver, only that they would not make for wholly accurate firing. The degree of inaccuracy at thirty-nine feet was highly significant, for this was the distance between Craig and PC Miles.

The information that John Parris had elicited was not for the purpose of establishing that another hand had held the gun that killed PC Miles. Parris, like everybody else in that courtroom, was unaware that there were any armed policemen other than Detective Sergeant Fairfax in the vicinity of the roof. Parris, working on the manslaughter defence, was bent on demonstrating to the jury that Miles had been killed accidentally by Craig. The thought that he had been killed accidentally by someone else did not apparently occur to anyone at the time.

Yet another singular aspect of the case for the Prosecution was that time somehow became telescoped. Christmas Humphreys said in his opening speech, 'The whole of the gun fight seems to have taken twenty to twenty-five minutes.' That may well be as it seemed to him, but even a cursory examination of the police depositions reveals that it took considerably longer. The police were at Barlow & Parkers by 9.25 p.m. at the very latest. They may well have been there five minutes earlier, as Mrs Ware had seen the two youths climbing over the gates at 9.15 p.m. and she stated during the trial that they arrived 'in about four minutes'. Her husband had run to the phone box in his road. The distance from Tamworth Road to the police station is about half a mile. Even with the most generous allowances for Mr Ware and the police car, Fairfax would have been over the iron gates of the wholesalers' several minutes before 9.25 p.m. PC James Ross did not arrive at the wholesalers' until 9.55 p.m., but he was still in time to hear several shots. On two occasions he heard Craig shout. On one occasion Craig raised his arm and fired in Ross's direction, who was by then standing in Upper Drayton Place. Undoubtedly Ross had arrived at Barlow & Parkers before Fairfax bundled Bentley downstairs, went right down to the ground, was given a gun and then made his way upstairs to continue the fight. It would have taken Ross at least ten minutes to get round the block and witness all this. This means that Craig did not dive from that roof before 10.05 at the very earliest. The overall duration of the battle, therefore, is forty minutes, maybe longer, but certainly very close to double the time estimated by Christmas Humphreys and accepted without question. One can only speculate as to the effect all of this would have had on the minds of the jury. Had the information about Craig's revolver been used to illustrate not only the high improbability that he could deliberately kill at thirty-nine feet, but the probability that another hand had held another gun (and in forty minutes the police had had time to call out an armoured division), then the ultimate verdict should have been 'Not Guilty'.

When Christmas Humphreys was re-examining his ballistics expert he took pains to establish that, inaccurate or not, if the gun had been fired at somebody standing six feet away the person would have been hit. Although this was highly relevant to the attack on Fairfax, it was irrelevant as far as this trial was concerned; the two teenagers were on trial for murder, not attempted murder.

Humphreys then attempted to relate the same degree of accuracy to the shot allegedly fired at Miles.

HUMPHREYS: Now, we do not know exactly where Craig was standing, but give him the maximum distance of forty feet away: if he fired at such people as are coming out of the staircase head, and fired more than once with correct ammunition, was there a reasonable chance of hitting them, or one of them or some of them?
NICKOLLS: I think it would be an extremely dangerous thing to do.

It might well have seemed to Christmas Humphreys that the sands from under his feet at that moment were beginning to shift uncomfortably. He was, however, about to receive help from an unexpected quarter.

LORD CHIEF JUSTICE: Mr Humphreys, this is a case in which an officer of justice was murdered, shot.
HUMPHREYS: Yes, my Lord.
L.C.J.: Very different considerations, as you know, apply where an officer of justice in the course of the execution of his duty is killed.
HUMPHREYS: Yes, my Lord; but, with great respect, I was following up with this witness what I imagine to be – I may be wrong – the beginning of a certain line of defence.
L.C.J.: Well, if that defence is run I shall tell the jury that that is no defence at all.
HUMPHREYS: If your Lordship please. My Lord, that is the case for the Prosecution.

John Parris was later to write, 'All this which took place in the hearing of the jury was, of course, scarcely the happiest note on which to call evidence for the Defence, especially since the Judge had, in his first remark, begged the very question the jury were trying.'

With a glance to his parents, Christopher Craig walked slowly to the witness box. His demeanour contrasted sharply with that of the sixteen-year-old boy who had held the police at bay with a gun for at least forty minutes. Now his manner was in keeping with the conservative clothes that Parris had so shrewdly insisted upon. Gone was the bravado and the capacity for great evil, the Court saw only the gentle, shy, bible-class-attending boy. This was no act, for within Craig were several people. His answers were given in a voice that was little more than a whisper. Lord Goddard and Christmas Humphreys, in particular, had great difficulty in hearing him. During his examination-in-chief, Humphreys five times interrupted to clarify what Craig had said, while Lord Goddard interrupted eleven times, either for the same purpose, or to ask questions of his own.

The reason for all the interjections that Lord Goddard made throughout the entire trial is not so obvious. On even the most favourable interpretation, over two hundred and fifty interjections during the day and a half that evidence was given, resulted in evidence being produced that was harmful to Craig and Bentley, or damaging to their case. Quite obviously the Lord Chief Justice did not share the view of one of his predecessors, Lord Hewart, who said, 'The business of a judge is to hold his tongue until the last possible moment.' One looks in vain for a further two hundred and fifty interjections from Lord Goddard that resulted in evidence being produced which supported or helped Craig and Bentley. *In fact, one looks in vain for a single interjection that had this effect.* Is this normal trial procedure? I would like to think that very little of what took place at No. 2 Central Criminal Court during the second week of December 1952 was normal trial procedure.

Frank Cassels had expressed the fear to John Parris during their pre-trial conference that if Craig was put into the witness box his cross-examination could result in damage being done to Bentley's defence. Superficial examination of the interchanges between Humphreys and Craig would appear to justify that fear. Craig stated that as the police were surrounding the warehouse and Fairfax was climbing the drainpipe, he had told Bentley that he had a gun and ammunition. Humphreys rightly considered that this clearly showed that Bentley knew Craig had a loaded revolver prior to the shooting. When he made his final speech to the jury he hammered this point home. What he did not do was to follow through the logic of Craig's admission. If Craig told Bentley that he had a gun and ammunition only a few minutes before his friend was grabbed by Fairfax, Bentley clearly had no knowledge of this fact before that moment. Craig's evidence makes it quite clear that it had not been a gratuitous comment. He was informing Bentley for the first time that he'd brought the gun and ammunition. If he had told Bentley before they had embarked on their journey to Croydon, Bentley would have stayed in Norbury. Clearly, when he learned about the gun and ammunition, there was precious little he could do about it, except give himself up. It is understandable that Humphreys should choose to ignore this; it was not his function to do Defence Counsel's work for him. Against that it could be argued, and I would argue, that if a trial is not to secure a conviction but to discover the truth, then justice is only served well if *all* concerned work towards that end. Frank Cassels saw the logic but could do little with it while Bentley insisted that he did not know at any time prior to the first shot that Craig was armed, and Bentley did insist just that, not only in the witness box, but for the rest of his life.

Craig was quite prepared to tell the truth in the witness box. The sixteen-year-old admitted that he and Bentley had associated after their fathers had forbidden the continuation of the relationship. He told the Court how many guns had passed through his hands over the years. He told the Court where he had obtained the ·45 revolver. He told how he had sawn a piece off the barrel so that the gun would fit into his pocket. He told how he had collected the ammunition, that had been found in the attic of his house, from the rifle range at Caterham Barracks. He told how he and Bentley had set out that night to break into a butcher's shop. He told how he had made the knuckleduster. He admitted that he knew that Fairfax was a police officer before the first shot. Although apparently the only one to know, he told how many shots he had fired on the roof. He admitted, in fact, a great many things that he could easily have suppressed. It is interesting, therefore, to note a few of the things that he did deny. He denied that Bentley had any prior knowledge of the gun and ammunition and continued to deny it, although closely questioned by Prosecuting Counsel and the Judge on this point. He denied that Bentley told him not to use the gun, a remark that Bentley too denied making. He also stated categorically that Bentley did not say 'Let him have it, Chris'. He denied firing directly at PC Miles, and said that all of the shots that he had fired in the direction of the roof entrance had been directed over the garden of No. 30 Tamworth Road. Despite this he accepted that he had killed Miles, although he also stated that the first time he knew he had, was on Wednesday, 5 November, when the assumption that Craig had fired the bullet had become a 'fact' via the national press.

As John Parris listened he must have regretted brushing aside Frank Cassels' arguments. Whatever effect Craig's evidence had on Bentley's defence, his honesty undoubtedly destroyed to a great extent the defence that Parris had been at such pains to build up. Ironically, in Bentley's case, it was his dishonesty that was to destroy him.

When Bentley went into the witness box his total illiteracy prevented him reading the oath. As the Clerk of the Court intoned, Bentley duly repeated his words.

Of Bentley's performance in the witness box little could be added to the two following descriptions. Arthur Smith, in his biography of Lord Goddard, said: 'Bentley emerged from these proceedings as little more than a kind of zombie.'

Reginald Paget, QC, MP, said in *Hanged and Innocent*, 'It would not be correct to say that Bentley made a fool of himself in the witness box – God had already done that for Bentley.' Unlike Craig he would not admit that they had set out that night with the intention of breaking into a butcher's shop. Bentley's version was that they had merely gone to Croydon for a walk round, and that when his friend had climbed over the gates of Barlow & Parkers he had merely followed without a word being spoken. To Bentley's simple mind this explanation obviously seemed highly rational; to the jury it must have sounded absurd. These, and a number of other lies, must have seriously diminished the possibility of the jury believing Bentley on the aspects that really mattered. He did finally admit that he and Craig were intent on theft. But by then it was too late.

If the cross-examination of Bentley by Christmas Humphreys, and Lord Goddard had been conducted under the Marquis of Queensberry's rules, it would soon have been stopped to avoid Bentley taking further punishment. Under a hail of rhetorical questions, he stumbled from denial to denial. Looked at objectively, the cross-examination was virtually a speech to the jury. At one point, forgetting momentarily that Bentley was totally illiterate – he had just seen him take the oath – Humphreys asked Bentley to read the statement he had made to the police, and had to be reminded by Lord Goddard that the youth could not read, so he was obliged to read it out loud himself. When Bentley protested that the statement had been obtained by the police in answer to questions that they had asked, Humphreys, surprisingly, agreed with him. Perhaps he was, by now, too full of righteous indignation to realize that in so doing, he was calling two of his own witnesses liars.

Every police witness had confirmed the Prosecuting Counsel's opening remarks that 'Bentley was under arrest and in custody at the time PC Miles was shot'. Just three references in Bentley's evidence dealt with this aspect.

They are dealt with in Chapter 6, for they were to form an integral part of Bentley's Appeal.

The last part of the cross-examination accurately reflects what Bentley had to contend with in the witness box, and also perhaps why he was sunk without a trace.

HUMPHREYS: And you were still on the roof when the shooting was going on?
BENTLEY: Yes, Sir.
HUMPHREYS: Your mind was still with Craig?
BENTLEY: My mind, Sir?
HUMPHREYS: Yes.
BENTLEY: No, Sir.
HUMPHREYS: You were doing nothing to stop him doing what you had come up to do together – break in?
BENTLEY: We'd come to break in, not to kill, Sir.
HUMPHREYS: You had had your weapons taken away from you by the police?
BENTLEY: I gave him the knuckleduster, Sir.
HUMPHREYS: He found the knife?
BENTLEY: Yes, Sir.
HUMPHREYS: And had taken it away from you?
BENTLEY: Yes, Sir.
HUMPHREYS: And you couldn't do a thing?
BENTLEY: No, Sir.
HUMPHREYS: You did nothing to stop him from shooting?
BENTLEY: No, Sir.
HUMPHREYS: In fact you incited him to do something further; you shouted, 'Look out, Chris. They're taking me down.'
BENTLEY: That was in case he shot me, Sir.
THE LORD CHIEF JUSTICE: You were only thinking of your own skin, you mean?
BENTLEY: If he shot me there were two other police officers with me.
HUMPHREYS: You were frightened he might shoot at the police and hit you by mistake?
BENTLEY: He might have hit anybody, Sir.

HUMPHREYS: The police didn't matter! In fact Sergeant Fairfax, having been hit, takes you behind the staircase head for cover, and then you volunteer the remark when McDonald comes up – I think I have already put it to you, and you say you didn't say it – 'I told the silly bugger not to use it'; but did you also say to the officers later 'Look out! He'll blow your heads off'?

BENTLEY: I can't remember saying that, Sir.

HUMPHREYS: You knew he was a thoroughly dangerous and irresponsible person with a gun in his hand, didn't you?

BENTLEY: At that time when he was shooting, yes, Sir.

HUMPHREYS: And well before you got on the roof?

BENTLEY: No, Sir.

HUMPHREYS: And when you thought you were being taken down, you incited him further, so that you might get away from the police?

BENTLEY: If I'd done as you said, Sir, I might have been shot myself.

HUMPHREYS: I see – still thinking of your own skin. In other words, you were prepared to assist Craig to use such hitting with knuckledusters, or stabbing with daggers, or shooting with revolvers at the police as would enable you to escape if caught in the crime you were committing?

BENTLEY: No, Sir.

CASSELS: My Lord, that is the case for Bentley.

Bentley's cross-examination by Christmas Humphreys should stand for ever as a perpetual monument to emotional rhetoric. Why Frank Cassels allowed the Prosecuting Counsel to run on unchecked is difficult to imagine. Humphreys' righteous indignation leaps off the page; his performance transcends normal cross-examination. In theory a man is innocent until proved guilty, but it would be more accurate to say that Bentley was treated in precisely the reverse manner. I believe that one reason for this is that not one jot of the information contained in the previous chapter, and only a fragment of Bentley's statement to his solicitor, John Stevens, was used by Cassels. In that statement, Bentley told how, after Fairfax had been shot, he had stayed by his side and pulled his jacket to one side to see how badly the officer was injured. He told how he called out to Craig at that moment, 'You bloody fool.' Then, after Fairfax had recovered and they had walked to the roof-entrance wall, Fairfax had said, 'If you stand there you should be safe', which Bentley did. Earlier in his statement, he said that upon the approach of Fairfax he had walked out from behind the lift-head and *given himself up*'. Quite clearly Bentley was submitting to arrest and was accepting the fact. When PC Miles fell, virtually at Bentley's feet, and was subsequently pulled behind the wall, Craig had called out, 'Is he dead?' To which Bentley replied, 'Yes he is, you rotten sod.' All of this would have had a powerful effect on the jury if it had been brought out in evidence; none of it was.

Because of the implications raised by Craig's defence, the jury withdrew while Counsel discussed a point of law with Lord Goddard. It will be remembered that Parris had based his defence of Craig on the premise that Miles' death was accidental and not the result of a deliberate act. If this contention was allowed to go forward to the jury then there was a possibility that in the case of Craig the verdict would be reduced to manslaughter. As the legal argument developed, John Parris cited various cases that in his opinion supported his point of view. One of the cases, Rex *v.* Appleby, was astonishingly similar to that of Craig and Bentley; these similarities were not discussed during the legal argument but they are worth recording.

In 1940 two men, Appleby and Ostler, tried to break into a warehouse. They were surprised by the police as they made their getaway. Appleby was unarmed but was later alleged to have said, *'Let him have it,* he is all alone'; whereupon Ostler produced a gun and shot the officer, who before dying told a colleague of Appleby's remark. The words he used were largely instrumental in hanging him. John Parris was later to comment on this singular fact in *Most of my Murders*. 'It is a strange coincidence that, in

202

the only two reported cases this century of joint liability for the murder of a police officer, exactly the same words should have been used. The case of Appleby is, of course, one that anybody would look up if they wanted to know whether, if one of two house-breakers does the shooting, the other can be found guilty of murder.'

This was not, of course, the reason that the case of Appleby was now being quoted in the Old Bailey. During Appleby's unsuccessful appeal various other cases had been quoted and it was these that Parris was pinning his hopes on. It says volumes for his powers of persuasion that Lord Goddard, who was disposed at first not to let the issue of manslaughter go to the jury, finally agreed to leave open a possible verdict of manslaughter.

Having clarified the law in relation to Christopher Craig, Lord Goddard defined Bentley's position. It was agreed that in his case different considerations arose, and that, before he could be found guilty, it had to be established beyond all reasonable doubt that (in the words of the Lord Chief Justice), 'He must be aware that Craig was armed, and the jury must be satisfied that he intended with Craig to offer violent resistance.'

This definition of the law with regard to Bentley was accepted without question by Prosecuting and Defence Counsel.

So, after the lunchtime adjournment on the second day, Christmas Humphreys rose to make his final speech.

Realizing from the legal argument before lunch that Parris would cite Rex *v.* Appleby in his final address to support his contention that Craig was guilty of no more than manslaughter, Humphreys shrewdly decided to spike his opponent's guns, and began by citing the same case. But he was citing another extract, to demonstrate that Craig was undoubtedly guilty of murder.

With regard to the very great number of contradictions in the evidence of the various police witnesses, Humphreys had this to say:

'You will bear in mind that the evidence is not entirely the same; some heard one phrase which others did not hear, and some remembered a particular phrase slightly differently, and you may think that this is inevitable in the course of a gun fight in the dark, with the consequent excitement' – which should surely stand as a definitive example of British understatement.

Having advised the jury, albeit in a perfunctory manner, to consider the police evidence with caution, Humphreys attacked Craig for having the temerity to say in the witness box that some of the police evidence was incorrect. He then quoted a number of remarks attributed to Craig as he lay in a hospital bed, and concluded that they indicated that the boy's only regret was that he had not shot other policemen. In view of Craig's attitude on the roof and in the hospital, and of his remark about Fairfax on the first day of the trial, this would appear to be fair comment. During this attack on Craig, however, the Prosecuting Counsel selected only those parts of Craig's evidence that supported his case and used them to illustrate his own arguments. Those parts of Craig's evidence that did not suit his case, or contradicted it, were discounted as untrue. Humphreys concluded the argument, 'I say no more upon the case concerning Craig. I ask you to say that it is beyond argument.' He then turned to Bentley.

'Bentley is quite a different proposition. Two men are charged together with being concerned in a common enterprise, as a result of which Police Constable Miles was killed, but you must find a verdict separately against each, because different considerations apply. It is right that in respect of Bentley he never had a gun in his hand, and he was, except in the case of Sergeant Fairfax, a substantial distance away from Craig while he was firing, and was, in fact, physically speaking, almost at the receiving end of Craig's line of fire at the time Police Constable Miles was killed. You will bear that in mind. You will also bear in mind that to some extent it is difficult to say now to what extent Bentley was under arrest. I opened to you in

Bentley's favour that during the actual murder of Police Constable Miles he was physically under arrest. Bentley will not have it; Bentley is saying he was not, that he was not being held, that he was free to get away, and in such case, if there is any assistance to him in the story that he was actually physically controlled at the time when Craig shot Police Constable Miles, that assistance no longer applies, because he has knocked it from under his feet. He now says he was not under arrest, so that you need not trouble with that item of assistance to him any longer. But he has agreed that he knew they were going to break into that warehouse; whether he knew moments before they got on to the roof or whether he knew perfectly well, as he says in his statement, it is quite clear that he knew they were going to that warehouse for that purpose; he has agreed that he was in a common enterprise of crime with Craig.

"The all-important matter for you to consider is the evidence that he knew Craig had upon him a loaded gun. You will have to consider, on the one hand, the evidence of a number of police officers and Craig, and on the other hand Bentley's word; because Craig there has let him down. Craig says, "We discussed the gun before it was ever fired for the first time." I will not trouble you in detail with all the statements which at different times he made to the police officers. Of course, the most important is the deliberate incitement which began the shooting; did he, or did he not, say right at the beginning of the incident to Craig while he was with Sergeant Fairfax, "Let him have it, Chris"? Three separate police officers – McDonald at the bottom of the drainpipe, Fairfax at the receiving end of the bullet, and Harrison away to the right, as you look at the plan, on the roof – heard that statement. Therefore it was shouted. Bentley asks you to say he did not hear it and that it was not said. If it was said, what does it mean but that he knew that Craig had a gun, and he was urging him to use it? Why? Because he had been arrested. "Let him have it, Chris." And what was the answer showing that Craig understood that incitement, but a bullet which

205

hit Sergeant Fairfax? If you believe that, you need not look much further, but in fact, at a later stage, if you believe the evidence for the Prosecution, he is saying, "I told the silly bugger not to use it." What does that mean except that there had been prior conversation about the gun, and he expressed some opinion about it? Then again, "He's got a ·45 Colt and plenty of ammunition for it too." So he not only knew he had a gun, but he knew it was loaded, and he knew what the gun was.

'Were those statements made, or have all these officers dreamed this evidence for the Prosecution against this young man? If they were made, what does it mean except that he knew perfectly well that that gun was loaded?

'But in case you think that in the excitement of the fight on the roof in the dark these officers might have imagined things, you get the evidence of two more policemen when it is all over and they are all down on the ground and Bentley is being put in the car, and nobody has got any weapon and there is no more excitement. What does Bentley say? "I knew he had a gun, but I didn't think he'd use it. He's done one of your blokes in."

'Well you have got all that evidence of all those officers and Craig's frank admission, against Bentley's bare denial that he did not know that Craig had a gun, and can you believe he did not know it when you have heard from Craig of his boasting and bragging of his great arsenal of guns, how he wants to be a gunsmith, that he carried it about, and showed it off at school, and swapped with other boys at school, that four or five other boys at school had guns, and a friend he has known for years seems to be the only person who did not know it. Do you believe it?

'But at least Bentley was deliberately armed, was carrying a murderous dagger which he admits would tear the lining of the pocket of his coat – he said it was an old coat – and he was given a knuckleduster on the way to the premises. You shall look at it. When I asked Bentley in terms "Why did you accept it?" he had no reply. What do you think? Why do you think he accepted it unless in order that he might use it if he found it necessary, if the police came near them in the course of the house-breaking they were about to commit? And if Bentley is going to accept a murderous knuckleduster, he is already carrying of his own volition a murderous dagger, are you going to believe he did not know that Craig not only had some other weapon but also a gun? That is for you to say. Craig himself on oath has said that he told Bentley before a shot was fired that he had a gun, and so you have got, I repeat, the evidence of all the officers and Craig against Bentley's bare word; and if you believe those officers, three of them from different points in the darkness, Bentley is actually inciting Craig to begin the shooting in the course of which nine bullets were fired and two police officers were hit.

'Members of the jury, there is only one further observation. Whether or not Bentley was physically in custody and actually held by a police officer throughout the fight, when the officers go to take him down, to show that his mind is still with Craig in their common enterprise and avoiding arrest, you have his statement, "Look out, Chris! They're taking me down", and the answer is a shot in their direction. At no time, or for one moment, throughout the whole of that twenty or twenty-five minutes did Bentley make a sound, either shouting to Craig or even to the police officers, to show that his mind had ceased to be with Craig, and that he was trying to stop Craig shooting and to throw away the gun.

'So you have these two men charged jointly with the murder of this Police Constable. It is the only issue you are trying. They are both sane in law, inasmuch as no attempt whatsoever has been made to suggest to you that they are not. They are both, therefore, young though they be, responsible, like any other citizen, in law, for what they do. You have sworn to return a verdict according to the evidence. What may or may not be the result of your verdict is no concern of yours or any other person in this court, and I must ask you, in accordance with the oath that you have taken, to return a verdict on this indictment of guilty of wilful murder against each of these two young men.'

That is a verbatim record of the Prosecuting Counsel's closing remarks concerning the case against Derek Bentley.

Tony Parker, commenting on Christmas Humphreys' performance when he led the Prosecution in the case of Michael Davies, wrote, 'He moved from facts to opinions and back again in rapid succession throughout, and it is difficult to escape the conclusion, so vehemently did he pile on his scorn, that he was at times personally carried away.'

As a description of Humphreys' performance during the Craig/Bentley trial it cannot be bettered. His comments concerning Bentley's remarks about the issue of his arrest fly in the face of reality. His comments on Craig's statement that Bentley had prior knowledge of the gun should be assessed against Craig's evidence. He quotes Craig saying 'We discussed the gun before it was ever fired for the first time.' Here is the cross-examination covering that aspect of Craig's evidence.

HUMPHREYS: You told him when you were on the roof that you had a gun?
CRAIG: Yes, Sir, when I saw the police.
HUMPHREYS: So before there was any shooting you told him in terms you had a gun?
CRAIG: Yes, Sir.
HUMPHREYS: And it was loaded?
CRAIG: Yes, Sir.
HUMPHREYS: *Was there any discussion about it being used?*
CRAIG: *No, Sir.*

As to the vital remark 'Let him have it, Chris', contrary to Humphreys' contention, McDonald was not at the bottom of the pipe when he heard the alleged remark, he was nearly level with the roof, trying to get his footing to climb down. By placing him at the bottom, the time-lag between

208

the shouts and the shots was thus eliminated. Humphreys also implied that all three officers had sworn that they had heard Bentley make the remark, and that against this was Bentley's bare denial. As has been previously noted, PC McDonald, although pressured by Lord Goddard, refused to commit himself. The fact that Craig, too, had stated categorically that the remark was not uttered, was completely ignored by Christmas Humphreys.

Also ignored is the disturbing absence of PC Alderson from the witness box. The jury heard all about his two colleagues, who had sworn that Bentley while in their car had remarked, 'I knew he had a gun, but I didn't think he'd use it.' Of PC Alderson not a word of reassurance that he had deposed a similar statement, but unfortunately had not been available. He simply melted into the ranks of the policemen missing at the Craig/Bentley trial – PC Pain, PC Bugden and possibly many more.

And it was not enough for the Prosecuting Counsel to refer to the knife and knuckleduster in factual terms, for him they became a murderous dagger, a murderous knuckleduster with a murderous spike, and yet again there was a reference to a murderous dagger. The jury were, or should have been, solely concerned with facts, not emotive expressions. Sir Malcolm Hilbery, in *Duty and Art in Advocacy*, said, 'An advocate must not open any fact as a fact in the case which he is not in a position to prove.' Yet Humphreys, referring in his opening speech to the moment when Bentley was bundled downstairs by the police, said: 'At that moment the police began to take him downstairs and he shouted "Look out, Chris; they're taking me down". The reply was a further burst of firing. You, gentlemen of the jury, will have to interpret all the evidence in this case, and you will have to interpret that further observation by Bentley; made, although he is technically under arrest, while he is still on the roof where the fight is going on and, to all intents and purposes, in the presence of Craig. He is being taken down by the police officer and he calls out "Look out, Chris; they're taking me down". Was that a further invitation? Cry for help? Challenge? What was it? The result was clear: a further burst of firing by Craig.'

He also read out a number of the statements that Craig had allegedly made in hospital, saying before he read them that they were not in dispute.

The 'burst of firing' proved during the course of the trial to be pure hyperbole. PC Harrison stated that he heard *one* shot. Bentley, Detective Sergeant Fairfax, PC McDonald and PC Jaggs heard *nothing*. Not only did Humphreys lead as a fact something that he was never in a position to prove, he compounded the error during his closing speech by totally ignoring the four witnesses who declared that not one shot had been fired in answer to Bentley's remark.

Not only were the statements allegedly made by Craig subsequently disputed, they were hotly disputed.

If one thing is quite clear about Bentley's behaviour on that roof it is that he submitted to his arrest and that his mind, what there was of it, ceased to be with Craig. Even if one accepts the police evidence as being completely and totally true and Bentley and Craig's evidence as completely and totally false, Christmas Humphreys' final remarks are in my view a travesty of the truth.

Sir Malcolm Hilbery, in the book previously quoted, made the following points about the role of prosecuting counsel.

'If he is prosecuting, a particular attitude towards his work in hand is required of the Barrister. As a prosecutor it is his duty to see that every material point is made which supports the prosecution case or destroys the case put forward for the defence. But as prosecution counsel he should not regard his task as one of winning the case. He is an officer of justice. He must present the case against the prisoner relentlessly but with scrupulous fairness. He is not to make merely forensic points or debating scores. There is, perhaps, no occasion when the Barrister is called upon to exhibit a nicer sense of his responsibilities than when prosecuting.'

I leave the reader to judge whether Christmas Humphreys exhibited a particularly nice 'sense of his responsibilities'.

The Prosecuting Counsel sat down, and John Parris rose to make the only speech that the rules of English justice allowed him. After telling the jury that they must decide the case on the evidence and not on remarks such as 'Craig gloried in murder', he attempted to dispel the prejudice that surrounded the name of Christopher Craig throughout the country. It was an impossible task – as impossible as the task of rebutting the overwhelming amount of evidence that existed against Craig. The sixteen-year-old boy, as his Counsel said, had become the national symbol of wayward youth. 'The nation's uneasiness and anxiety about the state of their youth had become focused in him.' Craig listened attentively as his Counsel quoted Tom Paine: 'We must see that our enemies do not suffer injustice.' Parris's one hope lay in convincing the jury that the death of Miles, though admitted by the defence to have been caused by Craig, was an accident, and he cited Rex *v.* Appleby to support his contention that Craig was guilty only of manslaughter. (It must have confused the jury somewhat to have had the same case cited by Prosecuting and Defence Counsels, the first to illustrate that Craig was guilty of murder, the second to illustrate that he was not.) Doubtless this is an example of the law's flexibility that one hears so much about.

Undaunted by the enormity of his task, Parris succeeded in casting serious doubt on the credibility of much of the police evidence. He cited a number of the contradictions, though not all of them by any means: that would have taken days, not hours. As his speech reached its climax, Lord Goddard intervened.

LORD CHIEF JUSTICE: Mr Parris, I think it is only right I should tell the jury that what you are saying to them – no doubt with the best of intentions – is not the law. If all your hypotheses were right, the defence of accident is

211

not open to him, for the reason I shall explain to the jury, and it would be murder.

PARRIS: My Lord, the defence base it on the case of Appleby.

L.C.J.: You have misread it.

To make it abundantly clear that he had not misread it, Parris quoted from the case: 'If in the course of a struggle, he accidentally caused an injury . . . '

L.C.J.: A man does not accidentally cause an injury if he shoots. The act has got to be accidental.

But John Parris was not a man to be deterred by the Lord Chief Justice of England. If Lord Goddard wanted to argue law in an open court, he was prepared to give him an argument.

PARRIS: As I understand it, it was the injury which was accidental. Members of the jury, it is said on behalf of the defence that this was an accident, a tragic accident, and not a deliberate act of murder. May I conclude with one final thing? If this boy had the intention to murder police officers, as is suggested, why did he not kill Sergeant Fairfax when Sergeant Fairfax was within three feet of him, or six feet, on two occasions? I ask you if possible, members of the jury, to return in this case a verdict of manslaughter, which, in the submission of the defence, would be consistent with justice and law.'

If it is true that a trial is a clash of personalities and that one personality, either counsel or judge, will dominate, then for two days John Parris had given as good as he had received. But the last word was to be Lord Goddard's. Meanwhile, however, Frank Cassels rose to speak on behalf of Bentley.

By now, the Bentley family, who had for two days been sitting patiently waiting in the corridor, had realized that they were not going to be called to give evidence. While their son had been on trial for his life they had not heard a word of the case. The world of Kafka had become their world. Totally uncomprehending of the very real danger that their son was in, they were supremely confident that these strange proceedings would result in his returning home. So, it was not until Frank Cassels was making his closing remarks to the jury, that the Bentley family finally got into that courtroom.

Frank Cassels began by reminding the all-male jury that a separate verdict was required for Bentley, and that if, after hearing the evidence, they considered that Craig was guilty of no more than manslaughter, they could not then find Bentley guilty of murder. Consequently, he said, the assumption he had to make in addressing them was that they would find Craig guilty of murder. He went on: 'But, as has been indicated to you, the position with regard to Bentley is quite different in this case: he did not have the gun, he did not fire a shot, and in fact, in spite of what my learned friend Mr Humphreys has said, it may be that describing Bentley's position, at the time when the shot was fired that actually killed Police Constable Miles, as being under arrest, is an accurate description. It was suggested that Bentley had swept the ground from under his feet in relation to that suggestion because he said in the witness box that he was not being held all the time. I will explain to you in due course why I, in defence of Bentley, make that point.'

Cassels then explained the point of the 'joint adventure' principle – that, although the defence admitted that there was joint intent to steal, he would dispute joint intent to use violence.

The point of the case, he summarized, was that 'You have to be satisfied here of two things, first of all that Bentley knew that Craig carried a gun – that is the first matter – and the second matter is: you have to be satisfied that Bentley, knowing that Craig carried a gun, incited him, or counselled him, or inspired him – whatever word

213

you like – to use violence; in other words, to use the gun to resist arrest.'

Cassels then passed to the events on the rooftop prefacing his remarks with this very pertinent observation: 'As my learned friend has suggested, in the heat of battle (or perhaps a more apt expression might be "in the course of any struggle") it is very difficult for those who are taking part in the struggle to put clearly before the members of a jury such as you, something like a month later, an accurate description of what took place, and I am sure that in a serious charge such as this, the most serious that can be brought against any person, you will say to yourselves: "We must be quite certain that we have clearly formed in our minds a picture of what took place on that roof in the evening of Sunday 2 November."'

He also warned them to listen carefully to the evidence and then ask themselves whether it confirmed the Prosecution's allegations – this was a formal move intended to remind the Court that reasonable doubt would suffice for the defence.

'You will remember,' he went on, 'that it is common ground in this case that never at any time at all on that roof did Bentley offer violence to any police officer.' It was remarkable behaviour for one who was, according to the Prosecution, inciting his friend to use violence, that he made no attempt to offer violence to any of the three policemen, Fairfax, McDonald or Harrison, who were within striking distance, nor to rejoin Craig under the cover of the gun, nor indeed to leave the target men.

He then referred to the moment when Fairfax assisted McDonald on to the roof. 'There was a wonderful opportunity, was there not, for a man who wished to be violent towards police officers, for a man who wished to assist his armed colleague in shooting police officers, or at least doing them some injury, so that they might avoid arrest, to take some violent action towards the police officers, or, if he did not wish to do that, there was a wonderful opportunity for him to rejoin his armed colleague, having first sounded

214

some warning to him that he was going to do so. He did not do anything of that kind, members of the jury, and that is what you have to consider in this case, just as much as you have got to consider the various remarks attributed to him either on the rooftop or subsequently when arrested.'

Then, to emphasize this point, Cassels described the moment when PC Miles was shot. 'Both Sergeant Fairfax and Police Constable McDonald went to pull him from where he had fallen, round behind the staircase head – this is the evidence of the police, not the evidence of Bentley – and during that particular time, as Sergeant Fairfax agreed, Bentley was free; he was not being held (if he was held at any time) by either of those police officers, and their attention was on something else; but, you know, again there is no suggestion that Bentley tried to rejoin Craig, no suggestion that he ever tried to move away from the police officers or to get away from them, no suggestion that at any time, when he had every opportunity, you may think, to use some sort of violence if he was so inclined; he never did so, but remained there doing nothing while those two police officers pulled Police Constable Miles' body from the line of fire.'

If Frank Cassels had established, during his examination of Bentley, the evidence contained in the teenager's statement to his solicitor about his conduct on the roof, Bentley's concern for the wounded Fairfax, his bitterness towards Craig, these would have been powerful weapons to use in his final speech, but this vital evidence lay dormant and unused. Referring to the vital remark 'Let him have it, Chris', Cassels astonishingly compounded the error made by Christmas Humphreys when the Prosecution Counsel had implied that all three officers had heard Bentley say it. 'All three of them have said quite clearly that they heard Bentley say "Let him have it, Chris!" – and that, of course, as my learned friend has told you, is the all-important remark in this case, because I venture to suggest to you that if you are not satisfied that that remark was made by Bentley it will go a long, long way in helping you come to a decision so far as Bentley is concerned. Now, those three police officers say that they heard the remark made. As against that, you have the evidence of Craig, who says, "I never heard it", and he was certainly standing almost as close to Bentley as was Detective Sergeant Fairfax, and you have heard the evidence of Bentley, who said "I never said it". And you have this in addition, have you not, members of the jury? – and I do suggest it is important: was Bentley's behaviour from that point onwards the behaviour you might have expected from a man, one of two, who had broken into premises, or had tried to break into premises, who knew that his colleague was armed, who himself had invited his colleague to let the police officers "have it", and whose colleague had in fact let the police officers "have it"?'

Bentley, he reminded them, had even remained close to Fairfax when the latter was shot. 'Was that the behaviour of a man who had instigated or incited his armed colleague to let the police officer 'have it"?'

Counsel also pointed out that, although the Prosecution had made much of the fact that Bentley had been carrying a knife and a knuckleduster, he had not made the slightest attempt to use either weapon. ' . . . in my submission, when you have formed in your mind a picture which indicates that a man has the opportunity to use violence if he so desires, and he does not use violence, that is a matter which you have to consider.'

In a final reference to the vital remark, Cassels said, 'If you are satisfied that that was said, you have to ask yourselves, "What does it mean? What is the correct interpretation we should put upon it? Must we put upon it the interpretation that the Prosecution asks us to put upon it, that it means he knew Craig was armed, and he was inviting Craig to use that weapon on the police officer, or is there some other interpretation which is not capable of that strong meaning that can be put upon it?"'

It would have been highly relevant to point out to the jury that Bentley could easily have declared that he *had* made the remark, and that he had meant by it that Craig should *surrender* the gun. Bentley's entire conduct from the moment the remark was alleged to have been made was absolutely consistent with this interpretation. The fact that Bentley had not chosen such an easy, logical way out, but chose, rather, to publicly test the honesty of two policemen, was surely a powerful confirmation that, in this area at least, he was telling the truth. As I say, this point would have been highly relevant – but it was not made.

'Then you know, members of the jury,' Cassels went on, 'there are two other remarks which are attributed to Bentley. It is an odd thing, is it not, members of the jury, that when he said, according to the police officers, that he told Craig not to use the gun, they say that only means that he knew he had a gun and that does not contradict the previous allegation that was made that he was inciting Craig to use it. You see, according to one of the police officers (and, surprisingly, not according to the other police officer who was there at the time), according to PC McDonald and not Sergeant Fairfax, while they were behind the staircase head Police Constable McDonald heard Bentley say, "I told the silly bugger not to use it", but apparently Sergeant Fairfax did not hear that remark. There may be some explanation of it; it may be he was preoccupied with something else at the time; but does that remark mean that this man was inciting his friend to use the gun, or does it mean that he was in fact telling him not to?

'Then, members of the jury, subsequently, there is that remark which is attributed to Bentley by one police officer: "He has a ·45 Colt, and plenty of ammunition too." According to a second police officer who heard that remark, he said: "It's a Colt, and he's got plenty of ammunition"; and I am sure it will not have escaped your notice that yet a third police officer said he heard *Craig* say, "It's a ·45 Colt", and *he* did *not* hear Bentley say it.'

It was true, Cassels admitted, that that last policeman came on the scene later, but it was extremely hard to remember, some time after the event, what was said during a twenty-minute gun battle, and by whom. 'You have to consider again that point when you are considering whether the police officers have correctly attributed to the various speakers (or whatever word you like to use) on the roof that night the particular words they have given in evidence, either yes or no.'

Yet again Cassels had repeated one of Humphreys' errors, saying that the rooftop battle had taken only twenty minutes. There is no doubt whatsoever that it lasted nearly twice as long. Though his remark about the fallibility of memory is highly pertinent, Cassels failed in my view to make the most of it.

He then proceeded to Bentley's alleged cry of 'They're taking me down, Chris!' The Prosecution, he recalled, had described this remark as an incitement to Craig to fire, but was it? Bentley had already seen one policeman shot dead. He knew that he would be in Craig's line of fire when they brought him out from behind the staircase head to take him downstairs. Could his shout not have been a warning to Craig *not* to fire? In any case, the barrister added, only one of the several policemen standing next to Bentley said that the remark had provoked a shot.

Bentley's Counsel then examined the youth's alleged remark in the police car: 'I knew he had a gun, but I didn't think he'd use it. He's done one of your blokes in.' 'Well, of course he knew that one of the police officers had been done in; he'd seen PC Miles' body hauled from just by that door to safety by PC McDonald and Sergeant Fairfax, and it isn't surprising that he thought that one of the police officers had been killed. But the rest of the remark is the important part, so far as the Prosecution are concerned. There were three police officers in the car, members of the jury, and you have seen a large number of police officers giving evidence in this case. We have heard from two of those officers. We have not heard from the third one who was there. You are, perhaps, entitled to wonder why. You may wonder whether or not that police officer heard the remark which was made, according to the other two, by

218

Bentley. If you are satisfied that that remark was made, "I knew he had a gun, but I didn't think he'd use it", does that confirm the evidence of other officers who are supposed to have heard this man say "Let him have it, Chris", or is it a remark by a man who knew, perhaps as a result of the first shot that was fired, that Craig had a gun, but he did not think he would use it?'

This was a good point, for it cast general doubt on the credibility of the two policemen who had been in the car. Had he and the jury been aware that PCs Pain and Bugden were within earshot at the time when Bentley was supposed to have shouted 'Let him have it, Chris' he might have been able to cast similar doubt on the credibility of Fairfax, Harrison and McDonald – but Pain and Bugden, like Alderson, had not given evidence.

'Then, members of the jury, you have the statement that was made by him at the police station. When you come to consider that statement, as I am sure you will, you will remember this, will you not, members of the jury: this man, although he is nineteen years of age, cannot read. It may be, and probably is, his own fault, but he cannot read, and he cannot write anything more than his own signature. You have heard the Police Inspector in this case, Mr Smith, say that this man is very much below, or below, average intelligence. You have got to consider all that. You have had an opportunity now of seeing him in the witness box. Do you really think he could dictate from his own mind to the police officers that whole statement so that they might write it down? Do you think there was not some little jogging along, some little questioning – I do not say it was improper – by the police officers in order that that statement might be taken? You know, members of the jury, it is an extremely disjointed one, because it seems to flash from one particular incident to another. There are one or two places in the statement where there is no sort of context about it. If you have an opportunity of looking at the statement, on the last page of it there appear these sentences, and my learned friend referred to

219

one of them and said that thereby he knew he was going to break into these particular premises. But, you know, the sentence beforehand reads like this: "The policeman then pushed me down the stairs, and I didn't see any more. I knew we were going to break into the place. I didn't know what we were going to get – just anything that was going." Does that seem to indicate that that was dictated by this rather illiterate young man to the police officers, or was it the result of some questions they asked? – because, you know, in one part of the statement he says, "I didn't know he was going to use the gun", and in a subsequent part he says, "I didn't have a gun, and I didn't know Chris had one until he shot". Which of those two statements are you going to believe? Which one are you going to accept as being the truth?'

This was well argued, but the jury would have been in an even better position to evaluate the statement if Bentley's mental subnormality had been established.

'You heard Bentley give evidence this morning in the witness box, and you will have formed your opinion as to what sort of person he is. You heard him cross-examined by my learned friend, and heard his answers to his questions. I am not going to comment upon his evidence, but you will remember this, members of the jury, in this case as in every other one: *it is not for men who are charged to prove to the jury's satisfaction that they are innocent. So far as Bentley is concerned, it is for the Prosecution to prove to your satisfaction, first of all, that Bentley knew that Craig had a gun before the first shot was fired, and then it is also for the Prosecution to prove to your satisfaction that Bentley did something that indicates that he was in agreement with Craig using that gun or being violent towards the police officers in order to resist arrest. It is not for him to satisfy you (or, as my learned friend Mr Humphreys said in addressing you just now, to make you believe) that he did not know that Craig had a gun. You have to be satisfied by the Prosecution that he did know that Craig had a gun, and if you are not satisfied, in my submission, in relation to one of those things, well, then, your verdict in regard to Bentley is a verdict of Not Guilty.*'

One could not look for a clearer statement of the principle of reasonable doubt, as it applied to this case, than that. Cassels finished his speech with these words.

'Now, members of the jury, just one other matter: the decision on the facts in this case is your responsibility, and your responsibility alone; the facts are for you, and for no one else, and you have to form, each one of you, your own opinion. In my submission to you, you can only convict Bentley if each one of you is satisfied, or sure, whichever word you like to use, that you are doing the right thing. You will only convict on the evidence which you have heard in this court yesterday and today. You will not judge this case on any preconceived picture you may have formed, either by newspaper articles or by anything you may have heard about it outside that jury-box. You have a very serious responsibility in this case, members of the jury, which you will have to discharge in due course, and you can only, as I said before, in my submission, find Bentley guilty of this offence if you are satisfied and sure, each one of you, (a) that he knew Craig had the gun, and (b) that he instigated or incited Craig to use it. Members of the jury, in my submission, considering fairly and squarely the whole of the evidence forming a picture in your own minds of what took place on that roof that night, it has not been proved with that satisfaction which you should have in a case such as this that Bentley is guilty, and I am asking you to say he is Not Guilty, of murder.'

All that remained before the jury retired to consider its verdict, was Lord Goddard's summing-up. John Parris was convinced that if the jury retired that afternoon, their verdict on Craig would be manslaughter, in which case Bentley could not be found guilty of murder.

Frank Cassels had made the point, when questioning the accuracy of the police evidence, that it was unlikely that the police would have been able, after the excitement of the gun fight, accurately to assemble in their minds all that had been said. 'I do not suppose for a moment, members of the jury, that now, at twenty-five minutes to four this afternoon, you would be able to transcribe accurately the words that were used by my Lord or either of my learned friends something like, perhaps, half an hour ago.'

It was a valid point, and the Judge took it to heart, it seemed. During the lunchtime adjournment the second day, Lord Goddard's clerk, Arthur Smith, had advised John Parris that the Judge intended to sit that day until a verdict had been returned. But now, as Frank Cassels sat down at 3.40 p.m., the Judge said:

'Gentlemen of the jury, I never like, in so serious a case as this, to start a summing-up in the evening and then have to resume it in the morning, so we will adjourn now until tomorrow morning at 10.30.'

The gap of nineteen hours between Counsels' speeches and the Judge's summing-up would not have mattered if the jury had been supplied with transcripts of the trial, or even just of the final speeches, when they retired; but as has been previously noted, this facility was considered superfluous.

On Thursday, 11 December 1952, at 10.30 a.m., the members of the Court took their places for the final day of the Craig/Bentley trial.

LORD CHIEF JUSTICE: Now, members of the jury, in many respects this is a very terrible case, and it is one, therefore, that it is desirable you and I should approach in as calm a frame of mind as we can.

Lord Goddard's summing-up is recorded in full in Appendix III. Suffice it to say here that the 'calm frame of mind' produced such expressions as 'a dreadful weapon', 'the wickedness of taking out a revolver . . . and firing it when he is on an unlawful expedition and the police are approaching him'. 'He said that he hated the police because they had got his brother twelve years, which seems to show that his brother was convicted for a very serious offence to receive a sentence of that length.' (Craig did not admit this remark.) 'It may be – and, indeed I think it is – probable that you will see there is no room for manslaughter in this case.' 'Have you ever seen a more horrible sort of weapon?' 'You have got a dreadful heavy steel bar.' 'Then did you ever see a more shocking thing than *that*?' 'You may wonder why he said "I'm only sixteen". Possibly you may know that the law does not allow a capital sentence to be passed on a boy of sixteen. Was it a boast? "Aha! Come on! I've got a gun. I can't be hanged." You will think of that.'

Lord Goddard's summing-up contained both a dangerous confusion of thought, and a number of inaccuracies. An example of the latter occurs in the Judge's reference to the ruling of his Victorian predecessor, Mr Justice Brett. Goddard remarked that in that case a police officer had been killed by a kick; in fact it was not a police officer that had been killed, but a passer-by. Undoubtedly the passer-by could expect the same protection in law that was accorded to police officers while assisting in an arrest, so in essence Lord Goddard was correct, but in detail he was incorrect. A small point – but under the circumstances one is justified in demanding from the trial judge precision, exactness and complete and total impartiality.

The Judge stated, incorrectly, that PC Miles was killed by the third shot. Phrases like, 'The aiming does not seem bad, does it? Three shots, two police officers hit, one fortunately slightly, the other hit between the eyes, so that the blood gushed out and he fell dead instantaneously', are very powerful – perhaps more powerful than one might expect from a judge's impartial summing-up – but they were based on a false premise. Lord Goddard's attitude when he was advised that he had been incorrect is recorded on pages 226-7.

The theatricality of putting the knuckleduster on his hand and showing his clenched fist to the jury, the request to have the knives handed up to him so that he could jab the air with them as he made his points, these were

223

gambits that Lord Goddard frequently used when he sat in judgment and they were extremely effective. In this trial they might have seemed more impartial if he had also put on Fairfax's jacket and waistcoat, indicated the tear and commented on the likelihood of a ·455 bullet being fired at the owner at a range of less than six feet and travelling *across* the surface of the skin to harmlessly rest in his braces. This may sound an absurd suggestion; is it less absurd for the Lord Chief Justice of England to brandish knuckledusters and knives at a jury?

His categorical statement that all three police officers heard Bentley say 'Let him have it, Chris' has already been cause for comment.

Lord Goddard made, too, a curious equation of bravery with honesty. John Parris, commenting on this aspect, said, 'Of course, courage is not the same virtue as truthfulness and many a brave man might be a liar, especially if his emotions were lacerated by the murder of a companion for whom he had affection and knew that the killer himself was bound to escape with his life.'

Quite obviously Lord Goddard found the task of following the evidence beyond him. He placed the shots that had been fired at Harrison as the policeman crawled along the sloping roof *after* the death of PC Miles. Amazingly, he completely failed to comment on the absence of PC Alderson, though Frank Cassels had, quite rightly and properly, *stressed* this singular fact. Even more amazing is Lord Goddard's reference to *three* officers in the car who had sworn they heard Bentley say 'I knew he had a gun but I didn't think he'd use it.' All the exchanges about the missing third officer, all Cassels' remarks about the absence of the third officer, flew entirely over Lord Goddard's head. In his mind three officers had gone into the box and sworn this vital piece of evidence. It is significant that in the edited version of the Craig/Bentley trial (in Hodges' *Famous British Trials*) Lord Goddard altered 'three' to 'two'. Fortunately the verbatim transcript still exists to prove otherwise. In such a way are errors that affect human life masked from the public by the men who make them.

The two references, during Cassels' cross-examination of Shepherd and Smith, to Bentley's mental capabilities were known by Lord Goddard, from his reading of the Brixton Prison Medical Officer's report, to be only the tip of the iceberg. One would not expect the Judge to do Defence Counsel's work for him, but in view of the fact that Frank Cassels made particular reference, in his final speech, to Bentley being below average intelligence, one would expect the trial judge to comment on this salient fact; he did not.

One of the most astonishing aspects of Lord Goddard's summing-up is the manner in which he dealt with Bentley's defence. For all that defence's fatal deficiencies, it surely justified better treatment than it received. Lord Goddard spoke for forty-five minutes. The only reference he made to Bentley's defence was, 'In the case of Bentley, Bentley's defence is: "I didn't know he had a gun, and I deny that I said, 'Let him have it, Chris.' I never knew he was going to shoot and I didn't think he would."' To dispose of Frank Cassels' speech to the jury in such a peremptory manner is quite remarkable. One would not have been surprised if the figure of Justice that stands on top of the Old Bailey had taken a walk down the Strand until the Craig/Bentley trial was over.

The comment that follows that two-line reference to Bentley's defence is equally illuminating. 'Against that denial, which, of course, is the denial of a man in grievous peril, you will consider the evidence of the three police officers who have sworn so positively that those words were said.'

It could be argued that it was perfectly proper to remind the jury immediately after a passing reference to Bentley's defence what the Prosecution case rebutting that defence was. It could also be argued that greater impartiality would have been manifest in the summing-up if previously, when stating the Prosecution case in great detail, he had

225

immediately referred to the Defence case. It would have indicated impartiality if Lord Goddard had also reminded the jury that Christopher Craig, a young man who was not in grievous peril, had also stated categorically that Bentley did not utter those fateful words. On the central issue of whether Derek Bentley had made that statement it was two against two, not, as Lord Goddard concluded, three against one. The odds against Bentley living to celebrate his twentieth birthday had been steadily lengthening since the start of the trial.

When Lord Goddard had finished summing up, the following interchange occurred.

PARRIS: My Lord, before the jury retire, might I invite your Lordship to correct one mis-statement of fact?

L.C.J.: Certainly.

PARRIS: Your Lordship said that Sergeant Fairfax said it was the third shot which was the fatal one. That would appear to be so from his deposition, but he said in evidence that it was the seventh or eighth.

L.C.J.: Did he?

PARRIS: That appears in his cross-examination, my Lord.

L.C.J.: It may well be. I will just see.

PARRIS: My Lord, may I give you the exact words?

L.C.J.: This is my note: 'As he fell there was a second shot, and I pulled Bentley before me as a shield.' Then he said he felt Bentley and found the knuckleduster. 'Then Bentley said "He'll shoot you". Craig had followed us to about twenty feet or something, and then retired to the top corner. I heard McDonald coming up. I shouted to Craig "Drop your gun". McDonald said "What sort of gun has he got?" Before I could reply, Bentley said "He's got a ·45".'

PARRIS: It is in cross-examination, my Lord. May I give your Lordship the note taken by my learned friend? 'The shot that hit PC Miles was not the first shot. There were six or seven shots before the fatal one.'

L.C.J.: I have not got that, but be it so. It may not have been the third. It may have been the fourth, it may have been the fifth, it may have been the sixth. I do not know that it very much matters. It at any rate was a shot that he fired after he heard those police officers coming up the staircase. The shot, therefore, which killed Police Constable Miles must have been fired in the direction of the staircase. It does not really seem to me to matter very much whether it was the third shot, or the fifth shot, or the sixth shot.

This interchange is a perfect illustration of the vital need for verbatim copies of the transcript to be made available *during* the trial. It must be remembered that the jury were not even allowed the facility of making notes. The Judge, even *with* that facility, was ignorant of how many shots had been fired before Miles was killed. John Parris, even with the aid of Frank Cassels' notes, was ignorant of how many shots had been fired before Miles was killed. It is quite clear from the trial evidence that Sergeant Fairfax gave that there were eight or nine shots before the fatal one. It is equally clear that *prior to the fatal shot Craig had fired only four*. If this fact had been appreciated by Counsel, Judge, and jury, the ultimate outcome of the trial would have been vastly different.

The jury's sole function, to arrive at a just verdict based solely on the facts, was made infinitely more difficult by Lord Goddard's performance.

The Judge then turned back to the jury.

'Will you consider your verdict? Would you like any of these? [The exhibits.] Would you like the statement? I ought to remind you, but it does not really matter, because Bentley has been in the witness box and really repeated his evidence on oath, that strictly speaking the written statement is not evidence against Craig, but the evidence he has given in the witness box is all part of the evidence in the case. Will you tell me, gentlemen, if you would like any of the exhibits? Do you want any of the weapons?'

There was a look of consternation on the Judge's face when the foreman of the jury stood up and asked for Sergeant Fairfax's coat and waistcoat.

227

I have remarked at the beginning of this chapter the interest that the Craig/Bentley trial had for the general lay public. Throughout the trial the courtroom was also packed with members of the legal profession. One of them, a young barrister named Anthony Samuelson, described to me what transpired when the foreman of the jury made his request to see Sergeant Fairfax's jacket and waistcoat.

'Lord Goddard completely lost control of himself. He quite literally screamed at the members of the jury. "You will remember you are not considering the wounding of Sgt Fairfax. You are considering the murder of a policeman." When he uttered the words "murder of a policeman" he smashed the knuckleduster that was on his hand down on the bench. The jury at this point had nearly all gone out; only a few of them heard and saw this frightening display.'

This account comes, not from a person unversed in courtroom procedure, but from a member of Lord Goddard's profession. It should convince any reader still in doubt about the matter of Lord Goddard's determination that his point of view should prevail in this trial.

The jury retired. The time was 11.15 a.m. The whole trial, including the four long final speeches, had taken less than ten hours.

The courtroom gradually cleared until all the main participants, save one, had gone to the corridors. The exception was Lord Goddard, who was to try the next case. It was surely no mere coincidence that it was to be that of Norman Parsley.

Parsley pleaded guilty to the armed robbery that he had committed with Craig. Prosecuting Counsel J. S. Bass, who had been assisting Humphreys, left the Judge in no doubt as to the identity of Parsley's accomplice. The grammar school boy, having pleaded guilty, cast all the blame on his absent friend. He declared that he had come under the influence of Craig's 'magnetic personality'. When he had heard the evidence Lord Goddard said to the boy standing in the dock:

'It is true you are only sixteen and it is true that you were in company with a young lad who is apparently a serious criminal. But I say at once, if you had been over twenty-one I would have sent you to prison for twelve years.

'You covered your face with a mask, took a revolver, and with another armed lad you went to a house and terrified an old lady who might have had a heart attack and died on the spot, and then equally terrified her old husband for the sake of getting what you could. You have not once expressed regret for what you have done. I, and other judges, will do our best to let young men know what will happen to them if they do this sort of thing.'

Lord Goddard then sentenced Norman Parsley to four years' imprisonment. So that young man, who had until recently had high expectations of entering a university, instead found himself entering one of Her Majesty's prisons.

Shortly before 12.30 p.m. it was announced that the jury were returning. As the court filled rapidly there was a buzz of expectation. The jury had been considering their verdict for seventy-five minutes. In view of the direction given to them by Lord Goddard it was inconceivable that they would return any other verdict on Craig than that demanded by the Prosecution. Virtually all of the seventy-five minutes must have been spent discussing Derek Bentley. By the time the jury were seated the listeners were overflowing into the corridors. Conversation halted abruptly as the Clerk of the Court walked up to the foreman of the jury.

CLERK OF THE COURT: Members of the jury, are you agreed upon your verdict?
FOREMAN: We are.
CLERK: Do you find the prisoner Christopher Craig guilty or not guilty of murder?

FOREMAN: Guilty.

CLERK: Do you find the prisoner Derek William Bentley guilty or not guilty of murder?

FOREMAN: Guilty, with a recommendation to mercy.

CLERK: You find both prisoners guilty, and that is the verdict of you all?

FOREMAN: It is.

CLERK: Christopher Craig, you stand convicted of murder, have you anything to say why sentence should not be passed according to law? Derek William Bentley, you stand convicted of murder, have you anything to say why sentence should not be passed according to law?

There was no reply. In total silence the black silk square was placed on the Lord Chief Justice of England's bewigged head. Bentley stood watching the ritual, blank and uncomprehending, still wearing his overcoat despite the heat in the courtroom.

During the reign of Queen Victoria Lord Goddard had entertained his schoolfriends in the dormitory at Marlborough by reciting the death sentence. It had been a qualified success.

L.C.J.: Derek William Bentley, you are nineteen years of age; it is my duty to pass upon you the only sentence which the law can pass for the crime of wilful murder. The sentence of the Court upon you is that you be taken from this place to a lawful prison, and thence to a place of execution, and there you suffer death by hanging, and that your body be buried within the precincts of the prison in which you shall have been last confined before your execution; and may the Lord have mercy on your soul.

CHAPLAIN: Amen.

L.C.J.: Take him down.

Bentley turned for a moment, appeared to stumble, and then he was gone. As the black silk square was removed from the Judge's head Christopher Craig waited, standing on exactly the same spot where his brother Niven had stood less than two months previously. Expecting more than a mere formal passing of sentence, the reporters in the press seats waited, pens poised, for a phrase that would make a good headline. They were not to be disappointed.

'Christopher Craig, you are under nineteen, but in my judgment, and evidently in the judgment of the jury, you are the more guilty of the two. Your heart was filled with hate, and you murdered a policeman without thought of his wife, his family or himself; and never once have you expressed a word of sorrow for what you have done. I can only sentence you to be detained until Her Majesty's pleasure be known. I shall tell the Secretary of State when forwarding the recommendation of the jury in Bentley's case that in my opinion you are one of the most dangerous criminals who has ever stood in that dock.

'While the jury were out considering their verdict in this case I had to deal with another boy whom you led into it holding up an elderly couple at the point of revolvers and stealing from them; and it is quite obvious that the people in this country will not be safe if you are out of prison. I shall recommend the time which I suggest to the Secretary of State that you shall be kept in confinement. The sentence upon you is that you be kept in strict custody until the pleasure of Her Majesty be known. Take him down.'

As the sixteen-year-old Craig turned to walk down to the cell, his face broke into a smile.

It grew as his eyes searched the courtroom for his parents. For a moment he stood smiling across the courtroom at his father; then he was gone.

'Now,' said the Lord Chief Justice, 'let Detective Sergeant Fairfax, PC McDonald and PC Harrison stand forward. Will you stand with them, Chief Inspector. The conduct of the men of Z Division on this night in arresting these two desperate young criminals is worthy of the highest commendation and the thanks of the community to the police for their gallant conduct. They are all deserving of commendation, but I have asked these three officers in particular to stand forward, as they showed such commendable courage on that night. It is no light thing to face a burglar or house-breaker in the dark when he is armed with a revolver and firing in the way he did. I doubt not that all your comrades who were there that night would have shown exactly the same courage that you did; it so happened that you three officers were exposed to the worst of it, and had, therefore, I suppose in one way one may say, more opportunity of showing the courage and resolution that you did. The thanks of all law-abiding citizens ought to be tendered to you.'

It was a fitting tribute to men who had, indeed, demonstrated extraordinary bravery. Fairfax and Harrison could count themselves particularly fortunate to have lived to hear that tribute. The bravery that they and their colleagues showed on that wet, dark night of Sunday, 2 November 1952, cannot, and should not, be questioned. The fact that I have questioned their recollection in no way diminishes their courage. But in view of the many serious contradictions contained in the police evidence, I had no alternative but to cast doubt upon it.

So, on 11 December 1952, ended the trial of Craig and Bentley. It has been said that the clamour surrounding the subsequent attempts to get Bentley reprieved has tended to mask the fact of his guilt, and that he had, after all, been found guilty in a fair trial. I sincerely hope that this chapter has demonstrated the fallacy of that particular view.

As the reporters rushed to the telephones, Mr Bentley walked slowly from the court. Waiting in a nearby café were his wife and two remaining children, nine-year-old Dennis and twenty-one-year-old Iris. They had confidently expected that Derek would walk from the courtroom a free man. Now their hopes even for his survival were pinned on five words: 'with a recommendation to mercy'. Five words had put the rope round his neck: 'Let him have it, Chris.' Were the jury's five words enough to cancel the other five?

232

One can only speculate on how those twelve men, then dispersed, felt on the morning of Bentley's execution. One can only speculate as to what their verdict would have been had they known that their recommendation to mercy would remain so many empty words.

In *Duty and Advocacy*, Sir Malcolm Hilbery wrote: 'A jury is twelve ordinary citizens, with probably little or no training in consecutive thought. They will be largely if not entirely swayed by emotion. But remember that in all probability they do not think so. The less training or capacity for reasoning they have, the more certain it is that they will pride themselves on being susceptible only to strict logic and impervious to mere emotion.' In finding Bentley guilty, that jury showed a frightening facility for standing logic on its head; they had shown a truly remarkable – or perhaps only too human – susceptibility to mere emotion. But they did display one undoubted virtue. In recommending mercy, the jury betrayed that it had a conscience. That attribute was to be singularly lacking in the Home Secretary, Sir David Maxwell Fyfe, as will become apparent in Chapter 7.

6

The Season of Goodwill

The morning after the trial had finished, the *Daily Mirror* voiced the thoughts of many thousands of people in a front-page article headed *Will Bentley Hang?* Defining the official attitude of the Home Secretary, the article quoted a memorandum that the Home Office had recently laid before the Royal Commission on Capital Punishment. The memorandum said: 'The Home Secretary always attaches weight to a recommendation to mercy by the jury. He would be very reluctant to disregard such a recommendation if it is concurred with by the judge.'

The newspaper article went on to quote further evidence given by the Home Office before the Royal Commission, to the effect that very occasionally the Home Secretary recommended a reprieve because he felt that, in spite of the verdict, there was a shadow of doubt of the prisoner's guilt.

(A number of other factors also influenced Home Secretaries when deciding whether or not to recommend a reprieve, and these are dealt with in a subsequent chapter.) The point that the article made, which was undoubtedly missed by most of its readers was that: 'Out of every hundred murderers convicted between 1900 and 1948 but recommended to mercy, seventy-five were reprieved.'

If the point was missed, it was because it was unwittingly concealed. It was that, *in spite of a recommendation to mercy*, twenty-five convicted murderers in every hundred were still hanged. Reprieve after a jury had recommended mercy was by no means automatic. Few people in this

234

country thought at this stage that Bentley would hang, and when it was announced the following morning that he would appeal the majority were quite content to leave it at that, feeling certain that he would win his appeal. This was a view shared by many, although as we shall see, by no means all.

Now that Derek Bentley stood with virtually one foot on the scaffold, the realization dawned in Fleet Street that there was copy in the Bentley family. They had been almost totally ignored by the press until the final day of the trial, all attention centring on Craig. But with Harry Procter guarding the Craig family there was little potential in that area.

So not long after the trial Bentley's parents found themselves in the offices of the *Sunday Dispatch*. Talking to the press was a novel experience for them; it was to become all too familiar during the next forty-seven days.

After they had given the *Sunday Dispatch* enough copy to fill the front page, they returned to their Norbury home to try to grasp the full meaning of the verdict.

The Craig family were assisted in their hour of need by the tenacious Harry Procter. Aided by his assistant, Madeline MacLoughlin, and the chauffeur-driven Rolls-Royce, he had spirited Christopher Craig's parents, and his sister Lucy, directly from the Old Bailey to a riverside inn at Shepperton. His purpose was hardly therapeutic. He was obsessed with the fear that the 'opposition' would get at the Craigs and ruin the *Sunday Pictorial*'s exclusive. So the Craigs had to be kept out of circulation until the *Pictorial*'s own had been boosted. It is just one of the many astonishing facets of the entire Craig/Bentley episode that intelligent people, and Mr and Mrs Craig were undoubtedly highly intelligent, allowed themselves to be manipulated by Procter. The only rational explanation is that they were emotionally off-balance. Procter wrote his story and showed it to the Craig family. Even by his own standards he had excelled himself. It was written with some first-hand knowledge of Craig, for, posing as a relation of the youth, Procter had managed to get himself into Brixton Prison on one of the occasions when the boy's parents were visiting him. The opening lines of the piece make Procter's intrinsic ability clear.

'Christopher Craig was lying in bed in a small gloomy cell at Brixton Prison. The pale yellow walls around him gave a sinister pallor to his white face. He tossed back his coal-black hair, turned his strikingly handsome head. What a handsome youth! I thought. And then he grinned and broke the spell. As I saw the left lip curl, and the impudent flicker creep into his eyes, I knew I was watching just another of those brass-faced little hooligans of which this post-war world is so bitterly ashamed. A lazy, cowardly, selfish young lout.'

There was much more in a similar vein. Procter saw it as his role to write about criminals with contempt. In his view they must be cheapened and ridiculed. (One wonders if he still held that view some years later when he himself was sentenced to prison for drunken driving.) Understandably, the Craig family did not appreciate Procter's 'candid pen-picture' of their son, but they agreed it ought to be published. Whether they would have agreed if they had known Procter's capacity for bending the truth is doubtful. Below his article, the newspaper reproduced a school report which showed the remarks against Craig's English tests. They were in keeping with the article, indicating that Craig, as well as being bottom of his class, was thoroughly lazy and had no inclination to improve his poor ability in this subject. The bottom half of the report, however, was not shown, depriving the *Pictorial*'s readers of the information that, although Craig's abilities in certain subjects left a great deal to be desired, his ability in others was well above average.

Another omission that could have had a considerable effect on public opinion concerned Procter's pre-trial prison conversation with Christopher Craig. 'Before you shot the policeman,' Procter said, 'did you hear Bentley shout to you "Let him have it, Chris"?'

'No,' said Christopher Craig. 'He never did. No, he never did.' Procter pursued the point. 'This is very important. Think about it carefully. Are you absolutely certain that Bentley never shouted to you "Let him have it, Chris"?'

'No,' Craig insisted. 'Derek never said it.'

When Procter finally revealed this aspect of his interview with Craig to his waiting public it was a full five years too late to have any effect on Bentley's fate. Referring to Craig's remarks, Procter commented, 'This was before the trial, this was long before the sixteen-year-old boy knew anything about what might happen to Derek Bentley.' One can only speculate why Procter suppressed this piece of information until long after Bentley's execution. Did it, perhaps, not fit in with his paper's editorial policy?

On the Friday evening, Procter received news from his London office. The paper required a further article. They wanted Captain Niven Craig to condemn his own son and put his name on the story of condemnation. Dutifully Procter went to his hotel bedroom and wrote the article, based on the many remarks that Craig's father had made to him over the past few weeks. This was subsequently phoned in to the *Pictorial*. The editor considered the article 'a brilliant human document', but he still insisted that Mr Craig sign his name above the story and also sign it on every page.

Niven Craig at first flatly refused to have anything to do with it, but eventually on the Saturday morning he agreed to sign it, provided it was treated seriously and not sensationally. The following day he read just how seriously the *Sunday Pictorial* had treated it. In black, two-inch headlines the paper proclaimed, *MY FAILURE: BY CRAIG'S FATHER*.

The story was sub-titled 'Why I Have Failed by Niven Mathews Craig'. That was the end of Procter's friendship with Christopher Craig's father. But Procter had not yet touched the Bentley family.

If the other papers were debarred from obtaining first-hand quotes from the Craigs they more than made up for it, with headlines like this one, from the *Sunday Dispatch* the weekend after the trial: *THE UNTOLD STORY BEHIND CRAIG AND BENTLEY*.

It went on to tell a story that was indeed untold at the trial: of how, the week before the death of PC Miles, Mr Bentley had gone to his local police station and asked that his son be given police protection from Craig at a dance the two youths were going to attend. Mr Bentley feared that Craig might attack his son. He asked for help in keeping the two youths from associating with each other. The article lacked the flair of the *Pictorial*'s coverage, but it compared favourably with its rival in the field of distortion. Purporting to have been written by Mr Bentley, but actually by Len Cotten, the article put all the blame on Craig. Derek Bentley had tried this technique at the Old Bailey without success, but perhaps what failed with the jury succeeded with *Sunday Dispatch* readers. Then again, remembering that the *Sunday Dispatch* is no longer with us, perhaps it failed in that area too.

The other Sunday papers, deprived of an entrée to either the Craig or Bentley households, contented themselves with a variety of pertinent observations. Virtually all of them, with the strange exception of the *Pictorial*, reported the wedding of Craig's sister Lucy, which had taken place on the Saturday two days after the trial. Regretfully, there were no photographs of the smiling couple, as a guest had been disagreeable enough to smash the camera of the one photographer who had had the temerity to discover the location of the wedding.

One of the few responsible articles was in the *Reynolds News*. It concerned the pittance that was doled out to the widows of policemen. Not surprisingly, this article was written by an ex-policeman, Tom Fallon. This topic was, as Chapter 1 of this book indicates, a cause for constant agitation by the police throughout this entire post-war period. Had 50% of the energy, that was expended in the newspapers that particular weekend in vilifying Craig, been channelled towards this problem, it is highly likely that public opinion would have been stirred and Mrs Miles would have received rather more than £2 16s. (£2.80) per week. Thousands of pounds were spent during the Craig/Bentley trial to bring to justice the men allegedly responsible for her husband's death. Could not some of this money have been more usefully employed by the widow? For all the justice that it bought, she might as well have had the money.

The readers of the *Sunday Chronicle* were treated to an article by James Dow, who was of the opinion that somewhere along the line someone had failed. A strategically placed photograph of Mr and Mrs Craig alongside the headline left the reader in no doubt as to who, in the opinion of Mr Dow, that someone was. His solution to the problem was somewhat more original. He feared that Craig might be released after a mere five-year sentence, and that there might be other Parsleys and other Bentleys for him to dominate. Dow's solution was to make parents responsible in law for the crimes committed by their sons (presumably the daughters of England were above reproach). He also wondered if the law should not be altered so that the 'rogue beasts in the herd could be put down' whatever their age. His final question was, 'Should the law not be altered so that Craig, the ringleader, could have been hanged?'

Cheek by jowl with this article was another, in which Beverly Nichols expressed some strong views on one particular aspect of the case. 'It seems faintly ironic that the young brute with the knuckleduster should be lapped in the luxury of pentothal in case he should suffer a twinge when they were setting his wrist. As tax-payers, you and I pay for that pentothal. Is it inhuman to suggest that our money could be put to a better purpose than narcotics? Maybe it is. But there are times when inhumanity becomes almost an essential duty.'

In the national press there was a total absence of any comment, responsible or otherwise, on the morality and legality of the Bentley verdict. The nineteen-year-old, having stood in Craig's shadow throughout the trial, was destined to stay there a little longer. There would come a time when his name, and his alone, would scream out from the headlines, but it would be for a reason that no man on earth could desire.

But meanwhile there was the season of goodwill to celebrate, Christmas 1952. For the Bentleys, the daily visits to their son in the special block at Wandsworth Prison had taken on a nightmare routine. One visit melted into the next. His mother had noticed, the first time she saw him after the trial, that his shoelaces had been removed and he was no longer wearing a tie. The realization of why the regulations forbade these items brought home her son's situation. On Christmas Eve she took him a parcel of fruit but was not permitted to leave it. Quite obviously Mr Nichols was not the only one to feel that 'there are times when inhumanity becomes almost an essential duty'.

During this happy, festive time there was hardly any newspaper comment about the young man who now had only one month to live. Sweet novelty had become sour commonplace.

By the end of December it was known that the Appeal hearing would be on 12 January 1953. The Bentley family were convinced that the sentence of death would be quashed. They would have been less confident if they had overheard a conversation which took place a few days before the hearing, between Frank Cassels and Lord Goddard. They chanced to meet near the Law Courts, and in a jocular manner the Lord Chief Justice of England asked Bentley's Counsel to 'take it easy on me during the Appeal'. In his opinion, he said, Bentley would ultimately be reprieved, either as a result of the Appeal or by the subsequent intervention of the Home Secretary. But Cassels did not share his optimism. He considered that Bentley would not be reprieved. He also considered that Bentley *should*

240

not be reprieved. In his opinion Bentley deserved to hang.

Six days before Bentley's Appeal was due to be heard, it was announced from St James's Palace that the policemen, Fairfax, Harrison, McDonald and Jaggs, were to be awarded medals for the parts they had played in the rooftop battle. With the announcement came a long citation giving details of the events on the Croydon roof. That the awards were merited is beyond doubt. But the timing of the announcement is very significant. Coming less than a week before Bentley's Appeal, it must have seemed to support the belief that the Appeal was mere ritual, and the result a foregone conclusion. The psychological effect of the announcement on those intimately concerned with the Appeal, particularly the Appeal Judges, is easy to imagine. Why was the announcement of the awards not delayed until after the result of the Appeal was known? Why was it not delayed until the Home Secretary's deliberations were known? Why was it not delayed until after Bentley's execution? Had the Executive already resolved in their minds the question of Bentley's fate?

The public interest in the trial that had resulted in all-night queues outside the Old Bailey, was now repeated at the Appeal hearing at the Law Courts. But the hundreds of people who queued for many hours on 12 January were to be disappointed. After the main participants had themselves waited over four hours they were advised that their Lordships were still occupied with another case. So the grim charade had to be repeated the following day.

The Appeal was heard on the morning of 13 January. It is doubtful whether Derek Bentley understood a single word of it. Those who consider that in England justice must not only be done, but must be seen to be done, would do well to remember that an Appeal hearing is not presided over by an independent body devoid of any connection with the trial judge. It is presided over by his brother judges. In view of the fact that the trial judge was also the Lord Chief Justice, this ensured that the three Appeal judges were junior to the trial judge. The situation is not unlike one in which three directors of a company are asked publicly to state that their managing director has made a mistake. It was perhaps situations such as this that had led one member of the legal profession bitterly to describe these hearings as presided over by a 'Court of Criminal No-Appeal'. In reply to any criticism of a particular judge's behaviour, the reply all too often was 'No fault is to be found with this impeccable summing-up.'

The men who were to sit in judgment on Bentley's Appeal were Mr Justice Croom-Johnson, Mr Justice Ormerod and Mr Justice Pearson. The men who were to oppose Frank Cassels' arguments were his opponents at the Old Bailey trial, Christmas Humphreys and J. S. Bass. It will be recalled that the solicitors acting on behalf of Craig and Bentley had attempted, at the Croydon hearings, to obtain two counsel for each of the accused. This plea had been rejected, so that John Parris and Frank Cassels, acting quite independently of each other, had had to contend with two Prosecuting Counsel. The rules of English Justice, cherished by many, perpetuated this unequal situation at the Appeal hearing.

Frank Cassels, opening on behalf of Bentley, outlined the bare details of the Old Bailey trial. This résumé drew from Mr Justice Croom-Johnson the comment, 'We have all read these papers. We are all fully aware of the circumstances of the case, and the point is quite a short one, is it not?'

There were in fact two grounds upon which Bentley was appealing, but they were indeed short. Frank Cassels came immediately to the first: That the learned judge failed adequately to put Bentley's defence before the jury in his summing-up. Analysis of Appendix III shows just how apt this complaint was. Cassels quoted Lord Goddard's two-sentence summary of Bentley's defence and then rightly observed that it was much more than this. Then, further to justify his complaint of the Lord Chief Justice's summing-up, Cassels went through a number of the points that he had made to the Old Bailey jury.

When Counsel referred to Bentley's version of the conversation in the police car, Croom-Johnson interrupted, 'He said what the gun was?' It was the first indication of just how well the senior Appeal judge had read the trial transcript. The evidence relating to that alleged remark concerned the events on the rooftop, not the events in the police car. When Cassels gently pointed out to Croom-Johnson that he was in error, the judge adopted an attitude not unlike Lord Goddard's when he had been corrected by John Parris. He ignored the fact that he was himself in error, saying, 'All this was a matter for the jury, wasn't it, including the fact that according to one witness at least, if the jury chose to accept his evidence, this prisoner had said what kind of gun it was Craig was carrying.' This had nothing whatsoever to do with the point that Cassels was making about the trial judge's treatment of Bentley's version of what was said in the car. Persevering with the point, Frank Cassels then gave a verbatim reading of exactly what Bentley's version was, concluding with the comment, 'That was one of the major issues in this trial as to this Appellant's knowledge of the fact that his companion was armed with a gun. There was no reference of any sort to the Appellant's evidence in relation to that.' Mr Justice Ormerod then read out Lord Goddard's two-sentence reference to Bentley's defence, commenting after he had done so, 'Doesn't that cover it? I agree it is short.'

This was the first chink of light shed by the Appeal judges on the possibility that perhaps Lord Goddard had given the youth's defence too short a shrift. Cassels warmed to his theme, pointing out how much detail that the Lord Chief Justice had given to the Prosecution case, pointing out the twenty-four-hour time lag that had occurred between Bentley's evidence in the witness box and the summing-up. He then turned to the trial evidence of the statement that Bentley had made to the police; again he quoted the verbatim record of Bentley's evidence, referring as he did so to Bentley's illiteracy, none of which had been touched upon in Lord Goddard's summing-up. There was undoubtedly a total conflict between the Prosecution version and Bentley's, as to exactly how that statement had been obtained, and what had actually been said. Mr Justice Croom-Johnson commented that this was the type of controversy that arises in a great number of cases, and asked Frank Cassels if the statement was eventually handed to the jury. He was advised that the twelve good men and true did not avail themselves of the opportunity of reading the statement when they retired to consider their verdict.

Croom-Johnson then extolled the merits of trial by jury, but Cassels, sticking to the point at issue, pointed out that when there is a difference of opinion about a prisoner's statement, that difference should be squarely put before the jury in the summing-up. This drew from Croom-Johnson the retort, 'You don't seem to leave much to the discretion of the trial judge, do you? Surely it is for the learned judge to decide what he is going to lay before the jury, and so long as it is done, I will use an expression of my own that you won't find in the books, fairly and squarely, that is sufficient.'

Frank Cassels, having summarized the first ground of the Appeal, moved to the second issue. This was that the jury should have been advised to consider when the joint adventure that Craig and Bentley were upon, ceased to be a joint adventure. In view of the fact that Bentley had been under arrest for at least fifteen, and more probably twenty-five, minutes when PC Miles was killed, it was a highly pertinent point, and one that Lord Goddard had completely failed to mention during his summing-up. Croom-Johnson's comment was, 'A judge in the course of summing-up cannot deal with every little point; the judge must be allowed a little latitude, mustn't he?'

That 'little point' should have saved Bentley's life. That 'little point' concerned an issue that at the time of Bentley's case had never been resolved in English law. Doggedly

Cassels soldiered on; as no reference had been made to this issue during Lord Goddard's summing-up, he argued, it was not unreasonable to assume that the jury, upon retiring, had not concerned themselves with the fact that at the time the fatal shot was fired, and for some considerable time before, Bentley was under arrest and being held by the police officer. Observed Mr Justice Ormerod, 'Bentley himself denied that on oath.' Cassels corrected him: 'He said on oath that he was not being held all the time.' Ormerod pressed the point. 'He was not being held at the time the fatal shot was fired.' Cassels then clarified Bentley's evidence on this point, that the youth in effect said that he was held some of the time but not all of the time, as PC McDonald and Detective Sergeant Fairfax had confirmed on oath. When Miles fell and his colleagues had gone to his aid, Bentley had been briefly free from physical restraint.

In conclusion Frank Cassels said, 'This was a man who had up to the time of the fatal shot been under arrest or in custody, was held, whichever word you would like to use, by those two officers, and the jury should have had put before them this consideration, whether that did not affect this man's responsibility for this crime if the jury were satisfied that the shooting of Miles was part of the joint adventure.'

It is quite obvious from the various remarks made by the Appeal judges exactly what their opinions were of the validity of the two grounds of Appeal. Any further comment was superfluous. But further comment there was from Christmas Humphreys. Humphreys, of course, felt that Bentley's defence had been put fairly by Lord Goddard to the jury. The fact that it had been dealt with by the Lord Chief Justice in two short sentences was in Humphreys' opinion 'perfectly reasonable'. Discussing the events on the rooftop, Humphreys came to the surprising conclusion that all Bentley disagreed with in the case for the Prosecution were the words 'Let him have it, Chris'. (In fact Bentley disagreed with virtually the entire Prosecution case.) Humphreys skirted quickly over the alleged conversations in the police car. Cassels had completely failed to mention the missing PC Alderson, and Humphreys was certainly not going to remind him of this glaring weakness in the Prosecution's case.

Then, discussing the arrest issue, Christmas Humphreys said, 'There is no doubt that Bentley was arrested by a police officer on the roof, who then kept him under cover from the murderer, searched him and removed from him the two weapons, the dagger and the knuckleduster. Thereafter, though the police officer was under deadly fire, he was managing to have some consideration for the live body of the man under arrest, and he did so and got him behind the staircase head. Thereafter, he was technically under arrest but not in the sense of being physically held, and, the jury may have thought, for the good reason that only a consummate fool would have put his head out from behind the staircase head because the result of doing so would have been a shot from Craig. Nevertheless, in one sense he was under arrest. In another sense I was amazed to find that the case for Bentley was that he was not under arrest and was free to go to the assistance of Craig and did not do so.'

The consideration that Fairfax had for 'the live body of the man under arrest' was, on Fairfax's own evidence, to use it as a shield to protect his own body. During the trial both Lord Goddard and Christmas Humphreys had been scathingly critical of Bentley because he had done nothing after his arrest to dissuade Craig from continuing the fight. Now, at the Appeal 'only a consummate fool would have put his head out from behind the staircase head'. As for Bentley's case in respect of the 'arrest issue', Humphreys justified his remarks by reading Bentley's verbatim evidence concerning this aspect. I shall take up this point in a moment.

Humphreys then justified his contention that even though Bentley had been arrested he was still acting in the joint enterprise by citing Bentley's remark when he was rushed towards the staircase head with a number of police officers sheltering behind his body. 'Look out Chris, they're taking me down.' The reply from Craig, Humphreys asserted, was a shot in the direction of the police officers. If nothing else Humphreys was consistent. In his final speech to the jury he had ignored the uncomfortable fact that only one officer alleged that the reply from Craig was a shot, and Bentley and three other police officers had heard nothing. Now he ignored that fact again.

His final point was a remarkable demonstration of mind-reading. He referred to Lord Goddard's remarks: 'What does matter is whether Bentley shouted in the first instance, "Let him have it, Chris", because if he did, then you can consider whether that does not show, firstly that he knew that 'Chris' had the revolver, and, secondly, was calling upon 'Chris' to use violence to prevent arrest.' In Humphreys' opinion what Lord Goddard had meant by those remarks was, 'The arrest point doesn't matter very much one way or the other.'

Disputing the Prosecuting Counsel's contention concerning Craig's reaction to 'Look out, Chris, they're taking me down', Frank Cassels quoted Fairfax's evidence to show the inaccuracy of that contention; he could also have quoted the evidence of PCs McDonald and Jaggs, and of Bentley. Humphreys subsequently apologized, but that, apparently, did not sway the Appeal judges.

Having considered the arguments, Mr Justice Croom-Johnson delivered the Appeal judgment. In the opinion of the Appeal judges, Lord Goddard's summing-up had been a model of perfection. They could see nothing wrong with it. 'The idea that there was a failure on the part of the Lord Chief Justice to say anything short of what was required in putting that sort of case to the jury is entirely wrong.' The first ground of the Appeal therefore was accordingly dismissed. So was the second ground. The Appeal judges considered that, 'this is nothing more than an ordinary Appeal in a murder trial, an ordinary Appeal which is, in our judgment, without foundation and which is accordingly dismissed.'

The hearing had lasted less than one hour. The rush to judgment was now complete, with some help from the Appeal judges.

At the outset of the Appeal the senior judge, Mr Justice Croom-Johnson, stated categorically, 'We have all read these papers. We are fully aware of the circumstances of the case.' In view of that contention a number of his subsequent remarks are inexcusable. He admits that he was incapable of discovering how many shots were fired, and at what targets; after struggling with the task for a long time, he says, he gave it up! This from a senior judge at the Appeal. Defending his inability to understand the evidence he cites the Lord Chief Justice's remarks during his summing-up, that, 'it is impossible for anybody to say with accuracy how many shots were fired or how many particular witnesses heard those shots that were fired.' *These remarks do not appear anywhere in the trial judge's summing-up.*

In his judgment, Croom-Johnson differed from Lord Goddard in his interpretation of the law. It will be recalled that the Lord Chief Justice had stated quite clearly that 'Bentley must be aware that Craig was armed, and the jury must be satisfied that he intended with Craig to offer violent resistance'. This, during Croom-Johnson's judgment, is reduced to 'he must know that his companion in the adventure is armed'. True, later on in his judgment he qualified this to, 'the prisoner must know that the other man is armed and know what was the adventure they were upon'. If this is intended to mean *exactly* the same as the Lord Chief Justice's ruling, I am afraid it is too subtle for me.

Inaccuracies abound throughout the judgment, but two are particularly remarkable. During the hearing there had been considerable discussion about the alleged conversation in the police car that was taking Bentley to

Croydon Police Station. Frank Cassels had stated quite correctly that while the trial judge had gone into the police version in detail, he had not done the same with Bentley's version. Indeed, Lord Goddard had made no reference at all to Bentley's version during his summing-up. It will be recalled that, during the summing-up, Lord Goddard had mistakenly referred to *three* police officers swearing that they had heard Bentley say in the car, 'I knew he had a gun, but I didn't think he'd use it though.' It had of course been only two. The fact that the other officer, PC Alderson, never made a statement and never gave evidence, was totally neglected by Lord Goddard. Croom-Johnson was to compound this error in an astonishing remark made during the course of his judgment.

'The matter was carefully put, adequately put and properly put by the Chief Justice, and it was then for the jury to decide Aye or No. Did they accept the prisoner's denials or did they accept the evidence of two witnesses who spoke affirmatively to statements made by the Appellant and, I think, another witness who was not able to give the main evidence, but did depose to hearing the words or similar words spoken by somebody.'

Those words perfectly illustrate the quality of the Appeal judgment. The fact that the three Appeal judges considered that the matter was adequately put by Lord Goddard during his summing-up to the jury is surprising enough. What stretches credibility beyond breaking point is the reference to PC Alderson as being 'not able to give the main evidence, but did depose to hearing the words or similar words spoken by somebody'. *No such deposition was ever filed in court.*

If Derek Bentley was cocooned in stupidity from the realities of what was happening, it was merciful protection.

Like any good clown, Croom-Johnson had saved his best trick for the end. Giving his judgment on the second ground of Appeal, 'the joint adventure' issue, Croom-Johnson turned common sense on its head and jumped on it. 'It is a little difficult for Mr Cassels because his own client was asked specifically at the hearing whether he was under arrest at the time when this shot which killed Miles was fired. He would not have it. He said that he had not been arrested, that he was not under arrest, that the police officer had not detained him, and all the rest of it. In the face of that it seems to us that it is idle to suggest that this point, if it be the point, about the arrest is one which the jury could take into consideration and about which the Chief Justice ought to have directed the jury. The answers given in cross-examination by an individual on trial do sometimes have the result of destroying the possibility of a good point of law being persisted in, which the learned counsel has endeavoured to get on its feet before a jury, and it seems to us that there is nothing in this point on either of the two grounds.'

Barrister John Parris was later to write, 'Almost every word of that part of the judgment is inaccurate, as can be seen by a transcription of the material parts of the evidence . . . The judgment of Mr Justice Croom-Johnson was, therefore, not an accurate version of the evidence, and the basis on which the second ground of Appeal was rejected was wholly wrong.'

Reginald Paget, QC, MP, was later to write, 'To dispose of this vital question which affected life or death in such a manner was surely astonishing. I do not believe that even upon the strictest law Bentley, in the circumstances of this, was responsible for a murder which he did not commit and which was committed by another more than a quarter of an hour after he had surrendered.'

Barrister Charles Duff was later to write, 'Bentley was, in fact, safely under arrest when Craig fired the fatal shot.'

Criminologist Rupert Furneaux was later to write, 'It was a curious but an important point that, at the time when Miles was killed, Bentley was in custody. A person is under arrest from the moment he is touched by a police officer.'

250

Lord Justice Devlin, dealing not with the Bentley case, but with the general issue, was later to write, 'Arrest and imprisonment are in law the same thing. Any form of physical restraint is an arrest and imprisonment is only a continuing arrest.'

Only three passages in Bentley's evidence refer to this aspect. The first occurred when he was being questioned by his own Counsel.

CASSELS: What happened after you got behind the stack?
BENTLEY: Sergeant Fairfax come and took me, Sir, because I couldn't see nothing where I was standing, Sir, and he come and took me, Sir, and walked me across the roof, Sir.
HUMPHREYS: I can't hear.
CASSELS: Sergeant Fairfax came and took you and walked you across the roof?
BENTLEY: That's right, Sir.
CASSELS: When Sergeant Fairfax came and took you, did he say anything?
BENTLEY: He said, 'I'm a police officer. I've got the place surrounded.'
THE LORD CHIEF JUSTICE: What did he say?
BENTLEY: 'I'm a police officer. I've got the place surrounded.'
CASSELS: When Sergeant Fairfax took hold of you, did you make any effort to struggle?
BENTLEY: No, Sir.
CASSELS: Or any attempt to strike him?
BENTLEY: No, Sir.
CASSELS: At the time when Sergeant Fairfax got hold of you, did you know that Craig was armed?
BENTLEY: No, Sir.
CASSELS: Did you say anything before any shot was fired?
BENTLEY: No, Sir.
CASSELS: What happened between the time Sergeant Fairfax took hold of you and the time the first shot was fired?

BENTLEY: Well, I don't know what happened on Christopher's side, Sir, but Sergeant Fairfax had me and nothing happened. We just walked along the roof.

THE LORD CHIEF JUSTICE: Did you break away from him once?

BENTLEY: No, Sir.

CASSELS: Did you say 'Let him have it, Chris'?

BENTLEY: No, Sir.

CASSELS: Up until the time a shot was fired did you know that Craig had a gun?

BENTLEY: No, Sir.

CASSELS: What happened when the shot was fired?

BENTLEY: Sergeant Fairfax leaned on me and fell over, like that, Sir. He didn't touch the floor though, Sir.

CASSELS: What did you do when the shot was fired?

BENTLEY: I stood by Sergeant Fairfax.

CASSELS: You stood by Sergeant Fairfax?

BENTLEY: Yes, Sir.

CASSELS: Did you make any attempt to get away from him?

BENTLEY: No, Sir.

CASSELS: Did you make any attempt to strike him while he was on the ground or while he was falling?

BENTLEY: No, Sir.

CASSELS: After the shot was fired, did you see where Craig was standing?

BENTLEY: Yes, Sir, just a little way from the lift-shaft, Sir.

CASSELS: Did you make any attempt to join Craig?

BENTLEY: No, Sir.

CASSELS: What happened when Sergeant Fairfax recovered from the shock?

BENTLEY: He got up, Sir, well, leaned up, Sir, and put me behind that staircase.

CASSELS: Did you make any attempt to get away from him?

BENTLEY: No, Sir.

CASSELS: Is it right, as he says, that he searched you and found the knuckleduster and the knife?

252

BENTLEY: I gave him the knuckleduster, Sir; I took it out of my pocket myself.

CASSELS: From that time until you were taken downstairs by the police, did you remain behind the staircase head?

BENTLEY: I did, Sir.

CASSELS: Were you being held all the time by the police officers?

BENTLEY: No, Sir.

Then, in cross-examination Humphreys referred to the moment when Fairfax got hold of Bentley.

HUMPHREYS: Then he grabbed you?

BENTLEY: Yes, Sir.

HUMPHREYS: And you knew you were grabbed by a police officer when you were trying to commit a crime, didn't you? Arrested? You know what that means?

BENTLEY: Yes, Sir.

HUMPHREYS: And while you are *arrested* you do your best to break away, and he, with you in *custody*, pursued Craig round the stack. Is that right?

BENTLEY: No, Sir.

HUMPHREYS: At any rate, you broke away from him, didn't you?

BENTLEY: No, Sir.

Then later in cross-examination:

HUMPHREYS: According to you, when you were over by the staircase you weren't being held by a police officer. Is that right?

BENTLEY: That's right, Sir.

HUMPHREYS: So that you weren't under arrest at the time?

BENTLEY: I was standing there, Sir.

HUMPHREYS: But you weren't being held?

BENTLEY: No, Sir.

HUMPHREYS: You were quite free to run away if you wanted to?

253

BENTLEY: Yes, Sir.
HUMPHREYS: And you were still on the roof when the shooting was going on?
BENTLEY: Yes, Sir.

It is quite clear that Bentley accepted that he was under arrest, that he had been arrested, and that he was being detained by a police officer. Despite Humphreys' attempt to confuse the issue by equating 'grabbed at' with 'arrested', there is no doubt that Bentley had been arrested. On the evidence contained in his statement to the police he considered he was. 'I should have mentioned that after the plain clothes policeman got up the drain-pipe and arrested me, another policeman in uniform followed and I heard someone call him "Mac". He was with us when the other policeman was killed.' This by any standards is vital evidence in the 'arrest' issue. *It was not once referred to during the entire Appeal. Also entirely ignored was the fact that the Lord Chief Justice considered that Bentley's evidence in the witness box was a reiteration of his statement.* Immediately before the jury retired to consider its verdict, Lord Goddard made the following remarks: 'Will you consider your verdict? Would you like any of these? Would you like the statement? I ought to remind you, but it doesn't really matter, because Bentley has been in the witness box and really *repeated his evidence on oath*, that strictly speaking the written statement made is not evidence against Craig, but the evidence he has given in the witness box is all part of the evidence in the case.' It is manifest, from the remarks that Lord Goddard made, that in his opinion Bentley had stated in the witness box that he was under arrest. It is manifest, from Christmas Humphreys' trial statements, that the Crown Prosecutor considered that Bentley was under arrest. On the evidence given by Detective Sergeant Fairfax he was. On the evidence given by PC McDonald he was. On the evidence given by PC Jaggs he was. On the evidence given by PC Harrison he was. The fact that Bentley was not literally being held all the time – for

254

example when Fairfax and McDonald released him to pull the dying policeman to cover – led the youth to say that he had been free to run away. The fact that he did *not* run to Craig illustrates quite clearly that he was accepting that he had been arrested, and that he was not prepared to make an issue of it. The issues raised at the Appeal hearing appeared to be beyond the powers of understanding of the Appeal judges.

The conclusion is inescapable that Croom-Johnson in his judgment of the Appeal, was not giving an accurate version of the trial evidence. The basis on which the second ground of Appeal had been rejected was wholly and totally wrong. Moreover the three Appeal judges suddenly attributed to Bentley the wisdom of Solomon. The feeble-minded epileptic with the mental age of eleven had, for a brief moment during the trial, acquired infallibility. In their opinion Bentley had said he had not been arrested, that he was not under arrest, that the police officer had not detained him; and Bentley must be right and everybody else wrong. Apparently he had also acquired a method of communication with the learned Appeal judges that circumvented the transcript of the trial, for no such assertions by Bentley appear in the verbatim reports. If God does indeed move in mysterious ways he could still learn a thing or two from those Appeal judges. They not only had access to a police deposition that does not, and never did, exist, they also had evidence from Bentley that does not, and never did, exist. The judicial murder of Derek Bentley had now been given its official seal of approval.

7

'Help me, please help me!'

The Appeal judges dismissed Derek Bentley's Appeal on 13 January 1953. The date for his execution was 28 January. But his family were completely confident that their son would be reprieved. It was a belief they shared with the majority of people in this country.

Quite apart from all the information that has been published and made public for the first time in this book, there was overwhelming evidence that had been made public at the time to justify that belief. The fact that he had been under arrest for fifteen minutes before PC Miles was killed. The fact that he did not have a gun. The fact that the jury had recommended mercy. The fact that the Lord Chief Justice of England had concurred with that recommendation. The fact that the Lord Chief Justice of England had stated that Craig was the more guilty of the two. The fact that the more guilty of the two would live while the less guilty died. These facts, and many more, buoyed not only the Bentley family's hopes, but also those of the majority of their countrymen and women. This was England in 1953; the second Elizabethan age was dawning. We were not a barbarous nation. Had not this country been a principal architect of the Judgment at Nuremberg? Ensuring that even the Nazis who survived the Second World War received 'just and fair trials'? Our sense of justice, mercy and humanity was second to none. A few days before the Appeal the Bentleys had taken a friend's advice and begun to organize a petition to the Home Secretary, though they felt it was probably a waste of time.

256

After the Appeal judges had pronounced judgment it seemed less like a waste of time, and they set to work in real earnest. There then occurred a remarkable phenomenon. The petitions virtually organized themselves. People, the ordinary people of this country, wrote to the Bentleys in their thousands, protesting at what they considered an appalling injustice. These were not the fine legal minds of this country. Not men and women capable of quoting Rex *v.* Appleby, or Mr Justice Brett, they were people capable of applying that virtue so highly prized by Lord Goddard, 'common sense'. They believed that it would be wrong for Derek Bentley to hang. They wrote, not only from all parts of Great Britain, but quite literally from all parts of the world. Mail arrived by the sackful, and the GPO were obliged to create a special delivery service. Two secretaries volunteered to help sort the avalanche of letters. The GPO installed a telephone in the Norbury house, and it rang continually from the moment it was installed until well after the fight had been lost – there were never less than five hundred calls per day, all conveying the same message: 'Your son must not hang.'

This was not merely an anti-capital-punishment campaign; indeed, many who approved of capital punishment shrank from this particular hanging. It was not a campaign inspired by the press; *indeed it was in spite of the press, for without exception they considered that Derek Bentley should hang.* This was a remarkable example of spontaneous action. Vast numbers of the people in this country had made up their minds, independently of newspaper opinion, independently of political pressure groups, indeed independently of each other, that to allow the execution of Derek Bentley to take place would be to allow injustice to reign unchallenged. Most remarkable of all, until the very eve of execution there was no public indication that any of the Establishment agreed with this view.

Shortly after the death of PC Miles the public's sympathies were solely for the dead policeman and his widow. This resulted in violent scenes at Croydon Magistrates'

Court (see Chapter 3), but even then the hostility had been directed at Craig, not at Bentley. That in itself was a tacit acceptance that Bentley was not responsible for the policeman's death. Now that death was to be avenged by the death of Bentley. The British public, applying its own common sense, came to the inescapable conclusion that the two did not equate. And so they wrote in their thousands to the national newspapers. Not all of them considered that a miscarriage of justice was about to occur, but the ratio demanding that Bentley should be reprieved was never less than eight to one. Six hundred reprieve forms, each capable of containing one hundred signatures, were distributed by Mr Bentley. Car stickers proclaiming 'Bentley must not die' were in evidence all over the country.

It is important to remember that in the England of 1953 professional protesters and professional agitators were unknown. The public reaction to the sentence of death passed on Bentley was the forerunner, the first post-war manifestation of public protest on such a scale. We have, in the last few years, seen huge public protests about the Vietnam War, a war in which Britain is not directly involved. At the time of the Bentley case the Korean War was raging. Thousands of British soldiers were fighting in Korea, many hundreds of them died, yet there was virtually no public protest. Awareness of moral issues was obviously not the public's forte at the time. It took the issue of the hanging of a nineteen-year-old, feeble-minded epileptic to arouse public protest on such a scale.

The Bentleys had originally hoped to obtain a thousand signatures on petition forms asking the Home Secretary to grant their son a reprieve. Before he was executed the number of signatures had risen to one hundred thousand. Many thousands more wrote to their MPs. Many thousands more sent telegrams to their MPs and to the Home Secretary. Many thousands more, like one group of thirty civil servants, sent their own petitions direct to the Home Secretary. It was then, and remains, the greatest public protest against the execution of a man for murder.

It was all aimed at one man, Sir David Maxwell Fyfe; and as the execution day drew nearer he sat in the Home Office and brooded on the decision he had to make.

Meanwhile Derek Bentley also waited, sitting in the condemned cell at Wandsworth Prison and guarded round the clock. He displayed at this time an awesome courage. The nineteen-year-old boy whose teachers and friends had considered a coward, now greeted his parents calmly on their daily visits, joked and laughed with his warders as he waited for his reprieve to be announced. The meetings with his parents were like impromptu parties. Bentley talked quietly to his parents and his sister Iris of ordinary, everyday things. He asked them how his dogs were, how his young brother Dennis was behaving. And as he talked a man named Pierrepoint was making a note in his diary that he would be away from his North of England home towards the end of January.

John Parris was at this time not only a highly successful barrister, he was also prospective Socialist candidate for Bradford North. On 18 January he rose to speak at a political meeting, choosing as his theme 'Crime and Punishment'. Parris had already shown during the Craig/Bentley trial that he was not a man to be inhibited by Lord Goddard; as he spoke, he again showed that quality. 'The present emotional campaign for the reintroduction of flogging has been almost entirely instigated by Lord Goddard.' Continuing, Parris said, 'It is undesirable that anyone holding high judicial office places himself in a position where he must be criticized for political utterances.' With the press reporters busily scribbling, the Leeds barrister warmed to his theme. 'I cannot say anything about the manner in which Lord Goddard conducts criminal trials. But I am entitled to say that many of his recent utterances in the House of Lords are sensational and untrue nonsense, so much so, that many of the members of that House regard them with complete contempt.' Parris concluded with the observation that Lord Goddard's comments on the flogging issue were 'paranoiac outbursts'.

For a barrister to attack the Lord Chief Justice of England in this manner was very rare and John Parris was subsequently to pay a high price for displaying such courage. A few months later he was suspended from practising at the Bar for four months. He was suspended, according to the masters of the Bench of Gray's Inn, not for making a political utterance, but because he had been reported in the press as saying, 'Unfortunately, I am precluded from expressing in public the universal consensus of opinion in the legal profession in which he [Goddard] conducts criminal trials.'

In suspending Parris, the Masters of Gray's Inn displayed a touching belief in the infallibility of the Press. The speech had been extensively reported in the national press, but only the *Yorkshire Post* carried the offending remarks. It was on this 'evidence' that Parris was suspended.

As the January days hurtled by, MPs began to interest themselves in what had, by then, become known as 'The Bentley Case'. The Bentleys met many of them, and all promised to do everything in their power to secure a reprieve. A week before the execution date, Bentley's parents, still awaiting word from the Home Secretary, started to fear that, despite everything, their son might hang. Although the vast majority of the post that was daily arriving at their house was from people declaring their belief that Bentley must be reprieved, there were one or two notable exceptions. One of these was a parcel addressed to Mrs Bentley. It had been carefully wrapped. After undoing the many layers of paper, Mrs Bentley found a small card. On it was written 'Your son needs this.' Lifting the lid of the box, Mrs Bentley saw a length of rope tied in the shape of a noose. She collapsed. For the first time the awful implications of what might happen were brought quite literally into the Bentley home. As if in confirmation that their fears were only too well founded, there came the news on 22 January that they had been denied the right of appeal to the House of Lords. The Attorney General, Sir Lionel Heald, refused to grant the necessary fiat (certificate). The privilege of appeal to the House of Lords was normally granted when it 'raised a point of law of exceptional public importance and it was in the public interest that such an appeal should be brought'. The issue of when a joint adventure ceased to be a joint adventure, which had been one of the main points of appeal, *had never been decided by an English Court*. Tens of thousands of people were publicly saying that Bentley must be reprieved, yet the Attorney General, a paid servant of the people, refused to allow an appeal to the House of Lords. All that was left now to prevent Bentley being launched prematurely into eternity was the Home Secretary, Sir David Maxwell Fyfe. As Mr Bentley was later to write, 'Now we were on our knees asking for mercy.' There was precious little time for that mercy to be dispensed.

Two days later, on 24 January, Dr Denis Hill could bear the waiting no longer. It will be remembered that Dr Hill, a recognized authority on human brainwaves, had examined Derek Bentley at the Maudsley Hospital prior to his Old Bailey trial, and established that Bentley was an epileptic. Now he was tormented by the thought that the epileptic was about to be hanged. He wrote to the Home Office, leaving them in no doubt as to the implications of Bentley's epilepsy.

On the same day that Dr Hill wrote to the Home Office, Mr Bentley received in the huge welter of mail one particular telegram that puzzled him. The telegram read, 'See me at once.' The name of the sender was Mrs Sarah Bartley of 65 York Road, Southend-on-Sea, Essex. The woman was unknown to the Bentley family, but after discussing it with his wife Mr Bentley phoned for a hired car and set out for Southend. Eventually, after what seemed an eternal journey, he arrived at the address. Mrs Bartley, an elderly woman, showed the puzzled man into her home.

261

She apologized for causing him the inconvenience of such a long journey and explained that she would have travelled to London if she had not been an invalid. Then she dropped a bombshell. 'My brother is the Home Secretary. I have written to him asking him to spare your son's life. Have no fear, Mr Bentley, Derek will not die.' Numbly Mr Bentley attempted to grasp the implications of the conversation. Mrs Bartley continued, 'I have sat in this room, night after night, thinking about you, praying for you. After I had written to my brother I thought I must let you know at once.' Mr Bentley was filled with hope. If the Home Secretary's own family considered that his son's execution would be a cruel injustice, then surely humanity would prevail and Derek Bentley would be reprieved? 'He will not die,' she went on, 'go home and tell your wife. It will comfort her.' They continued to talk for over an hour and from their conversation Mr Bentley was able to draw a measure of faith and hope.

To this day Mr Bentley believes that Mrs Bartley was indeed the sister of Sir David Maxwell Fyfe. The sad fact is that she was not. Whatever her motivations, whatever her reasons, what she told the frightened, desperate man was totally untrue.

On the morning of 26 January, with less than forty-eight hours left before the execution, the Bentley family were still awaiting news from the Home Office. They were still receiving an enormous quantity of letters and telegrams by every post, but from the Home Secretary there was nothing. At lunchtime there was a ring at the front door. It was yet another reporter. Since the Appeal had been rejected the Bentley household had not been free of reporters for one minute. Some of them quite literally moved in. Not only those from British papers, but reporters from America, Germany, Sweden, France and many other countries, were the Bentleys' constant companions during those days. This young reporter was just another to add to the fold. Mrs Bentley was about to bring him in and give him a cup of tea, but he was in a hurry to ask his question. 'Is it true,' he asked, 'that the Home Secretary has refused to grant a reprieve?' Mrs Bentley, near the point of collapse, called her husband. 'No,' he said, they had heard nothing. The young reporter seemed as disturbed as the Bentleys, and muttering that his paper had got the news that morning, he apologized and quickly left. For a moment the Bentleys were too stunned to think, then Iris wondered aloud if a letter had come through the ordinary post. The amount of mail coming into the Bentley household at this time was so enormous, that each fresh sackful of letters and telegrams was dumped into the bath and then sorted. The family hurried upstairs to the bathroom and frantically began to wade through the pile. Eventually Mrs Bentley came across an envelope bearing the insignia OHMS. Her husband tore it open. It said:

Sir,

I am directed by the Secretary of State to inform you that he has given careful consideration to the petition submitted by you on behalf of your son Derek Bentley, and I am to express to you his deep regret that after considering all the circumstances of the case he has failed to discover any sufficient ground to justify him in advising Her Majesty to interfere with the due course of law.

I am, Sir,

Your obedient servant,
(Signed) *F. A. Newsam*

The Home Office decision concerning their son's life had been delivered through the ordinary mail, with the pools coupons, the circulars, the thousands of letters pledging support. It had been posted on Saturday and eventually arrived in the welter of mail on the Monday. The Communication concerning the life or death of their son did not, in the eyes of the Home Office, justify a special messenger.

It is a revealing indication of the amount of conscience, the amount of compassion displayed by the Home Secretary. Quite apart from the implicit callousness of such an action, it had the effect of reducing by two days the amount of time in which effective action could be taken to counter the decision.

Recalling this moment when they learned of the Home Secretary's decision, Mr Bentley said, 'I do not want to describe what happened to my wife and daughter after I had read the letter out to them, but I shall hear their screams as long as I live.' A doctor was called immediately and both women were given sedation. Later that day, when they had sufficiently recovered, all three of them went to Wandsworth Jail to see Derek. As they walked into the interview room, all were near the point of collapse. They knew that he had already been advised of the Home Secretary's decision, and they feared the effect the news might have had on him. Yet again he was to give them strength. His smile was strained, he looked paler, but he still appeared to be cheerful. The nineteen-year-old epileptic with the mind of a child was displaying the courage of a man, courage that most men would surely find completely beyond them in such a situation. Or was he still, with less than thirty-six hours to live, unaware of the strange and horrible thing that was to happen to him? It seems unlikely. His remarks as he talked to his parents appear to indicate only too well that he was fully aware.

'Dad, I'm not afraid to die, because I'm innocent. As long as you keep your chin up I'll keep mine up, whatever happens. Everybody knows I didn't kill Mr Miles, so I've got nothing on me conscience. I know I did wrong going with Craig. I didn't know what he was going to do. I wouldn't kill anything, you know that Dad, don't you?'

Then, a moment later, for the first and only time, he broke down and exclaimed, 'Help me, please help me!' If Derek Bentley ever understood what was to happen to him, it was at this moment. Painfully his family tried to reassure him. They told him that his case was to be debated in the House of Commons on the following day. They told him of all the important people who were convinced that he should, and would, be reprieved. It must have been difficult for Derek to grasp the fact that he was to be the subject of a debate in the seat of British democracy. Had he ever been advised of the outcome of that debate, it would have been totally beyond his powers of comprehension. How would he have understood the Speaker's ruling that the House of Commons could not debate whether or not Derek Bentley should hang until after he had hanged?

Returning to their home, the Bentleys were advised that Mrs Craig had some new evidence that might help their son. There had been no contact between the two families since that fateful night in November; now the mother of the young boy who, in the Bentleys' opinion, was the sole cause of their son's fearful predicament, wanted to meet them. For the Bentleys, this ordeal was every bit as great as the one they had just suffered at Wandsworth Prison. Ironically, the evidence that Mrs Craig had was not new, but the Bentleys were prepared to clutch at any straw. It was really a reaffirmation of what Craig had said in the witness box at the Old Bailey. Derek had not said 'Let him have it, Chris'. He had not shouted to the police that Craig had a ·45 and plenty of ammunition. And Bentley always called him (Craig) Kiddo or Kid. (This last statement is in fact incorrect; although Bentley usually used these names for Craig, he did on other occasions call him Chris.) Whether Craig, who was himself in a highly emotional state by this time, was aware of what he was saying, was a moot point. The night before his friend was hanged, he declared that he wanted to die with Derek. To the Bentley family, with their backs to the wall in the fight to keep Derek alive, any help was welcome, from whatever quarter. They arranged with Mrs Craig that on the following day they would all go to the Home Office and lay this 'new evidence' before the Home Secretary.

The following morning they all presented themselves at the Home Office and advised Sir Frank Newsam of

Craig's statement. Mr Bentley stumbled his way through the interview. Newsam promised to put the information before Sir David Maxwell Fyfe within the hour.

One of the reporters who had been in constant attendance at the Bentley home now took a dazed and bewildered Mr Bentley to lunch; it was Harry Procter. As he sat there eating, Mr Procter calmly said that if, on the night before Derek Bentley was hanged, he wrote a final letter to his family, the *Sunday Pictorial* would 'pay generously for permission to publish that letter exclusively the following Sunday'. Mr Bentley, by now too numb to grasp the full implications of Procter's offer, accepted it.

Among the many thousands of people who were shocked by the Home Secretary's decision was a man who had played an active part in ensuring that Bentley was found guilty of murder. That man was Lord Goddard. From the moment that the trial had finished he was convinced that Bentley would be reprieved. But as the days went by without word from the Home Office, the Lord Chief Justice of England became more and more disturbed. When it was finally announced that there would be no reprieve, he was profoundly distressed. He had felt sure that there would be one; perhaps if he had been less sure, and if he had known then that Sir David Maxwell Fyfe would not consult him before announcing his decision, he would have attempted to exercise a greater degree of impartiality during the course of the trial.

Undoubtedly the fact that he was completely convinced from the very outset of the case that Bentley would ultimately be reprieved had greatly influenced Lord Goddard. It had enabled him to treat the proceedings at the Old Bailey almost as a symbolic ritual. Confident in the belief that whatever the outcome, the hapless Bentley would live, the Lord Chief Justice of England indulged himself to the full.

During my interview with Lord Goddard there was only one truly pathetic moment. We were talking about the public's opinion of his performance as Lord Chief Justice. Looking at me, he said, 'It's not an easy job, you know.' I wondered then, and still wonder, if it was made harder by having to live with the fact that, more than any other single person, he had placed the rope around Bentley's neck. Sure that the Court verdict would be reversed, he had played his symbolic game, and now it was too late. He had done his work too well, and it could not be undone. The democratic machinery was moving into top gear, and nothing could stop it.

Dr Denis Hill had still received no reply to his letter to the Home Office. He telephoned the Home Office and requested permission to publish the EEG findings on Derek Bentley. As all three examinations had been undertaken while Bentley was under the ultimate control of the Home Office, such permission was essential before he could make the findings public, as he had been acting on behalf of Brixton Prison when he acquired the relevant information. The Home Office refused to give permission, resorting to the time-honoured cliché that to advise the public of Bentley's mental condition 'was not in the public interest'.

A telegram to Winston Churchill on board the *Queen Mary* returning from America; a letter to the Queen asking her to intercede – these had proved of no avail to the Bentley family. It will be remembered that Churchill had taken the unprecedented step of demanding a full police report, forty-eight hours after the death of PC Miles. The Prime Minister's reply to the Bentleys' plea was simply, 'I have forwarded your telegram to the Home Secretary without comment.'

All that was left now was the debate in the House of Commons. On the evening of 26 January Sydney Silverman, the fiery Labour Member for Nelson and Colne, had gone to the Table Office and presented a Motion that, when debated, would almost certainly result in a massive vote in favour of a reprieve. Of this there was no doubt whatsoever. Over fifty MPs signed that Motion before it was presented, many more signed it afterwards, hundreds of others had pledged themselves to vote for it. The feeling all through the House was that the result of the debate was a foregone conclusion. So it was with high expectations that Mr Bentley and his daughter Iris went to the House of Commons on the afternoon of 27 January. They were met by Sydney Silverman, who informed them that the Motion had been removed from the Order Paper on the Speaker's instructions. Silverman advised the Bentleys that he intended to fight Speaker William Morrison's ruling. He was as good as his word.

The House of Commons was packed to the doors when he rose at 3 p.m. Addressing his remarks specifically to Speaker Morrison, Silverman stated that he wished to ask about the Motion that he had sought to put on the Order Paper the previous evening. The rules of procedure of the House are such that Silverman was prevented from discussing the merits of the Motion; all he could do was question the Speaker's decision to remove it. The Speaker's action, Silverman said, involved the whole matter of the authority of Parliament and the right of Parliament to control the Executive in any action which a Minister takes, particularly in matters where the Royal Prerogative of Mercy is involved.

He recounted how on the previous day, shortly after 7 p.m., he had taken to the Table Office the Motion: 'That this House respectfully dissents from the opinion of the Home Secretary that there were no sufficient reasons for advising the exercise of the Royal Clemency in the case of Derek Bentley; and urges him to reconsider the matter so far as to give effect to the recommendation of the jury and to the expressed view of the Lord Chief Justice that Bentley's guilt was less than that of his co-defendant Christopher Craig.' When Silverman delivered his Motion, he recalled, it had already been signed by about fifty MPs from both parties; during the course of that evening signatures supporting the Motion grew to over two hundred including those of many who held high office. The Motion had been accepted by the Speaker's clerks without question; Silverman remained in the House until 8.30 p.m. During that time no question had been raised by the Speaker's clerks concerning the Motion, but at a quarter past ten that night – too late to do anything about it – Silverman had been advised by phone that, on the Speaker's instructions, it had been removed from the Order Paper and therefore could not be the subject of debate. Consequently what was taking place now on the afternoon of 27 January was a debate about a debate.

As Silverman started to ask for the reason, he was interrupted by the Speaker, who referred him to a particular page of Erskine May, the Parliamentary bible of rules, procedure and precedent. Unimpressed, Silverman declared that this did not relate to the current issue. He cited what, in his opinion, were the only two possible reasons in Erskine May to justify the removal of a Motion, neither of which related to his abortive Motion. The first was where a Motion's sole purpose was the annoyance of a Member, and was clearly inapplicable. As for the second, he went on, 'Whether the Motion was wholly out of order, it has been established and I think would not be contested in any quarter, that a Minister's action in the advice which he tenders to the Crown is, like any other action he takes, action for which he is responsible to the House of Commons. There is no doubt about that at all.'

All eyes were upon the small, silver-haired figure. As he developed his argument, telegrams were constantly being delivered into the Chamber to many of the MPs, and the pile at Silverman's feet fanned out ever larger as he spoke. 'Nobody has ever doubted that when a Minister presumes to offer advice to the Crown upon the exercise of a Royal Prerogative, he is responsible to the House for the advice he tenders. The exercise of the Prerogative of Mercy in

269

this country is not an arbitrary act as it might be in some totalitarian State; it is as much subject to the constitutional principles of a Parliamentary democracy as any other act by any other person. It is not beyond challenge.'

He accepted that there had, in the past, been considerable controversy over exactly when such Ministerial action could be challenged. It was a question of timing, but, he felt, the matter had been resolved; once a Minister had given advice to the Crown, that advice could be questioned in the House. That was the situation in general. Turning to the particular, he asked: 'Is it to be said that this House may have its way – that the Home Secretary shall be responsible to the House for the advice he has given – but only when it is too late to overtake it? Is the House to wait until Bentley is dead before it is entitled to say that he should not die?'

Even if this was the situation, a debate on the morrow would by any definition be in order, and it did not justify the *permanent* removal of the Motion. Under a crowded press gallery, Silverman confidently declared, 'This is a matter which arouses interest of the deepest kind, not merely in the House. I venture to think that if it were possible to put such a matter to the vote today, there would be an overwhelming majority of this House who would think that the Home Secretary had decided wrongly. I have here more than two hundred telegrams, from all sorts of people all over the country, all of them except one holding the decision to be wrong, and that one telling me only that the Home Secretary would probably tell me to mind my own business.' Throughout his speech he had spoken quietly. He had no need to shout, for the only sound in the chamber, other than his voice, was the cautious to-ing and fro-ing of officials delivering yet more telegrams to the listening assembly. Now, for the first time his voice rose to a shout as he unleashed the emotion that he had been suppressing.

'Sir, I *am* minding my own business! That is why I am raising this question with you. It is the business of all of us if this boy hangs when we think he ought not to hang. This is a Parliamentary democracy, and we are all responsible for what occurs.'

He did not wish, he concluded, to debate the merits of the matter. That he would do just as soon as the Speaker decided the House may debate it. But in removing the Motion the Speaker had exceeded his authority.

Silverman sat down, and attention focused on the Speaker. His authority had been challenged in no small way. William Morrison was comparatively new to the office of Speaker, having taken the Chair in 1950. Silverman had presented a strong case, and many MPs wondered if the Speaker would find it unanswerable. By now there was not an inch of space on the benches; many members were standing to witness this life or death debate. Morrison, known to his colleagues as 'Shakes' because of his liking for quoting the Bard, addressed the House in his round Scottish tones.

'I have listened to what the honourable member said, and I fully appreciate the deep feeling that exists in many parts of the country on this matter . . . In his case, the Motion of the honourable member, which I saw late last night, dealt with the case of a capital sentence which is still pending, and there is a long line of authorities of all my predecessors saying that, while a capital sentence is pending, the matter should not be discussed by the House.' This, then, was the kernel of the Speaker's argument. The House of Commons could not say that Bentley should not hang until he had hanged. The Speaker cited a previous ruling to justify this unedifying doctrine, a ruling which found no favour with Sydney Silverman, and he immediately contested it. He was not alone in his objection. Reginald Paget, another Labour MP, rose to question it, stating categorically that such a Motion had never been ruled out of order before. Paget, like Silverman, was a member of the legal profession, but never in his many courtroom appearances had he been so devastating as on that January afternoon.

'The second submission that I would make to you is to ask your guidance and assistance. I think the great condemnation which we made of the German people was that they stood aside and did nothing when dreadful things happened. We are a sovereign assembly. A three-quarter-witted boy of nineteen is to be hanged for a murder that he did not commit, and which was committed fifteen minutes after he was arrested. Can we be made to keep silent when a thing as horrible and as shocking as this is to happen? I ask your guidance because I feel that the great mass of honourable members here feel with me that we ought to be provided with an opportunity to try to prevent this dreadful thing happening.'

Before the Speaker could react to this plea, yet another Labour MP, Leslie Hale, was on his feet. He too challenged the Speaker's ruling, and with particular reason. The precedent that the Speaker had cited had arisen directly from a Motion that Hale himself had attempted to move in 1947. Referring to that precedent, he said, 'You will remember that until 1916 or so, it was almost commonplace to raise questions of the Royal Prerogative, and historically speaking, this power was taken away from the House because we were executing so many decent Irishmen.' This drew from the Conservative benches the first indication that they had tongues in their heads; a number of them objected loudly, but Hale, undeterred, went on to make his point. 'Indeed, that is precisely what happened – that it became a burden on Ministers to defend themselves at that time. Since then successive Speakers have ruled that Questions cannot be asked about the Royal Prerogative until the Minister's advice has been given.' Maxwell Fyfe's decision was lamentable, he said; but it went beyond the question of 'this unhappy youth's life'. What the Speaker had done, he argued, was to take away from the House the one method of raising a matter that could not be raised in any other way – such as the challenging of the Royal Prerogative. He reminded the House of Chuter Ede's announcement, during the 1948

Above, Crown Prosecuting Counsel Christmas Humphreys – later a judge. Below, pathologist Dr David Haler, who carried out the post-mortem examinations on both PC Miles and Derek Bentley.

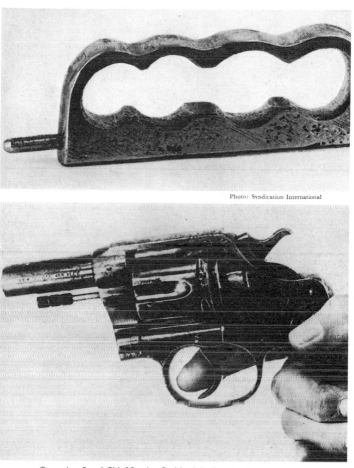

Opposite, Lord Chief Justice Goddard during the Old Bailey trial.
Above, the knuckleduster that Craig gave to Bentley – not used by
either of the two teenagers, but used by Lord Goddard during the
trial. Below, Craig's ·455 Eley revolver – his 'Colt 45'. With its
sawn-off barrel it was inaccurate to a degree of at least six feet at a
range of 39 feet, the distance between Craig and Miles.

Left, after the trial Derek Bentley's parents visit him in Wandsworth Prison. Centre, l to r, Harry Procter, Lucy Craig (Christopher's sister), Madeleine McLoughlin (Procter's assistant), Mrs Craig, Mr Craig. Right, Lord Kilmuir of Creich, the former Sir David Maxwell Fyfe (in this picture, wearing the Lord Chancellor's robes after being sworn in to that office in 1954). As Home Secretary he made the final decision that Derek Bentley should die.

Photo: Paul Popper

Photo: PA

Photo: UPI

Left above, Sidney Silverman, MP, ardent campaigner against capital punishment and for Bentley's reprieve; below, Albert Pierrepoint, the public hangman, by whose hand Derek Bentley died. Right, an outraged crowd tears down the notice of Bentley's execution from the gates of Wandsworth Prison.

In 1966 the Home Office gave permission for Bentley's reinterment. He now lies in Croydon Cemetery, Mitcham Road, a few yards from where PC Miles's ashes were scattered.

debates on the Criminal Justice Bill. It will be recalled that, after Silverman's amendment suspending hanging for five years had been passed by the Commons, Chuter Ede, the Home Secretary, announced that until the amendment had been ratified by the Lords he would exercise the Royal Prerogative of Mercy on any person found guilty of murder. As Hale pointed out, the House could, if it so wished, have put down a Motion saying it did not agree with this action; this was made clear after Lord Goddard's attack on the Home Secretary. They chose not to do so, yet it was a Ministerial decision affecting not one life, but many, that would be directly affected by the Royal Prerogative. 'Once we have a situation where a Home Secretary can say "I am going to defer to the views of the House of Commons and am going to suspend capital punishment in deference to its decision", then, surely, it cannot be argued that this is not a matter in which there is Ministerial responsibility to the House of Commons.' If it could be so argued, 'then this was the gravest invasion of the rights and privileges of the House made over the past three hundred years'.

The Speaker's action, Hale said, could be taken to suggest that the Speaker was protecting a member of the Government. Conservative members again objected vociferously, but Hale was not going to let them stop him. He concluded that the Speaker did not have the power to stifle the debate and that, 'Here was a matter referring to Ministerial conduct and a matter of grave public urgency on which the public are deeply moved, and most of them deeply shocked. In these circumstances, I submit that the Motion should have been on the Order Paper today.'

The Speaker, having failed to impress the Labour benches with a 1947 precedent, now delved further back into Parliamentary history, citing rulings from as far back as the Lipski and Maybrick cases of 1887 and 1889. He must have been reasonably confident that no member would jump up and question these rulings on the basis that he had himself instigated those particular debates, and that they were not relevant to the issue of Derek Bentley's life.

273

Still no Tory MP showed the slightest inclination to speak. The next man to catch the Speaker's eye was Aneurin Bevan. He was prepared, he said, to accept the Speaker's bizarre ruling that no attempt could be made to stop Bentley's hanging until he had hanged. He considered the precedents that the Speaker had cited as unassailable. What worried him was the directive to remove Silverman's Motion from the Order Paper on the grounds that it was out of order. This prevented members of the House from justifying in debate why they considered their particular Motions were in order. This, in Bevan's view, was a very serious step and one that should not be blurred with the issue of whether they could discuss the Royal pleasure before it had been exercised.

While the Speaker was pondering this attack from a new quarter, Silverman sprang to his feet again. He had been busily conferring with friends and hurriedly writing. Now he advised the Speaker that he wished to move the Adjournment of the House under Standing Order No. 9: 'To call attention to a definite matter of urgent public importance, namely the decision of the Home Secretary not to advise Her Majesty to exercise the Royal Prerogative of Mercy in the case of Derek Bentley.' Moving the Adjournment was another gambit to attempt to force a debate on the Bentley case. Silverman took his hastily written Motion to the desk in front of the Speaker and handed it to one of the clerks. It was passed to the Speaker who studied it silently. Had Silverman finally found the device that would unlock the door and allow reason and logic to prevail? The answer was not long in coming. The Speaker ruled that the same precedents that had stifled the initial Motion would suffice to silence this one.

Yet another Labour MP stood up, Desmond Donnelly. He also wished to move the Adjournment of the House: 'To call attention to a definite matter of urgent public importance, namely the action of Mr Speaker in directing that the Motion submitted by the honourable member for Nelson and Colne should not appear on the Order Paper today.'

274

This was a direct attack on the Speaker, but its intention was the same as Silverman's – to force an Adjournment – to discuss the Bentley case. Again those anxious to save Bentley's life were thwarted. It was ruled by, of course, the Speaker himself – that the actions of the Speaker could not be the cause for the Adjournment of the House. The final death pangs of the non-debate consisted largely of accusations and denials that the Speaker had been got at, that Maxwell Fyfe had brought pressure to bear on him to remove Silverman's Motion – all of which he strongly denied. In this atmosphere of recrimination the arguments dwindled away. Rules of conduct and civilized democratic procedure had sapped Derek Bentley's last hopes. As the next item on the agenda, the Argentine Meat Agreement, was raised, MPs crowded from the Chamber.

Throughout the entire debate the Home Secretary had sat like a figure of stone, the men around him equally silent. It was this scene that one writer had in mind a few days later when he wrote of a 'Tory contempt for conscience'. Perhaps their silence was due to the awareness that the legislative machine had taken over, and no matter how much they wanted to they could not stop it. 'A motion can be put down on this subject when the sentence has been executed . . . After the sentence of death has been executed, the Minister responsible may be criticized on the relevant vote of Supply, or on the Adjournment. I have stated that this is the practice of the House, and I cannot alter the practice of the House.'

If the Tory silence upset some people, then the Labour vociferousness upset others. The following day the *Evening Standard* wrote, 'It is clear that the Speaker yesterday had no choice but to rule Mr Silverman's Motion out of order. And Mr Silverman knew this before he instigated the emotional scenes in the House.'

After the non-debate Sydney Silverman left the Chamber and joined the Bentleys. He attempted to explain to Mr Bentley what had transpired. He might just as well have tried to explain the Virgin Birth, as the workings of a debate that reminds one of nothing so much as a passage from Voltaire, and Mr Bentley had never even had the advantage of reading Voltaire.

One of Silverman's great virtues was his inability to recognize defeat. He told the Bentleys that a deputation of six MPs, led by himself and Bevan, intended to take a Petition, signed by over two hundred members of the House, to the Home Secretary, in order to put fresh arguments to him. The petition read:

'We, the undersigned members of the Commons House of Parliament, believing the advice tendered by you to Her Majesty the Queen in the case of Derek Bentley to be grievously mistaken and out of accord with the natural justice of the case, urge that even now you will advise Her Majesty to exercise the Royal Prerogative of Mercy so that the sentence of death upon him be not executed.'

Mr Bentley told the group of MPs that he would return to the House as soon as possible, but first he and his family must pay Derek a visit. (The House of Lords, meanwhile, with a fine sense of priorities, had been debating the seating arrangements for the Coronation.)

Returning home with Iris to collect his wife, Mr Bentley told her of the day's events and reassured her that there would soon be news of their earlier efforts, when they had laid Craig's 'new evidence' before Sir Frank Newsam. Silently she handed her husband a letter that had been delivered a few minutes before his arrival. It had come from the Home Office, this time by special messenger.

'I am directed to inform you that the Secretary of State has given the fullest consideration to your representations, but very much regrets that he has been unable to find any grounds for modifying the decision previously communicated to you.'

Like its predecessor it was signed by Newsam. Without comment or discussion the Bentley family prepared to leave for the last of their daily visits to the condemned block at Wandsworth Prison.

*

Earlier that afternoon, while the Labour Members in the House had been in full cry, another man had gone to see Derek Bentley. Upon arriving at the prison he had not spoken to Bentley, however, but merely watched him exercising in the closed yard with his guards, and as he watched he was busy with pencil and paper. And while Bentley walked, this same man set about rehearsing the work that on the following day he would perform on behalf of the people of this country. He had previously been advised of Bentley's height and weight. He ascertained the correct drop from a chart that gave him the length appropriate to Bentley's weight, and then went to make sure that there would be no unfortunate mishaps the next day. Helped by his assistant and using a sack that weighed approximately the same as Bentley, he checked that the simple apparatus functioned perfectly. The lever was pulled, and the solid oak doors upon which Bentley would stand both fell at exactly the same moment.

It was thoughtful of him to rehearse while Bentley was in the exercise yard. If the boy had been in his cell he would undoubtedly have heard Albert Pierrepoint, the public hangman, working in the next room.

Now, as Bentley waited to see his family, Pierrepoint observed him through a peephole, making a final check to ensure that he had estimated the drop correctly. Mr Pierrepoint undoubtedly earned every penny of his £10 fee.

When the Bentley family were shown into the interview room the teenager was his usual cheerful self. As at all their meetings, there was a thick piece of glass between Bentley and his parents. He was calm, speaking naturally and without effort. Not once did he mention what awaited him next morning. In a little more than twelve hours his life was to be extinguished, but he talked quietly about everyday plebeian things, the only subjects that he was capable of talking about. His mother gave him a newspaper cutting that showed a photograph of his dogs. He was delighted, and asked her to stroke them for him.

Talking later of that final visit, his father said, 'God must have given him great strength then.' Perhaps, but God had also decreed that Bentley should go through life with a congenital lack of intelligence, and for the first time in his life it was an asset. Eventually his family rose to leave. As they walked away Derek Bentley called out, 'See you tomorrow.'

Outside the interview room Mr Bentley collapsed. His wife and daughter helped him to walk out of the prison. Outside, the two women also collapsed, and all three were virtually carried to the waiting car. They did not go home to rest, however, but to the House of Commons to continue the fight. The youth in the condemned cell now had eleven hours to live.

At the House of Commons they were met by Sydney Silverman, who told them of the arguments that had been put before Maxwell Fyfe when the petition had been presented. The Home Secretary had listened for forty-five minutes while Nye Bevan and his colleagues had argued for Bentley's reprieve. Bevan particularly stressed the important new element of public opinion that had risen to a crescendo throughout the country within the past forty-eight hours. The deputation had had the feeling that this and other arguments had impressed the Home Secretary. Sir David gave them their reply just before the House rose. He had given careful consideration to their point of view, the reply said, and had not listened with a closed mind. 'I am well aware that you have added further points of emphasis, but all the same feel that there is not sufficient reason to change my mind. The balance is still the other way.' Slowly the Bentley family walked from the House of Commons.

By now there were spontaneous demonstrations all over London. As the family walked into Parliament Square, they were greeted by a huge crowd shouting, 'Bentley must not hang, Bentley must not hang.' Another large crowd was at this moment marching down Whitehall towards the Home Office. Yet another demonstrated outside the building in Great Peter Street that they believed to be the private residence of Maxwell Fyfe, and another demonstrated outside the home of Sir Anthony Eden. These were not political demonstrations; the crowds were drawn from all political loyalties, all classes, all colours, all creeds. The whole capital seemed to be on the verge of civil strife.

And while protesting thousands ran through the streets, Derek Bentley was dictating a last letter for his family to one of the warders who had been constantly at his side.

At one o'clock in the morning Mr Bentley received a phone call from the police. They were having trouble controlling the crowds, and it was thought that an appeal from Mr Bentley might pacify them. With his daughter Iris he set out once again from his South London home, and arriving in Central London they moved from crowd to crowd urging them to disperse. 'My family and I thank you from the bottom of our hearts,' Mr Bentley declared. 'We shall always be grateful to you. But nothing more can be done. My son is now in God's hands.' But the crowds were in no mood to be pacified. One huge group demanded that Mr Bentley lead them to Buckingham Palace. He felt it would be a useless gesture, and declined. Eventually, at three o'clock in the morning, the Bentleys returned home. They had fought with every ounce of their strength and will, but time, as it always must, had run out. They sat in the room that Derek Bentley had left on that Sunday evening a lifetime ago. There was no more time for fighting, there was now only a time for death. As they waited they pondered in their own way on the quality of English justice.

The morning of 28 January was bitterly cold in London. By 8.30 a.m. nearly a thousand people had gathered outside Wandsworth Prison. Mr Pierrepoint had already made a final check of the equipment in the execution shed, working quietly this time, for all that separated him from Bentley was a thin metal wall. The rope was coiled, fitted to the chain that hung from the overhead beam and secured in position by a piece of pack-thread which would break as Bentley's body dropped. As the clock moved inexorably towards 9.00 a.m. the tension outside mounted, there were scuffles and then fights between sections of the crowd and the police who were guarding the prison.

Inside, the Governor warned his staff that a near-riot situation was developing outside the gates. There were genuine fears that the crowd might attempt to break into the prison and try to succeed where Parliament and the majority of the country had failed.

Outside a motor cyclist from the Post Office appeared with a telegram. Thinking that a last-minute reprieve had been granted the crowd gave a huge cheer.

In a playground at a Luton primary school, children stood counting down to the hour – a scene that had its counterpart in many places throughout the British Isles.

At five minutes to the hour a small group of people gathered outside the condemned cell. Inside with Bentley was the Prison Chaplain, the Reverend Ball. They prayed together, watched by the two warders who had been the youth's companions for the past hour. Outside the door waited a number of prison warders, Governor Lawton, the Under Sheriff of the County of Surrey, C. R. Wigan, the Prison Medical Officer, James Murdoch, a hospital orderly, the prison engineer; and Albert Pierrepoint and his assistant.

On the stroke of nine, the cell door was opened, and Governor Lawton turned to the Under Sheriff and said simply, 'Your prisoner, Sir.' Pierrepoint entered the cell and shook hands with Bentley. The hospital orderly gave the youth a large cup of brandy, which he drank, then Pierrepoint's assistant pinioned his arms above the elbows. The two prison warders then led the way to the execution shed, not through the cell door, but through a wall of the condemned cell that slid away to reveal to Bentley that he had been living virtually in the execution shed.

By now Bentley was crying silently. He was guided to a chalk-mark on the trap. Taking his last look at the men gathered about him he sobbed, 'I didn't say it. I didn't tell Chris to shoot that policeman.' Pierrepoint placed the white cap over Bentley's head, then put the noose around the youth's neck and adjusted it. His assistant meanwhile had been securing Bentley's legs with a leather strap. Pierrepoint gave a sign for everyone to stand well clear of the trap, then he kicked the release bolt from the lever. The heavy oak doors dropped open and life began to leave the body of Derek William Bentley. The time that elapsed from the moment that Pierrepoint entered the condemned cell until the moment that Derek Bentley's body was swinging silently in space was less than twenty seconds. He was left hanging for sixty more minutes, to ensure that the last spark of life had been squeezed from his body. The heart in the body of an executed person has been known to continue to beat for twenty minutes. Just eighty-six days had passed since Derek Bentley had left his home and taken a threepenny bus ride to oblivion.

As Bentley had been walking those few steps to the gallows the crowd outside the prison had fallen silent. Mrs Van Der Elst, a well-known campaigner for the abolition of capital punishment, declared, 'Let us be with him at his time of need.' The men in the crowd removed their hats. There was one minute of total silence, then the crowd sang 'Abide with me' and the 23rd Psalm, 'The Lord is my Shepherd'. For a time they were quiet and orderly; then the gates swung open and a warder came out with two notices in a glass case that he attempted to put up on the green prison gates. One notice declared that the judgment of death on Derek William Bentley had been executed. The other notice stated that Bentley had been subsequently examined by the Prison Medical Officer and was dead. The warder was immediately engulfed in a surging crowd trying to grab the notices. For five minutes, aided by the police, he struggled to hook the board on the gates. Three men forced their way past the police, grabbed the frame and smashed it against the gates. Glass showered over the police and the struggling crowd. Another warder appeared and attempted to straighten the smashed frame, now hanging drunkenly on the gate; he was dragged away by the crowd. There was fighting and the police were pelted with coins. As police helmets went flying three more men burst through and actually managed to get inside the prison, but were dragged out again by the police and the warders. Several other men were chased down the main road by yet more police. For a while it appeared that the police and prison officials would be swept away and that the crowd would pour unimpeded into the prison, but finally the officials managed to close the gates. After a further fifteen minutes' fighting, the demonstration, unique of its kind in this country, was over. By lunchtime all that remained of this last bitter protest was the smashed notice-board hanging from one hook.

By lunchtime too, the Coroner's Inquest on Derek Bentley had been completed. By one of those quirks of English Law, it was customary for a pathologist, once involved in the case, to follow it through to its bitter end. Thus it was that Dr David Haler, the man who had carried out the post-mortem on PC Miles, now gave evidence of a similar examination of the body of Derek Bentley. Dr Haler told the court that there was 'no injury to the head, and the brain was perfectly normal. The cause of death was a fractured neck and crushing of the cord.'

The Coroner asked 'That means instantaneous unconsciousness and *practically* instantaneous death?' to which Dr Haler replied simply 'Yes.'

(With regard to the evidence of the autopsy that Bentley's brain was normal, it was confirmed to me by Dr Haler himself that the abnormalities which Bentley suffered from would not have been revealed by the examination.)

*

The following morning the letter that Harry Procter had bought before it had been dictated arrived at the Bentley home.

Dear Mum and Dad,

I was glad to see you on my visit today but I was a little disappointed that Rita [a girl friend] could not come. I got the rosary and the letter and I saw the photo of the dogs. Iris looked quite nice surrounded with all those animals. I couldn't keep the photo because it was a newspaper cutting.

I told you Mum it would be very difficult to write this letter, I can't think of anything to say except that you have all been wonderful the way you have worked for me.

Thank Rita for writing to me, tell her I am thinking of her. Don't forget what I told you today. 'Always keep your chin up', and tell Pop not to grind his teeth. Oh! I mustn't forget to thank Lil and Bert for writing and coming to see me. Give my love to them both and to everybody else that we know. Tell Ronnie [a close friend] to keep away from the boys and to stay on his own.

I hope Dad has some more televisions in. I forgot to ask him how things were on the visit. Dad and I used to have some fun on that one of Leslie's, he certainly had some spare parts for it.

Oh, Dad! Don't let my cycle frames get rusty they might come in handy one day 'cause old Sally [a bicycle] has got a cracked frame and I want you to change it before something happens to you, and Dad, keep a strict eye on Dennis if he does anything wrong, though I don't think he will but you never know how little things can get you into trouble, if he does, wallop him so that he won't be able to sit for three weeks. I am trying to give you good advice because of my experience.

I tell you what Mum, the truth of this story has got to come out one day, and as I said in the visiting box that one day a lot of people are going to get into trouble and I think you know who those people are. What do you think Mum? This letter may sound a bit solemn but I am still keeping my chin up as I want all the family to do.

Don't let anything happen to the dogs and the cats and look after them as you always have.

I hope Laurie and Iris get married all right, I'd like to give them my blessing, it would be nice to have a brother-in-law like him, we could have some fun together. We could have gone round the club and drunk ourselves to a standstill on the great occasion of them being married, tell him to lob out my flower, tell him to keep my mac clean and my ties. Laurie and I used to have some fun up at the pond till four o'clock in the morning, by the café. I always caught Laurie to pay for the pies, he never caught me once. That will be all for now. I will sign this myself.

Lots of love,
Derek

8

Lessons Learned?

Thus died Derek William Bentley, hanged so that the people of this country could sleep more easily in their beds, secure in the knowledge that they were protected from murderers by the full strength and power of the law. Ironically, his death had precisely the adverse effect: it deeply troubled many people, and gave impetus to a movement that ultimately succeeded in abolishing capital punishment.

In the days and weeks that followed the execution, the Establishment, ignorant of the implications, carried serenely on. Detective Sergeant Fairfax received the George Cross, Police Constables Harrison and McDonald the George Medal, Police Constable Jaggs the British Empire Medal (Civil Division). The King's Police Medal was awarded posthumously to Police Constable Sidney George Miles, and presented to his widow by the Queen. Police pensions remained unchanged. The Establishment had yet to learn that you cannot smoke a medal. The State considered £2 16s 4d a week sufficient for Mrs Miles.

In the House of Commons, Labour MP M. Follick attempted to learn just how backward Craig and Bentley had been at school. He also asked the Minister of Education, Florence Horsbrugh, for a summary of their school attendance records, and how far their truancy had been affected by their inability to read. Straight answers to these questions would undoubtedly have escalated Question Time in the House to a major debate that day. Florence Horsbrugh declined to give straight answers. She did not think that she ought to give information about the records of individual pupils in the matter either of school attendance or of literacy. One Minister had already successfully stopped an attempt to make public Bentley's epilepsy; now another Minister was ensuring that the public remained ignorant of just how feeble-minded the nineteen-year-old boy had been. Further questions revealed that she did not think one could justify the amount of work that would be entailed in establishing the correlation, if any, between illiteracy and truancy. The Minister was also incapable of giving an immediate answer to the question of a correlation between backwardness in reading and delinquency and crime. The Minister, it seems, was incapable of a lot of things that day.

A few days later, Sydney Silverman attempted, yet again, to get a debate on Derek Bentley's execution. In view of the previous ruling, that he could not question the rightness of the execution until it had taken place, he must have felt that he was now completely in order. The Speaker felt otherwise; once more Parliamentary procedure deprived Silverman of an answer to this problem.

Bentley's execution left not only unresolved problems, but unanswered questions. Why, in the face of such enormous pressure, in the light of the then known facts, in the name of justice, humanity, compassion and pure common sense, had one man set his face against the majority of the people of this country and refused to recommend a reprieve? One of the principles that Lord Goddard had called upon during the 1948 House of Lords debate on hanging had been that of 'Vox populi, vox Dei'. The voice of the people is the Voice of God. In Lord Goddard's view the voice of the people proclaimed loudly in 1948 that hanging must be retained. It was therefore his opinion that the Commons and the Lords should submit to the will of the people. Both Houses of Parliament and the Government of the day endorsed Lord Goddard's opinion. Less than five years and one change of Government later, the will of the people was contemptuously brushed aside, and Derek Bentley was executed.

The grounds upon which a Home Secretary might exercise the Royal Prerogative of Mercy and recommend a reprieve were, at the time of Bentley's case, as follows:

1. Youth has always been considered a ground for exercising the Prerogative of Mercy. Nobody under the age of eighteen can be executed. Those near that age are normally reprieved save in very exceptional circumstances. Physically, Bentley was nineteen. Mentally, he was at the very most eleven.

2. When the leading actor in a murder cannot, for whatever reason, be executed, it has always been the practice to reprieve his associates. Thus, when Ley and Smith were found guilty of the Chalkpit Murder (see Chapter 1) Smith was reprieved by the Home Secretary after Ley had been found guilty but insane. Derek Bentley is the only man in our legal history who has been executed for a crime for which he was only vicariously responsible, when the principal could not be executed.

3. Persons considered insane are automatically reprieved. The defence of insanity was defined by the M'Naghten Rules, which have already been the subject for comment in this book. Under them this defence was only allowable when by reason of mental illness a person was considered *wholly* irresponsible for what he had done. In cases where the mental illness was such as to diminish responsibility without removing it altogether, insanity was not a defence, but the person was usually reprieved. Three years after Bentley's execution the then Home Secretary, Major Gwilym Lloyd George, stated categorically, 'People who are suffering from any degree of mental abnormality which reduces their moral culpability are reprieved'. There was an absolute obligation for the Home Secretary to hold a Statutory Medical Enquiry if there was reason to believe that the prisoner under sentence of death was insane. It was also the practice to hold an enquiry whenever there was anything to suggest that the condemned person was mentally abnormal. The information in Chapter 4 indicates how serious Bentley's mental abnormality was. And also

how relevant his epileptic condition was. If the issue of his fitness to plead had been raised, there is overwhelming evidence to suggest that a jury would have found him not mentally fit to stand trial. Equally, there is overwhelming evidence to support the view that on this ground alone Bentley should have been reprieved.

4. The report of the Commissioners of Criminal Law in 1839 and the Report of the Royal Commission in 1878 both recommended that the definition of murder should be altered to exclude cases such as Bentley's, where a man is held responsible for a death which he never intended nor desired. The law was not altered, because it was felt that the Prerogative of Mercy could be trusted to cover such cases as these. It will be recalled that the doctrine of constructive malice that was applied to the Craig/Bentley case had not previously been used in this century.

5. It has occasionally been thought right to commute the sentence of death in deference to a widespread or strong local expression of public opinion, on the ground that it would do more harm than good to carry out the sentence if the result was to arouse sympathy for the offender or hostility to the law. Vox populi, vox Dei?

6. The Secretary of State always attached weight to a jury's recommendation to mercy, and was very reluctant to disregard it if it was concurred in by the trial judge. When passing sentence on Craig, Lord Goddard publicly agreed with the jury's opinion that Craig was the more guilty of the two. He subsequently advised the Home Secretary that he felt Bentley should be reprieved (and was extremely distressed when he was not). Before Bentley, there had only been six recorded cases in this century where the sentence of death had been carried out after the trial judge had concurred with the jury's recommendation to mercy.

7. When there is a 'scintilla of doubt' as to the guilt of the accused, the Home Secretary has invariably advised commutation. In Bentley's case there is not merely a scintilla – it is more like a mountain.

*

Bentley's case assembled in the very highest degree every ground upon which the Prerogative of Mercy may be exercised. The rush to judgment was only equalled by the rush to execution. *There are good grounds for believing that a Statutory Medical Enquiry was not carried out in Bentley's case. I am certain that all the relevant medical evidence on Bentley was not considered, and was not placed before Sir David Maxwell Fyfe.*

It will be recalled that a few days before the execution Professor Sir Denis Hill (as he now is) wrote to the Home Office, leaving them in no doubt of the implications of hanging an epileptic. He received the following reply. The letter was from the Home Office and is dated 27 January 1953. It arrived too late for its contents to be usefully contested by Sir Denis.

'Dear Dr Hill,

'Thank you for your letter of 24 January about Derek Bentley. I appreciate the terms in which you have written and quite recognize why you were anxious to bring this particular point to my notice.

'I can, however, give you an assurance that full regard was paid to the medical side of the case and that all the relevant information was before the Home Secretary when he came to his decision.'

The letter is signed by Sir Frank Newsam, Permanent Under-Secretary to the Home Office. *The remark that all the relevant information was before the Home Secretary is untrue. I am quite convinced that a number of the documents in my possession, documents that are highly relevant to Bentley's medical history, were never seen by Sir David Maxwell Fyfe, nor was the information contained in them made known to him – for example, Dr Munroe's report on Bentley. I challenge the Home Office to prove otherwise.*

When Lord Goddard remarked to me that 'Bentley's execution was an act of supreme illogicality; the responsibility for that act must rest with Fyfe', his Lordship was doing more than give a staggering exhibition of hypocrisy. He was, to my mind, declaring how ably he had been assisted in the destruction of Bentley by the Home Secretary.

A study of the grounds upon which successive Home Secretaries exercised the Royal Prerogative of Mercy only increases one's bewilderment as to why, in Bentley's case, it was seen right and proper that he should hang. Until, that is, one understands this one simple thing: he was hanged for one reason and one reason alone, to encourage the others, his fellow teenagers. He was hanged to encourage the others, the police force of this country.

In 1964, Sir David Maxwell Fyfe, by then Lord Kilmuir, published his autobiography. Just two passages in it refer to Derek Bentley.

The first, a very short one, refers to the days when Fyfe was a young barrister-at-law. 'In the July of 1923, I appeared in my first murder case at Manchester Assizes. This was a poor person's defence, in which a Mr Geddes had been instructed as a solicitor and sent the papers to me. The case had certain features in common with the *cause célèbre* of Craig and Bentley in 1953, when I, as Home Secretary, had to consider the matter of the Prerogative of Mercy in Bentley's case. It was agreed that my client had not fired the fatal shot, but he had had a revolver in his possession, and had fired some shots over the heads of the crowd which had secured the escape of his companion who had committed the murder, although he himself had been captured. Thus it became an arguable point as to whether there had been a joint design and agreement to use all possible force, because although my client was carrying a gun, he had not used it with the intention of hurting anyone. It was not a strong case, but I made the best of it and went to the Court of Appeal, and eventually my client was reprieved. Whether this was because of my advocacy or because his evidence was wanted in another case is not for me to speculate upon.'

Later on Fyfe refers to the time when he considered Bentley's case. 'During that week I was engaged upon the gravest of the manifold responsibilities of the Home Secretary, which prompted Mr Tom Driberg to call me "the man who rations mercy". Derek Bentley and Christopher Craig, aged nineteen and sixteen respectively, had set out to break and enter and steal from a premises in Croydon; Craig carried a loaded revolver, Bentley a knuckleduster and a knife. Disturbed by the police, a miniature battle took place on the roof of the premises; Bentley was caught by a police officer, and shouted "Give it to him Chris", whereupon Craig shot and killed another police officer. Both were found guilty of murder, and their appeals were dismissed by the Court of Criminal Appeal. Craig was too young to be hanged, and the decision before me was whether Bentley – who had been recommended to mercy by the jury – should be reprieved or whether the law should take its course.

'The exercise of the Royal Prerogative of Mercy is a sombre responsibility in any circumstances. The Home Secretary has to consider the evidence of the trial, medical reports, family or other private circumstances which may be relevant to his decision, and police reports; he must ponder the available precedents, the legal as well as the personal considerations, and, most subtle and difficult of all, the possible consequences of his decision upon public opinion. In the Bentley case I had the additional question of the possible effect of my decision upon the police force, by whom the murder of a police officer is justly regarded as the most heinous of crimes. The Home Secretary cannot – or should not – reach his terrible decision as if it were merely a matter of studying legal, medical, and personal files in his office. It cannot be emphasized too strongly that he is intervening in the due process of the law; to decide, in short, if those processes ought to be diverted. His decision may bring the law into public hatred or contempt, and this factor is of great – although not overriding – importance. And, in spite of the documents submitted to him and the advice available to him, the final decision is his alone. It is a bleak, solitary, miserable position for any sensitive or imaginative man, and I am sure that most Home Secretaries have approached their decision as I did, with an overwhelming anxiety to find factors which could justify a recommendation for mercy.

'After brooding unhappily over the problem for what seemed an interminable period, I decided that Bentley's case did not warrant the recommendation for mercy. My decision was announced on Monday, 26 January, and brought down on my head a storm of vituperation without parallel in my career. Public opinion alternated violently throughout the Bentley–Craig affair. After the murder there was an intense revulsion against the perpetrators of the crime, which lasted until after the dismissal of the appeals; then the implications of a situation in which one boy who had fired the shot was reprieved because of his age while the other who had not, was sentenced to death, provoked an articulate and highly charged reaction. Sympathy was abruptly switched from the unfortunate policeman and his family to the youth who faced execution.

'On the evening of the 26th the telephone calls began. One charming lady telephoned to inform my wife – after referring to the Bentley case – that she was an invalid who did not sleep well, and that she proposed to ring up every half-hour. Eventually all incoming calls had to be cut off by the Post Office.

'On the next day hundreds of telegrams and thousands of letters poured in to the Home Office and later to the House of Commons. On that day the majority were against my decision, I should think by a proportion of three or four to one.' Fyfe then records details of the 'non-debate', concluding: 'feelings were running high on the Opposition side, and a certain amount of semi-hysteria was manifest. According to one newspaper, the only movement that I made the whole time was to bow when Bevan said that he did not suggest that I had approached the Speaker in any way. The newspaper comments of my appearance were, of course, over-dramatized, but they present an interesting picture after the passage of time.

'After the discussion in the House was finished, I went on with my work. I was due to be the guest of the Burns Club to propose the "Immortal Memory", but I felt that it was not the occasion to attempt a speech on a poet whose humorous poems formed a great part of his output and success. I went home to dinner and was then informed that a number of Members wished to see me, in order to make another appeal for Bentley, whose execution was fixed for eight o'clock on the morning of Wednesday, 28 January. I went back to the Home Office and received the deputation, which consisted of Aneurin Bevan, Lynn Ungoed-Thomas, who had been Solicitor General in the Labour Government (and who is now a judge), Silverman, Paget, McEntie and Glenvil Hall. There were three ex-Ministers and three back-benchers. Bevan argued simply, and with subtlety and skill, that "You've probably considered all these points, the new point that I ask you to consider is the expression of public opinion."

'I think that Bevan's point was probably an honest one, but he was not forgetful of the effect which the idea of acting contrary to an outburst of public opinion might have on some politicians. The deputation left me at about nine, and I sent a letter, written by myself, to Bevan. It reached the House at about a quarter to ten. I went home and, after a few lunatic calls, we had the telephone switched off again. An episode that evening, which had its humorous aspects, was that a hostile and rowdy crowd went to serenade and demonstrate at the block of flats where we had lived until the previous February. The only political figure left in the building was Lord Silkin, the most mild Socialist Peer who ever supported a confiscatory measure, and we could not help, even at that dreadful moment, smiling at this example of sporadic injustice.

'Curiously enough, the next day, which was the day of Bentley's execution, the tenor of my postbag dramatically changed and the proportion of the letters and telegrams was

293

reversed, and roughly three to one in favour of my decision. An interesting speculation is what constitutes the motive. I think it is that the hysterical people are more ready to write and the second wave were people who thought that I had been subjected to unfair pressure in meeting a difficult situation and were only spurred to write by reason of this thought. In a sense, one might say that popular sympathy with the 'underdog' had swung from the dead policeman to Bentley and finally to myself.'

There then follows an account of the Home Secretary's engagements in Wales the weekend after the execution. Scotland Yard had apparently received information that an attempt was to be made on his life. Extensive security arrangements were put in hand, but the information must have been ill-founded for there is no further mention of it.

'On the next day I went on to Bangor and there I was told that there might be some demonstrations. In the event, only one man asked for the reason for my decision in the Bentley case. I replied that it was not the practice to give reasons behind the advice tendered to the Sovereign by the Home Secretary in regard to the Prerogative of Mercy. There was a spontaneous outburst of applause from the hall and the questioner himself came to the platform to apologize and shake my hand. I have no doubt that the emotional, indeed frenetic, nature of the abuse hurled at me by the abolitionists, to say nothing of the nauseating scenes outside the prison where Bentley was executed, had created a powerful counter-feeling in the country.'

I would have preferred to make no comment on the above passages, for it is my belief that if ever a man condemned himself out of his own mouth then Fyfe does. Certain basic points, however, have to be made.

In the first passage Fyfe compares an armed man, firing a gun to assist a murderer's escape, with Bentley, a youth who did not possess a gun and had been under arrest for at least fifteen minutes when PC Miles was killed. It is particularly ironic in that the man to whom Fyfe compares Bentley was reprieved.

In the second passage Fyfe vividly illustrates the level of his thought processes. This man, who decided that Bentley must die, records in some detail all the information about the case that was available to him. The pity is that he does not appear to have read it. Lord Goddard told me that not only did Maxwell Fyfe not consult him, he did not consult anyone. A pity; had the Home Secretary taken advantage of the help of others he might not have remained so badly misinformed of the facts. The most important remark of the trial, which hanged Bentley, and which many, many people during the past sixteen months have quoted to me verbatim, is misquoted by Fyfe. Here, briefly, are just a few of the errors contained in that second passage.

The remark that Bentley was alleged to have made was 'Let him have it, Chris'. Not, 'Give it to him, Chris.'

Upon the alleged remark Craig did not 'shoot and kill another police officer'. He allegedly shot and wounded Detective Sergeant Fairfax. *It was at least fifteen minutes later, fifteen minutes after Bentley had been arrested, that PC Miles was killed by an unidentified bullet.*

Fyfe makes several references to 'appeals'. Craig did not appeal, nor was he sentenced to death and reprieved, as Fyfe also said.

Even the time of execution is incorrect, it was not 8.0 a.m, but 9.0 a.m. There are a number of other inaccuracies; I have recorded enough to indicate Fyfe's contempt for facts. The incompetence, the inaccuracies with which officialdom had surrounded Bentley from early life dogged him to his death and beyond.

The insinuation that Nye Bevan was motivated by a fear of losing votes, made by a man who at the General Election of 1951 had a majority of 1,707 about a man who at the same General Election had a majority of over 22,000 is simply disgraceful.

Fyfe's memoirs, reeking with pomposity, self-importance and an indifference for the truth, also provide invaluable insights into the working of the Home Secretary's mind. They provide one of the keys to the reason for Bentley's execution. '*In the Bentley case I had the additional question of the possible effects of my decision upon the police force, by whom the murder of a police officer is justly regarded as the most heinous of crimes.*'

That it should be 'just' for the police force to consider the killing of one of their number any more heinous than, say, the killing and sexual assault of a child, is difficult for me to accept. Nevertheless that police attitude was, and still is, a fact. Not only did the law of England place a sliding scale of values on human life, as Lord Goddard's summing-up also made clear, it was a judicial attitude that received wholehearted endorsement from the police.

Lest the reader think me unduly intolerant of the Home Secretary's remembrances, and that one should not expect him to be able to quote verbatim eleven years after the event, it should be pointed out that Fyfe makes it quite clear in the Preface of his book that the material for his book was taken from confidential records *made at the time of the events in question*. An ironic postscript to this aspect is that Fyfe's obituary in *The Times* (28 January 1967) states that one of his particular virtues was his 'astonishing memory'.

In Chapter 1, I have mentioned the murder of PC Edgar, and the reaction to that murder. When Edgar's murderer was reprieved because of the temporary suspension of hanging, there was uproar in the police force. A number of police officers resigned, and the reaction of the force at large played a vital part in scotching the attempt to abolish capital punishment. In Maxwell Fyfe's remarks one can see an echo of that uproar. The pressure brought on him to recommend a reprieve is well known, because so much of it was exerted publicly. (It is interesting to note in passing that Fyfe considered that that pressure came solely from emotional, semi-hysterical abolitionists. His estimate that prior to the execution the people were against him by three or four to one flies in the face of all known evidence

– the figure was never less than eight to one. I do not argue with what he found in his postbag after the execution, but his postbag is more than outweighed by what many MPs found in theirs. Huge numbers of people who considered capital punishment desirable, drew back from Bentley's execution. This fact is recognized by all, it seems, except Maxwell Fyfe.)

The public pressure that was brought upon Fyfe to change his mind is well known. What is not known is the private pressure that was certainly brought upon him to let Bentley hang. It is difficult to believe that the Home Secretary was not prevailed upon by members of the police force not to yield. It is obvious from the Home Secretary's remarks that these were the very people he sought to encourage by Bentley's execution. The man who held Bentley's life in the palm of his hand and dropped it was also, of course, the supreme head of the police force.

The police were not the only people that Bentley's hanging was designed to encourage. It was also aimed at his fellow teenagers, in a different way. The post-war crime explosion, and particularly the wave of juvenile violence, was the other factor that influenced Fyfe's decision that Bentley must die.

The execution expediently demonstrated the Executive's determination to solve the problem of juvenile crime, particularly crimes of violence, once and for all. The Executive felt that Bentley's death would encourage the youth of this country to think twice before they went out armed with revolvers, knuckledusters, coshes, knives, razors and chains. His death would also encourage the professional criminal, thinking to escape from the full consequences of his actions by giving a gun to a juvenile, to think again. His death, in fact, was a categorical statement of intent to all delinquents: 'If his death does not encourage you to mend your ways, then take care; you may be the next to hang.' Derek Bentley had become the scapegoat for a whole generation.

One can, I suppose, imagine a shudder running through the ranks of juvenile delinquents in this country. 'If they can hang someone as innocent as him,' they might have reasoned, 'they can hang anyone.' If there was such a shudder it was short-lived. The supreme indecency in the hanging of this innocent youth lies in the fact that the very people his death was intended to impress were singularly unimpressed.

It could be reasoned that if Bentley's execution was to have an inhibiting effect on the youth of this country, then nowhere would this be more noticeable than in the areas nearest to his Norbury home. Clapham Common is but a short bus ride from Norbury. On the evening of 2 July 1953, I was on that common when seventeen-year-old John Beckley was stabbed to death. This was the culmination of a fight involving ten youths of the kind then known as 'teddy boys'. Beckley's body suffered nine knife wounds – three cuts, six stabs. I saw him as he lay on the pavement after the fight, wearing what I first thought was a red shirt; then he moved his arm slightly, revealing a patch of white; it had been a white shirt. An hour later he was dead. Within days the suburb had been dubbed 'Little Chicago' by the press. The teddy boy cult had produced its first murder, just five months after Derek Bentley's execution – an execution that had taken place in the self-same Borough where Beckley was stabbed to death.

Seven days after the death of John Beckley, Lord Goddard spoke at the Lord Mayor's banquet for the Judges at the Mansion House. In view of his opinions on Bentley's execution, and in view of what had just taken place on Clapham Common the following passage from his speech is of particular interest.

'There are signs, not great signs, but there are signs that the wave of violent crime is to some extent receding. I think I can say that I attribute that, at any rate to a great extent, to the firm attitude of the Home Secretary in refusing to interfere with the due course of justice in a recent case in which great pressure was brought on him at the beginning of the year.'

This was the official confirmation from the Lord Chief Justice of England that Bentley had been hanged to encourage the others – Lord Goddard obviously felt that Bentley's death had encouraged them. It speaks volumes of Lord Goddard's opportunism that he could cite a case in which he passionately believed that an executed man should have been reprieved. Presumably in the week preceding that speech he had had no contact with the outside world, for the news of what had taken place on Clapham Common had apparently not reached him.

Lest it be thought that that was just one tragic swallow in the summer of 1953, I must emphasize the fact that crimes of violence did not recede in that year. The figures for the year indicate a rise of the order of one hundred. True, that was the smallest increase for several years, but it was still an increase and a substantial one – hardly the impression that Lord Goddard's listeners at the Mansion House would have gained. The fallacy of his argument, and the futility of Bentley's execution, was further demonstrated when the 1954 figures for crimes of violence revealed a 7% increase on those of the previous year. The figures continued to rise. Eventually, in 1957, Lord Goddard admitted, in another Mansion House speech, that 'crime was never higher'. An official admission that Bentley's death had failed to produce the desired results.

That failure had been recognized by Maxwell Fyfe much earlier on. Since the increase in crimes of violence, in the year of Bentley's execution, showed the smallest increase for some years, one might wonder if the idea of hanging a Bentley every year ever occurred to Fyfe. Exactly one year after the judicial murder of Bentley the Home Secretary had a superb opportunity to put that notion to the test.

The Clapham Common murder involved at least ten youths, but, curiously, it resulted eventually in only one youth being found guilty of murder. The fact that he was one of the few youths involved who was old enough to be hanged is, I believe, no mere coincidence. Twenty-year-old Michael Davies had been found guilty after a mistrial, a second trial, a Criminal Court of Appeal and a hearing in the House of Lords (a privilege that had not been extended to Bentley).

Davies spent ninety-two days in the same condemned cell at Wandsworth Prison that had been Bentley's last home on earth. As Davies waited for his fate to be decided he had ample time for contemplation. He was later to recall that time.

'I wasn't giving a lot for my chances then. I was a bit younger than those two [a reference to two young men who were executed while Davies was in Wandsworth] but I started thinking about Derek Bentley, and how he was younger than I was. He was only seventeen or eighteen and they'd topped him, though he was completely innocent, and they'd got far less reasons for doing it to him than they had to me.'

Almost exactly a year to the day after the Home Secretary decided that Bentley must die, he decided that Davies could live. As the Clapham boy said, 'they'd got far less reasons for doing it to him than they had to me'. Many people agreed with that.

I believe Michael Davies owes his life to Derek Bentley. I believe the Home Secretary shrank from being the centre of a public storm for the second time in a year because he realized that he had made a terrible mistake when considering the question of Bentley's fate. He also recognized the futility of the argument that to hang Bentley was to encourage the others. That recognition saved Michael Davies. The two decisions show an alarming inconsistency; even Michael Davies recognized that. The demonstration of Executive strength had failed to impress. It had failed to encourage. It had failed.

I have quoted in this book extracts from two Royal Commissions. One of them, the Royal Commission on Capital Punishment, had finished sitting before Maxwell

Fyfe was obliged to consider the case of Derek Bentley; indeed, by that time the bulk of their report was at the printers. The Home Secretary undoubtedly had access to their findings, a number of which were based on information supplied by his department. In considering Bentley's possible reprieve a number of the Commission's findings are highly relevant:

'We recommend by a majority (six to five) that the statutory age-limit below which a person may not be sentenced to death should be raised from eighteen to twenty-one in both England and Scotland.

'Any test of criminal responsibility must take account of the fact that, where a grave crime is committed by a person who is so grossly disordered mentally that he could properly be certified as insane, the presumption that the crime was wholly or largely caused by the insanity is, in ordinary circumstances, overwhelmingly strong, and there is an equally strong presumption in the grosser forms of mental deficiency and of certain epileptic conditions.

'We consider (with one dissentient) that the test of responsibility laid down in England by the M'Naghten Rules is so defective that the law on the subject ought to be changed.

'If an alteration were to be made by extending the scope of the Rules, we suggest that a formula on the following lines should be adopted. "The jury must be satisfied that, at the time of committing the act, the accused, as a result of disease of the mind or mental deficiency (a) did not know the nature and quality of his act or (b) did not know that it was wrong or (c) was incapable of preventing himself from committing it.'

'Although this formula might not prove wholly satisfactory, we consider (with one dissentient) that it would be better to amend the Rules in this way than to leave them as they are.

'We consider (with three dissentients) that a preferable amendment of the law would be to abrogate the M'Naghten Rules and leave the jury to determine whether at the time of

301

the act the accused was suffering from disease of the mind or mental deficiency to such a degree that he ought not to be held responsible.

'The tests of insanity on arraignment, and of insanity as a defence, should make no distinction in law between mental deficiency and insanity. In practice there are wide variations of mental capacity and of responsibility among mental defectives; and it will be for the jury to decide in each case whether the degree of mental defect is such that the accused ought to be held unfit to plead or not criminally responsible.

'The sentence of death ought not to be carried out on any person who is certifiable as a mental defective.

'Where the murder is carried out by a person suffering from epilepsy in circumstances that do not justify his being held to be wholly irresponsible on the ground of insanity, the question of the death penalty being carried out should be approached with a presumption that, if not the epilepsy itself, then the underlying abnormality of the brain may have provided the link in the chain of causation which led to the crime.

'In England and Wales the mental state of every prisoner charged should be examined by two doctors, of whom one at least should be a psychiatrist who is not a member of the prison medical service and the other usually an experienced member of that service.

'The law of England should be amended so as to abolish the verdict of guilty but insane and substitute one of acquittal on the ground of insanity.'

Many of the Royal Commission's other recommendations were also highly pertinent to Bentley's case. The impact that these would have had if the report had been published at the beginning of 1953 instead of in September of that year is not difficult to imagine. Derek Bentley would not have been hanged. The fact that a number of those recommendations were not subsequently adopted by the Government and incorporated into our legislation is irrelevant to the issue of Bentley's reprieve. Those recommendations, representing, as they do, the conclusions of an independent body which had considered the aspects of Capital Punishment for four years, would, if published before Bentley's execution, have swept away the last vestiges of the arguments that justified it. The psychological effect on all sections of society would have been profound. It is significant that when Fyfe considered the case of Michael Davies the Report had been published, and was, therefore, public knowledge.

The Royal Commission on the Law relating to Mental Deficiency and Mental Illness published their report in 1957. Their main conclusion was that the Mental Deficiency Act was so obsolete that it should be entirely repealed.

Doubtless the reader will derive comfort from the fact that the events recorded in this book took place over eighteen years ago. He may well think that they were the inevitable product of those early post-war years. This is indeed true. *It is equally true that it could happen again. In many areas not only has there been no improvement, there has been a marked deterioration.*

The figures for crimes of violence at the time of the Craig/Bentley case were at an all-time high, and were the cause of much head-clutching and soul-searching. The figures for crimes of violence in the year of Bentley's execution were 7,083, which was considered frightening at the time. The figures for 1969 were 37,818, an increase of over 500%. If the 1953 figure represented a crime-wave, then the 1969 figure represents a flood.

In 1949 there were 166 schools for educationally subnormal children, attended by 15,000 ESN children. A further 12,000 ESN children were waiting for places. For all handicapped children there were 491 special schools attended by over 40,000 children. Over 22,000 children were waiting to obtain admission. The real figure of those waiting was undoubtedly much higher, for many children were not classified as handicapped because of the futility of adding to an already massive waiting list. By 1969 there were 464 schools for educationally subnormal children, attended by 51,000 ESN children. Nearly 10,000 more ESN children were waiting for other children to leave. *Over 4,500 had been waiting for more than a year*. By 1969, for all handicapped children there were 963 schools attended by nearly 85,000 children. Over 21,000 were waiting to obtain admission. Again the real figure is undoubtedly higher.

The Education Act of 1949 makes it quite clear where the buck stops with this problem. The responsibility for ensuring that all handicapped children are given the appropriate schooling lies with the Local Education Authorities. If a few parents took the appropriate legal action, the results would be interesting. The Local Education Authorities have not, of course, been idle. In the twenty-year period to 1969 the number of ESN schools more than doubled, and the number of all types of special schools nearly doubled. *But the waiting list of children in 1969 was still at the 1949 figure*. No progress in real terms has been made. There are still thousands of educationally subnormal children drifting through school, as Bentley drifted through school. There is very strong evidence that the rise in crimes of violence and the rise in the numbers of ESN children are directly linked.

Incredibly, at the time of Bentley's case the number of delinquent children (that is, those who had been caught, tabulated and put into various regimes) who were educationally subnormal was not known. Nobody, it seems, had thought it relevant. Even more incredibly, the number of ESN delinquent children is *still* not known. Still, it seems, nobody thinks it is relevant. The number of offenders who suffer from epilepsy is not known. One begins to wonder what is known, apart from the fact that crime in this country is our greatest single problem. As a society we are obsessed with the effect rather than the cause.

Conditions in the police force are only marginally better than they were in those early post-war years. We still expect its members daily to put their lives at risk for a pittance. Police widows' pensions are still pathetically inadequate. The police are still gagged and forbidden to express their views in public, and they continue to resign with an alarming frequency.

The problem of the cure of epilepsy and the public's attitude towards epileptics is profoundly depressing. How little has been achieved in the control and eventual cure of the illness Hippocrates called 'the sacred disease' can be gauged from the fact that its sufferers cost this country £25 million a year in treatment, sickness benefit and absence from work. The bulk of this money is undoubtedly an important lifeline for the country's 300,000 epileptics, but it does nothing to remove the stigma imposed by an ignorant, prejudiced society. A survey in 1969 revealed that 23% of British people think that epileptics should not be employed in jobs like other people, and, nauseatingly, that 15% would not like their child to play with an epileptic child.

No one can doubt the correlation between the level of intelligence in an individual and his criminal inclinations. That is not to say that highly intelligent people do not commit crime, but the vast mass of men and women, boys and girls who come before the Courts of this country are demonstrably of below average intelligence. It may satisfy some basic need in ourselves to insist that these people be punished harshly; it does little for those whom we punish.

Many members of the medical profession with whom I have discussed Bentley's history have described it as a classic case; to them it followed an all too familiar pattern. How familiar the pattern is, can be ascertained from an exhaustive survey conducted recently on the Isle of Wight. The main purpose of the survey was to investigate the education, health and behaviour of school-age children living on the Island, with the ultimate aim of giving a comprehensive picture of 'handicaps' within this group of children. The research team's main conclusion was that, in a population which is slightly above the national average in intelligence and standard of living, one child in six had a chronic handicap of moderate or severe intensity.

Within the definition of 'handicaps' used by the research team, both Craig and Bentley qualified. By that definition there are at this moment in England and Wales *one million, three hundred thousand children suffering from exactly the same 'handicaps' that Craig and Bentley had suffered from.*

The implications are too obvious to require comment. They also, incidentally, make nonsense of all official figures on handicapped children.

'There are features that give rise to a very real concern. For one thing, offences of violence have grown more rapidly in recent years than other crimes. For another thing – this gives me personally the greatest concern – it appears that about half the people found guilty of indictable offences are under the age of twenty-one and no less than a quarter of the people so found guilty are even under the age of seventeen. To my mind these are quite terrifying figures.'

That is an extract from a speech made by a Home Secretary. What is more terrifying than the figures is that the speaker was voicing the fears previously voiced by every post-war holder of that office. The speaker was Reginald Maudling, the speech was made during October 1970.

Many of the legal procedures recorded in this book, procedures that any rational person would consider outrageously unfair, are still with us. Trial transcripts are still not made available to juries. The 'poor prisoner's defence' system has, admittedly, been overhauled to ensure that counsel receives reasonable fees, but about 80% of all people summarily charged with indictable offences during 1970 had no legal representative whatsoever, simply because they were not advised by the courts of their basic rights. It wasn't because they didn't need representation, either: a 1969 survey showed that nearly 70% of those given custodial sentences (i.e. sent to prison, approved schools, etc.) were unrepresented. Even more horrifying, those least well equipped to defend themselves fared no better. In 1967 a survey of the inmates of Holloway Prison revealed that 78% of the prisoners suffering from mental disabilities had been legally unrepresented at their trials.

Some of the worst of these procedures have, thankfully, been abolished. Defence counsel now always gets the last word. The disastrous Court of Criminal Appeal that existed at the time of Bentley's case has gone – a much-needed reform resulting, I am sure, from performances by Appeal Judges like the one described in this book – and has been replaced by the Court of Appeal, Criminal Division, which is devoid of any connection with the trial judges.

It will, no doubt, be argued that these rules and systems, and the men who implemented them, were 'right for their time'. It will doubtless be claimed that Lord Goddard was 'right for his time' that by his strength he deterred the criminal fraternity of this country. But if it was considered right and proper that a man of Lord Goddard's inclinations should dominate the legal profession in the 1940s and 1950s, where then is our present-day Lord Goddard? If the behaviour, which I would term barbarous, of the Lord Chief Justice was justifiable at that time, what we need now, when crimes of violence are at five times their 1952 level, is presumably a new Judge Jeffreys. Either the former Lord Chief Justice was the wrong man, or the present one is.

The issue of corporal punishment is still very much with us. Indeed, Great Britain is the only democratic country in Europe that retains whipping in its schools.

Old vices, it seems, die particularly hard in this country.

One change, the most dramatic one, and one that Bentley's death was largely instrumental in effecting, was the abolition of hanging. The worst sentence that could today be imposed on a youth like Bentley, would be life imprisonment. But I believe that to be a temporary situation. I do not believe, as some do, and have publicly stated with unconscious macabre humour, that hanging is 'a dead issue'. It is far from being a dead issue. A significant proportion of the present Government are staunch supporters of Capital Punishment. Indeed, I believe there exists at the present time a majority in favour of it in the House of Commons. If the principle of Vox populi, vox Dei, means anything at all, then hanging will assuredly return, for its return is undoubtedly desired by the majority of the people in this country. A tacit acceptance of these facts is the gallows at Wandsworth Prison, the gallows from which Derek Bentley was hanged. Six years after the abolition of Capital Punishment that gallows is still there, waiting.

Although I believe that PC Miles was not murdered, there was without doubt one murder in the Craig/Bentley case: the judicial murder of Derek Bentley. That murder was ultimately responsible for a great deal of enlightened legislation. An analysis of the entire case by the Government could bring forth even further legislation. No amount of analysis, however, can remedy what was done in the name of English Justice on the morning of 28 January 1953. Analysis there must be, but there must also be a full official public investigation. We cannot bring Bentley back from the grave, but we can officially acknowledge that he should not have gone to it. I am convinced that Derek Bentley was innocent, that he was the victim of a terrible miscarriage of justice, that he was hanged for one reason, and one reason alone. To encourage the others.

*

308

'As a realist I do not believe that the chances of error in a murder case, with these various instruments of the State present, constitute a factor which we must consider . . . There is no practical possibility. The honourable and learned member asks me to say that there is no possibility. Of course, a jury might go wrong, the Court of Criminal Appeal might go wrong, as the House of Lords and the Home Secretary: they might all be stricken mad and go wrong. But that is not a possibility which anyone can consider likely. The honourable and learned member is moving in a realm of fantasy when he makes that suggestion.'

Sir David Maxwell Fyfe.
14 April 1948. *Hansard*, vol. 449, col. 1007.

This has been the true story of how one teenager moved into that realm of fantasy.

David A. Yallop
16 February 1971

EPILOGUE

On 18 November 1971, three days after this book was first published, Russell Kerr, Member of Parliament for Feltham, asked the then Home Secretary, Reginald Maudling, the following question: ' . . . Whether he has studied the recently published book by David Yallop concerning Derek Bentley, entitled *To Encourage the Others*, a copy of which is in his possession; and in view of the evidence it contains, whether he will now institute an inquiry with a view to a posthumous pardon being granted to this educationally subnormal young man?'

Replying on behalf of the Home Secretary, the Under Secretary of State, Mark Carlisle, confirmed that the Home Secretary had been sent a copy of the book, was having it studied and was not yet ready to reach any conclusion.

Thus it was, eighteen years after Speaker Morrison's ruling that Parliament could only discuss whether or not Bentley should hang after he was hanged, that the question of Bentley's fate and the justness of his execution again became the topic of conversation in the House of Commons.

On 2 December 1971, MP William Price asked the Home Secretary how many letters he had received requesting an inquiry into the Bentley/Craig case. Mr Maudling advised him that he had received 'five, from two correspondents'. Mr Price declared, 'In view of that answer I assure the Home Secretary that he will get another letter tomorrow morning.' Mr Price then referred to the evidence contained in this book, stating that it appeared 'to raise a number of

310

points of vital interest'. Asked by Mr Price to comment on that evidence, the Home Secretary told the House that it 'has been studied'. Evidently Mr Maudling was not in the vein to discuss what conclusions, if any, had been reached. His subsequent remarks were confined to further information about the five letters he had received. The Home Secretary was evidently of a mind to illustrate that the book had had little, if any, effect upon public opinion. Ironically a letter was already on its way to *The Times* that demonstrated perfectly the opposite.

On 10 December 1971, the following letter appeared in *The Times*:

Craig-Bentley case
From Mr W. G. Bentley and others
Sir, At the Old Bailey on 11 December 1952, sixteen-year-old Christopher Craig and nineteen-year-old Derek Bentley were found guilty of the murder of Police Constable Sidney Miles. Craig was sentenced by the trial judge, Lord Goddard, to be detained until Her Majesty's pleasure be known. Bentley was sentenced to death. It may be recalled that the trial and the subsequent events were the cause of great unease in this country and others, and many thousands of people petitioned the then Home Secretary, Sir David Maxwell Fyfe, to spare Bentley's life. Despite all their efforts, Derek Bentley was hanged at Wandsworth Prison on 28 January 1953.

Now, David Yallop, in his book *To Encourage the Others*, has amassed a vast amount of evidence, much of which was not produced at the trial of Craig and Bentley. Had this evidence been forthcoming at the time it would certainly have saved Bentley from the gallows and might well have saved Craig from an indeterminate prison sentence. With regard to the innocence of the two youths, we believe that a prima facie case has been established and we urgently call on the Home Secretary to open a public inquiry or grant a Free Pardon to Craig and Bentley.

311

As the author rightly says, 'We can never bring Bentley back from the grave, but we can acknowledge that he should never have been put there.' We believe it is the duty of Mr Maudling to make that acknowledgement without delay.

That a letter couched in such uncompromising terms should come from Derek Bentley's father was, perhaps, to be expected. That the letter was also signed by Louis Blom-Cooper QC, the former Lord Chancellor of England Lord Gardiner, publisher Livia Gollancz, authors H. Montgomery Hyde and Arthur Koestler, and also Nancy Silverman and Lord Soper was unexpected. If such a group of people could be convinced by the evidence, then surely it was only a matter of time before a public inquiry was opened or Free Pardons were granted to Craig and Bentley?

A few days later a second letter supporting the views of the first was published in *The Times*; this time the signatories were Brigid Brophy, Lord Byers and Ben Whitaker. *The Times*, evidently holding the view that it had done its democratic duty towards those of its readers who wished to comment on the Craig/Bentley case, shut up shop and published no more. The only reason that I know more were received is because a number of people wrote to me complaining that they had written to *The Times* expressing similar views and their letters had not been published. I was obliged to point out to these people that, unfortunately, or perhaps fortunately, I had no control over what *The Times* did or did not want to print.

On 20 December 1971, the indefatigable Russell Kerr again inquired of the Home Secretary as to whether he had yet reached any conclusions. The reply from Mark Carlisle was a masterpiece of brevity: 'Not yet.'

At precisely the same time as this interchange was taking place the Bentley family and I were discussing the case with Mr Harold Wilson. The kindness and sympathy accorded Derek Bentley's family was impressive. Even more impressive was the fact that Mr Wilson considered Derek's execution a terrible miscarriage of justice. It was an opinion he had held from the time of the case when his former colleague and close friend Nye Bevan had fought in vain to save the nineteen-year-old's life. The Leader of the Opposition declared that the new evidence confirmed his view that an innocent man had been hanged.

Whatever the contents of Mr Maudling's post might have been concerning the Craig/Bentley case, there was no doubting the mail the Bentley family and I were receiving. We received hundreds of letters; with one or two exceptions they all carried the same message: 'Derek Bentley was innocent; there must be a public inquiry.'

Petition forms demanding a public inquiry also began arriving at our respective homes. The number of signatures rapidly moved into the thousands. It seemed to me almost as if we had slipped back in time to early January 1953.

By the middle of February 1972, the task of creating for the BBC the television adaptation of this book had been completed. It had been a long and bitter struggle to ensure that the play became a reality. That it did was due entirely to the commitment of two men, director Alan Clarke and producer Mark Shivas.

On 24 February, Russell Kerr again raised the issue in the House of Commons. He asked the Home Secretary '. . . whether, having now had over three months to study the book by David Yallop concerning Derek Bentley, entitled *To Encourage the Others*, a copy of which was in his possession, he will now recommend the grant to him of a posthumous pardon in the light of the facts set out in the book and the representations made to him by Hon Members.' Replying on behalf of the Home Secretary, Mark Carlisle advised the House that 'My Right Hon Friend has not yet completed his study of the case.'

In fact Mr Maudling had had the book for *four* months and contrary to the impression that Mr Carlisle gave the House that day, the Home Office had done more than merely study the written evidence. On the instructions of the Home Secretary a secret police inquiry had been under way for some time. The reader may recall that in the open letter to the Home Secretary at the beginning of the book, I ask for a full public inquiry. What we now had was a secret police inquiry. With the greatest possible respect to the officers who undertook the inquiry, the decision to have the case investigated secretly by members of the police force was, in my opinion, a disastrous one. It is quite obvious that one of the key issues in the Craig/Bentley case is the conduct and behaviour of a considerable number of police officers. A secret police inquiry into aspects of the police investigation can hardly be described as justice being *seen* to be done.

On 28 March the BBC transmitted the television play. A book had been published that many wise people in publishing had declared would never and could never be published. Now a play based on that book, a play that many wise people in the television industry had declared would not and could not be transmitted, had been seen by millions of people. It seemed to me then that truth was on the march and nothing could stop it now. The television play was acclaimed both by the press and the public. There were just two exceptions to this national acclamation. One was a critical review in the *Daily Telegraph* that objected to the concept of drama documentary and referred to it as 'this bastard child of television'. The other came from pathologist Dr David Haler.

Prior to the publication of my book in November 1971, solicitors acting on behalf of my publishers, W. H. Allen, had wished to check a great many aspects of the evidence contained within my book, particularly the evidence that had been acquired as a result of my personal interviews. Many of these interviews, but by no means all, had been tape-recorded. One of the exceptions was the interview with Dr David Haler. I had foolishly assumed that this particular interview would not throw any new light on the Craig/Bentley case and I had therefore travelled to his Weybridge home without any recording equipment. I would observe that I have never since made such a naive assumption. I had a typewritten list of questions for the doctor and I recorded his answers in my own hand on paper. Stunned at the implications of what Dr Haler had told me, I telephoned him the day after the interview to confirm precisely what he had said to me. The salient parts of both the interview and the telephone call are as follows:

Interview carried out at Dr Haler's residence on 6 March 1971
YALLOP: I believe you knew PC Miles.

HALER: Yes, I knew him professionally. Our paths had crossed in a number of cases.

YALLOP: What kind of person was he?

HALER: He was a modest man, quiet and efficient. He was very well liked by his colleagues.

YALLOP: With reference to the post mortem you carried out on PC Miles, I understand that the bullet that killed him entered virtually the centre of the forehead and exited virtually out of the centre of the rear of the head. Is that correct?

HALER: Yes, that's quite correct.

YALLOP: Now you subsequently described during the Old Bailey trial and also on your original deposition the bullet as being of large calibre. I wonder whether you could be more specific on this? What for example did you mean by large calibre?

HALER: Well, it was bigger than a ·22.

YALLOP: Yes, but can you be more precise?

HALER: Indeed. The bullet was between a ·32 and a ·38 in calibre.

YALLOP: Is there any possibility that the calibre could have been bigger?

HALER: Oh no, putting it at ·38 is the very ultimate extreme.

YALLOP: Was it possible to ascertain from the nature of the wound from how far away the bullet had been fired?

315

HALER: Yes, it was close range.

YALLOP: Can you be more specific?

HALER: It was fired from a maximum distance of between six to nine feet.

YALLOP: Now the fatal bullet was in fact never produced at any time during the subsequent proceedings. From your knowledge of the wound and your ballistics experience how far would you estimate that the bullet would have travelled?

HALER: Well, it's very difficult to be precise. There are a number of external factors that have to be taken into consideration such as wind velocity of which I have no knowledge in this particular case but I think a maximum distance would be fifty yards.

Towards the end of the interview, I discussed the case with him in general terms.

YALLOP: It is manifest to me after a year and a half's investigation into this case that Derek Bentley was innocent. Many people believed in his innocence at the time of his execution. What were your feelings about the justness of his death?

HALER: Well, I am quite prepared to accept what you are saying about Bentley's innocence, but does it really matter? We all have to go some time, perhaps better earlier than later.

YALLOP: But surely wouldn't it be nice to think we had the illusion of choice?

HALER: Well none of us have. I've carried out post mortems on over sixty-five thousand people and they all probably felt until it was too late that they had choice. I mean, if Bentley had not have been hanged at nineteen, he may well have died for example in a car accident at thirty-five.

YALLOP: If indeed he had he may well have been grateful for the additional sixteen years.

Extract from telephone conversation Yallop/Haler
Sunday 7 March 1971

YALLOP: Dr Haler, I wanted to be quite certain that I have clearly understood you during our discussion yesterday. Did I understand you to say that the bullet that killed PC Miles was between ·32 and ·38 calibre?

HALER: Yes, that's quite correct.

YALLOP: And that the distance from which Miles had been killed was six to nine feet?

HALER: Yes, that's what I told you and that is correct.

The solicitors advised me that they wanted to show Dr Haler a transcript of these conversations. I told them I had no objection to his. They duly had a meeting with Dr Haler, showed him the transcripts quoted above and he confirmed that they were a true and accurate record of our conversations.

When the book was published it made front-page news throughout the country. It was also serialized in the *Observer*. There was no response from Dr Haler. Now, five months later after Dr Haler had been interviewed by senior police officers on behalf of the Home Office and after the television play had been transmitted, Dr Haler denied making the remarks that I had attributed to him. Inevitably solicitors' letters were exchanged, including the following two letters from the solicitors acting on behalf of my publishers, but not on behalf of me!

'Our clients, W. H. Allen & Co Ltd, have passed on to us your letter to them of 11 April.

'We have advised our clients that there is no allegation in the book that your client suppressed any evidence. It is on the contrary quite clear that nobody knew the calibre of the fatal bullet because it was never found and it is also quite clear that your client was not asked either by the prosecution or by the defence to give any evidence as to his estimate of the size of the fatal bullet.

'When Mr Yallop saw your client he made some

notes. When we saw your client we took a copy of the transcript of those notes and showed it to him. He did not seek to correct any relevant part of the notes.

'During our subsequent conversation with your client, he volunteered that he thought that the fatal bullet was probably a sten gun bullet as there were many of these available at the time when the incident occurred. He told us that a sten gun bullet would be of 9 millimetre calibre.

'That is the clear recollection of the two partners of this firm who saw your client and it is supported by the note made at the time.

'9 millimetres is approximately ·35 inches.

'We have in the circumstances advised our clients that they are under no liability whatsoever to your client in this matter.'

Their second letter was also sent without any prior consultation with me.

'Further to our open letter of even date, our clients, as reputable publishers, are naturally anxious that the book should state the position accurately.

'If, as appears to be the case, your client has after reflection altered the view which he expressed to the author and to us as to the probable size of the fatal bullet, then we have no doubt that our clients would be prepared to make appropriate amendments to any future editions or reprints of the book.

'We consider that a discussion would serve a useful purpose. If you agree, perhaps you would be good enough to telephone the writer, Mrs Scott Bayfield, so that mutually convenient arrangements may be made.'

Subsequently, again without any reference whatsoever to me, W. H. Allen and Dr Haler arrived at an agreement.

They paid no damages or costs to him and released the following statement:

THE CRAIG–BENTLEY CASE

The following statement is issued on behalf of Dr David Haler with the concurrence of W. H. Allen & Company Limited, publishers of David Yallop's book *To Encourage the Others*:

'Arising out of the book *To Encourage the Others* by David Yallop published by W. H. Allen, Dr David Haler, with the agreement of the publishers, wishes to emphasize that the calibre of the bullet which killed PC Miles was never established because the bullet was never found.

'Dr Haler was not asked at any time by the prosecution or the defence to give any estimate of the size of the fatal bullet. Dr Haler had no information which would have enabled him to give any definite evidence as to this beyond saying that it was apparent from the wound that it was caused by a bullet of large calibre. The precise calibre could not have been determined from the wound.'

By early April 1972 a great many other people were taking an interest in the Craig/Bentley case. Lord Goodman declared that he intended to raise the matter in the House of Lords. The gentle and sensitive Earl of Arran publicly committed himself to fighting for a public inquiry.

On 25 May in the House of Commons Russell Kerr yet again raised the issue. He asked: 'whether the Home Secretary had yet had an opportunity of seeing the BBC2 film *To Encourage the Others* produced by David Yallop; and whether, in view of the documented evidence it contains, he was prepared to recommend a public inquiry into the circumstances surrounding the trial and execution of 19-year-old Derek Bentley.'

Mr Maudling, in a written reply, said, 'Derek Bentley was sentenced to death in consequence of the verdict of a jury convicting him of the murder of Police Constable Miles. An appeal against that conviction was considered by the Court of Criminal Appeal but dismissed.

'It is not for me to review the evidence and arguments which have already been considered by the courts nor to comment on the application of the legal doctrine of constructive murder. These were matters for the courts and I cannot presume to re-try the case.

'I am concerned only to consider whether any material fresh evidence has come to light which was not before the courts and which might have affected the verdict, and it is on this basis that I have approached the matter.

'I have fully reviewed the facts of this case in the light of Mr Yallop's book and television production, and the Commissioner of Police of the Metropolis has at my request made some further inquiries into those matters on which it is suggested that new or different evidence is now available.

'In the light of these inquiries and of my study of all the facts I have found nothing to justify any action on my part in regard to the conviction, or to warrant more extensive inquiries.

'Mr Yallop's book and play propound the theory that Police Constable Miles was accidentally killed by a bullet from a police weapon. My inquiries show this to be quite contrary to the available evidence.

'Statements taken in the course of the original investigation make it clear that at the time that PC Miles was shot no police officer at the scene was armed and that police weapons were sent for only after he had been shot.

'Five ·32 calibre automatic pistols, each with eight rounds of ammunition were then issued to police officers and with the exception of that used by Detective Constable Fairfax all were returned unfired. The only ammunition not returned intact was the two rounds fired from that pistol after PC Miles had been wounded.

'Nor can I find any basis for the doubts that have been raised as to the calibre of the fatal bullet. These appear to have been derived from an opinion attributed to Dr Haler, the pathologist who performed the post mortem on PC Miles. He is said to have told the author that the wound could have been caused by a bullet of calibre between ·32 and ·38 (whereas the weapon that Craig was firing was known to be a ·445 revolver).

'Dr Haler has been seen and has made a statement in which he denies having expressed any such opinion. He adheres to the evidence which he gave at the trial that the wound was caused by a bullet of large calibre, and says that by this he meant a calibre of more than ·38.

'Former Detective Constable Fairfax has also been seen and made a statement in which he adheres entirely to the evidence which he gave at the trial and to which there is nothing that he is able to add.

'Apart from considering the material in Mr Yallop's book, I have also had inquiries made into statements made independently by a Mr Philip Lee, who claims to have been an eye witness of an alleged gun battle on the roof of the warehouse in Croydon on the night in question.

'Mr Lee has now made a long statement to the police describing fully what he claims to have seen and other consequential inquiries have been made to verify the details given in this statement. My inquiries show that this account of events is so inconsistent with other available evidence that I should not be justified in taking any action upon it.

'Although there are some understandable discrepancies of detail in the accounts of witnesses of the confused events on the warehouse roof, the essential facts of the shooting are clear.

'There is no information before me to cause me to think that the verdict of the jury was wrong.

'I am concerned only to consider whether any material fresh evidence has come to light which was not before the court and which might have affected the verdict, and it is on this basis that I have approached the matter.'

This then was the yardstick, the principle that governed the Home Secretary's attitude. By applying such a principle a great many vital considerations were automatically brushed aside. The appalling behaviour of trial judge Lord Goddard, the inept performance of the Appeal Judges, these and many other facts that may have a direct bearing on Bentley's fate were, quite literally, never even considered by Reginald Maudling. But if one is going to apply such a principle then surely one should apply it consistently.

With regard to the evidence contained in this book and the television adaptation, the police officers acting on behalf of Mr Maudling had seen fit to examine one fragment and one fragment alone: the possibility that PC Miles had been accidentally killed by a bullet from a police gun. Of the rest, nothing. Of the three police officers who failed to give evidence, Police Constables Pain, Bugden and Alderson, nothing. Of the fact that Derek Bentley was mentally unfit to plead, nothing. Of the fact that members of the public were in the vicinity during the gun battle and that one in particular was prepared to swear on oath that armed police went through her house to gain access to the roof, *before the death of PC Miles*, nothing. Of the fact that on Craig's evidence to me, Bentley had, *after being arrested*, put his own life in real jeopardy by attempting to persuade Craig to surrender, nothing. Of the fact that Bentley had been under arrest for at least twenty minutes at the time of PC Miles's death, nothing. Of the fact that the fatal bullet had not and never had been produced, nothing. Of the fact that the Home Office had prevented Sir Denis Hill from making Bentley's mental condition public before the execution, nothing. Of the fact that Prime Minister Winston Churchill had demanded a full report on the gun battle, a mere 48 hours after the events, nothing. Of the fact that the police officers acting on behalf of

Mr Maudling had, with regard to the evidence presented in this book, seen fit to interview just two people and only two people, nothing.

None of these facts were before the jury, yet none were now considered. Nothing demonstrates more graphically how pitifully inadequate the secret police inquiry was than the Home Secretary's remarks concerning Dr Haler and former Detective Sgt Fairfax. They had been seen and denied making the remarks to me that I contend they did make to me. For any logic or justice to apply, I should have been questioned and asked what my justification was for attributing statements to these two men that they now denied making. I was not questioned. Indeed, I have never been given an opportunity of discussing the issues raised in this book with any member of the Home Office nor with any member of the police force. When, late in 1972 Mr Maudling, having by then resigned his position as Home Secretary, was the subject of considerable comment during the Poulson inquiry, the former Minister complained: 'They are saying what they bloody well like about me. I do not have the opportunity to defend myself.' My heart went out to him – I knew just how he felt.

Neither the Bentley family nor myself have any connection with Mr Philip Lee. Indeed, I have never met the man. His story is so obviously riddled with errors of fact and inconsistencies, one wonders why the Home Office concerned itself with it rather than with the very real evidence of which there was an abundance.

On 25 April 1972, Mr Bentley and I went to the House of Commons to discuss the case with Mrs Shirley Williams. The Shadow Home Secretary made it abundantly clear to us that she deplored the secret police inquiry. In her view the evidence pointing towards Derek Bentley's innocence was so overwhelming that the granting of a posthumous pardon should happen immediately: it was quite unnecessary to go through the formality of a public inquiry.

Early in June it became known that Lord Goodman intended to raise not only the Craig/Bentley case but also the Hanratty case in a House of Lords debate. By that time I had taken part in a number of public discussions on the Craig/Bentley case in various parts of the country and in front of a large cross-section of the community. To judge from the many thousands who had made their views known to me, an overwhelming majority believed that in hanging Derek Bentley the State had executed an innocent man.

On the evening of 14 June 1972, Lord Goodman initiated the House of Lords debate on both the Craig/Bentley and Hanratty cases. A verbatim record of the debate will be found in Appendix I.

The words when read in cold print convey little of the atmosphere that was present in the House of Lords that evening. When Lord Goodman rose to speak, the air was electric with anticipation. The Chamber was full. Lord Goodman had chosen to raise not only the Bentley case, but also another murder case that has given rise to continuing unease and anxiety, the case of James Hanratty. He spoke for some forty-five minutes, unaided by notes. It was one of the most extraordinary examples of public speaking I have ever seen in my life. With remarkable fluency and speed, he enumerated just a few of the reasons that justified a full inquiry into the case of Derek Bentley.

Since the night of 2 November 1952, when PC Miles died on that Croydon rooftop, there have been many bizarre and extraordinary events in the Craig/Bentley case. The performance of Viscount Colville, the Government spokesman in that House of Lords debate, ranks as one of the most extraordinary and bizarre events of all.

When considering the requests for public inquiries into both the Craig/Bentley and Hanratty cases, Home Secretary Reginald Maudling clearly stated the basic principle that he had applied.

On 27 May 1971, Mark Carlisle, Under Secretary to the Home Office, referred to that principle (this was during a discussion of the Hanratty case): 'What must be the approach of the Home Secretary is whether there have come to light new factors which were not before the jury at that time and which, had they been before the jury, might have led to a different decision. The Home Secretary has to assess the weight and significance of those matters which the jury was not in a position to take into account.'

A year later almost to the day, Mr Maudling, as already recorded in this Epilogue, declared, when giving his decision on the request for a public inquiry into the Craig/Bentley case, 'I am concerned only to consider whether any fresh evidence has come to light which was not before the courts and which may have affected the verdict, and it is on this basis that I have approached the matter.'

We have already seen how this principle was promptly abandoned by Mr Maudling and his secret police investigators, without explanation. Now, astonishingly, Viscount Colville blurted out the explanation.

' . . . There may in a criminal trial be evidence which is available and is known to one or another of the parties at that time which for one reason or another they choose not to use. In those circumstances, I do not think that some years later, because somebody considers that they were mistaken in their choice of not using it, the existence of that evidence would be grounds for reopening the matter by way of public inquiry.'

Let every person who believes in our judicial system consider deeply those words. The reaction in the House of Lords on the night they were uttered was a gasp of disbelief. Lord Davies leapt to his feet declaring, 'That is very dangerous.' The Earl of Arran, visibly shaking with rage, remarked, 'I cannot understand how the noble Viscount has the audacity to say things like that.' But said it he had, and he meant every word of it, as his subsequent remarks clearly show. The latitude this gives to police, prosecution and, indeed, State, is enormous and frightening. With a few well-chosen words, Viscount Colville had sent English standards of justice hurtling back past the Star Chamber to the Dark Ages.

Viscount Colville subsequently made a remark that gives the whole wretched game away. It explains why there has been no public inquiry. It explains why the Home Office file on this case will not be made available to the public for seventy-five years.

'There was one other piece of evidence which was not mentioned in the summing-up but which was given in evidence and also told upon the matter. The fact of the matter is that, having heard the law described as I began just now, and having heard all the evidence, the jury did convict. I cannot see how I can possibly suggest that the Government should at this stage interfere and say that the jury were wrong, that the judge was incorrect in his summing-up and that the Court of Criminal Appeal should have said so, but did not, and that therefore we should now have an inquiry to re-try the case. Because, with the greatest respect, and however hard anybody feels about the result, that is the only result of a public inquiry that could possibly arise in that particular case. I do not believe that it would be a satisfactory precedent for anyone if this were to occur.'

If one is to believe the noble Viscount, the one and only reason that we have not had a public inquiry into the case of Regina *v.* Craig and Bentley is because it would result in Derek Bentley being found not guilty. It would result in the conclusion that this sad, inadequate youth was the victim of judicial murder.

As I write these words the fight for a public inquiry continues. It will continue until one takes place.

AN OPEN LETTER
TO THE HOME SECRETARY, 1990

Sir,

Although this is entitled an open letter to you, I would ask you to regard the entire contents of this book as an open letter to yourself.

I am asking you, as I asked your predecessor, Reginald Maudling, to find time to read this book. I am asking you, having read this book, to set up a full, independent public inquiry into the case of Derek Bentley. Your predecessor responded to my request by instructing through his Commissioner of Police a secret police inquiry into one fragment of the evidence contained within this book. With regard to that particular inquiry, I would observe that based upon the public statements of the then Home Secretary, the investigating police officers did not see fit to interview a number of crucial witnesses. I would include among these Christopher Craig and myself. Neither did they see fit to consider the very serious implications of a statement made by the then Director of the Metropolitan Police Laboratory, Lewis Charles Nickolls. In a book written by Mr Nickolls entitled *The Scientific Investigation of Crime*, published a mere three years after Bentley's execution, Mr Nickolls states that he identified one of the bullets that was discovered on the Croydon rooftop after the death of PC Sidney Miles as 'being a bullet from ·32 automatic ammunition'. An examination of the trial records will confirm for you that this bullet was not entered as an exhibit during the trial. Why not? An examination of the trial transcript will confirm for you that the fatal bullet that killed PC Miles was also not entered into the Court exhibits. Notwithstanding the conclusions arrived at by the investigating police officers in

1972, is it possible that we have finally identified the bullet that killed this brave and courageous police officer?

I would ask that any inquiries that you cause to be made are not confined merely to this aspect, important though it may be. Leaving this particular issue to one side, there is overwhelming evidence to justify a full independent public inquiry into this case. If we are to be confined to the principle that Home Secretary Reginald Maudling and his colleagues applied in 1971, that the approach of the Home Secretary is whether there have come to light new factors that were not before the jury at that time and which, had they been before the jury, might have led to a different decision, it is abundantly clear that there are many such new factors which you must consider.

If a jury's function is to arrive at a true verdict based on all the evidence, then the jury that served in the case of Regina v. Craig and Bentley were placed in an impossible and intolerable position. No evidence was presented to them concerning Bentley's mental condition. They were not advised to consider the implications of the indisputable fact that the unarmed Derek Bentley had been under arrest for at least twenty minutes at the time of the death of PC Miles. There were three policemen near the Croydon rooftop or with Bentley at vital moments on that evening of Sunday 2 November 1952. These three men, who are clearly identified within this book, never gave depositions or subsequently evidence at the trial. It is not enough to say, as Viscount Colville did, that Sir David Maxwell Fyfe had all the medical evidence before him before he arrived at his decision. We are talking about the evidence being available not to a politician, but to a jury of twelve. There are many other factors that have a direct bearing on this case. They are all contained within the pages that I ask you to read.

Doubtless you will send for the Home Office files on this case to study them. I would ask you to give the Bentley family and myself the same opportunity to study these files. The normal period before such files are made available for public inspection is thirty years. It is my understanding that a previous Lord Chancellor has placed a ban on the Derek Bentley file being made available for seventy-five years. It is also my understanding that the justification for this excessively long period is that disclosure of the file's contents may cause distress to the relations of Derek Bentley. Let me advise you that the Bentley family have been trying for many years to obtain access to these papers. Clearly they contain no information that can assist this or any previous Government in sustaining the belief that the sentence that was carried out on Bentley was just. If they did hold such information I am sure it would have been made public long ago. If justice is to be seen to be done in this case, I ask you to begin by making these files available.

Let me finally draw your attention to the remarks made by Viscount Colville in the House of Lords on the evening of 14 June 1972 when he was replying to the Government of the day and speaking specifically of the Craig/Bentley case.

'I cannot see how I can possibly suggest that the Government should at this stage interfere to say that the jury were wrong, that the judge was incorrect in his summing-up and that the Court of Criminal Appeal should have said so, but did not, and that therefore we should now have an inquiry to re-try the case. Because, with the greatest respect, and however hard anybody feels about the result, that is the only result of a public inquiry that could possibly arise in that particular case. I do not believe that it would be a satisfactory precedent for anyone if this were to occur.'

The respect in which the public of this country hold our judicial system will not be shaken if it is finally admitted that in the case of Derek Bentley the law produced a miscarriage of justice. On the contrary, if the law and the judicial system in this country is held in contempt, it is because of the failure of the executive to admit such miscarriages of justice. I look forward to an early reply.

Yours faithfully,
David A. Yallop.

April 1990

Appendix I

The House of Lords Debate, 14 June 1972

HANRATTY AND BENTLEY CASES

6.43 p.m.

LORD GOODMAN rose to ask Her Majesty's Government whether it is not desirable, in view of the social and legal implications, for an impartial review of the cases of Hanratty and Bentley. The noble Lord said: My Lords, I am most obliged to the Government for enabling this short debate to take place on what I regard as a very important matter. May I make a few preparatory remarks which I think need to be made to illustrate my approach to the matter? First, I should like to make it absolutely clear that this is in no way an attack, or even a criticism, on my part of our system of criminal jurisprudence. I believe that we have very splendid criminal courts, and that it is a rarity indeed for a man on criminal trial to suffer an injustice. I should like to make that point, because what we are dealing with are cases of a very exceptional nature. It is foolish to believe that any system of justice that can be devised by man is not open to fallibility. The suggestion here is that once in a decade, very occasionally, an injustice does take place in very special and unexpected circumstances, which are often beyond the predictions of ordinary lawyers and which cannot be safeguarded against by ordinary jurisprudential precautions. I believe this to be so in both the cases that I am mentioning today.

The second point is that my remarks imply no criticism whatever of the police. I have very little to do with crime, and frankly I have no interest in crime as such: it is a distasteful subject. There is no glory or credit in crime. Both crimes to which this debate relates were hideous ones. They both involved the death of innocent people – in one case a policeman, acting in circumstances of great heroism, and in the other case a potentially innocent citizen and the killing of a perfectly innocent young woman. Neither crime could be justified nor could any attempt be made to excuse it. That has nothing to do with the matter I am seeking to discuss.

The third disclaimer I should like to make is that I do not suggest by what I say any inadequacy on the part of defence lawyers. In both cases, having read a good deal of the transcripts and the presentation of the cases, it seems to me that the defence lawyers made a more than adequate fist of what they did. So far as the Hanratty case was concerned, they had a specially difficult job because they were seeking to assemble evidence almost minute by minute. I think it would have been difficult to have found people who would have discharged their duty more conscientiously than those who defended Hanratty. Those are the points which I think ought to be made at the outset of the relatively short observations in which I intend to indulge.

Very occasionally, as I have said, cases occur in our criminal courts in which, although they have been concluded, and concluded with the finality with which these cases were concluded, that is to say, by a capital sentence, there nevertheless remains a stir of public anxiety and concern. Where this happens and where that stir of public anxiety and concern fails to be allayed by the passage of time, it appears to be a pretty historic certainty that there is something that needs to be looked into. If you examine the occasional cases where this has happened, public concern is a pretty good index of the need for examination and re-examination. This has happened with very great rarity. It is difficult to put a finger on any number of cases of which this observation could be made; but where it has happened – as in the case of Oscar Slater, the case of Evans and a few others – time does not enable one to bury the situation. Hence I am completely unapologetic about the suggestion that has been made that it is an injustice to the survivors concerned in the individual cases to rake up the matter again. Well, it is not I who may cause injustice, but the circumstances. The matter will not allow itself to be buried. Hence, the justice to these people is to see whether the cases can be finally disposed of by a system of examination and inquiry which will be finally reassuring to the parties concerned. To be candid, this may be an impossibility. In both these cases the young men who met these tragic ends had respectable and devoted parents. Those parents have suffered the appalling tragedy of seeing the circumstances in which their sons died. I do not know the parents and I have not met any of the people concerned but it is quite clear, from the record of what has happened since, that they have devoted themselves unsparingly to seeking to procure a declaration of the innocence of their children and a declaration that the verdicts were wrong.

That is what one would expect and it indicates, if I may say so, the nature and quality of the parents. But it is not a factor that we can reasonably take into account; nor does it provide evidence one way or the other. However, what, to my mind, does provide a justification for raising this matter is that notwithstanding the years that have passed in each case, notwithstanding the fact that public statements have been made, seeking to provide reassurance from honourable Ministers and honourable officials, the public anxiety on this matter remains unaltered, unchanged, and at the same pitch. I do not think that in those circumstances as a general proposition, unless it is possible to show that the whole thing is a response to some organized lobby, which is not the case in respect of either of these cases, there is an onus on the Government to consider whether that circumstance by itself is not enough to justify a special inquiry into the case.

I do not intend to deal with the facts of each of these cases at any length. That would be an impossibility. I observe that the noble Viscount has appeared with a whole armful of thick files. I would regard myself as having done a grave disservice to the House if this Unstarred Question occasioned the necessity for him to read the lot, or any of them. I hope to seek to demonstrate that there are circumstances attaching to each of these cases without any expression of my own view as to the guilt or innocence of the young men that makes it desirable, wise and sensible that there should be a further investigation.

I should like to deal first with the case of Bentley. This is in many ways the simpler case so far as the facts are concerned, a case upon which it is possible to say that the form of inquiry could be a simple one. It is my belief that if a form of inquiry were adopted in the case of Bentley it might well suffice to have an independently-minded criminal lawyer of high standing who could investigate the existing facts as they are without investigating any further facts and who would, in my belief, very likely arrive at the conclusion from the transcript of the trial proceedings in the Court of Criminal Appeal that there was a manifest injustice for reasons that I shall seek to indicate. I do not wish to adopt the one or two conjectures, speculations and surmises that have appeared in recent publications. There have been recent books about both

333

these cases, very carefully and meticulously compiled, containing a good deal of speculation and suggestions about how the crime may have come about in circumstances other than the finding by the court. These are matters that I do not need to probe or concern myself with. For instance, in the Bentley case there is an interesting suggestion that certainly seems to have some circumstantial support, that the shot that was fired did not come from the gun of the young man Craig but came from the gun of one of the policemen who was engaged in the gun battle. It is my view that as a matter of law this would be irrelevant. If it were the case that the gun battle had been instigated by a criminal firing, by one person, to which the police responded, then it is my belief that in law if one of the police shots went astray and killed someone the person who instigated the gun battle would be as much responsible as if he had fired the shot himself. Hence this is not a matter, for a number of reasons, with which I shall concern myself. It is a matter which might well at some stage be investigated if it were thought desirable to do so because the Bentley facts speak for themselves so far as the necessity of an inquiry is concerned without looking for new and extra facts.

The circumstances of the case will be well known. There can have been few murder cases in this country that aroused greater interest and feeling. There were debates in the House of Commons, attempts to adjourn the House of Commons, and Motions to endeavour to persuade the Home Secretary of the day that it was his duty to reprieve the young man Bentley. All of them, for one reason or another, failed. The circumstances in which the Home Secretary reached his decision about advising Her Majesty as to the exercise of mercy are not matters that concern me at this juncture. What concerns me is that there appears to be an absolute abundance of evidence that on a properly conducted trial, weighing and assessing the evidence produced in that case, the jury would not have arrived at a verdict of guilty and that the circumstances of that verdict were to a large extent influenced by the nature of the judge's summing up.

There is something I want to say about the judge's summing up. A great deal has in recent months been said about the late Lord Goddard. It is not necessary for me to embark on any of the criticisms or comments that have been embarked upon in recent years about the general conduct of his trials. I had no personal knowledge of him. As a lawyer, on a number of occasions I heard cases in his court. I would only say – because I have some criticisms to make later – that I often felt that if I were engaged in a piece of personal litigation and was undoubtedly in the right, there is no judge before whom I would have preferred to have been tried than Lord Goddard. That is my assessment of the position. But everybody errs, Homer nods; and there can be little doubt that anyone who now, in the cold light of day and with the passage of time, reads his summing up in this case could hardly fail to arrive at the conclusion that this was not one of the most creditable performances of a distinguished judge. The summing up will at some stage need to be examined with some care to indicate why this matter ought to be the subject of examination.

Let me recite the brief facts of the crime. Undoubtedly there was a crime. Two young men, the young man Craig and the young man Bentley, had agreed – and this was admitted – to break into a butcher's shop in West Croydon. Craig, as it emerged, had a gun. The whole point of the case, and the whole area of controversy, turned on the question of Bentley's knowledge of whether Craig had a gun and when Bentley acquired that knowledge. That determined the verdict. If it had been established that Bentley did not know that Craig had a gun then it would certainly have been an inexorable consequence that Bentley would have been acquitted, unless possibly it could be shown that at some stage in the proceedings Bentley was urging him to use the gun having then come to the knowledge that he had it. That was not the Crown's case. The Crown's case was that these young men went together into the crime and either explicitly, or by implication from their course of conduct and the nature of the crime, both agreed that in the event of the police appearing, in the event of some attempt to apprehend them, Craig would use violence on behalf of both. That was the case. This argues a pre-arrangement between the two young men of a coherent and orderly character which would certainly be appropriate among professional criminals.

The point that one has to make – and I regret having to make it in circumstances where it might still be distressing to the members of the family – is that the young man Bentley was not an ordinary criminal. When he was in prison pending his trial and awaiting execution there were medical examinations. It emerges from the medical report that this young man aged 19 was expressed by the doctor to be nearly feeble-minded and to

335

have the intelligence of a boy of 11 or 12 years of age and to be hardly able to read or write. Against that medical assessment it is preposterous nonsense to suggest that those two boys set out with an organized, coherent plan whereby one of them had decided in advance carefully, cruelly and with calculation that the other would act in terms of violence if they were apprehended. It is preposterous nonsense, and I use no lesser words to say so. If you have a boy of this type of intelligence, is it really to be supposed that the cool, calm reckoning of professional criminals would have entered into his calculations? This boy was not a professional criminal. It is highly relevant to say this. This was a boy who had no record of violence; he had a criminal record and had been in an approved school.

Some while after his execution, the Home Secretary concerned in the matter was asked why no precautions were taken against the possibility of further violence by the young man after his tenure in the approved school, and the Home Secretary replied that in the approved school there had never been the slightest reason to apprehend that there would be violence on the part of the boy. He was not a violent boy. The circumstances of the crime confirm that fully. I do not intend to go into plans of where they stood or did not stand. Being inexpert and clumsy young criminals, the two boys were detected as they climbed on to the roof by a small child looking out of a window. The child called her father, and her father called the police. The police then climbed on to the roof and discovered the two boys, and the boy Bentley was promptly arrested. There is some conflict of testimony as to whether he came out by himself when challenged or whether he was dragged out.

There is no conflict of testimony that from that moment onwards he did not display a flicker of resistance or a flicker of violence. He was supine to the point of total timidity. He played no part in any physical action in relation to the police. I think this emerges incontrovertibly from the evidence. There is a slight conflict of evidence, but not relevant, about what happened when the boy Craig fired at the first policeman. The first policeman flung himself to the ground, and Bentley was flung with him or was thrown down by the policeman. This is really irrelevant in view of the later narrative, because Bentley obviously concurred in the whole situation and made no effort to escape. He was for all practical purposes under arrest. He was plainly under arrest. He had been apprehended by a policeman in the course of a crime.

There was an odd feature of the prosecution counsel's address because he had opened his case by saying that he accepted the possibility that the boy Bentley was under arrest at the time the crime was committed; but then in the course of cross-examining Bentley, Bentley asserted, as indeed was the case, that if he had wanted to he could have run away. This was indeed the case, because the policeman had left him by himself during most of the exchanges with Craig. He was alone. He could have run away. This boy was so cowed, so timid, so unwilling to commit any further breaches of the law, that he stayed exactly where he was for a period that has been variously estimated at 15 or 20 minutes. During the whole of the time this boy, whose behaviour if it were to vindicate the verdict of guilty required him to be designated as a positive desperado, had not moved from the position in which he was put by the policeman and had made no effort of any kind to assist the boy Craig.

The prosecuting counsel further stated that in view of Bentley's answer that he was able to escape if he had wanted to, Bentley was thereby rejecting the possible defence that he was under arrest and was himself asserting that he was not under arrest. This appears to me the oddest of propositions. It is equivalent to saying that if I, through some misfortune, am taken to a police station and imprisoned in a cell, I am not under arrest if the window is open by some chance and I can climb out of it. This was an extraordinary proposition but it appeared to have some weight in the proceedings, because there certainly was some doubt instilled in the mind of the jury as to whether, when incontrovertibly he was under arrest, it was considered that he was not.

In any event, the situation was this. There were against the boy Bentley — and this boy was convicted on a capital charge and hanged — so far as I can see, only two pieces of evidence. One was that he had in his possession two weapons. One of the weapons was a sheath knife and the other weapon was a knuckle-duster. He stated, and I think it was confirmed in evidence by the other boy, that the knuckle-duster had been given to him by the boy Craig. Nobody suggested that the boy had made any attempt whatsoever to use either weapon. Both, from the point of view of this crime, were totally irrelevant. It was difficult to see why they were introduced; and certainly difficult to see why they were introduced with the wealth of horrible detail that regaled the summing up of the Lord Chief Justice in relation to the matter. I will read to your Lordships in a moment what he said about the knuckle-duster. He said a good deal more about the knuckle-duster than he said about the whole of Bentley's defence, and this was a startling and surprising aberration.

In justice to the Lord Chief Justice, it is clear that he was strongly inflamed by the circumstances of the crime. He felt great anger about it. He obviously and legitimately, as we all should, felt horror that an innocent policeman had been killed in the course of his duty for a crime as futile and purposeless as this. But the strength of his feeling led him, I think, to the doing of a grave injustice to the boy Bentley. Because, apart from the question of the knuckle-duster, and apart from the question of the sheath knife, neither of which was used, the only relevant evidence against the boy was an allegation that he had used some words, when the boy Craig appeared from behind some partition with a gun to encounter the first policeman, such as: 'Let him have it, Chris.' Now these words were used in connection with the firing of the pistol and had no lethal effect. The pistol was apparently a ·45 and undoubtedly Craig shot at the policeman. Providentially that policeman was saved; the shot hit his shoulder and he was knocked over. He was, I think, happily not gravely hurt. This was a very fortunate outcome. But it is alleged that the boy Bentley gave him that encouragement at that moment of time.

That encouragement might give rise to two possibilities of criminal responsibility. The one I have already indicated is that there was a pre-concerted arrangement between the two boys that if they were apprehended, then Craig was to defend Bentley by the exercise of violence. I discard that as phenomenally unlikely, having regard to the mental state and condition of the boy Bentley and the extreme improvidence of the whole approach to the matter. The idea that you could read into an enterprise of this character even the providence of having made arrangements, express or implicit, as to how they were going to defend themselves in the event of arrest, is, I think, far-fetched and positively fanciful.

The next possibility which might inculpate the boy was that in relation to this particular situation, although he only then knew that the pistol was in the possession of Craig, he urged him to use it. If that were the suggestion, then one must remember that it was 15 or 20 minutes later that the actual lethal act, the firing, took place in consequence of which the unfortunate and very gallant policeman was killed. What one has to say to oneself is this: that the encouragement supposedly given 15 or 20 minutes earlier to the firing of one shot still remained as the inducement and incitement to Craig to fire the shot 15 or 20 minutes later when the other boy had been arrested, when he had totally withdrawn from the situation, when he had given no manifestation of any kind of supporting any further violence or illegality, despite the opportunities that existed for him. There were on the roof, as it emerged, because the police made use of them, milk bottles and bricks that had been thrown. It is not unreasonable to conjecture that there were other forms of weapons that might possibly have been used if there were a resolute young desperado determined to assist his colleague. In fact, the evidence is entirely to the contrary. The police evidence made no suggestion that this boy showed the slightest intention or desire or inclination to resume the controversy, to resume the battle.

Prosecuting counsel made another weird suggestion. What he said was that when the whole situation started the boy Bentley obviously had his mind with the boy Craig; that the two minds were as one, in unison, in determining to resist the onslaught. If in fact this were the case, that the words alleged, 'Let him have it, Chris', were used, or had the interpretation which was placed upon them, this certainly might have been a possibility at the outset. What prosecuting counsel then said, forgetting, if I may say so, the whole question of the onus of proof in criminal trials, was that there was no evidence from that moment onwards that the boy Bentley had withdrawn his mind. Whether he was expected to write a formal letter and send it to Craig to tell him that in the circumstances he no longer wished to participate in this enterprise – what action he was supposed to take to indicate that he was resigning from the partnership – will remain one of the unsolved problems of jurisprudence for years to come. There was nothing he could do. What he did do, quite clearly, was to indicate that he had resigned from the club from the very moment of his arrest. He did not stir; he did not resist; he gave no encouragement of any kind. What he did was to remain in a state, I imagine, of absolute terror, of shaking terror, while this appalling battle went on with a boy of a totally different calibre and character, about whom it would be quite inappropriate to make any comment. He has served the sentence. One earnestly hopes that he can be restored to a useful life – indeed, he has been restored to a useful life.

But the fact remains that the boy Bentley played no further part in the matter, and I think there was incontrovertible proof that, so far as he was concerned, he wanted no further part in the matter.

Now let us test the likelihood; because I am not saying that any policeman lied. It is not necessary for me to say that the policeman lied. All I am saying is that the inherent probabilities are strongly, and almost overwhelmingly, against what was suggested by the police. You have to look at the second statement that was attributed to the boy Bentley by the police. When arrested he was taken down to a police car. On the way down there was certainly a statement. It was not denied that as he was crossing the parapet – Craig was still firing – he called out, 'Look out, Chris. They're taking me down', by that, clearly meaning that he had no wish to be shot by his colleague on the way down. There is no other meaning attributable to those words. 'Look out!' was not a warning against any special or specific approach by the police, and the police did not suggest that it was. It was, 'Look out for me; I am going down.'

When the boy finally descended and was taken into the police car he is then alleged to have said, 'I knew he had a gun but I didn't think the idiot – or fool – would use it.' Reflect for a moment, my Lords. This is a boy who is supposed previously to have said in the hearing of the self-same policeman, 'Let him have it Chris!'. He is now saying to the self-same policeman, 'I knew he had a gun but I didn't think he would use it.' Is it remotely possible that those two statements can be reconciled – that the boy who had made the first statement could have made the second statement? He knew perfectly well that the policeman would have been aware of his violent exhortation to Chris to use the gun to shoot the policeman. How, then, could he have made the second statement? But the reports that he had made those two statements came from the same source, from the police.

I do not want to say much more about this case, my Lords. There can be added to the facts odd suggestions in cross-examination about whether or not he knew that there was a sheath knife. His cross-examination was one of brutal ferocity. Having regard to his mental state and IQ, the cross-examination should have been as careful, patient and humane as was consistent with extracting the facts. But that was not the form which this cross-examination took.

When one looks at the tragic summing-up – as I say, it does no credit to the reputation of a very great judge – one finds that there are circumstances which, at any rate to me, appear

340

incontrovertibly to establish the need for an inquiry. I have the summing up with me, but I will not read the whole of it. Consider, however, this portion:

> 'Now let us see what the evidence is in regard to Bentley. The first thing you have to consider is: Did Bentley know that Craig was armed?'

The evidence, and the only evidence, on this matter was quite simple: that Bentley had said he had not known that Craig was armed until Craig told him so when they were on the roof and when the police arrived; that Craig had said that Bentley did not know that he was armed. Craig had no motivation and one of the things that has been said about Craig is how he emerged as a transparently honest witness.

The judge went on:

> 'The great virtue of trial by jury is that jurymen can exercise the common sense of ordinary people. Can you suppose for a moment, especially when you have heard Craig say that why he carried a revolver was for the purpose of boasting and making himself a big man, that he would not have told his pals he was out with that he had got a revolver . . . ?'

The judge is asking the jury:

> 'Can you suppose for a moment . . . ? – '

and of course one can suppose for a moment, one can suppose for many moments, that he had not told his friend Craig that he had a revolver. The only evidence to show that he had told his friend Craig that he had a revolver was the evidence on this point supplied by the Lord Chief Justice, and nobody else.

Then we come to the next horrifying sentence:

> 'Is it not almost inconceivable' –

these were the actual words he used—

> 'that Craig would not have told him and probably showed him the revolver which he had?'

341

This is totally baseless speculation. There was not a word in evidence in the case to justify that comment to the jury. There was not a syllable of evidence which justified the suggestion that it was inconceivable that Craig should not have told Bentley that he had the weapon. We are told by the Lord Chief Justice that it was 'inconceivable'. The whole of the summing up is shot through and through with tendentious suggestions of that kind. I will read what is said by the judge about the knuckle-duster and the other weapons:

> 'Then see what Bentley had on him. Where is that knuckle-duster? Apparently it was given to him by Craig. Bentley was armed with this knuckle-duster. Have you ever seen a more horrible sort of weapon?'

That remark, my Lords, bore no evidence to the case at all; the knuckle-duster had not been used by anybody. The number of innocent children who never appear in a court but who must be possessed of knuckle-dusters probably exceeds many thousands, if not hundreds of thousands. If every child found in possession of a knuckle-duster or a lethal weapon had found himself arraigned at the Old Bailey in front of Lord Goddard, I shudder to think of the number of executions that might have taken place.

The Lord Chief Justice said:

> 'Have you ever seen a more horrible sort of weapon?'

I am quite satisfied that it would have been a most unworldly jury if they had not seen a more horrible weapon. He went on:

> 'You know, this is to hit a person in the face with who comes at you.'

We have some interesting speculation about what one does with a knuckle-duster that was never used by anyone and played no part in the crime and was admittedly belonging to the other boy and not to this boy with whom we are here concerned. The Lord Chief Justice goes on:

> 'You grasp it here, your fingers go through – I cannot quite get mine through.'

One is almost relieved that that was the case lest in his enthusiasm he might have found it necessary to demonstrate what one could do with the weapon. My Lords, I believe that in the whole history of summings up in criminal trials there can hardly have been a more inappropriate and improper passage in relation to the capital trial of an unfortunate youth whose association with the crime on any account was as tenuous as one could make it. That was the summing up presented to the jury.

I have no desire to keep your Lordships here all night discussing this matter. I conclude by saying that this case went to the Court of Criminal Appeal, normally a bastion of justice, a great protector of people who, by chance or misfortune, may have been wrongly convicted. In the present case the presiding judge in the Court of Criminal Appeal and the two judges who sat with him arrived at the sweeping conclusion that there was nothing to criticize in the summing up. That was the outcome of the appeal by this wretched youth. How any experienced judge, reading this summing up, could have arrived at the conclusion that there was nothing to criticize in the summing up passes my understanding and, I venture to think, passes belief. It is unnecessary and undesirable that one should stress the unfortunate features of this case: in so doing one might give rise to doubts and anxieties about our system of justice which I believe would be unjustified. Every so often something goes wrong, and in this case something went very badly wrong. In my view, it is due to the parents of this boy, and to our whole criminal system and the system of justice in this country, that this case should be carefully reviewed so that what I believe to be the justness of the situation can at least historically be restored. That is my view about the case of Bentley.

I come next to a more difficult case, that of Hanratty. This case in some ways aroused greater public anxiety and concern than does the case of Bentley. It is a difficult case and it is again a very horrible crime, happily a crime of a most unusual character. A man and woman are in a motor car in a quite isolated field, I think towards dusk, one evening. Another man appears almost from nowhere, a sinister figure with a gun, who climbs into the motor car and orders them to drive off. They drive and stop at various points; there are various incidents and episodes connected with the case, and at some appalling stage he shoots the man dead and then, later, shoots the woman. Happily, he does not kill her, although she remains, I fear and believe, still very seriously crippled. It was a most appalling crime and everyone's sympathy must go out to her, a person against whom not a whisper of criticism can be uttered, whatever role she may have played in the trial. Nobody has suggested that her participation in the trial was anything but totally honourable and public-spirited.

From that moment onwards a hue-and-cry arises for the arrest of the criminal. At one stage a man is arrested, but I believe that he is not charged. He is presented to an identification parade where the young woman does not identify him. It is important to point out that this is a man of whom it is later said that he made confessions for exhibitionist reasons. Unless he was a man with a remarkable gift of prophecy, he could not, in the circumstances that had happened, have involved himself in this case at the outset in the way he did if his motives were truly exhibitionist. There is nothing exhibitionist about the fact that the police sought him. There was nothing exhibitionist about the fact that this man had occupied a room, the same room in the boarding house or hotel that the ultimate accused had occupied. There is a question about whether or not he did occupy the same room but there was certainly evidence at one stage that he occupied room 4 and a later suggestion that he occupied room 24. I am prepared to waive this point. I am prepared to leave it on the basis that this man had stayed in the same small hotel – which is sufficient coincidence in itself, without necessitating identifying which room it was – in which the police had subsequently found the cartridge that had been fired from the gun. They found cartridges in that room in the hotel which had been occupied by this man.

This man subsequently made two or more confessions in very queer circumstances. He is alleged to have confessed to another man who is described in the book where the confession appears as a businessman. I do not want to identify him any further. What his motivation was is not known, but there is a highly substantial confession produced in handwriting from the man who stayed in the room who associated himself and apparently confessing to the crime.

VISCOUNT COLVILLE OF CULROSS: My Lords, the noble Lord really ought to be aware that this man did not stay in the room in which the cartridges were found.

LORD GOODMAN: I would not wish to dispute that particular point, if it is conceded that he stayed in the hotel—

VISCOUNT COLVILLE OF CULROSS: Yes, that is right.

LORD GOODMAN: – containing the room where the cartridges were found. That is quite enough to create the sufficiency of coincidence for the purpose I require in order to establish a *prima facie* case that there should be investigation.

If he did not stay in the room then various versions that have been put about are in fact inaccurate. That may well be the case and it would be surprising if it were not. I have no personal knowledge, and it would be quite wrong to establish the point when there is a clear contradiction from the Government Benches. It is the case that he stayed in this small hotel; it is not a great hotel; it is not a hotel where a number of people might gravitate quite ordinarily because they all go to the Savoy or the Dorchester. It is a small hotel in Maida Vale, and it would indeed be an odd chance that two men should select it by sheerest accident. But they might. It is an odd chance that a man who later confesses to the crime should stay there on the night of the crime. It is also, I believe, the case that the man who confessed to the crime was absent during the night of the crime from the hotel, and there were some equivocal exchanges between himself and the proprietor of the hotel as to what he had done during the night.

I wish to make this point clear. I am not suggesting that this man is guilty of the crime. What I am saying is that there is a sufficiency of coincidence to make one believe that if the circumstances now known had been known to the jury when they tried this case they would have been unlikely to arrive at the same conclusion. There is the coincidence that the man was in the same room; the coincidence that the man was arrested by the police for this crime; the coincidence that subsequently he confessed to the crime, and the coincidence that on a number of occasions he brought libel actions against people who alleged he committed the crime yet never pursued a single one. It is my belief that he has not brought a libel action against Mr Paul Foot who makes a clear-cut allegation that he is guilty of the crime. It is my belief that he has not challenged this fact. No one can regard those as unmaterial circumstances.

Here again, if the facts of the case as presented to the jury had been totally free, or substantially free, of doubt, these later circumstances might have much less relevance. I am not suggesting that this jury arrived at a perverse verdict because they arrived at a verdict on the basis of the facts they knew and not of the facts

I am retailing. If nothing more had been known, and if nothing more had emerged, I doubt whether anyone could really criticize the findings of the jury, because one of the peculiarities of the two cases of Bentley and Hanratty is that the normal suggestion made against any proposal to reopen a case, that the jury had an opportunity of seeing the accused, is totally irrelevant. It could not matter whether the jury saw Bentley or not. They knew the poor lad was a young criminal and that he asserted he had not got a gun and went on asserting it. Whether they saw him or not was quite irrelevant to the circumstances of the case.

The same is true in relation to Hanratty, because the jury would not have known of the circumstances of these confessions or of this startling coincidence; and in relation to Hanratty also the unfortunate young man had this situation to deal with: that he had not surrendered to the police, when they had made it known that they wanted to arrest him. The explanation he put forward was wholly plausible. It was that he was a criminal on the run; he thought the police wanted to arrest him for a crime, and he did not present himself to be arrested because it is not the technique of criminals to present themselves to be arrested; they wait to be found. That weighed against him, and undoubtedly it aroused prejudice against him. This is a case where, in the light of the confessions and coincidences, and in the light of the fact that if you examine the evidence critically, now knowing that it is peppered with these doubts and uncertainties; that you have another case, as you had in Bentley, of a boy who had never indulged in violence although he had a criminal career, there is more to be said. The police conceded that he had never indulged in violence although he had a criminal career. There was never any suggestion he had indulged in sexual violence of any kind; nor was he suffering from any kind of sexual frustration.

These are difficult matters, my Lords. One can examine them in much greater detail. There is more to be said in relation to those cases. They cannot be swept under the carpet and I do not believe that anything the Government say today will succeed in sweeping them under the carpet. The only thing that will satisfy public anxiety is a full and candid inquiry. Such an inquiry would do credit to our system of jurisprudence. It would not arouse the fear that we are all driving a great wedge into a situation where every criminal case can be reopened. The public is not concerned about every criminal case. There is concern about the rare case where the circumstances suggest that something has gone wrong with the best of human systems. That is what they are concerned with, and it is because of that concern that has been manifested so firmly, so strongly and so continuously over the years that I invite the Government, and the Minister who is to reply, not to close their minds to the possibility of considering an investigation. I do not necessarily ask the Minister to give his answer tonight, but I ask him to listen very carefully to the debate and to convey to his colleagues what has been said, and whether it is not wise for once to concede the possibility of error in judicial processes and, by so doing, to satisfy the public.

7.28 p.m.

THE EARL OF ARRAN: My Lords, I am no lawyer; I am no orator, and I shall stick strictly to my brief, which is to ask for a public inquiry into the circumstances of the so-called Craig and Bentley case. I am against post-mortems and these cases are, alas! exactly that. Next we shall be re-trying Crippen and the murderer of the 'brides in the bath'. What has been done cannot be undone – or so it is argued – and if there is one thing I have learned in life it is that there is no justice. I speak not about the law and its processes but of the cruelties of human and animal existence. But, my Lords, one does one's best and there are certain occasions when, in the name of human dignity, one is forced to protest. If one is to try to eliminate legal injustices, at least in the future, our first step should surely be to acknowledge the injustices of the past. The stubborn resistance that successive Governments demonstrate when attempts are made to reopen cases where there has been reasonable cause for doubt is notorious. Your Lordships will recall the, if you like minor, case of Commander Swabey, whose cause my noble cousin, the late Marquess of Salisbury, supported. It took fifteen years for Commander Swabey's name to be cleared. One has only again to think of the sixteen-year-old struggle before Timothy Evans was finally granted a posthumous Royal Pardon – and I emphasize the word 'posthumous'.

The Executive appear to adopt a singular attitude in such matters. Apparently when decisions concerning life and death are made, or were then made, the men responsible were seemingly guided by a mysterious infallibility. They were never wrong. But in fact sometimes they were wrong. Undoubtedly, as the noble Lord, Lord Goodman – to whom I think we are all very much indebted – said, mistakes have been made in capital cases and men and women who should still be alive are dead as a result

347

of fatal errors of judgement. It is not in fact only my opinion. Indeed, the present noble and learned Lord, the Lord Chancellor, said as much during a Commons debate in 1969, when he was, I think, Shadow Home Secretary. I have naturally informed him that I was going to mention the case.

THE LORD CHANCELLOR: Yes, my Lords. I should make it plain, however, that as the context shows, my remarks on that occasion related solely to the use of the prerogative and had nothing whatever to do with the question of guilt, and that is what the noble Lord, Lord Goodman, is raising by his Question. I do not want to interrupt the noble Earl, but he should not misuse what I was saying.

THE EARL OF ARRAN: No, my Lords, but I must quote the noble Lord verbatim. It may be that he was talking about the prerogative – indeed, he was talking about the prerogative and the wrongness of one man having to make one decision. Nevertheless, he said this:

'I think that in the past Home Secretaries have proved inadequate. With great respect to a distinguished succession of gentlemen of humane and civilized bent, I say that they demonstrably made mistakes. Oddly enough, the mistakes they made have erred occasionally in the direction of severity.'

And Mr Hogg went on:

'One has only to mention some of the cases – Evans, Ruth Ellis, Bentley, and for rather different reasons, even Hanratty, on whose guilt I do not wish to cast the smallest doubt.' – [OFFICIAL REPORT, Commons, 16/12/69; col. 1172.]

And the noble and learned Lord went on to make his case, which was, in fact, that no such great power should lie in the hands of one single man.

THE LORD CHANCELLOR: My Lords, the only point I was making was that this is a Question which relates to the guilt of two persons who were charged with murder. The passage to which the noble Earl refers – and he has not yet read it all, but he has read enough of it – shows that I was dealing solely with the prerogative of mercy, which has nothing whatever to do with guilt but assumes guilt. I do not want to spoil the noble Earl's speech, but it really is a misuse of my words to indicate that they have the smallest relation to the important subject now under discussion.

THE EARL OF ARRAN: My Lords, I have referred the noble and learned Lord to his quote, and he will not go back on that.

> 'With great respect to a distinguished succession of gentlemen of humane and civilized bent,'—

and he was referring to Home Secretaries—

> 'I say that they demonstrably made mistakes.'

I say again to the noble and learned Lord:

> ' . . . they demonstrably made mistakes. Oddly enough, the mistakes they have made have erred occasionally in the direction of severity.'

And he goes on to mention two or three cases. Those were the noble and learned Lord's words. I leave it to the House to decide.

THE LORD CHANCELLOR: I am bound to tell the noble Earl that he has not quoted me correctly. I began the passage as follows:

> 'At this point, I digress for a moment to the question of the prerogative of mercy. Whatever the result of the debate today – and certainly if it turned out that the House was not prepared finally to abolish capital punishment—'

and that was the subject of the debate—

> 'I feel that the Home Secretary should, on any view, cease to be solely responsible for the exercise of the prerogative.'

Then follows the passage which the noble Lord quoted. After

mentioning the case of Hanratty and saying, as the noble Lord read:

> '. . . on whose guilt I do not wish to cast the smallest doubt',

I went on to say:

> '. . . the Home Secretary in the isolation of his chamber deciding between life and death is attempting a job which ought not to be done by any one man. On any view of the prerogative of mercy, even on the basis of imprisonment, I should like to see a reprieve board advising the Home Secretary.'

I do not want to spoil the noble Earl's speech, but he really must abandon a point which is utterly without foundation and which has no relevance to the subject under discussion.

THE EARL OF ARRAN: My Lords, I ask the noble and learned Lord to stick to what he said, in whatever context it was made. He made these remarks, and he will not deny that he made them.

THE LORD CHANCELLOR: My Lords, I only ask that the noble Earl should quote them correctly and fully and not go off at a tangent. I am not seeking to depart from what I have said. I am only repeating what I said, and in particular repeating those parts of my remarks which the noble Earl did not see fit to quote.

THE EARL OF ARRAN: My Lords, would the House like me to repeat what the noble Lord said, or what Mr Hogg said at that time? I will gladly do so if your Lordships so wish. I thank the noble and learned Lord for his kindly interruption. Such an occasion as the noble and learned Lord the Lord Chancellor mentioned – and he did mention it – is the trial of Bentley and Craig and the termination of Mr Bentley's life by hanging. I will not speak of Mr Hanratty; his case is outside my scope and my knowledge. It may be that the noble Lord who is to follow me will be able to supply information on that point.

My Lords, I am not, publicly, at least, a champion of individuals. What we all do privately as Members of the Upper House of Parliament, with all that such a grave responsibility involves, is our duty and not to be bruited abroad. This is the first time that I have ever publicly supported in Parliament the case of an individual. I make this point because it simply emphasizes the importance that I attach to the case in question. I should further make it clear that I am no doctrinaire opponent of capital punishment. If it is satisfactorily proved to me that hanging is an effective deterrent to murder, then I will vote in favour of the reintroduction of hanging. So far, thank God!, it has not been proved. I apologize for the preamble. I have only made it lest your Lordships think that I am in some ways prejudiced.

May I turn to the case itself. Certain facts – and I think the noble Lord, Lord Goodman, has made them clear – are not in dispute. They are all recorded in a book called *To Encourage the Others* by Mr David Yallop. They have also been the subject of a BBC television play based on Mr Yallop's book. On 11 December 1952, Mr Craig, then 16, and Mr Bentley, then 19, were found guilty of the murder of Police Constable Miles. The judge was the late Lord Goddard, to whom I shall be referring later. Mr Craig was detained during Her Majesty's pleasure, and I am glad to say that since his release he is leading a useful and happy life. He has, to his credit, I think, not changed his name. Mr Derek Bentley was hanged.

Now, my Lords, to the stuff of the case. I will make four immediate points, no more. This is not the public inquiry which we hope to see set up. First, let me deal with the pathetic exercise, the secret police inquiry – why secret? why police? – into the case which the Home Secretary has recently caused to be held. This inquiry was confined seemingly to one specific issue, the calibre of the bullet and the possibility that Police Constable Miles had been killed by a fellow officer, in mistake of course. The inquiry heard evidence from only two witnesses, both of whom gave evidence at the trial, the pathologist, Dr David Haler and the ex-police sergeant Detective Sergeant Fairfax. This matter of the size of the bullet was one aspect, albeit only one, but an important one, although there are others which I shall mention to your Lordships. Was the wound inflicted by a ·32 or a ·38, or was it a ·45, which was Mr Craig's gun? On these points both Dr Haler and Sergeant Fairfax made statements which, although I cannot positively identify the voices because I have never spoken to those concerned, I have myself heard and seen. Dr Haler and Sergeant Fairfax now deny having made these statements, although in fact Dr Haler confirmed his statement to two highly-reputable members of the legal profession. These two legal gentlemen are prepared to testify to this. The author is prepared to make his recordings freely available to any public inquiry on the Craig and Bentley case.

Once again, my Lords, you must bear in mind that it was said in evidence at the trial that the shot came from a ·45 calibre revolver. On this I quote a statement from Dr David Haler, to the writer of the book, as recorded. I quote very briefly:

Yallop: Now you subsequently described during the Old Bailey trial and also on your original deposition the bullet as being of large calibre? What, for example, did you mean by large calibre?

Haler: Well, it was bigger than a ·22.

Yallop: Yes, but can you be more precise?

Haler: Indeed. The bullet was between a ·32 and a ·38 calibre.

Yallop: Is there any possibility that the calibre could have been bigger?

Haler: Oh, no. Putting it at ·38 is the very ultimate extreme.

Police officers who conducted the latest secret inquiry did not see fit to interview Mr Yallop or Mr Craig or any member of the Bentley family. They confined it to interviewing two witnesses, Dr Haler, the pathologist, and Sergeant Fairfax. Am I correct in that statement?

Viscount COLVILLE OF CULROSS: No; the noble Earl is not correct.

The Earl of ARRAN: Would the noble Viscount like to correct me?

Viscount COLVILLE OF CULROSS: In my final speech.

The Earl of ARRAN: That is as recorded in the newspapers. To come back to the inquiry itself, the two senior police officers, Detective Chief Inspector Smith and Detective Sergeant Shepherd, in charge of the investigation at the time of the Craig-Bentley case – I am not speaking of the latest inquiry but of the time of the trial – were grievously in error. They swore on oath during the trial that:

352

'Craig, within one hour of the gun battle, made vital self-incriminating remarks which constituted vital evidence.'

But Sergeant Fairfax, who was in the cubicle next to Craig, has clearly stated on tape:

'Craig was unconscious when he was placed into the ambulance. I travelled with him to the hospital. He remained in an unconscious condition for the rest of the night and well into the following day. He wasn't talking to anybody, either voluntarily or in any other way.'

I repeat the last sentence:

'He wasn't talking to anybody, either voluntarily or in any other way.'

This interview former Sergeant Fairfax now denies having given, as also does Dr Haler. But if these records are true statements (I repeat, I cannot personally vouch for them because I have never met the people concerned), it would appear that they are lying. Why, if they are not lying, have they not taken legal action over this highly actionable statement contained in Mr Yallop's book and in the film that was made from it?

The second point I want to make – it has been made already by the noble Lord, Lord Goodman, much better than I can do it – is the matter of Mr Bentley's mental age. I do not want to repeat it, but I think it was briefly this. At the age of 17 Mr Bentley had an IQ of 66 and a mental age of 9. At the age of 10, after a National Service medical, he was placed in the lowest possible grade – Grade IV – and totally exempted from National Service. This was after psychiatric examination. I apologize to Mr Bentley's parents if they are in the House, but I must give the facts. I know a little about these things.

The Brixton Prison medical officer, in his pre-trial report to the Old Bailey, indicated that Mr Bentley was sane, fit to plead to the indictment and fit to stand trial. But shortly before Mr Bentley's execution – this is very grave – Professor Sir Denis Hill, a world authority on human brain waves or the human brain, wished to make public the fact that Mr Bentley was an epileptic. In his opinion this fact alone should have ensured Mr Bentley's reprieve. The Home Office refused to give Sir Denis permission on the ground – I say this with appalling solemnity – that it would not be in the public interest. Why not in the public interest?

VISCOUNT COLVILLE OF CULROSS: The noble Lord said the Home Office did not give Sir Denis Hill the opportunity to do something. I did not hear what it was that he was not given the opportunity to do.

THE EARL OF ARRAN: The Home Office refused to give Sir Denis permission to give the facts to the Home Office or to have them stated or brought before those who were to decide the fate of Mr Bentley. I am glad to see that the noble and learned Viscount is taking very careful notes. The phrase is that it would not be in the public interest.

Thirdly, I must draw your Lordships' attention to two statements by Mr Frank Cassels, defence counsel for Mr Bentley. In one of them he said before the trial:

'I think both the little bastards ought to swing.'

In the other statement, made to the late Lord Goddard after the trial and before Mr Bentley's appeal, he said:

'I think he will hang and I think he ought to hang.'

Mr Cassels, as recorded in Mr Yallop's tape recordings, has freely admitted making these remarks. While referring to Mr Cassels' statement I must also refer to a statement by the late Lord Goddard, before the trial had even begun: I repeat, before the trial had even begun. In consultation with learned counsel Lord Goddard said that Craig was obviously guilty and could have no defence. Mr Parris, defence counsel for Mr Craig and I believe now a QC, is willing to confirm this.

Lastly, I come to the trial itself, conducted by the late Lord Goddard. If I may amplify what the noble and learned Lord, Lord Goodman, said, during that trial the late Lord Goddard interrupted the evidence no fewer than 250 times, on almost every occasion in a sense damaging to Mr Bentley and Mr Craig. He showed anger when asked by the foreman for a vital exhibit. He brandished the knuckle-duster (I think that is in confirmation of what the noble Lord, Lord Goodman, said) to the jury. His

45 minutes' summing-up contained only one sentence referring to Bentley's defence. It is none the less a fact that he expected Mr Bentley to be reprieved. He said so to Mr Yallop afterwards. I quote from his Lordship:

> 'Yes, I thought that Bentley was going to be reprieved. He certainly should have been reprieved. There is no doubt in my mind. Bentley should have been reprieved.'

Now the late Lord Goddard was not exactly an anti-hanger. In his evidence before the Royal Commission on Capital Punishment he said of the case of a certain Thomas Ley, in New South Wales:

> 'I have no doubt that the person was insane. His whole conduct showed a typical case of paranoia.'

Lord Goddard went on:

> 'Insane or not, he should have been hanged.'

In a nutshell, that was his Lordship's attitude.

My Lords, that is the evidence. I fear that I have wearied the House and the noble and learned Lord who sits on the Woolsack, and certainly I have wearied myself; but I hope that I have helped to establish a *prima facie* case for a public inquiry. I have tried to be factual and, against my ordinary nature to be unemotional. This is not a time for oratory. There is public unease, and when there is public unease there should be a public inquiry. We do not want any more of what I call these 'hole-in-the-corner' inquiries with interested parties – namely, the police – as the inquirers.

I ask these eight simple questions. First, with regard to the recent secret inquiry, why was the author of the book, Mr David Yallop, not questioned? Why was Mr Christopher Craig not questioned? Why was no member of Derek Bentley's family questioned? Second, why, for example, were Police Constables Pain, Bugden and Alderson, who were at the scene of the crime, not questioned? Alderson, in particular, who sat next to Bentley in the car on the way to the station, was not questioned? Third, why were Professor Sir Denis Hill, Mr Frank Cassels, Mr John Parris and many other people, whose evidence has a direct bearing on Derek Bentley's conviction and execution, not questioned? Fourth, why was one item covering a few hundred words, from

355

a book of some 100,000 words, the only piece of evidence – according to the newspapers – subjected to the latest police investigation? Fifth, why was evidence not taken as to the mental condition of Mr Bentley, though in fact such evidence was freely available? Sixth, why was the manifestly biased summing-up of the late Lord Goddard totally ignored?

Seventh, why, in short, during the latest police inquiry, was one aspect of the affair the only one taken into consideration when the other circumstances of the case were so unsatisfactory and, indeed, so horrifying? Eighth – and this is more or less a rhetorical question – why has neither Sergeant Fairfax nor Dr Haler taken legal action against Mr Yallop, who has accused them of having gone back on statements which he maintains were made? Either Mr Yallop is the biggest rogue unhanged, and is guilty not only of deceiving myself – and I do not count – but of causing me to deceive the High Court of Parliament, which is your Lordships' House and the highest Court in the land; or he is telling the truth, the whole truth and nothing but the truth. I do not expect the noble Viscount who is to reply to give the answers to those questions. Had I wished him to do so, I should have given him advance notice. I simply put them as questions for his right honourable friend to answer in the very near future.

My Lords, before I sit down, I think I should add a note about the climate at the time of the trial and the climate today. Your Lordships, or those of your Lordships who were alive at the time of the trial, will recall that at the time there was a feeling of anger about thuggery and acts of violence, particularly where the police were involved – I do not mean where the police committed violence, but where it was committed against them. The book by Mr Yallop is called *To Encourage the Others*. It is rightly so called. It was a matter of making an example and it is much the same today – probably rightly so. But it remains a fact that the then Home Secretary, Sir David Maxwell Fyfe (later the noble and learned Earl, Lord Kilmuir), did not consult Lord Goddard, the trial judge, which I understand is customary procedure, before denying Mr Bentley a reprieve.

VISCOUNT COLVILLE OF CULROSS: My Lords, that is not true. The noble Earl is simply incorrect factually.

THE EARL OF ARRAN: My Lords, the noble and learned

356

Viscount, Lord Dilhorne, to whom I spoke shortly before this afternoon's debate, said that it was customary procedure.

VISCOUNT COLVILLE OF CULROSS: Yes, my Lords. But the point is that the Home Secretary of the time did consult the trial judge.

THE EARL OF ARRAN: My Lords, I thank the noble Viscount very much. I am only too glad to be corrected. I submit to your Lordships that, despite the petition on Mr Bentley's behalf, the greatest public demand for the reprieve of a man in this country, the dice were loaded against him at the beginning, during the trial and at the end.

My Lords, I began by saying that I am against post-mortems – I still am. But it remains a principle of British justice, or rather of natural justice, that justice should not only be done but evidently be seen to have been done. To those who might ask, 'What is the use: Mr Bentley has been dead for 19 years?', I would say that although we cannot bring Derek Bentley back from the dead – and when I say 'we', I mean each and every one of us, for we are all responsible – we should never have put him there. As Voltaire said:

> 'To the living we owe our respect, to the dead we owe nothing but the truth.'

7.57 p.m.

LORD BROCKWAY: My Lords, I should like in a very special way to express my appreciation to the noble Lord, Lord Good man, for having raised this issue tonight. His authority in the legal field, and in many other respects, gives this debate a prominence which it could not otherwise have been given. Those of us who are concerned about one case or the other are deeply indebted to him. There is also a personal reason why I want to thank him. I first raised the issue of Hanratty's condemnation to death – perhaps 10 years ago – immediately after the trial. Yet ever since I have been silent about it and I do not think anything has been more on my conscience than that silence. It arose from the fact that legal proceedings were taken against me. I was not allowed to speak outside Parliament, and I felt it wrong to use the privilege of Parliament to say things which I could not say outside. Even tonight, I shall not trespass upon what may remain of that *sub judice* condition to make what is perhaps the strongest case on the innocence of Hanratty.

I became involved because the Hanratty case was so closely associated with Slough, which I represented in Parliament. My first concern was with a woman constituent who after the shooting was thought dead, lying at the side of the road, paralysed in both of her legs, the assailant having driven off. My first sympathy was with my woman constituent. Despite her paralysis she has very bravely maintained her work at the road research laboratory in Slough. No word that I will say tonight will be a reproach on her in any way whatsoever. There followed the trial at Bedford. I was disturbed in the proceedings of the trial by the contradictions in the identification of the supposed criminal. First there were doubts; then there were other considerations, and finally there was an identification on the ground of his Cockney pronunciation. I might say that I have heard on records the voice of someone else who has been concerned in this case and he had a Cockney pronunciation just as great as that of Hanratty who was identified on that ground.

At the trial I was not concerned about something which has since become very important. I refer to the alibi that Hanratty was in Rhyl when the murder took place. It was raised only at the later part of the trial, but subsequently the evidence that he was in Rhyl when he was supposed to have committed the murder became very strong indeed. My doubts during the proceedings of the trial were intensified when a newspaper man in Slough who was assigned to investigate the case came to me with his evidence, which was supplemented by that of others who had examined the case.

I ask your noble Lordships to believe that I approached this issue with an impartial mind. I sought to see all who were involved in the case. I saw the wife of the murdered man and her brother. I saw more than once the man who subsequently confessed that he had committed the murder. I saw the Catholic priests who were with Hanratty in the death chamber. I wish that it were possible to repeat what they said, but it would be denying their religious authority. I had interviews with Superintendent Kennedy and the detectives at Scotland Yard. I saw one Home Office secretary after another. After all that investigation, which I had sought to make on the broadest possible grounds in order to find the truth, I had no doubt whatsoever that Hanratty was innocent of the charge on which he was hanged.

That investigation led me to the view that the circumstances of the Hanratty case were these: a married man employed at the Slough research laboratory; an unmarried woman. Together they gave very valuable service in surveys of road traffic around the country. They were much together. These things happen and I am not going to condemn them. They fell in love. They made a practice of going to a public-house at Taplow and after that of going in their car to an isolated cornfield. On one occasion a man rapped at the window of the car and threatened them with a weapon. He got into the car and they travelled about Slough for nearly two hours. The charge is that the man had his weapon at the back of the first man all through that drive, I find that a little difficult to accept.

I have no doubt that the second man was asked to intervene in order to break up the affair. In the two hours that he argued, the suggestion that he threatened the first man with his weapon is removed by the fact that he allowed the man to get out of the car, buy cigarettes and return to it. What happened at the end of this? The man got out of the car at a petrol-station and was shot. The allegation was that the other man raped the woman, drove around, shot her and left her for dead. But she was in fact left paralysed. As a result of my investigations I have no doubt that that is the explanation of the affair; that it was an attempt to break up the association between the man and the woman. I am not suggesting that those who sought that intended that it should go to the extent of the murder of the man and the paralysing of the woman.

But when we come to the case against Hanratty let us remember that the first charge was made not against him but against another man. The charge against Hanratty was based on the fact that in this boarding house, exaggerated in terms of being called an hotel, cartridges were found in the room of Hanratty which identified him with the shooting. Whether the other man occupied the same room or not, he occupied the same hotel. I need not repeat the fact that, at the identification parade, the woman did not recognize Hanratty in the first instance, and recognized him only by a pronunciation in the second instance.

Viscount COLVILLE OF CULROSS: My Lords, it was at the same identification parade.

Lord BROCKWAY: Yes; I did not say otherwise. It gives me great encouragement that the Minister is so anxious to get up to correct things which need no correction at all. It suggests to me that the Minister himself is very doubtful about these cases. It has occurred in a previous instance.

VISCOUNT COLVILLE OF CULROSS: No, my Lords, it merely indicates that I have taken the trouble to do my homework, and I am trying to ensure that the House is given an accurate account of what occurred. I entirely appreciated that the noble Lord was referring to the same identification parade, but it might have been interpreted that there were two. I am merely ensuring, I hope, that the House has the facts accurately put before it; and if there is a mistake I must seek to correct it.

LORD BROCKWAY: I am grateful to the Minister – very grateful indeed. Now it is acknowledged about Hanratty that he had had a record of robbery. I have met his parents. They very movingly described to me how, in his younger years, he had had an accident which had affected his brain, and how, in those younger years, his character had changed after that accident. I think one of the reasons for doubting the Hanratty case is that mental inheritance. But never was he charged with an offence involving firearms. Never once in his whole story was there any suggestion that he had committed violence. There was the charge that the murderer had raped the woman after he had shot the man. There had never been any suggestion in the whole record of Hanratty's history that he had been guilty of any sexual assault at all. I mentioned earlier that during the proceedings at the trial I was doubtful about the alibi at Rhyl. It was raised only in the last moments of the trial, possibly because of the difficulty of the defence in meeting information which came in. But I say to the Minister now that the strength of the evidence that Hanratty was at Rhyl when he was alleged to have committed this crime is certainly strong enough to justify this request for an inquiry. Not one person, but people one after another say that he was there.

My Lords, some are saying that one ought not to raise this issue tonight because this man was hanged nearly ten years ago. I know the parents of Hanratty. In all my life I have rarely met a man or a woman of working class stock so fine, so noble and so good as Hanratty's parents. They are just the best of our working class. Many of us are interested in world questions – Vietnam, the Middle East, industrial struggles here – but every one of us who is a parent, if our son were charged and hanged for a murder which we knew he had not done, would, as a parent, forget Vietnam; as a parent we should forget the Middle East; as a parent we should forget industrial struggles here. Our whole life would be concentrated on vindicating the son who had been wrongly charged. That is the life of Hanratty's parents.

Here in Parliament we ought not to be so concerned with great foreign and domestic issues that we forget the individual personal dedication to a human being who belongs to us. I just want to say to those parents, if I am within their hearing, that the Minister may reply tonight as the Home Office has replied before, refusing even to have a public inquiry – not a police inquiry but a public inquiry – into this case; but even if the Establishment of our land so denies parents whose son has been condemned to death for murder when the evidence against that charge is so great, those parents can live the rest of their lives knowing that, whatever the Home Office, backed by Scotland Yard and its interests, decide, men and women, not biased but who have looked at this problem in an objective way – someone of the authority of Lord Goodman tonight – men and women of good will, of good feeling and of objective investigation, are quite sure that their son was not guilty of the charge which was made against him.

8.19 p.m.

LORD FOOT: My Lords, I have no doubt that your Lordships will be eager to hear the reply to be made by the Minister from the Government Front Bench, and I do not want to detain the House for more than a few minutes. Indeed, I do not want to follow the previous speakers in speaking about the merits of these two cases. I want to confine myself – and I must confine myself – to the case of Hanratty, because I have not sufficient knowledge to speak on the Bentley case.

Really, I have two limited purposes and objects in speaking to your Lordships at all. The first is that, in the Hanratty case, I want to stand up and be counted. I hope that no erroneous conclusion will be drawn from the fact that there are so few speakers on this Question tonight. It would be a great mistake for anybody to suppose that that indicates there is not widespread concern about the case. I suspect that one of the reasons why more noble Lords did not set their names down to speak is because we knew that this debate was to be initiated and introduced by the noble Lord, Lord Goodman. We all know in advance that if ever he takes anything up everything that should be said will be said;

and not only will everything that should be said be said, but it will be said with great panache and brilliance and with great philosophy in a way that is beyond the capacity of ordinary mortals like ourselves. I should like to emphasize what I believe to be the breadth and the depth of concern on the part of anyone who has studied this case: that this is one of those rare cases, as the noble Lord has said, where justice has in fact miscarried.

The other object which I have in mind is that I should like to make a few observations upon the reasons given by Mr Maudling, the then Home Secretary, last year when he refused a judicial inquiry into the Hanratty case after he had read Paul Foot's book, *Who Killed Hanratty?* I want to make it plain at the outset that in making what may appear to be critical observations on the reasons which the then Home Secretary gave I do not want to suggest that I think that he failed to give to the consideration of this case all the time that was required or, indeed, to approach it with the utmost sympathy. But I remain unconvinced by the reasons which the Home Secretary gave on that occasion, and as I apprehend it is likely that the noble Viscount may tonight follow him in the sort of answer which he gave on that occasion, I would like to anticipate what he is likely to say and express one or two observations about the Home Secretary's reasons.

In the beginning of the Home Secretary's statement in refusing that inquiry at that time – and I am quoting from the statement written into the OFFICIAL REPORT of another place for 28 October 1971. He started off by explaining what his approach to this matter was; and with this, with the utmost respect, I have no quarrel. He started off by pointing out that in cases of this sort it was for the jury to reach a verdict on the evidence which they had heard and that the Court of Appeal had subsequently dismissed Hanratty's appeal and it was not therefore for the Home Secretary to set aside the verdict of the court. There is nothing in that from which I dissent. He went on to say, again, if I may say so, quite rightly:

'But I have considered whether there are any grounds for my intervention on the basis of material which was not before them.' – [OFFICIAL REPORT, Commons, 28/10/71; col. 2051.]

That, again, my Lords, if I may say so, was entirely the right approach: to consider whether new relevant material has emerged since the trial which was never available to the jury, and whether that new material was of such weight and usefulness as to suggest that the verdict of the jury might have been unsatisfactory and wrong. There is one thing about the Hanratty case – there may be all sorts of arguments about the case – which is plain, and that is that since the trial a very great mass of new relevant material has come to light. The problem is that that material falls into two categories.

There is, first of all, the new material which has been uncovered by what I might call the private investigators who have given this case their attention. Lord Russell of Liverpool, and Paul Foot, in the most recent examination, suggest that there has been a great deal of relevant new material which has been uncovered by these private investigators. But at the same time, as the Home Secretary, Mr Maudling, made clear in that statement, this case has been reviewed in the Home Office under successive Home Secretaries over the years; and as Mr Maudling himself said, a great deal of information (that means information over and above the information available at the time of the trial) has been accumulated.

So we have two types of new material: that which has been exposed to the public by the private investigators, and, on the other hand, the material in the files of the Home Office. The importance of that is that it is not available for public inspection or public assessment, and in so far as it is evidence of witnesses it is the evidence of witnesses who have never been submitted to the scrutiny of cross-examination. The result is that when Mr Maudling went on to deal with Mr Foot's book he made two major points. He said first of all that:

'Mr Foot has not had full access to all the available material, and in some respects his arguments are based on premises that are not supported by the facts.'—

that is, facts known only to the Home Office.

Dealing with the alleged new material, he said:

'Other material which has been described as new evidence has proved upon examination to relate to matters which have already been the subject of investigation.'

He means that he has put this alleged new material contained in Mr Foot's book side by side with the secret facts, or alleged

363

facts, known only to the Home Office and makes the fair assertion (which there is no way of checking) that the premises and the so-called new evidence do not correspond with the secret information which he has accumulated. Mr Maudling went out of his way later on to say:

> 'I recognize and entirely respect the doubts which still remain in many minds, and I have considered carefully whether the appointment of a public judicial inquiry would help to resolve the issues.'

If that is so, does not the anxiety in the public mind arise in large measure from the fact that there is no impartial authority which can look at all the evidence – that is to say, the evidence uncovered by the private investigators and the evidence in the possession of the Home Office? These doubts can never be allayed until the public know that some impartial authority has been allowed to see all the evidence.

There was some new evidence given by Mr Foot which the Home Secretary did not dispute was new. It was largely evidence relating to the Rhyl alibi. It is somewhat curious, to my mind, to see the way in which that matter was dealt with by the Home Secretary in his refusal of an inquiry. He said this (col. 2052):

> 'My predecessors gave special attention to the possibility that Hanratty might have been at Rhyl at the time of the murder, and I have for my part examined with care all the additional evidence tending to support this alibi. At a trial, alibi evidence is subject to searching cross-examination to verify its relevance and reliability; and'—

these are the words to which I draw special attention:

> 'after close scrutiny I remain unpersuaded that any of the evidence produced since the trial could stand up to such critical examination, bearing in mind that the recollection of witnesses must necessarily become impaired by the passage of time.'

My Lords, with all respect to the Home Secretary, I find that an extraordinary reaction because one would not have thought that it was the duty of the Home Secretary to try to guess whether a particular witness was likely to prove convincing if he gave evidence under oath in a court of law. Surely, if you want to find out whether or not evidence is convincing, the thing to do is to put it to the test; to hold an inquiry in which the evidence may be subjected to scrutiny and cross-examination. Then you will discover either that it is convincing, in which case it would have been wholly right for it to be heard, or that it is unconvincing and valueless, in which case that would have been demonstrated, and it would have been a very useful exercise in clearing up the anxieties which exist.

At the end of the reasons for the refusal of this inquiry – I have covered them all, I think – Mr Maudling gave two specific reasons why he had concluded that a public judicial inquiry would not help to resolve the matters in issue. He said:

> 'I do not believe that any judicial tribunal can be expected to arrive at a convincing opinion as to the facts on the basis of the recollection of witnesses as to specific details ten years after the event.'

I have two observations to make upon that. In the first place, there is nothing unique, nothing really unusual, in cases being decided in the courts on the basis of the recollection of witnesses as regards events which took place years ago. Indeed, most civil actions, as the noble Lord will know, personal accident cases and cases of that kind, are heard very often two, three or four years after the events about which the witnesses have come to court to give evidence. And the courts have to cope with the situation. Naturally, the courts assess the value of the evidence bearing in mind how old and stale it is. But there is nothing unique about the judicial tribunal listening to evidence from witnesses about events which took place many years before.

The second reason given by the Home Secretary for refusing, or feeling that an inquiry would not be helpful, was:

> 'Secondly, there are fundamental objections to the use of such a procedure as a means to the informal trial of some other person outside the normal processes of law which would be inevitable in this case.'

My Lords, I understand the Home Secretary's apprehension on the point that an investigation of this sort might turn into a kind of indirect trial of some other person and that is indeed a danger against which we should guard. But I think the argument he uses is, first, dangerous and, secondly, it poses a difficulty which does not exist. When I say it is a dangerous argument I mean that this is a case where there is no dispute that a brutal crime was committed. The only matter which has ever been in issue in this case is whether it was Hanratty who was the criminal.

If it is going to be said that in cases of that kind – where the whole question in issue is not whether a crime has been committed but who committed it – you can never have an impartial or a judicial inquiry because there will always be in the background the question, 'Well, if he did not do it, who did?' You would be prevented from having a judicial inquiry however monstrous might be the injustice which had occurred. You cannot have an inquiry if that is to be the absolute rule.

The reason why I say I think that this is a false argument which raises an unreal difficulty is that it depends (does it not?) on what are the terms of reference, what is the remit you give to the inquiry. If you say, 'Your job is simply to answer the question: was it Hanratty who committed this crime? That is the limit and extent of your remit; you are not concerned with who else might have done it, you are concerned with whether he did it or not', you would then be putting to the inquiry the very question which the original jury had to answer, the only difference being that you would be asking the inquiry to give an answer to the question, not only in the light of the information available to the jury, but also in the light of all the information which has been uncovered since.

My Lords, I do not think that there is any difficulty in this matter. I think that the possibility of somebody being indirectly tried can be avoided, and I join with the noble Lord, Lord Goodman, in asking the Minister please not to close the door. I hope that nothing that has been said here tonight, where there has been a bit of feeling, will damage the possibility that the Home Secretary will have another look at both of these cases.

8.36 p.m.

BARONESS LEE OF ASHERIDGE: My Lords, I wish to detain your Lordships for only the briefest of moments at this late hour and after all that has been said so cogently and so eloquently, but distinguished as have been the speeches (we have had expert legal statements from the noble Lord, Lord Goodman, the noble Lord, Lord Foot and others; we have heard from the noble Lord, Lord

Brockway, detailed circumstantial stories of individual men and women he has known and dealt with and who suffered) it is very important that the Minister should keep in mind, if he will forgive my saying so, that he will also be replying to a large number of people outside this House. He will be replying to many people like me. I would not presume to comment on the legal points in this case, because I have not studied it and I have not had the personal contacts which other Members of your Lordships' House have had. But I have a conscience about it. I have been trying to remember – some of your Lordships may be able to quote them more accurately than I can – those haunting lines of Housman:

> 'Be still, Oh soul, be still
> And let injustice be,
> It is but for a day.'

But we cannot be still, we cannot let injustice be, and it is not just for a day.

My Lords, you cannot violate certain moods of the British people. Why is it that people like me, who do not know this case intimately, will not be silent about it? Is it not because the very basis of our legal system – I agree with everything that the noble Lord, Lord Goodman, said: the last thing in the world we want to do is to denigrate it in any sense – is that not only should justice be done but that it should be seen to be done? So I ask the Minister please to remember that we appreciate that he cannot say anything definitive this evening, but if he will consult his colleagues, if he will consult everyone who could have influence in this matter, he will be adding to his own distinction and to his Government's credit – and if he will listen to the haunting fear that so many of us have that there has been an injustice done.

8.40 p.m.

VISCOUNT COLVILLE OF CULROSS: I have been subjected to a number of moving appeals, not least from the noble Baroness, Lady Lee, who has just spoken. I do not in any way discount what the noble Lord, Lord Brockway, has done in that line either, or the feeling with which he did it. I am a little alarmed that the terms of the Motion and something that one of the noble Lords said should imply that I inevitably approach this case with a lack of impartiality. The same implication presumably applies to my

367

right honourable friend the Home Secretary. I knew nothing more about this case when I first started reading it than I rather suspect the noble Baroness, Lady Lee, knows now. I had read small parts of some of the material in the newspapers and I have taken the trouble to attempt to read and to learn the most voluminous amount of material, including both the book by Mr Foot and also the book by Mr Yallop and a great deal else, in order to try to equip myself to deal with this debate. Why I should be supposed to be partial in these circumstances I really do not know.

LORD GOODMAN: My Lords, I do not like to interrupt the noble Viscount but I hope that nothing I said conveyed the slightest suggestion that I thought that he or the Home Secretary were partial in the matter.

LORD BESWICK: My Lords, may I ask the noble Viscount, Lord Colville, to make it clear that there is not a Motion before the House at all. One reason why there have been few speakers here is that it is a Question that has been asked.

VISCOUNT COLVILLE OF CULROSS: The noble Lord, Lord Beswick, is perfectly right and perhaps I may be forgiven, having been here until the House rose early this morning, for making a minor technical slip. I quite agree it is an Unstarred Question. I am much obliged for being reminded of the fact. If I have misread the implications, the noble Lord, Lord Goodman, is not attempting to pursue them. That is all to the good and I am grateful for what he has said. I am also very much obliged for the three prefatory points that he made in his approach, in which he does not endorse the criticisms of some of the institutions of State and indeed individuals that have been, I am afraid, only too apparent in some of the material that I have had to read in the course of preparing for this Question.

It might be helpful for the House if I could just deal with the circumstances in which, by convention and as a result of trial and error, I think it has been worked out in what circumstances the Home Secretary can intervene in cases of this sort. I am delighted to hear from the noble Lord, Lord Foot, that he agrees with the first paragraph of my right honourable friend's statement in another place last October, when my right honourable friend made it perfectly plain that the Home Secretary is not a court of appeal from the Court of Criminal Appeal, nowadays the Court of Appeal (Criminal Division). The role of the Home Secretary – and this, I think, was implicit in, or at any rate cognate to, what my honourable and learned friend on the Woolsack said – is to do with the prerogative of mercy, and not to re-try cases. It is when new material comes before the public and is presented to any Home Secretary that he begins to get into a position where he can consider an inquiry, and not until then. I am sorry to say that in those circumstances the Bentley case simply never leaves the starting line. The only new information—

LORD GOODMAN: My Lords, I hesitate to interrupt the noble and learned Viscount, but I should like to make something clear. I have not invited the Home Secretary to do anything. I have invited Parliament, which is a supreme authority, to consider whether in circumstances where there are grave considerations pointing to someone's innocence – the technical questions of who does what in relation to reviving the case have no relevance at all – Parliament should not, in its full, complete and untrammelled authority, order an inquiry. The ambit of the Home Secretary's previous authority and the precedents in the matter are totally irrelevant.

VISCOUNT COLVILLE OF CULROSS: In that case I think I shall have to take refuge behind a technicality. If that is what the noble Lord, Lord Goodman, wants, this is not a suitable Motion for it. I have to answer this on the basis that it is a Question which is asked of Her Majesty's Government, and I am answering it with the assistance of those who advised me in the Home Office, because it is customary for the Home Secretary to deal with this sort of matter.

LORD GOODMAN: My Lords, this is really a matter of such importance that even at this hour I must pursue it. I did not invite this particular Minister, welcoming as I do his reply, to reply to this Question. If there is some more appropriate Minister who should have replied to it he ought to be here at this moment to reply.

VISCOUNT COLVILLE OF CULROSS: I think, with respect, I am probably the appropriate Minister to attempt to reply, but I cannot of myself commit Parliament to setting up a public inquiry as the result of an Unstarred Question, asked even by the noble Lord, Lord Goodman. This is not the procedure by which one does it and I have simply got to take refuge in that fact.

LORD GOODMAN: I do not think there is a case for irony in a matter of such social importance or that the fact that the Question is asked by me or anyone else has any particular relevance. What has very great relevance is that an enormous apparatus of technicality relating to the previous circumstances in which someone has seen fit to consider whether an injustice is done has no possible relevance to my inquiry. That is the point I want to make. I cannot see why, in relation to an Unstarred Question, the appropriate Minister should not come to answer the Question which is asked of him and not some other Question.

VISCOUNT COLVILLE OF CULROSS: I thought I was answering the Question that was asked of me. If the noble Lord wishes to pursue the whole matter by another procedure at another time we shall have to see what happens, but at the moment, if I may, I shall try to proceed with my speech. There are other occasions on which public inquiries of one sort or another have been set up after a trial has taken place and an appeal has been heard. I should have thought that it might have interested the House, in considering this matter, to know in what circumstances those public inquiries were set up and to consider whether they are precedents or parallels for doing the same here. If, at the end of the reply that I am now trying to give, any noble Lord considers that there should be new, totally different, machinery, other criteria and a complete change in the system, then I hope that he will put down constructive suggestions, Motions, Resolutions and anything else that is necessary. I am afraid that I propose to deal with this upon the basis of a fairly well-tried practice that has been going on for some time and has had the advantage of being looked at and considered by a number of quite wise people over a long time. That is what I propose to tell your Lordships about this evening.

LORD GOODMAN: My Lords, it is impossible for me not to intervene again, much as I regret it. May I now ask the noble and learned Viscount, Lord Colville of Culross, whether he is proposing to deal with this matter on the footing that, provided a well-tried procedure operates in this case, he and the Government are indifferent about whether the existence of injustices are not revealed? If that is so, may I say that we can all go home as there seems to be little point in continuing the discussion?

VISCOUNT COLVILLE OF CULROSS: My Lords, I am finding it extremely difficult to make a speech at all, let alone tell the noble Lord what I am trying to say. That intervention, if I may say so, does not really assist me to get on with the matter and it does not seem to me that anything I may say in answer to it is going to help us very much. I am trying to get on with the matter and I have told noble Lords how I am proposing to deal with it. If noble Lords do not want to listen to me, there is a perfectly good answer. They can remove themselves. But I am going to go on with this speech on the basis that I have started it.

As I said, it has been the practice for an inquiry to be set up when new evidence emerges. I had got to the point of saying that in those circumstances I am sorry to say that the Bentley case does not fall into that category. I have read the book by Mr Yallop. It is true that I did not see the equivalent film on television, but I have read the book from cover to cover. I think the noble Earl, Lord Arran, has been very convinced by it. I am afraid that I am rather less convinced by it, but this is probably neither here nor there because what one has to deal with is the question whether that book provides new evidence which would justify my right honourable friend in setting up a public inquiry.

THE EARL OF ARRAN: My Lords, if I may interrupt the noble Viscount, it is not a question of new evidence, but of evidence that was not sufficiently produced at the time of the trial. That is in fact new evidence, is it not?

VISCOUNT COLVILLE OF CULROSS: No, my Lords; I do not think that is so. I think there is a subtle distinction. There can be in a criminal trial evidence which was available, but for one reason or another was not chosen to be used. The existence of that evidence does not, I think, constitute a situation—

THE EARL OF ARRAN: If I may interrupt again, if there is evidence that was not produced at the time of the trial and a man was convicted and sentenced to death, does that not constitute evidence which should be heard now? That evidence was available at that time. Should we not hear it now?

371

Viscount COLVILLE of CULROSS: My Lords, I cannot possibly explain anything if I get halfway through a sentence and then I am interrupted. I was saying that there may in a criminal trial be evidence which is available and is known to one or other of the parties at that time which for one reason or another they choose not to use. In those circumstances, I do not think that some years later, because somebody considers that they were mistaken in their choice of not using it, the existence of that evidence would be grounds for reopening that matter by way of public inquiry.

Lord DAVIES of LEEK: That is dangerous.

The Earl of ARRAN: I cannot understand how the noble Viscount has the audacity to say things like that.

Viscount COLVILLE of CULROSS: It is fairly basic legal arrangement in the Court of Appeal, and it also applies further afield. If the noble Earl does not agree with me, then I am sorry, but that is what I am informed and that is my own experience in the matter. If, however, there is evidence which was not available to anybody at the trial, but only becomes available afterwards, then if that evidence seems to be sufficient, I think that there could be a case for reopening the matter by way of public inquiry.

The question in the Bentley case then arises: is there such new evidence?

The Earl of ARRAN: I am so sorry, my Lords, but I really must—

Lord DENHAM: My Lords, I think we are getting very much out of order. This is an Unstarred Question, admittedly on a subject of great importance on which a number of noble Lords feel very strongly indeed, but my noble friend really has not had a chance to make more than two consecutive sentences. I think the House probably would appreciate it if my noble friend could carry on with his speech.

Viscount COLVILLE of CULROSS: My Lords, I do not mind giving way to noble Lords, but the fact remains that I must try to keep this speech within some bounds of time, and if

I am continuously interrupted I shall simply have to take material out of it, because I cannot keep the House here for ever. I was attempting to say that if new evidence emerges which was not available to anybody at the trial, then this may give grounds for a subsequent public inquiry. What one wants to see is whether in the Bentley case such new evidence has become available.

There are, to the best of my knowledge, two sources from which such evidence has been suggested. One is in the book by Mr Yallop, and the other is in, I think, a newspaper article where a certain gentleman called Mr Lee has come forward. I do not want to go in great detail into these matters, but certainly in Mr Yallop's books some of the points mentioned by the noble Earl, Lord Arran, were raised: the question of the calibre of the bullet and, as a result of that, the question whether it may have been fired by one of the police guns which came upon the scene rather than by the gun held by Craig. We have heard Lord Goodman's view upon the relevance of this, and I do not know that I should be very happy to dispute with him on the legal point. But I think, perhaps, for the benefit of those who have been interested in this, I should say a few words. The inquiries that we have carried out show that there can be no doubt that there were no police weapons in the area at the time when Police Constable Miles was shot. We have carried out extensive inquiries to see whether this could be so, and there is no doubt that the first gun that arrived upon the scene was that which was carried by Sergeant Fairfax when he went upstairs, having taken Bentley down; and the only two cartridges that were fired from any of the five police weapons issued that evening were fired from that gun by him. That, I am afraid, is the end of that line.

There was also the question of Mr Lee, who said that he had seen certain parts, or perhaps the whole, of the incident from the house nearby. This statement also has been investigated extensively, and I am sorry to say that there is absolutely no evidence whatever to support what Mr Lee alleges. Moreover, it would have been impossible for him to see from the window from which he said he saw. If he climbed on to the roof, then he was an athlete of no mean achievement, because a policeman could not do it in broad daylight: and, in any case, if he was on the roof he could not have seen into the area where the action took place, because it was shielded by the lift shaft or the skylight – I am not sure which. That, I am afraid, is the calibre of that evidence.

When one goes beyond that, one takes oneself, I fear, back to the question of what might have happened at the trial rather than the grounds of new evidence which has come to light since. The noble Lord, Lord Goodman, was very interested in what happened at the trial, and I am not surprised, because if one wishes to criticize the matter, then I have no doubt that that is a very good place to start. The noble Lord did it, if I may say so, with great delicacy, and a good deal more delicacy than has been shown in some other quarters on this subject. I applaud him, and was glad to hear the way that he did it.

But even assuming that the noble Lord put the case in the way that I am sure everybody would expect him to do, as well as it is possible to do it, one has to face the fact that, if one wishes to reopen the trial on the basis that it was not properly conducted; that there was something wrong with the summing up; that the Court of Criminal Appeal (as it then was) was wrong in saying that there was nothing wrong with the summing up, then one is becoming a court of appeal from the Court of Criminal Appeal. It may be that the noble Lord will say that the Home Secretary should not do that but somebody else should. But, at any rate for the purposes of answering this question, I am afraid I cannot advise the Home Secretary or try to influence him to turn himself into that sort of body.

I would just say this to the noble Lord, Lord Goodman, about the summing up. Of course it is perfectly true that Lord Goddard made the remarks that were attributed to him by the noble Lord, Lord Goodman. But the question that was before the jury, as I understand it, was one of constructive murder. I, too, have been reading the summing up, and I should like to quote a short passage from it. What Lord Goddard said was this:

'Is there evidence from which you can properly infer that these two youths went out with the common purpose not merely to warehouse-break but to resist apprehension, even by violence, if necessary. That is all. It is, I repeat, no answer if you come to that conclusion'—

he was speaking to the jury—

'for one of the two accused to say, "Yes; but I did not think he would go as far as he did."'

374

We have already heard that on this question of the knowledge that Craig had the gun the then Lord Chief Justice suggested inferences about what might have happened before the two young men arrived at the shop that they finally decided not to break into. We have also heard that he described how Bentley had those two weapons. We have heard what the Lord Chief Justice said was perhaps the most serious piece of evidence against Bentley: those words, 'Let him have it, Chris!'. The noble Lord, Lord Goodman, also referred (and this is also mentioned in the summing up) to the statement which was vouched to by two of the policemen in the trial, where Bentley said:

'I knew he had a gun but I did not think he would use it';

and the noble Lord pointed the contrast between those two.

In addition to that, in the summing up there was a statement that he made at the police station:

'I didn't know he was going to use a gun.'

This was contradicted by another statement:

'I didn't know Chris had a gun until he shot . . .'

That was a flat contradiction of the previous statement. There was also the evidence which, strangely enough, was not in the judge's original summing up but was brought in only after one of the defence counsel had drawn attention to a mistake that Lord Goddard had made. This was the evidence that Sergeant Fairfax shouted to Craig, to drop the gun. Police Constable McDonald, another of the officers in the case, said to Fairfax:

'What sort of gun has he got?'

And before Fairfax could reply, Bentley said:

'He's got a ·45.'

That was in evidence: it was cross-examined. It was in the evidence given by two of the police officers, both Fairfax and McDonald vouched for it.

Lord GOODMAN: I am so sorry, but I must interrupt. The Minister said – and I think this is a crucial matter – that the Lord Chief Justice, in his summing up, pointed the contrast that I made between the original statement, 'Let him have it Chris!' and, 'I knew he had a gun but I did not think he would use it.' I have no recollection that he did more than address the attention of the jury to those statements and suggest that one reinforced the other. I do not believe anyway that the judge, in his summing up, did not point the contrast between the two, the fact that they were inconsistent.

Viscount COLVILLE of CULROSS: My Lords, I believe that the noble Lord is quite right, but I am just coming to the point. This is what a trial by jury is for. It may be that at the end of the day, after they have delivered their verdict (and the noble Lord, Lord Goodman, knows this as well as I do) that the Court of Criminal Appeal, or the Court of Appeal, will say that the summing up was faulty in law. The time to take up that point is on appeal to the Court of Criminal Appeal. I am merely telling the House that the jury had before them the selection of facts which I have been telling the House about.

There was one other piece of evidence which was not mentioned in the summing up but which was given in evidence and also told upon the matter. The fact of the matter is that, having heard the law described as I began just now, and having heard all the evidence, the jury did convict. I cannot see how I can possibly suggest that the Government should at this stage interfere and say that the jury were wrong, that the judge was incorrect in his summing up and that the Court of Criminal Appeal should have said so but did not, and that therefore we should now have an inquiry to re-try the case. Because, with the greatest respect, and however hard anybody feels about the result, that is the only result of a public inquiry that could possibly arise in that particular case. I do not believe that it would be a satisfactory precedent for anyone if this were to occur.

Lord DAVIES of LEEK: My Lords, I am grateful to the noble Viscount for giving way. Nothing has been said about the ambiguity of the phrase, 'Let him have it, Chris!' That was not taken into consideration at the time. I should like that to be put on the Record.

VISCOUNT COLVILLE OF CULROSS: My Lords, it was because I was fully aware that the phrase was capable of more than one interpretation that I took the trouble to look up what else was said which might have borne upon this subject, and that is why I have wearied the House by reading it over. Incidentally, the other alternative for the interpretation of that phrase is

'Do give it to him, Chris.'

But what was it that Bentley was asking Craig to give to Fairfax? It does not necessarily mean that one is led to the opposite conclusion. I agree that there are two interpretations, but one is not necessarily innocent, as one might at first think, set in the legal context.

LORD DAVIES OF LEEK: My Lords, I should like to thank the noble Viscount for his courtesy in giving way.

VISCOUNT COLVILLE OF CULROSS: I did take this point, my Lords, and that is why I went into further detail.

Now I must come on to the Hanratty case. This has been considered many times by successive Home Secretaries. It has been considered twice in Parliament; once on a Motion of (I think) the noble Lord, Lord Brockway, and once on a Motion of this House. Successive Home Secretaries, despite the growing volume, first of all of alibi evidence, and secondly of the increasingly complex, diverse and, I am afraid, not altogether consistent confessions by Mr Alphon. Successive Home Secretaries have still come to the conclusion that there is nothing on which they could properly take the opportunity of reopening this matter by way of public inquiry.

Now again I must deal with some of the technicalities of this. The noble Lord, Lord Foot, if I may say so, went into this in some detail. I am going to digress from some of the problems that my right honourable friend touched upon in the rather short statement. There is no doubt that in this case new evidence is available now that was not available at the trial, although in fact a certain amount of what I think is popularly thought to be new evidence was available at the trial but was not chosen to be used by the defence, for reasons no doubt best known to themselves. It is not by any means all in this case, and a great deal has happened since; but I do not think it ought to be thought that the whole of the real alibi evidence which was available at the trial is comprehended in the amount which was actually tendered to the court. There was a great deal more, and some of it was not used. But there was also a good deal which has since been produced. We now have to consider this in the light of the kind of inquiry which might be set up.

This kind of post-trial inquiry would be, as I have said, primarily concerned with new matters which were not known at the time of the trial, and the basis derives from the Home Secretary's responsibility to exercise his prerogative. This is a constitutional matter. It is all very well for the noble Lord, Lord Goodman, to say that Parliament ought to set up a public inquiry, but I suppose that what those who are genuinely concerned in this matter would really like to see at the end of the day is a pardon for Hanratty. I do not think that anybody but the Queen herself, advised by her Ministers, has the prerogative of mercy and can therefore issue that pardon. So inevitably my right honourable friend is saddled, and, to a lesser extent I myself, with answering for this matter.

For that very reason, and to try to satisfy those who wish this matter to be pursued, he can in the exercise of his responsibility to the necessity for advising the Queen, arrange for inquiries into the facts of the case if it is thought necessary and appropriate, and very occasionally he can appoint a judge or a member of the Bar to consider all the information available, and I think to do so in public. It is however a fairly exceptional procedure and a good deal rarer than is commonly supposed. There have been several such inquiries in capital cases, but with the exception of one, into the case of Timothy Evans, they have all been carried out as a result of urgent information or new material that came forward before the man was executed in order to enable the Home Secretary to receive new advice for the purposes of recommending a reprieve. Only in the case of Evans was this done in public after the execution, and that was the Brabin Tribunal which was presided over by Mr Justice Brabin. It was appointed in the wholly exceptional circumstance that another man living in the same house, Christie, was later discovered to be a multiple murderer and confessed to the murder of Mrs Evans – a very clear new fact to come about.

The experience of that one inquiry has served to demonstrate very clearly the difficulties of attempting to get at the truth so many years after the event. This is where the noble Lord, Lord

Foot, comes very much into it. I would not suppose that one would fail to take account of the sort of evidence that would be likely to come before the inquiry. If it is a matter of the fading recollections of an accident it is quite true that the mind grows dim and the memory not so bright as it used to be; but in this case, an alibi case, we are dealing with fleeting glances of recognition which took place ten years ago. We are doing so in the circumstances where, ever since, there have been people asking questions in the locality, trying to find out about things, showing photographs and generally examining and investigating the whole state of affairs. There is a considerable difference in the *ambiance* of the evidence one is thinking about there.

But let me revert to what Mr Justice Brabin found in the way of difficulties in the case of his Tribunal. He said:

'Stale evidence is often bad evidence. When recollection begins to fail imagination often take its place and a witness is sometimes unable to distinguish the one from the other. A witness doing his best to tell the truth may, without realizing it, be it giving evidence for in his imagination, but giving it with the same confidence and demeanour that would mark his evidence if it were accurate. There comes a time when recollection almost entirely vanishes and imagination of one witness is competing with that of another in recounting events which both have really forgotten. It can happen that what is spoken about as reality is in the main make-believe.'

Later he goes on:

'In this inquiry the events of 1949 have been checked against other evidence and accounts given over 12 years ago. The evidence shows various influences have had an effect on some of those who gave evidence and over the years people have had different motives for seeking to mould general and particular trends of thought. Some of the evidence has been buffeted during that time.'

It is no use disregarding the practical experience of Mr Justice Brabin on the previous occasion. I ask your Lordships to consider whether the material which the noble Lord, Lord Foot, specifically referred to, the limited area of the real alibi (and I appreciate what he said about that), is not peculiarly susceptible to just those difficulties that the judge has spoken about in that passage.

Lord FOOT: My Lords, if I may interrupt the noble Viscount, does he not agree that if you appoint a legal authority of distinction, a person familiar with the criminal courts, to conduct the inquiry, possibly with assessors, he is perfectly capable of making his own estimate of the value of any witness who comes before him, and the evidence that that witness gives; and, indeed, is in a very much better position, having the witness before him, seeing him examined and cross-examined, of testing the value of that evidence than the Home Secretary, or the noble Viscount, sitting in the Home Office and reading Mr Foot's book.

Viscount COLVILLE of CULROSS: Once more, in trying to deal with this by stages, I have not yet reached the point where we have run into another difficulty. I understand what the noble Lord says about this. The fact remains that we have to remember that, when Mr Justice Brabin finished that inquiry, he could not, as a result of the problems that I have just described, come to the conclusion beyond reasonable doubt; and the only thing he could do was to come to a conclusion – even in that case – on a balance of probabilities: the civil test rather than the criminal test. This must be a serious consideration to be borne in mind.

Unfortunately, this is not the only difficulty, and this is where I take the matter further. The noble Lord, Lord Foot, is perfectly right: it may be possible, and no doubt would be extremely desirable, to try to define the terms of reference of the inquiry. Unfortunately, I do not think that that is what everybody wants to do. I do not know whether I was right in interpreting the noble Lord, Lord Brockway, but whether or not he thinks that it was Alphon who was responsible, I seem to detect that at any rate the whole of the motive and the story that is implicit in Alphon's confessions appeals to him as being more likely to be the truth than the theory which has been put forward and which was accepted by the jury. I am not suggesting that he is accusing Alphon; I am saying that he accepts that this is the story which he considers more probable.

Lord BROCKWAY: My Lords, the Minister will agree that I have been very careful to make any remark on those lines in this debate. I would say that the theory which I put forward for the murder was based not so much on Alphon's confessions as on my conversations with all the persons concerned which I described while I spoke.

Viscount COLVILLE OF CULROSS: My Lords, I was careful myself not to impute to the noble Lord any suggestion that he was accusing anybody. I was identifying the theory which in fact happens to be the theory put forward also by Mr Alphon in one form or another.

I would also suggest that those of your Lordships who have read Mr Paul Foot's book, and particularly its final words, would find in it an indication that the public inquiry for which Mr Foot (not the noble Lord, Lord Foot; Mr Paul Foot) is asking is one which, in effect, would bring Alphon to informal trial. One has only to think of the difficulties that have occurred in some of the Tribunals of Inquiry Act cases, where people have been accused in circumstances where there was not a criminal trial. There was a recent case on the V & G inquiry, where there were all sorts of complaints about accusations being made. That was under a Tribunal of Inquiry where the witnesses were capable of being subpoenaed, put on oath, and dealt with generally in the way that they would be dealt with in a court of law. The sort of public inquiry that could be set up in this case would not be susceptible of subpoena of witnesses; the witnesses would not be on oath; there would be no protection for them; they would not be privileged. I should have thought that there was the gravest danger that a public inquiry in this case would be likely to turn into a para-judicial trial. And I am afraid that the person who would be very liable to be tried would be Mr Alphon. I feel that this is an exceedingly dangerous thing to encourage, and I am very much afraid that this is what would happen.

Since I am talking about the 1921 Act, in case anybody thinks that that would be the right way to proceed, I should add that the Statute is so phrased that it would not be capable of being used in these circumstances, even if both Houses so considered that otherwise it would be a suitable method of handling the whole affair.

Lord GOODMAN: My Lords, I apologize for troubling the Minister but I wonder whether I might ask him this question. He raised, validly, the question of a public inquiry in relation to someone who might seemingly be under accusation at the trial. Clearly, that is a highly objectionable course if there is a prospect of a man thereafter being charged. Supposing one accepts that there is no prospect of anyone being charged. How would the position be worse if the inquiry contrived to secure that Hanratty was cleared and then left the position as it was? Why is it then so obnoxious that matters have been raised that reflect upon the possible guilt of somebody else?

Viscount COLVILLE of CULROSS: My Lords, I should have thought that was because they reflected upon the possible guilt of someone else who was in no position to defend himself adequately against this.

Baroness PHILLIPS: He would be accused, my Lords.

Viscount COLVILLE of CULROSS: My Lords, he would not be accused. This is the whole point. The whole procedure would not be a trial of somebody else. It would be an attempt to exonerate Hanratty, which in the process would have the effect of putting somebody else on trial. I am very sorry, but I do not think that this is the right way to handle this matter. I believe it to be a real danger and one which is simply not acceptable.

My Lords, I do not think I ought to go into further details about these matters. Fortunately, noble Lords have not wished to speak about details of these cases very much. I hope that the noble Earl, Lord Arran, understands from what I said earlier why it is that I do not specifically answer his eight questions. I will tell him what the compendious answer is. In the case of, 'Why did not Fairfax and Dr Haler sue for defamation?', the answer is, I do not know; it is not for me to say, it is up to them. In the case of all the other questions, the investigation that would be made in the terms as I put it would only be confined to new evidence, and that would only concern Sergeant Fairfax, Dr Haler and Mr Lee, and the policemen who were in charge of issuing the guns and counting the ammunition when they came back; and that is what the inquiry did go into.

The Earl of ARRAN: My Lords, I know that the noble Viscount is a most patient man, and I hope that a patient House will realize that the point I am trying to make here is that evidence suppressed at the time of the trial is in fact new evidence. That is the point I am trying to establish.

Viscount COLVILLE of CULROSS: I suspect that the noble Lord is now talking, among other things, about medical evidence. Whether or not the defence lawyers, who are quite heftily attacked, as is almost everyone else, by Mr Yallop in his book, were right in the way they handled their cases is something one cannot go into now. The fact of the matter is that the medical evidence was before Sir David Maxwell Fyfe, as he then was, including documents from Sir Denis Hill, as he now is, and all the material was before the then Home Secretary when he had to make his truly dreadful decision. I cannot see how that material could go into a public inquiry now. As I say, it was before the Home Secretary at the time.

I think I have answered most of the questions specifically asked of me in the debate. I hope that noble Lords will not think that I have been impatient in dealing with interventions; that is certainly not the impression I want noble Lords to have. While I plainly admit that it is not for me to say whether there will or will not be a public inquiry into either of these cases—

Lord DAVIES of LEEK: Oh!

Viscount COLVILLE of CULROSS: I said that it was for my right honourable friend to make the decision in this case. All I can do is act as the vehicle for the views of your Lordships. I am bound to conclude that I should be very hesitant indeed in letting your Lordships go home tonight thinking that there was any likelihood of a public inquiry taking place into either of these cases.

Lord DAVIES of LEEK: The noble Lord is concluding on a rather preemptory note. The issue is not whether the noble Lord or his right honourable friend in another place makes a decision in this matter. This is something for Parliament to decide. We want to find a means by which Parliament can make this decision. I would have expected the noble Lord to show more humanity from the point of view of finding a formula by which Parliament can discuss this issue – I am anxious not to raise the temperature of the debate – and reach a majority decision on whether an inquiry should take place.

Viscount COLVILLE of CULROSS: The noble Lord has made the point and I hope that in answering it I shall be answering the last question on this matter, because this is an Unstarred Question. I have been interrupted during my reply on more occasions that I can recall anyone being so interrupted when dealing with an Unstarred Question.

The noble Lord, Lord Davies of Leek, asks whether there is another way of dealing with this matter. It must be apparent that I have put forward some serious practical difficulties, one of convention and constitution and others of practice, practicality and fairness to people who might be involved. The ingenuity of the British is well-known. If noble Lords or right honourable and honourable Members of another place can think of a completely new piece of machinery which would be suitable for dealing with this matter, and they find that it does not suffer significantly from the difficulties from which the present pieces of machinery known to us suffer in this respect, then I am sure that my right honourable friend and the Government would consider it. The trouble is that I do not know what it might be. I have gone through the complete range of those known to me and those who advise me and I have told your Lordships of the difficulties. I assure the House that if new pieces of machinery are found, I will consider them. I cannot say more.

Appendix II

Dr Matheson's Second Report on Derek Bentley's Mental Condition

8664. BENTLEY, Derek William,   H.M. PRISON,
aged 19 years   Brixton
Central Criminal Court, Murder
No. 27 in the Calendar.

At the request of the Director of Public Prosecutions I have to report as follows on the mental condition of the above-named. He was received into custody at this Prison on 3.11.52. I examined and interviewed him immediately on reception. He was placed under close mental observation in the Prison Hospital where he has remained since.

I have had further interviews with him. He has been seen daily by myself or a colleague. I have read the daily reports of the Hospital Officers who have had him in their care. I have interviewed his father. I have read and studied the following reports.

1) A report from the Warden of Kingswood Training School, where he was from 27.10.1948 to 28.7.1950.

2) A report dated 16.11.49 of an Electroencephalographic examination which was carried out at the Burden Neurological Institute, Stapleton, Bristol, by A. L. Winter, Assistant Electroencephalographer.

3) A report by Dr James A. Munroe, Physician in Psychological Medicine, Guy's Hospital, where the prisoner was a patient when a baby, from 30.6.33 to 10.7.33 and where he was examined on two later occasions, viz. 20.6.49 and 9.8.49.

4) A report from Mr C. F. Towes, Welfare Officer for Home Office Schools, who had the duty of supervising the prisoner after he was released on licence from the Kingswood Training School on 28.7.50. During this period of supervision, Mr Towes made 31 visits to the prisoner's home. On 16 of these visits he had interviews with the prisoner himself.

5) A copy of a letter sent by the Ministry of Labour and National Service to the prisoner's father on 19.11.52.

6) A report of the result of an Electroencephalographic examination carried out at the Maudsley Hospital on 27.11.52 by Dr Denis Hill.

7) The police report and depositions.

Family History (informants – the prisoner, his father, Mr Bentley, and the police report).

His father and mother are alive. The prisoner is the third eldest of a family of five. The youngest brother died as an infant and was a Mongol, this is a form of feeble-mindedness accompanied by characteristic physical abnormalities.

The father informs me that he knows of no morbid mental history on his side of the family. The police state that on the mother's side there is a history that a cousin of his mother's suffered from epilepsy. This history, taken in conjunction with the birth of a Mongol to the prisoner's mother, suggests that the stock on the mother's side is not good.

Personal History (informants – the prisoner, his father, Mr Bentley, the police, and the medical authorities, Guy's Hospital).

Within 24 hours of being born the prisoner was admitted to Guy's Hospital suffering from pneumonia. As a result of treatment he recovered and was discharged after 10 days. He was a difficult child to rear on account of his bad temper.

School

At the age of 3 he started attending a Nursery School. He afterwards attended the Secondary Modern School at Norbury. After 7 months at this school he was transferred to another school by order of the Local Authority as he was a source of trouble to both teachers and other pupils. His attendance record was bad and the school could not get co-operation from his parents. He stayed at this school for just over a year and then returned to the Norbury Secondary School. There he stayed until March 1948 when he left having reached the Inferior Top Class. The Headmaster there found him backward and workshy but he did not consider him to be feeble-minded. At that time he was very slow in learning to read and write. While at school he took no interest in games.

As a result of a finding of Guilty at a Croydon Juvenile Court in September, 1948, he was committed to Kingswood Training School, Bristol; while there his IQ was estimated to be at 66 and that he had a reading age of 4½ years. There, too, he was found to be lazy and indifferent to training and it was found that he showed no interest in learning but was content to drift along doing as little as possible.

During a period of home leave in 1949 he attended, on two occasions, Guy's Hospital. He had been sent to the Out-Patient Department for investigation of his complaint of constant head-aches. Dr Munroe considered that he might be feeble-minded but that he did not co-operate well in the examination. He recommended that he be returned to the Approved School for further training. He was taken back to the Kingswood Training School and in November of that year (1949) he was examined by the Burden Neurological Institute. The result of an Electroencephalographic examination suggested very strongly that he suffered from 'petit mal', a form of epilepsy.

On release from the school on licence in July 1950 he came under the care of Mr C. F. Towes, Welfare Officer for Home Office Schools. Mr Towes visited his home 31 times and on 16 of these visits interviewed the prisoner himself. Mr Towes reports that he formed the impression that the parents were over-indulgent to the prisoner and he, Mr Towes, found it difficult to get full co-operation from the parents and from the prisoner.

He did not work from the time of his release from the School until 1951. During this period his father says he was trying to get him employment with the Electricity Authorities with whom he, the father, worked. During this period of unemployment the prisoner spent a good deal of his time at home repairing radio sets, etc. During this period too he had trouble with his ears.

In March 1951 he got employment with a firm of furni-ture removers. He remained there for a year; this is the longest period he has been in one job. When he left this employment in March 1952, the reason given was that he was finding the work too heavy for him. Just before he left this employment he was examined on behalf of the Ministry of Labour and National Insurance. The Medical Board who examined him placed him in Grade Four as they had before them a report from the family doctor that he suffered from 'petit mal'.

From March to May 1952 he was unemployed and the Welfare Officer reports that his attitude became more unco-operative than ever.

In May of this year he started work with the Croydon Corporation Cleansing Department. He appeared to be making an effort to do his best and to improve in his conduct. But this effort was not maintained and after a month's employment as a dustman, at a wage of £6 15s 0d a week, he was considered so unsatisfactory that he was re-employed as a road sweeper at a lower wage of £4 7s 0d a week. He was no more successful at this than his previous employment and in July 1952 he was dismissed. Since then he has been unemployed.

Medical History

As already noted, as a baby he suffered from pneumonia. His father tells me that while still an infant he had several falls on his head, but says they were never very serious.

Between the ages of 3 and 5 (his father cannot be sure of the exact age) he had a fit. From the description the father gave to me it would seem that this could have been a major epileptic fit. His father said he had 4 similar fits, the last one being when he was aged about 8 years. Since the cessation of the fits the prisoner states he has often suffered from headaches.

During the early part of the air attacks on London the houses in which the family were living were damaged and on one occasion, the father says, the prisoner was buried by debris.

At puberty he suffered a good deal from acne and boils in his ears.

Sex and Habits

No history of marked perverse sexual habits has been elicited. He has associated with girl friends but denies ever having had sexual intercourse. His usual associates were boys of a younger age than himself.

He says he always has been a heavy smoker, and that from time to time he has taken alcohol, sometimes beer, sometimes spirits.

Present Condition

Physical examination on the day of his admission (3.11.52) showed no evidence of old or recent disease.

388

His ears were dry and showed no infection. He is of asthenic build, i.e. he is loosely built and his body muscles are poorly developed.

At interviews he has been rational and has shown no evidence of insanity.

His account of the alleged offence corresponds with the statement he made to the police.

At all times he said that he did not know that his co-defendant was armed.

At interviews he gives the impression of a youth of low intelligence. He is careless in his attitude and although expressing great concern at the position in which he now finds himself, he does not, in my opinion, show any real appreciation of the peril in which he stands. His attitude is, that he has always hitherto got out of serious trouble and that, on this occasion, he will again be successful.

Mental tests which involve educational training show him to be just above the level of a feeble-minded person.

He is illiterate and cannot read or write.

Tests which do not involve a scholastic knowledge give him a mental age of between 11 and 12 years.

In view of his past history which, in my opinion, indicates that he has been allowed to grow up without any discipline or educational training, his present low intelligence is an educational defect rather than an innate defect. The social incapacity and failure which his history reveals is also, I think, the result of the absence of any discipline or training. It should be pointed out, however, that when he was at the Kingswood Training School, efforts were made to discipline and train him but the Warden states that he was always being encouraged by his father not to co-operate but continually to make complaints.

At no time while he has been under observation at this Prison has he shown any evidence of epilepsy, either of grand mal or major epilepsy, or petit mal; nor has he shown any signs of having any minor epileptic manifestation. His conduct, while under observation in the Ward, has been that of an undisciplined young boy.

On account of his inability to read properly, he spends a good deal of his time looking at 'comics' and picture papers. He tries to mix with the other inmates of the Ward but, as a rule, they do not like his company on account of his arrogant, boastful conversation.

The result of the Electroencephalographic examination at the Maudsley Hospital was compatible with and suggestive of a diagnosis of Epilepsy. No focal abnormality occurred to suggest acquired brain damage.

Summary

The picture he now presents is of an immature youth who has never been subjected to any discipline and has been allowed most of his life to have his own way, whether good or bad.

Although there is a history suggestive of epilepsy which is supported by the Electroencephalographic findings, I have failed from my personal observations to find any evidence of epilepsy. If he did, in fact, suffer from epilepsy, I am of the opinion that, at the time of the alleged offence, he was not suffering from any form of epilepsy.

His conduct before, during and after the alleged offence was always purposive.

I have been unable to find any genuine loss of memory or degree of mental confusion which occur during an epileptic manifestation.

I do not consider that he is a feeble-minded person under the Mental Deficiency Acts.

I am of the opinion that he is:
1) Sane;
2) Fit to plead to the indictment;
3) Fit to stand his trial.

J. C. M. Matheson
Principal Medical Officer.

Appendix III

Lord Goddard's Summing-Up

THE LORD CHIEF JUSTICE: Now, members of the jury, in many respects this is a very terrible case, and it is one, therefore, that it is desirable you and I should approach in as calm a frame of mind as we can.

Here are two lads, one of sixteen and one of nineteen, admittedly out on a shopbreaking expedition at night, armed with a Service revolver, a dreadful weapon in the shape of a knuckleduster, and two knives which may or may not be described as daggers – one of them I should think certainly could be – and the result is that a young policeman is shot dead while in the execution of his duty. You may think it was almost a miracle that others were not shot too. One of them, we know, Sgt Fairfax, was wounded, but fortunately only slightly.

Now let us put out of our minds in this case any question of films or comics, or literature of that sort. These things are always prayed in aid nowadays when young persons are in the dock, but they have really very little to do with the case. These two young men, or boys, whatever you like to call them, are both of an age which makes them responsible to the law – they are over fourteen – and it is surely idle to pretend in these days that a boy of sixteen does not know the wickedness of taking out a revolver of that description and a pocketful of ammunition and firing it when he is on an unlawful expedition and the police are approaching him. You will remember that so far as Craig is concerned, by his own words he supplied a motive for what he was doing, for he said that he hated the police because they had got his brother 12 years – which seems to show that his brother was convicted for a very serious offence to receive a sentence of that length.

Now there are one or two preliminaries to which I call your attention, though it is hardly necessary. The first one is hardly necessary, because you know as well as I do that in all criminal cases it is for the prosecution to prove their case, and it is said correctly that it is not for the prisoners to prove their innocence. In this case the prosecution have given abundant evidence for a case calling for an answer, and although the prisoners do not have to prove their innocence, when once a case is established against them they can give evidence, and they can call witnesses, and then you have to take their evidence as part of the sum of the case. The effect of a prisoner's evidence may be to satisfy you that he is innocent, it may be it causes you to have such doubt that you feel the case is not proved, and it may, and very often does, have a third effect: it may strengthen the evidence for the prosecution.

The second thing that I have to remind you of is that you have to consider the case of both of these youths separately. Different considerations will apply, and do apply, in the case of Bentley and the case of Craig. I say different considerations apply – you have to apply different tests. Then, of course, as you have been properly warned, any question of fact in the case is entirely one for you, not for me. I have to direct you as to the law, and you will have to consider the facts and apply the facts in accordance with the law as I tell it to you.

Now let us take first of all the case of Craig: It is not disputed, and could not be disputed, that he fired the shot which killed that Police Constable. You are asked to say that the killing was accidental, and that therefore the offence is reduced to manslaughter. Gentlemen of the jury, it is the prerogative of the jury in any case where the charge is of murder to find a verdict of manslaughter, but they can only do it if the evidence satisfies them that the case is properly reducible to one of manslaughter – that is, not with regard to any consequence that may happen, but simply whether the facts show that the case ought to be regarded as one of manslaughter and not of murder; but when I have explained to you the considerations of law which apply in this case, it may be – and, indeed, I think it is – probable that you will see that there is no room for manslaughter in this case. However, it is a matter for you.

Now, the law of this country with regard to murder is this: If a person does an act towards another wilfully – that is to say, intentionally – which a reasonable person would know may cause death or grievous bodily harm, and death results, that is murder, and you can see, if you think of it for a minute, that that is merely a matter of common sense. If I were to whip out a revolver and point it at you and shoot one of you gentlemen, and killed you, it would be no answer for me to say 'Oh, I did not mean to kill him;

I only meant to wound him.' The fact is, I am doing a dangerous thing with a dangerous weapon. The same with a revolver or a dagger: if I am doing an act which I know may cause grievous bodily harm, though I may not intend to do more than grievous bodily harm, and death results, that is murder. If in an ordinary case – I say 'Ordinary case', a case in which no police officer was concerned – you thought a prisoner only meant to fire wildly, and was not aiming at anybody, but simply letting off a revolver in a grossly negligent way, so negligent that it deserved punishment, and death resulted, that would only be manslaughter, but you would have to consider all the facts before you could come to that conclusion, as to whether he was merely firing wildly or whether he was firing with a deadly intent.

But, gentlemen, there is another and further consideration in this case to which I want to direct your particular attention: Miles, the dead man, was a police officer, and the law for centuries – in fact, ever since there has been law in this country – has given special protection to police officers while in the execution of their duty, or perhaps it is more accurate to say that in the case of the killing of a peace officer – I use the expression 'peace officer' which is the old expression in English law for the modern police constable; he is in exactly the same position as the old parish constables were before there was any regular police force, and who were the only peace officers in the country – in the case of a peace officer who is killed, the law does not give the accused the same defences as in the case of other persons; it takes one away, and I am going to direct you that this is the law: 'If a police officer has arrested, or is endeavouring to arrest (and that includes coming on the scene for the purpose of arresting) a person, and the arrest, if effected, would be lawful, and that person, for the purpose of escaping, or preventing or hindering the arrest, does a wilful – that is to say, an intentional – act which causes the death of the officer, he is guilty of murder, whether or not he intended to kill or do grievous bodily harm.'

Now, will you bear that in mind – and I will read it to you again: 'If a police officer has arrested, or is endeavouring to arrest (which includes coming on to the scene for the purpose of arresting) a person, and the arrest, if effected, would be lawful, and that person, for the purpose of escaping, or preventing or hindering the arrest, does a wilful act which causes the death of the officer, he is guilty of murder, whether or not he intended to kill or to do grievous bodily harm.'

In that case the only possible way of reducing the crime to manslaughter is to show that the act was accidental, and not wilful – the act.

Now I cannot do better to illustrate this than to read to you a few lines from a direction given by one of the greatest Judges of Victorian times – Mr Justice Brett, who was afterwards Lord Esher – to a jury in a case where a police officer was killed by a kick – not a kick on the head. A kick in the ordinary way would not be grievous bodily harm; it might hurt, it might wound, but it would not be grievous bodily harm. A kick is not like a blow with a fist, is not anything approaching the use of a deadly weapon; but unhappily, the kick, though it was not intended to kill, did kill a police officer, and this was the direction that the jury were given: 'If the prisoner kicked the man intending to inflict grievous bodily harm, and death ensued from it, he was guilty of murder. That is what I told you first. If the prisoner inflicted the kick in resistance to his lawful arrest, even though he did not intend to inflict grievous injury, he was equally guilty of murder, but if in the course of a struggle he kicked the man not intending to kick him, then he was only guilty of manslaughter. Now, you see, there you get the difference – the deliberate kick. Though it was not intended to do grievous bodily harm, if it was a deliberate kick and caused the death of a police officer, that was murder. If it was not a deliberate kick, but it merely so happened that the prisoner's knee or foot came into contact with the police officer's body owing to a struggle, then it was an unintentional act, and that would only be manslaughter.'

Now, there is no question here but that the arrest, or the attempted arrest, by the police officer or the police officers who were there was lawful. These two young men were engaged in intending to carry out a felony – that is to say, warehouse-breaking – and it was not only a lawful arrest; it was an arrest which the police officers were bound to make if they could; so it was a lawful arrest, and, therefore, if in the course of a lawful arrest the prisoner does an act which kills the police officer, that is murder, unless the act – that is, the firing of the pistol – was accidental.

Now, was it a wilful act which caused the injury? As I told you, the question is not whether the result was accidental in the sense that more harm was caused than was intended. A person who is doing such things as firing off revolvers at police officers cannot say: 'Well, it was accidental that I killed him, because I

394

never intended to kill him.' T...
deliberate act, a wilful act.'

Now that I have explained the law to you, ...
will have some difficulty, as I do not hesitate to s...
in understanding what defence there can be in the case o...
prisoner Craig. There he was on this roof, armed, his revolver
was loaded, when he took it there he had spare ammunition
from which at some time he reloaded it, and you heard, too, that
some of this ammunition had been specially filed down to fit the
revolver. There he was on the roof with a loaded revolver, firing
off shots until his revolver was empty, and then he reloaded the
revolver and continued to fire, because, as you know, the revolver
contains six chambers and he fired altogether nine shots, and two,
I think, that were found that had not detonated; so in all he tried
to fire eleven. If that is not a deliberate act, a deliberate firing, it
is difficult to understand what would be. But you will remember,
and you will bear in mind, that we are only concerned with the
death of Police Constable Miles on this indictment, and Police
Constable Miles, you will remember, was killed by the third shot
which this youth fired. You will bear in mind Detective Sergeant
Fairfax's evidence. He told you of the firing. The first shot was
when he first got on to the roof and had arrested, or had attempted
to arrest, Bentley, and it was the first shot that hit Sgt Fairfax.

Let me help you to come to a conclusion whether this man was
deliberately firing at the officers. The very first shot that he fired
hit a police officer, fortunately doing him very little harm. The
second shot that was fired, according to Sgt Fairfax's evidence,
was when Bentley was on the ground, because you will remember
that what the police officer said was that the first shot caused him
to spin round and fall to the ground, and he brought Bentley to
the ground. Sgt Fairfax got up, and while Bentley was on the
ground he was trying to pull Bentley up, or get him as a shield,
when the prisoner fired a second time. Then other police officers
were heard, because the prisoner himself told you he heard police
officers coming up the stairs, and then the third shot was fired in
the direction of the stairs, and Police Constable Miles fell dead.
The aiming does not seem to have been bad, does it – three
shots, two police officers hit, one fortunately slightly, the other
hit between the eyes, so that blood gushed out and he fell dead
instantaneously.

Then you know that Police Constable McDonald appeared.
He had appeared, I should have said, before Police Constable

...cDonald out for
...g. The next shooting
...her very gallant officer,
...orking his way on his back
...e prisoner, and if you accept
...ence – it is a matter for you, but
...fired at least twice in his direction,
...ks he heard strike the brickwork. Still,

only other thing I need remind you about
is ... ...aid, according to the evidence of the police
office... ...will remember that Sgt Fairfax, having dragged
the dead body of Police Constable Miles into the doorway,
went downstairs, and by this time reinforcements had arrived
and brought a revolver or an automatic for the police, and
when Sgt Fairfax at once went back to the roof armed with
the automatic he called out to Craig that he had a pistol, and
thereupon, according to Sgt Fairfax's evidence, if you believe
it, the prisoner said: 'Come on, you coppers! Let's have it out!'
Police Constable Jaggs told you that he shouted 'Come on, you
brave coppers! Think of your wives!', and to Police Constable
Harrison he said: 'I'm Craig. You've just given my brother 12
years. Come on, you coppers! I'm only 16.' You may wonder
why he said: 'I'm only 16.' Possibly you may know that the law
does not allow a capital sentence to be passed on a boy of 16. Was
it a boast? – 'Aha! Come on! I've got a gun. I can't be hanged.'
You will think of that.

I do not think it is necessary to go through all that he said in
hospital. Enough he said on the roof, in all conscience, if you
believe it, to show that that boy, inspired, apparently, by a deadly
hatred for the police, was meaning, so you are asked to find and
to assume – to infer, I mean – that he meant to kill the police if
he could and he did kill one.

Now, gentlemen of the jury, think of those facts together. Is
it possible – if it is, you will always find a merciful verdict if
you can – to say that that shooting was accidental? I have told
you that you have got to find, before you can reduce this case
to manslaughter, that the shooting was accidental, not that the
result of the shooting was accidental – quite a different matter.

Well, now I turn to Bentley. Members of the jury, these two
youths are tried together, and they are both tried for the murder
of the policeman. It is quite unnecessary, where two or more

persons are engaged together in an unlawful criminal act, to show that the hand of both of them committed the act. The simplest illustration I could give you – after all, this is only a matter of common sense – is this: If two men go out housebreaking, it is a very common thing for one of them to break into a house and the other to stand outside and keep watch, but they are both taking part in the unlawful enterprise, and therefore they are both of them guilty, so if one stands outside so that the other may hand out the loot to him, he is not guilty merely of receiving stolen property; he is guilty of breaking in, because he is a party to the breaking in; and where two are engaged on a felonious enterprise – and warehouse-breaking is a felony – and one knows that the other is carrying a weapon, and there is agreement to use such violence as may be necessary to avoid arrest, and this leads to the killing of a person or results in the killing of a person, both are guilty of murder, and it is no answer for one to say 'I did not think my companion would go as far as he did.'

Now you can only judge whether there is an agreement to use such violence as may be necessary by looking at what happened and all the circumstances of the case, but I do remind you that it is no excuse and no defence to say 'I knew he was carrying a loaded revolver' – if you find he was – 'that he was carrying a loaded revolver, or a revolver, but I didn't think he would use it.' If one is carrying a revolver and the other knows that he intends to use some degree of violence, it is no answer, if that violence results in death, to say 'Well, I didn't think he would go as far as that.' What you have to consider is: Is there evidence from which you can properly infer that these two youths went out with a common purpose not merely to warehouse-break but to resist apprehension, even by violence if necessary? That is all. It is, as I repeat, no answer, if you come to that conclusion, for one to say: 'Yes, but I didn't think he would go as far as he did.'

Now let us see what the evidence is with regard to Bentley. The first thing that you have to consider is: Did Bentley know that Craig was armed? Now, you know, because I sit on the Bench and you sit in the jury-box it is not necessary that we leave our common sense at home. The great virtue of trial by jury is that jurymen can exercise the common sense of ordinary people. Can you suppose for a moment, especially when you have heard Craig say that why he carried a revolver was for the purpose of boasting and making himself a big man, that he would not have told his pals he was out with that he had got a revolver? Is it not almost inconceivable that Craig would not have told him, and probably shown him the revolver which he had? That is quite apart from what Bentley said afterwards. I should think you would come to the conclusion that the first thing, almost, Craig would tell him, if they were going off on a shop-breaking expedition, was: 'It's all right. I've got a revolver with me.'

Then see what Bentley had on him. Where is that knuckleduster? Apparently it was given to him by Craig, but Bentley was armed with this knuckleduster. Have you ever seen a more horrible sort of weapon? You know, this is to hit a person in the face with who comes at you. You grasp it *here*, your fingers go through – I cannot quite get mine through, I think – and you have got a dreadful heavy steel bar to strike anybody with; and you can kill a person with this, of course. Then did you ever see a more shocking thing than *that*? You have got a spike with which you can jab anybody who comes at you; if the blow with the steel is not enough, you have got this spike at the side to jab. You can have it to see, if you like, when you go to your room. It is a shocking weapon. Here was Craig armed with a revolver and that sheath knife. Hand me that sheath knife – the big one. One wonders, really, what parents can be about in these days, allowing a boy of 16 – they say, perhaps, they do not know, but why do not they know? – to have a weapon like this which he takes about with him? It is not a new one, you can see; it is pretty well worn. That was the thing that Craig was taking about. Where is the other knife? Here is Bentley with a smaller knife, but you can feel it is sharp and pointed. What is he carrying that with him for in his coat, not even with a sheath on it?

Can you believe it for a moment although Bentley had said he did not know Craig had the gun? You are not bound to believe Bentley if you think the inference and common sense of the matter is overwhelming that he must have known that he had it. Now, of course, the most serious piece of evidence against Bentley is that he called out, if you believe the evidence, to Craig 'Let him have it, Chris!', and then the firing began, and the very first shot struck Sgt Fairfax. Gentlemen, those words are sworn to by three police officers – Sgt Fairfax, Police Constable McDonald, and Police Constable Harrison; they all swear that they heard Bentley call that out, and that then the firing started. There is one thing I am sure I can say with the assent of all you twelve gentlemen, that the police officers that night, and those three officers in particular, showed the highest gallantry and resolution; they were conspicuously brave. Are you going to say they are conspicuous liars? – because if their evidence is untrue that Bentley called out 'Let him have it, Chris!', those three officers are doing their best to swear away the life of that boy. If it is true, it is, of course, the most deadly piece of evidence against him. Do you believe that those three officers have come into the box and sworn what is deliberately untrue – those three officers who on that night showed a devotion to duty for which they are entitled to the thanks of the community?

Now the other statement on the roof, the other exclamation of Bentley on the roof, is nothing like so important. He shouted out 'They're taking me down, Chris'. Whether that was an invitation to Craig to go on shooting or whether it was an invitation to Craig to stop shooting lest his (Bentley's) body should suffer, is a matter which really does not matter: by that time Police Constable Miles was dead. What does matter is whether Bentley shouted in the first instance 'Let him have it, Chris!' – 'Let him have it, Chris!' – because if he did, then you can consider whether that does not show, firstly, that he knew that 'Chris.' had the revolver, and, secondly, was calling upon 'Chris.' to use violence to prevent arrest.

Then in the car first of all he said 'I knew he had a gun' – that is sworn to by three officers – 'I knew he had a gun, but I did not think he'd use it.' As I have told you, if he knew he had a gun, and knew he was taking the gun for protection in their common unlawful enterprise, or to prevent arrest by violence, Bentley is as guilty as Craig; he is as guilty in law as Craig.

Then in his statement he said: 'I didn't know he was going to use the gun.' Again, if he said that, it shows that he knew it. If he knew that he had the gun, can you believe he did not know he had ammunition? Why did he have ammunition? Why did he have the gun? Why did he have the ammunition? You will remember that at one stage the officers said that Craig on the roof told them he had a ·45 and lots of ammunition. I think they said something about 'blowing your head off' – 'He'll blow your head off'. Then later in his statement he said he did not know 'Chris.' had a gun till he shot. That, of course, is quite inconsistent with what he said earlier in his statement. You can have the statement when you go to your room, if you like. He did say 'I didn't know he was going to use the gun', and then he said afterwards 'I didn't know Chris. had one until he shot.' It does not seem very consistent, but, as I say, the real thing is, is it not, as a matter of common sense, can you believe for a moment that if Bentley had gone on that expedition with this boastful young ruffian who said he carried a gun for the purpose of making himself out bigger than he was, he would not have told Bentley he had the gun? What had he got the gun for, and what did Bentley think he had the gun for?

Members of the jury, that is the whole case. The prisoner's defence, as I told you, is, Craig asks you to reduce the offence to manslaughter. I have pointed out to you the difficulties that there are in accepting manslaughter. Manslaughter can only be accepted here if you think that the whole thing was accidental. How it can be said to be accidental I confess seems to me to be extraordinarily difficult. In the case of Bentley, Bentley's defence is: 'I didn't know he had a gun, and I deny that I said "Let him have it, Chris". I never knew he was going to shoot, and I didn't think he would.' Against that denial (which, of course, is the denial of a man in grievous peril) you will consider the evidence of the three police officers who have sworn to you positively that those words were said.

Gentlemen of the jury, I started by saying this was a terrible case. It is dreadful to think that two lads, one, at any rate, coming, and I daresay the other, from decent homes, should with arms of this sort go out in these days to carry out unlawful enterprises like warehouse-breaking and finish by shooting policemen. You have a duty to the prisoners. You will remember, I know, and realize, I know that you owe a duty to the community, and if young people, but not so young – they are responsible in law – commit crimes of this sort, it is right, quite independent of any question of punishment, that they should be convicted, and if you find good ground for convicting them, it is your duty to do it if you are satisfied with the evidence for the prosecution.

I have reminded you of what the defence is, and I think I have sufficiently reminded you of what the prosecution's case is, and with those words I will ask you to go to the serious and solemn duty that you have of considering your verdict.

SOURCE ACKNOWLEDGEMENTS

A Handbook of Hanging, Charles Duff (Executors of Mr Duff's Estate)

All Extracts of House of Lords and House of Commons Debates (HMSO)

Children in Care 1959, Cmnd 194 (HMSO)

Children in Care 1970, Cmnd 4559 (HMSO)

Duty and Art in Advocacy, Rt. Hon. Sir Malcolm Hilbery (Stevens)

Education 1900–1950 (HMSO)

Education, Health and Behaviour, Michael Rutter, Jack Tizzard & Kingsley Whitmore (Whitmore)

Epilepsy in Society, Office of Health Economics

Famous Criminal Cases (I), Rupert Furneaux (Wingate)

Fire Arms in Crime (HMSO)

Hanged and Innocent, Sidney Silverman, Reginald Paget, Christopher Hollis (Gollancz)

Juvenile Delinquency, J. D. W. Pearce (Cassell)

Lord Goddard, Eric Grimshaw & Glyn Jones (Wingate)

Lord Goddard, Arthur Smith (Weidenfeld and Nicolson)

Miscarriages of Justice, C. G. L. Du Cann (Frederick Muller)

Most of My Murders, John Parris (Frederick Muller)

Murdered on Duty, Belton Cobb (W. H. Allen)

My Son's Execution, William Bentley (W. H. Allen)

Police Chronicle 1948

Police Review Year Books 1940, 1951, 1952

Political Adventure – The Memoirs of the Earl of Kilmuir (Weidenfeld & Nicolson)

Scotland Yard, Sir Harold Scott (Deutsch)

Silent in Court, Susanne Dell (G. Bell & Sons)

Statistics of Education, (HMSO) 1969. Vol. I, Schools

The British Medical Journal, 18 January 1949

The Criminal Prosecution in England, Lord Devlin (Oxford University Press)

The Ploughboy, Tony Parker (Hutchinsons)

The Report of the Ministry of Education (HMSO) for the year 1950, Cmnd 8244

The Royal Commission on Capital Punishment (HMSO) 1949–1953, Cmnd 8932

The Royal Commission on the Law Relating to Mental Deficiency and Mental Illness (HMSO) 1954–1957, Cmnd 169

Trial of Craig and Bentley, Ed. by Montgomery Hyde (Wm. Hodge)

The Unquiet Mind, William Sargant (Heinemann)

The Verbatim Transcript of the Trial of Craig and Bentley, kindly loaned by the Director of Public Prosecutions

That this book exists is due to many people, and to all of them I am deeply grateful. In particular, I must single out three: John Silver, who suggested the initial investigation, and subsequently gave greatly of his time; William Bentley, who was responsible for having made available to me a great deal of material; and finally Marie, who for nearly two years by her help, encouragement and understanding sustained me through even the blackest moments.

I should also like to thank the following people:

The Librarian and staff of the Central Library and Central Reference Library, Harrow.

The staff of the British Museum Newspaper Library, Colindale.

The Editor and staff of the *Police Review*.

The Secretary and staff of Guy's Hospital.

The Secretary and staff of the Lambeth Hospital.

The staff of the Maudsley Hospital.

The Secretary of Croydon General Hospital.

The staff of the Inner London Education Authority.

Dr James McManus.

The Secretary of the Burden Neurological Institute.

The General Medical Council.

Dr Nicholas Jazwon, formerly Casualty Officer, Croydon Central Hospital.

Dr William Sargant, Physician in charge of the department of Psychological Medicine at St Thomas's Hospital.

Professor Sir Denis Hill, M.B.B.S., F.R.C.P., D.P.M., Professor of Psychiatry at the Institute of Psychiatry.

Mr Michael Berger, B.A., Dip. Psychol., Lecturer in Psychology at the Institute of Psychiatry.

Mr William Yule, M.A., Dip. Psychol.

The Clerk and staff of the Croydon Magistrates' Court.

Detective Sergeant Frederick Fairfax.

Dr David Haler.

Dr Gordon Hatfield, formerly Medical Officer at Croydon General Hospital.

Detective Chief Inspector Smith.

Detective Sergeant Stanley Shepherd.

Christopher Craig.

William Bentley.

Lillian Bentley.

Iris Bentley.

Christmas Humphreys.

Frank Cassels.

John Parris.

Lord Goddard.

Norman Parsley.

Mr F. H. Clogg, Headmaster of Norbury Manor School.

Mr K. R. Bonnetto, Deputy Headmaster of Norbury Manor School.

Messrs George Walpole & Co., shorthand writers to the Central Criminal Court.

Mr J. Wood of the Office of the Director of Public Prosecutions.

Philip Jenkinson.

Kenneth Allsop.

Mr Jones, Manager of Barlow and Parkers – scene of the Croydon gun-battle.

The Secretary of the John Ruskin School.

The Secretary of the Camrose Avenue High School.

The Secretary of the Friar Street School.

The Executors of the estate of Mr John Stevens, Derek Bentley's Solicitor.

Messrs Cherer and Co., shorthand writers to the Appeal Court.

The Secretary of the Ingrams School.

To all other organizations and individuals whom I have not mentioned, but nevertheless gave vital help, I would like to record my gratitude.

Index

Advocacy, Duty & Art in, 209–11, 233

ALDERSON, PC James Leslie, 83, 85–6, 185, 209, 249, 355

ALPHON, Mr, 377, 380–81

Appeal
  of Bentley, 241–55, 320, 326, 329, 333, 343, 374
  Court of Criminal, 28–30, 242, 307, 362, 369, 376
  of Hanratty, 362
  to House of Lords, 261
  Judges (*see also* Croom-Johnson, Ormerod, Pearson), 242, 247–8

Appleby, Rex v., 202–4, 211

Archbold, 109

ARRAN, Earl of, 319, 325, 347–57, 371–2, 373, 382

ATTLEE, Rt. Hon. Clement, 28

BALL, Reverend, 280

Ballistics evidence, 64, 73–5, 191–3

Barlow & Parkers, 21–5, 58–61

BARTLEY, Sarah, 281–2

Barton, Dick, Special Agent, 32

BASS, John, 183–4, 228, 242

BAXTER, PC Alan, 43

BAYFIELD, Mrs Scott, 318

BEATTIE, PC, 45, 104

BECKLEY, John, 298

BENNET, J W, 106

BENTLEY, Albert, 91, 98, 136

BENTLEY, Dennis, 116, 232

BENTLEY, Derek,
  Appeal, 241–55, 320, 326, 329, 333, 343, 374
    to House of Lords, 261

BENTLEY, Derek *(cont.)*
  Arrest, 22–4, 62, 69, 78, 109, 168–9, 250–55
    reference during Appeal to, 245–7
    comments on, 250–51
  Attitude to violence, 56–7, 119, 138–9
  Behaviour
    on rooftop, 210, 214–16
    after shooting, 97, 158
  Birth, 114–15
  Break-in at Barlow & Parkers, 21–2, 58–60
  Cautions received, 83–4, 93, 95–6
  Criminal activities
    early, 123, 124–5
    with Craig, 51, 137–9
  Croydon Courts, appearance at,
    Juvenile, 123, 124–5
    Magistrates', 101, 106–7
  Croydon Police Station
    detention at, 87, 90, 102
    journey to, 83–5
  Defence Counsel to, *see*
    Cassels, Frank
  Education (*see also* Schools attended), 115–24, 285–6
  Employment, 136–8
  Epilepsy, 115–17, 120, 128–32, 137, 147, 157–61, 353
  Execution, 279–81
    riots against, 280, 281–2
    House of Commons debate on, 286
  Family background, 115–16
  House of Commons, question in, 310–11
  House of Lords, debate on,

BENTLEY, Derek *(cont.)*
    324–6, 329, 331–43, 346,
      347, 348, 350–57, 368–77
  Illiteracy, 96, 117–20, 125,
    136, 189, 190–91, 198–9
  Inquest on, 282
  IQ tests received, 125–7, 148
  Kingswood Approved School
    detention at, 125–9
    release from, 134–5
  Medical Enquiry, Statutory,
    289
  Medical history, 115–20,
    128–32, 134–7
  Medical reports on, 118,
    128–9, 131–2, 142–50,
    154–60, 161
    full text of, Brixton Prison,
      353, 385–90
  Medical treatment received at
    Bristol Child Guidance
      Clinic, 129
    Burden Neurological
      Institute, 131–2, 149–50
    Guy's Hospital, 115, 118,
      128–9
    Lambeth Hospital, 116
    Maudsley Hospital, 142, 150
  Mental health, 57, 121, 125–9,
    131–3, 135–7, 148, 158–9,
    353
  National Service Medical
    Board, 136–7, 353
  Nicknames for Craig, 265
  Prisons, detention in
    Brixton, 111, 114, 353
      family visits 102, 240
    Wandsworth
      family visits, 259,
        264, 276, 277–8
      letter to parents, 283–4
  Relationship with Craig,
    53–4, 77–9, 138
  Reprieve
    demonstrations for, 278–80
    House of Commons debate
      on, 267–75

BENTLEY, Derek *(cont.)*
  Reprieve *(cont.)*
    petitions for, 256–9, 261,
      262–3
    petition to Home Secretary,
      276, 278
    refusal of, 263, 276, 278
  Rooftop, on, 22–4, 60–74,
    77–80
    remarks uttered, 22–4, 63–9,
      72, 77, 109, 236–7
    reference to during trial, 86,
      181–2, 200–201, 205–7,
      215–16, 218–19
  Schools attended
    Camrose Avenue, 116
    Friar St Elementary, 115,
      118
    John Ruskin, Walworth, 117
    Ingrams, 120–23
    Norbury Manor, 118–23
  Solicitor, *see* John Stevens
  Statement, 78–9, 92–7, 140–41
    reference to during trial,
      189–91, 219–20, 227
  Trial, 163–79, 180–232
    arrival at Old Bailey, 163
    defence counsel's speech,
      212–21
    evidence given, 199–202,
      251–4
    Judge's summing-up, 221–8
    prosecution speeches,
      166–70, 203–8, 209–10
    sentence, 230, 311
    verdict, 229–30
BENTLEY, Iris, 91, 114, 116,
  185, 232, 263, 268, 279
BENTLEY, Joan, 114, 115, 116
BENTLEY, Lillian and William,
  111–12, 116–17, 312–13
  Derek Bentley
    letter from, 283–4
    prison visits to, 102, 111–12,
      240, 259, 264–5, 277–8
    reprieve, petition for, 258
    trial of, 164, 178, 212–13, 232

BENTLEY, Lillian and William
(cont.)
  Winston Churchill, plea to, 267
  Home Office, visit to, 265
  police search of home of, 91
BENTLEY, Roger, 122–3
BENTLEY, William (see also
  Lillian and William), 279
  attending House of Commons
    debate, 268, 275–6, 278
  fight with education
    authorities, 121
  letter to The Times, 311–12
  newspaper stories given by,
    235, 238–9, 266
  visit to
    Mrs Sarah Bartley, 261–2
    Croydon Police Station, 98
    Shirley Williams at House of
      Commons, 323
BESWICK, Lord, 368
BEVAN, Aneurin, 274,
  278, 292–3, 313
Black market, 26–7, 33
Blom-Cooper, Louis, QC, 312
BONNETTO, K R, 121–2
BRABIN, Mr Justice, 378–9, 380
Brabin Tribunal, 378–9, 380
BRETT, Mr Justice, 223
Bristol Child Guidance Clinic,
  129
British Medical Journal, 129
Brixton Prison
  detention of Bentley, 102, 114
  medical report on Bentley,
    142–6
  full text of report,
    Appendix II, 353, 385–90
BROCKWAY, Lord, 357–61,
  366–7, 377, 380–81
BROPHY, Brigid, 312
BROWN, PC, 103
BUGDEN, PC, 60, 65,
  68, 86, 185, 209, 355
Burden Neurological Institute,
  131–2, 149–50
BURNS, J L, 126–7

BYERS, Lord, 312

Camrose Avenue School,
  Edgware, 116
Capital Punishment
  abolition of, 35–7, 308
  attitude of Lord Goddard to,
    37–9
  Parliamentary vote on, 35–6,
    39
  Royal Commission on, 132–3,
    151–2, 161, 300–302, 355
  Home Office memorandum
    to, 234
CARLISLE, Mark, 310, 312–13,
  324–5
CASSELS, Frank, 112, 155–6,
  354–5
  Derek Bentley
    appeal of, 241–50
    attitude towards, 189–90,
      240–41
    comment on execution of, 18
    trial of
      conduct of defence,
        178–80
      cross-examinations of:
        Derek Bentley, 251–3
        Det. Sgt Fairfax, 173–7
        PC Mcdonald, 181–2
        Det. Sgt Shepherd,
          189–90
        Det. Chief Insp. Smith,
          190–91
      final speech, 86, 213–21
  brief given to, 108, 190
  Lord Goddard, conference
    with, 110
  John Parris, conference
    with, 110–11
Chalkpit murder, 38, 287
CHASE, James Hadley, 32
Chief Constables' Association, 33
CHRISTIE, John, 378
CHURCHILL, Winston,
  104–5, 267, 322
CLARKE, Alan, 313

CLOSE, Det. Inspector, 91

COLVILLE of Culross,
Viscount, 324–6, 328, 329,
333, 344–5, 352, 354–7,
359–60, 367–84

Commons, House of
Derek Bentley
debate on execution of, 286
debate on motion for
reprieve, 267–75
petition to Home Secretary,
276, 278
request for enquiry into
case of, 310–11

Capital Punishment, support
for abolition of, 35–7

Criminal Justice Bill, passage
through, 34–7

Lord Goddard, attack of, 39

Conservative Women's Central
Advisory Committee, 46

Corporal Punishment, 34–5,
37–8, 39–41, 44–6
campaign for return, 105
comment on by Howard
League for Penal Reform, 46
legislation for return, 46
Magistrates' Association
decision on, 47, 105

COTTON, Len, 238

Court of Criminal Appeal, 28–30,
242, 307, 362, 369, 376

CRAIG, Christopher, 327
articles on, 235–40
attitude to police, 152–3, 178
break-in at Barlow & Parkers,
21–2, 58–60
cautions received, 88, 90, 96
childhood, 48
criminal activities
early, 50
with Derek Bentley, 51, 137–9
with Norman Parsley, 51
Croydon Magistrates' Court,
appearance at, 106–7
Defence Counsel, see John
Parris

CRAIG, Christopher (cont.)
drugs given to, 102–3, 188–9
education, 122, 285–6
gun collection of, 56, 92, 122,
138
Colt ·45, 22–3, 55, 73–4
House of Commons, question
in, 310–11
House of Lords debate on
Hanratty and Bentley cases,
334–42, 347, 350–55, 373–7
medical treatment received, 83,
87–9, 102–3
at Maudsley Hospital, 150,
154
mental health, 57, 103–4,
150, 152, 154
nicknames for, 265
Prisons, detention in
Brixton, 111
Wakefield, 154
visits from family, 111
relationship with Bentley,
53–4, 77–9, 138
rooftop, on, 22–5, 60–67,
68–74, 77–81
Shepherd, Det. Sgt, interview
with, 87–8
shots fired at, 74, 81
shots fired by, 177
at PC Fairfax, 22–5,
63–7, 68–9, 81
at PC Harrison, 23–4, 70–71,
79
at PC Miles, 73–6
Smith, Det. Chief Inspector,
interview with, 90–91
suicide attempt, 81
trial of, 163–78, 180–232
arrival at Old Bailey, 163
defence speech, 211–12
evidence given, 196–8, 208
Judge's summing-up, 221–8
prosecution speeches,
166–70, 203–8, 209–10
sentence, 230–31, 311
verdict, 229–30

CRAIG, Lucy, 111, 164, 235, 238
CRAIG, Niven Mathews, 48, 111
  at trial of Christopher Craig, 164
  evidence given, 170–72
  newspaper stories given by, 164, 235–8
  police search of home, 92
CRAIG, Niven Jr, 48–50
CRAIG, Mrs Niven, 48, 107, 111, 164, 265
Crime figures, 29, 31, 33, 45, 299, 303, 306
Crime, post-war, 30, 33–5, 42
Criminal Justice Bill, 40–42
  passage through Parliament, 34–9
Criminal Prosecution in England, The, 89
CRIPPEN, Dr, 347
CROOM-JOHNSON, Mr Justice, 242–4, 247–50, 255
Croydon Courts
  Juvenile, 123, 124–5
  Magistrates', 101, 106–7
Croydon Police Station
  detention of Bentley, 87, 90
  guns issued from, 72

Daily Express, 32, 36
Daily Herald, 32
Daily Mail, 40, 99, 101
Daily Mirror, 31, 32, 234
Daily Telegraph, 314
DAVIES of Leek, Lord, 325–6, 372, 376–7, 383, 384
DAVIES, Michael, 208, 300
DAY, Mr Justice, 46
Defence Counsel
  to Derek Bentley, *see* Frank Cassels
  to Christopher Craig, *see* John Parris
Defence, Poor Prisoner's, 107–8, 306
DENHAM, Lord, 372

DENHAM, PC Vincent, 89, 103
DEVLIN, Lord Justice, 89–90, 140, 251
DILHORNE, Lord, 356
Doctrine of Constructive Malice, 109, 168
DONNELLY, Desmond, 274
DOW, James, 239
DRIBERG, Tom, 291
DU CANN, C G L, 16, 179–80
DUFF, Charles, 16, 250

EDE, Chuter, 35–6, 38–41, 272
EDEN, Sir Anthony, 40
EDGAR, PC Nat, 34
EDGAR, Mrs, 43
Education
  Act 1944, 120–21, 132, 304
  of Bentley (*see also* Derek Bentley), 285–6
  of Craig (*see also* Christopher Craig), 285–6
  ESN Schools, 303–4
  Minister of, 285
  survey on, 305–6
EISENHOWER, General, 104
ELLIS, Ruth, 39, 348
Empire News, 164
Epanutin, 130
Epilepsy (*see also* Derek Bentley), 129–31, 305
Erskine May, 269
EVANS, Timothy, 39, 332, 347, 348, 378
Evening Standard, 275
EVES, Roger, 41, 42

FAIRCLOUGH, Father, 31
FAIRFAX, PC Frederick, 60–61, 112, 323, 356, 377
  award given, 241
  commended by Lord Goddard, 231–2
  evidence of, 62–5, 172–7, 320, 351–3, 375, 382
  on rooftop, 22–5, 61–7, 68–81
  in hospital, 83, 87–9

FAIRFAX, PC Frederick (cont.)
shots fired at, 22, 63–9, 81
shots fired by, 25, 74, 81, 320, 373
wound sustained by, 63, 64, 81, 188
FALLON, Tom, 238
Famous British Trials, 224
FAZEY, Frank, 54, 93
FIDOE, John, 134
FINLAY, Edward, 45–6
FOLLICK, M, MP, 285
FOOT, Lord, 361–6, 368, 377, 378–80, 381
FOOT, Paul, 345, 362, 363, 364, 368, 380, 381
FRASER, Inspector, 43
FREEBODY, Dr, 187–8
Friar St Elementary School, 115, 118
FUCHS, Klaus, 41
FURNEAUX, Rupert, 250
FYFE, Sir David Maxwell, 39, 89, 139, 261, 311, 328, 336
autobiography, 290–96
conduct during debate on reprieve, 275
at funeral of PC Miles, 106
petition from House of Commons to, 276, 278
pressures on, to execute Bentley, 296–7
refusal of reprieve, 263, 276, 278, 334, 356–7, 383
speech in House of Commons, 9, 309

GANDHI, Mahatma, 27
GARDINER, Lord, 312
GIBSON, Sergeant, 42
GODDARD, Lord, 30, 112, 322, 351
amendment on birching, 39–41
appointment as Lord Chief Justice, 28
attack on House of Commons, 39

GODDARD, Lord (cont.)
attacked by John Parris, 259–60
attitude to Capital Punishment, 37–8
attitude to reprieve of Bentley, 17, 266–7
biography of, 17
conference with Defence and Prosecuting Counsel, 110
interview with author, 17, 266–7
maiden speech in House of Lords, 37–8
speeches at Mansion House, 43–6, 298
trial of Bentley & Craig
arrival in Court, 164–5
commendation of Police, 231
definition of Bentley's legal position, 203
interchange with John Parris, 226–7
interruptions during, 181–2, 186, 196, 211–12, 354–5
passing sentence, 230–31, 311
summing-up, 77–8, 221–8, 243–5, 247, 334–5, 337–8, 341, 342, 356, 374–5, 376; full text of, Appendix III, 391–400
trial of Roger Eves and James Watson, 41–2
trial of Norman Parsley, 228–9
warning to criminals, 28–9
GOLLANCZ, Livia, 312
GOODMAN, Lord, 14, 319, 323–4, 331–48, 351, 353–4, 357, 361, 366, 367, 368–71, 373, 374, 375, 376, 378, 381–2
GREENO, Superintendent, 92
GRIMSHAW, Eric, 17
Guns, issued to police, 72, 74, 80, 177
Guy's Hospital, treatment of Bentley, 115, 118, 128–9

HAILSHAM, Viscount, Lord
  Chancellor, 348–50
HALE, Leslie, MP, 272–3
HALER, Dr David, 105
  evidence of, 186–7, 351
  inquest on Derek Bentley, 282
  inquest on PC Miles, 75
  interview with author, 75,
    314–17, 318–19, 321, 323,
    351–3, 356, 382
HALL, Glenvel, 293
Handbook on Hanging, A, 16
Hanged and Innocent, 16, 199
HANRATTY, James, 39, 324,
    331–3, 343–6, 348, 350,
    357–66, 377–82
HARRISON, PC, 60
  award given to, 241, 285
  commended by Lord Goddard,
    231–2
  evidence of, 66–7, 73–4, 182–4
  on rooftop, 23–4, 62–7, 70–71,
    73–4, 76–7, 79
  shots fired at, 70–72, 77, 79
HENDERSON, Sir David,
    151–2
HEWART, Lord, 196
HILBERY, Sir Malcolm, 49,
    209–10, 233
HILL, Professor Sir Denis, 142,
    149–50, 161, 355
  letter to Home Office, 261,
    267, 322, 383
  reply from Home Office,
    289, 322, 353–4
HODGES, William, 224
Home Office, 30
  letter from Sir Denis Hill, 261,
    267, 322, 383
  memorandum to Royal
    Commission on Capital
    Punishment, 234
  permanent under-secretary to,
    see Sir Frank
    Newsam
  reply to Sir Denis Hill,
289, 322, 353–4

Home Office (*cont.*)
  visit from Craig and Bentley
    families, 265–6
Home Secretary, *see* Chuter
  Ede, Sir David Maxwell Fyfe,
  Major Gwilym Lloyd George,
  Reginald Maudling
HORSBRUGH, Florence, 285
House of Commons, *see*
  Commons, House of
House of Lords, *see* Lords,
  House of
Howard League for Penal
  Reform, 46
HOWE, Earl, 47
HOWES, Mr and Mrs, 51
HUMPHREYS, Christmas, 112
  Derek Bentley
    appeal of, 242, 245–7
    trial of
      cross-examinations:
        Derek Bentley, 199 201,
          253–4
        Christopher Craig,
          196–8, 208–9
        Niven Craig Snr, 170–72
        Det. Sgt Fairfax, 172–3
        Dr Freebody, 187–8
        Lewis Nickolls, 194–5
      opening speech, 166–70,
        209–210; final
      speech, 203–8
  conference with Lord Goddard,
    110
  Prosecution of Michael
    Davies, 208
HYDE, H Montgomery, 312

Ingrams School, 120–23

JAGGER, PC, 43
JAGGS, PC, 71, 79, 241, 285
JAZWON, Dr Nicholas
  evidence of, 185–6
  interview with author, 188
JENKINSON, Philip, 33
John Ruskin School, 117

411

JONES, Glyn, 17
Judges' Rules, 95, 189
Jury
    exhibits wanted by, 65, 227–8
    facilities available to, 179, 222
    selection of, 165
    verdict of, 229–30

KENDALL, Councillor, 45
KENNEDY, Superintendent,
    358
KERR, Russell, 310, 312, 313,
    319
Kingswood Approved School,
    125–9
    letter to Bentley family, 134–5
    report on Bentley, 127, 134
Knuckleduster, 23, 24, 55, 63, 69
    reference to, during trial, 200,
    209, 216, 223–4, 252–3
KOESTLER, Arthur, 312

Lambeth Hospital, treatment of
    Bentley, 116
LAWTON, Governor, 280
LEE of Asheridge, Baroness,
    366–7, 368
LEE, Philip, 321, 323, 373,
    382
LEY, Thomas, 38, 287, 355
LIPTON, Marcus, MP, 139
LLEWELLYN, Lord, 38
LLOYD GEORGE, Major
    Gwilym, 287
Lord Chief Justice, see Lord
    Goddard
Lords, House of
    appeal of Derek Bentley, 261
    debate on corporal
        punishment, 47
    debate on Hanratty and
        Bentley cases, 14, 324–6,
        329, 331–84
    passage of Criminal Justice
        Bill, 37–8
    vote on abolition of Capital
        Punishment, 39

Lunacy and Mental Deficiency
    Acts, 150
MACDONALD, Det. Constable,
    105
MACLEOD, Det. Constable, 105
MACLOUGHLIN, Madeline,
    164, 235
Magistrates' Association, 47, 105
Malice, Doctrine of Constructive,
    109, 168
MATHESON, Dr, 114, 146–9
    report on Bentley, 142–9,
        154–9, 161; full text of,
        Appendix II, 385–90
MAUDLING, Reginald, 14, 327
    demands for public enquiry,
        313, 322–6, 328, 362–5
    open letter to, 15–20
    reply to question in House of
        Commons, 310–12, 319–22
    speech on crime figures, 306
Maudsley Hospital, 142, 150
MAXWELL FYFE, Sir David,
    see Fyfe
May, Erskine, 269
McBAIN, 28
McDONALD, PC, 60–61
    award given, 241, 285
    climbing to roof, 62–3, 65–6
    commended by Lord Goddard,
        231–2
    evidence of, 65–7, 70–71, 73–4,
        180–82, 375
    on rooftop, 23–4, 71–4, 76
McMANUS, Dr, 117–18
Mental Deficiency, Lunacy
    and, Acts, 150
Mental Illness and Deficiency
    Royal Commission
        on Law, 125–7,
        303
Metropolitan Police Force, 31,
    36–7
    pension to police widows,
        43, 239, 285
    Royal Commission on Police
        Powers and Procedure, 89

412

MILES, PC Sidney, 52, 60, 72,
83
award given, 285
death of, 24–5, 73–6, 183–4,
311, 315, 319, 320–21, 322,
324, 327, 351, 373
funeral of, 106
inquest on, 105–6
MILES, Mrs Sidney, 90,
100–101, 105–6, 285
Miscarriages of Justice, 16, 180
M'Naghten Rules, 133–4, 287
MONTGOMERY HYDE,
H, *see* HYDE
MOORE, Alfred, 43
MORRISON, Herbert, 40
MORRISON, William, 268,
271–5, 310
Most of My Murders, 202
MUDIE, John McMain, 38
MUNROE, Dr James, 118,
128–9, 132
MURDOCH, James, 280
My Death is a Mockery, 52
My Son's Execution, 138

National Chamber of Trade, 46
News Chronicle, 32
NEWSAM, Sir Frank, 263,
265–6, 276
NICHOLS, Beverly, 239–40
NICKOLLS, Lewis, 191–5, 327
No Orchids for Miss Blandish,
32–3
Norbury Manor School, 118–23
Headmaster of, 122

Observer, 32
ORMEROD, Mr Justice, 242–3,
245

PAGET, Reginald, QC, MP, 16,
199, 250, 293
speech for reprieve, 271–2
PAIN, PC, 60, 65, 68, 86,
185, 209, 355
PAINE, Tom, 211

PARKER, Tony, 208
PARRIS, John, 102, 108,
112, 224, 354–5
brief given to, 109–10
Frank Cassels, conference
with, 110–11
comments
on execution of Bentley,
17–18
on inquest of PC Miles, 106
on Judgment on appeal, 250
Christopher Craig, trial of
challenging of jury, 165–6
cross-examinations of
Niven Craig Snr, 170–71
Det. Sgt Fairfax, 173–7
Dr Nicholas Jazwon, 185
PC McDonald, 180–81
Lewis Nickolls, 191–3
final speech, 186, 211–12
interchange with Lord
Goddard, 226–7
Lord Goddard
attack on, 259–60
conference with, 110
Most of My Murders, 202
PARSLEY, Norman, 54, 92–3
robbery committed with Craig,
51
trial of, 228–9
PEARCE, J, 123–6
PEARSON, Mr Justice, 242
Penal Reform, 34
Howard League for, 46
PESKETT, Reverend, 45
Phenobarbitone, 130
PHILLIPS, Baroness, 382
PIERREPOINT, Albert, 259,
277, 279–81
Police Chronicle, 32, 37
Police Force, *see* Metropolitan
Police
Police Review, 95, 101
POOLE, Derek, 42–3
Poor Prisoner's Defence, 107–8,
306
Post Office frauds, 29

Post-war crime, 29–30, 33–5, 42–3
PRICE, William, 310–11

REYNOLDS, Dr Doris, 128, 135, 137, 157
Reynolds News, 238
ROBERTS, Sgt Edward, 83–5
Rooftop battle
  Christopher Craig's version, 63–5, 68–74, 76–82
  Daily Mail report on, 99–101
  duration of, 193–4, 217–18
  Police Review report on, 101
  Prosecution version, 23–5, 60–63, 65–8
ROSS, PC James, 194
Royal Commissions on
  Capital Punishment, 133, 151–2, 161–2, 300–303, 355
    Home Office Memorandum to, 234
  Law relating to Mental Illness and Deficiency, 125–7, 303
  Police Powers and Procedure, 89
Royal Prerogative of Mercy, 268–9, 272, 287–8, 291
RUSSELL of Liverpool, Lord, 363

SALISBURY, Marquess of, 347
SAMUELSON, Anthony, 228
SARGANT, Dr William, 134, 155
Scientific Investigation of Crime, The, 327
SHEPHERD, Det. Sgt Stanley, 87–8, 92, 140
  evidence of, 189–90
  interview with Craig, 87–8, 90
SHEPHERD, PC Thomas, 103
SHIVAS, Mark, 313
SILVERMAN, Nancy, 312
SILVERMAN, Sydney
  amendment on abolition of Capital Punishment,

SILVERMAN, Sydney (*cont.*)
  35–6, 37–9, 41
  debate on execution of Bentley, 286
  motion for reprieve, 267–71, 274–6
  petition to Home Secretary, 276, 278
SIMON, Lord, 46
SIMONDS, Lord, 47
SLATER, Oscar, 332
SMITH, Arthur, 198, 222
SMITH, Det. Chief Inspector John, 87, 104, 121, 140
  evidence of, 190–91
  interview with author, 191
  interview with Craig, 90–91
SMITH, Lawrence, 38, 287
SMITH, PC, 103
SOPER, Lord, 312
Stanford-Binet Scale, 126
Star, The, 32
STEPHENS, PC Henry, 83
STEVENS, John, 155–7
  brief offered to Frank Cassels, 102, 108–9
  statement from Bentley, 114, 140–41
STEWART, PC, 25, 79, 83
Street of Disillusion, The, 164
Sunday Chronicle, 239
Sunday Dispatch, 235, 238
Sunday Express, 105
Sunday Pictorial, 164, 235–7, 238, 266
SWABEY, Commander, 347

THOMAS, Donald, 34, 36, 38-9
THOMAS, Lynn Ungoed-, 293
Times, The, 32, 311, 312
To Encourage the Others, quoted in House of Lords debate on Hanratty and Bentley cases, 351–2, 356, 368, 373
Trials
  Derek Bentley and Christopher Craig,